Franciscan Solitude

Edited by

André Cirino, OFM, and Josef Raischl

Franciscan Solitude

Edited by

André Cirino, OFM, and Josef Raischl

The Franciscan Institute
St. Bonaventure University
St. Bonaventure, New York

1995

Library of Congress Catalog Card Number:
95–60674

Publishers Note:
The individual essays in this volume have often been based on the same reference material. The first citation of a reference is given in full; all subsequent references are given in an abbreviated form. A complete bibliography of sources is provided at the end.

ISBN 1–57659–006–2

Cover Design
    Mark Lisle
    Cavalier Lisle Art and Design
    Boston, MA

Printed in the United States of America
    BookMasters
    Ashland, Ohio

We dedicate our work

to Bernadette,
Jona and Elia
for patience and loving support;

and
to John,
Angela and Ralph,
Ralph,
Jessica and Jerry,
River,
Samantha and Stephen
John and Dana
for their constant love.

Table of Contents

Preface

In the concluding words of the *Earlier Rule,* Francis prays:

> And I ask God that He who is all powerful, Three and
> One, bless all those who teach, learn, retain,
> remember, and put into practice all these things, each
> time they repeat and perform what has been written
> here for the salvation of our soul, and to love deeply,
> to guard and cherish them.

I believe that we have witnessed in recent decades many
epiphanies of Franciscan consciousness that arise from individual
and corporate dedication to the task Francis described in the
words above: "teach, learn, retain, remember. . . ."

It is not the province of the classroom lecture *(teach)* alone to
produce a renewed reality of charismatic initiative. It is the
result of actually living again—*retaining, remembering, practicing*
—the Life and Rule that Francis engendered. It is the
determination to *cherish, guard, love deeply* the life expressed in
the *Rule* so that it becomes incarnate again with the light of
Christ's power and presence. Something so loved and cherished
attracts others and creates a circle of influence that may, at
times, appear almost magical in its properties.

This kind of determined exploration into the profound
meaning of traditions and texts—texts that are the results of
living, not the dry bones of archaic recollection—has resulted in
the publication of this anthology, *Franciscan Solitude.* André
Cirino and Josef Raischl have journeyed not from theory to
experimentation, but conversely, from personal involvement in
hermitage experiences to studious reflection on its meaning for
today's Franciscan family.

Their research is a form of servanthood. They have taken a
theme of intense personal interest and experience; and worked
hard to explain it by scholarly research and written evaluations
of serious pastoral experimentation.

The short, almost cryptic, "Rule for Hermitages" that forms the heart of this collection (chapter 3) is an example of the rediscovery of a whole way of Franciscan Gospel living that has been unknown by generations of Franciscans. Franciscan scholarship brought this text back into prominence thirty years ago. Works included here by Kajetan Esser and Ignatius Brady witness the restoration these eminent leaders effected in their writing and teaching, and allow us to delve deeply into the "innards" of the text itself.

Hardly had this little *Rule* found its way into collections of Francis's writings published after Vatican II, when original and ingenious attempts to experiment with its contents began to emerge. The appearance of the "Rule for Hermitages" was matched by the emergence of religious sensibility in the West that sought to restore ways of praying in solitude. Franciscans who were part of this movement founded *ritiros*, houses of prayer and hermitages. Some of these brothers and sisters had little explicit awareness of the deep historical and theological foundations upon which they were building. Nonetheless, they intuitively sought ways to introduce an eremitical element into personal and communal prayer life. The fifth chapter of *Franciscan Solitude* chronicles several of these honest and ordinary "experiments" that have contributed greatly to our knowledge. The projects described demonstrate the daily effort to *put into practice* this marvelous legacy.

As those who attempted these projects shared their successes and failures, continued study emphasized the solitude experience as central to the life and mission of Francis. The entries in the first two chapters offer ways of understanding the historical underpinnings of the hermit life that attracted him. The editors have gathered rich examples of reflection and historical documentation on this ancient form of Christian life and its medieval expressions. Articles by Conti and Mertens focus more precisely on the particular stamp which Francis placed upon the hermitage tradition. We are coming to appreciate fully Francis's remarkable amalgamation of prayer in solitude and in a fraternal, relational context.

A variety of interests is served by special studies. Gatti's intriguing investigation of the property rights and politics of the Carceri through the years will delight history buffs. Pasztor and Casagrande invite us to glimpse the world of the medieval women hermits, thus enlarging our grasp of early feminine Franciscanism. Conti stresses the contemporary theme of evangelization and its rootedness in the hermitage spirituality. The Raischls offer a wonderfully innovative approach for married couples who want to savor this Rule.

Each writer allows a unique perspective to emerge. Confirmation of efforts to restore the hermitage ministry to a central place in our lives is one by-product of careful reading. Another benefit is a renewed enthusiasm for the task of finding means to translate the genius of the early Franciscan movement into meaningful paradigms for a postmodern Christian diaspora. The applications of the "Rule for Hermitages" to modern people and places has become an exciting locus of the powerful blessing Francis envisioned for those who would dare to *repeat and perform* what he had prescribed.

This last assertion is based on personal experience. During the time in which this publication was developing, my own congregation took the bold step of inaugurating a hermitage ministry. Over the last twenty years several of our members asked for the establishment of a hermitage on our convent grounds. Others, lacking an opportunity at home, received permission to spend lengthy periods in hermitages operated by other religious groups. Finally, we found means to build three small hermitages in a pine woods on our Mt. Providence campus. André Cirino assisted us by providing a workshop on the hermitage tradition for both architect, Richard Keller, and contractor, Steve Catranel. These men caught the infection of our enthusiasm and built simple but durable and comfortable dwellings for women and men in search of solitude.

Since the inception of the ministry we have had an enthusiastic response from the people of the Pittsburgh area and beyond. Most heartening to us has been the eagerness of local lay persons and Protestant clergy to avail themselves of this oasis of contemplation. Thus we feel deeply joined to this renaissance of the eremitical aspect of our vocation.

Weekly I rejoice as I see the light of a hermitage burn in the scented darkness of our woods. I remember the potent benediction of Francis. My heart reaches out to all those who likewise labor in projects such as this volume to refound our charism in its fullness. May the readers of this publication become part of the refounding energy that binds us to one another as we *put into practice all these things.*

Margaret Carney, OSF
October 4, 1995

Foreword

"THE TWO WHO ARE MOTHERS . . . " (RegEr 2)

Francis and Clare were fond of the *mother* image. Their *Rules* describe how the brothers and sisters are to love one another through the use of the *mother* symbol. The brothers and sisters used the *mother* symbol to describe Clare and Francis. Francis's familiarity with the *mother* symbol is quickly evidenced by its inclusion in this verse of the "Rule for Hermitages."

Taking the symbol of *mother* for ourselves as editors and authors, we can see in retrospect that we have been called to the same role with this book. We *conceived* the idea for this anthology in 1988 when studying in Rome at the Capuchin Franciscan Institute. While one of us was busy collecting material, the other spent some ten days in hermitage to experience the depth of the solitude we desired to share. Once the data—both academic and experiential—had been collected, we realized we were *pregnant*.

We desired our *child* to have an international perspective. So during our *pregnancy* we searched for material from various languages that we thought important to have available in the English language. As a consequence, our *child's* background is Italian, German, and American. Then we contacted several people both to translate and to write various articles for this book. By June, 1993, all the necessary translations and new articles were in our hands.

And in December 1993, we met in Eichstätt, Germany, and *gave birth to the child* you have in your hands. And just like any new parents, we had to decide on a *name* for our *child*. Since there has been discussion among scholars regarding the title of this document by Francis, Esser gave "this small work a title that is meaningful: *Regula Pro Eremitoriis Data*." Laurent Gallant, OFM, encouraged us to search for the name of our anthology in the word *eremis*, which Francis used in the first line of this

work. The meaning is *solitude*. So we named our *child*
FRANCISCAN SOLITUDE since this writing stems from Francis's
experience in solitude.

To the many people who have *gifted our child* we wish to
express our gratitude. First we acknowledge our translators:
Nancy Celaschi, OSF; Aaron Pembleton, OFM; Eric Kahn, OFM;
and Berard Doerger, OFM. Nancy not only translated for us, but
gave strong personal support. Both Nancy and our good friend
Don Aldo Brunacci offered tremendous help in tracking down
permissions for reprinting certain texts. And may Aaron, who has
died, be at peace.

We thank our writers: John Kerr, TOR; David Liedl,
TOR; Mary Catherine Gurley, OSF; Raphael Fulwider, OSF;
Baptiste Westbrook, OSF; Leonilda Avery, OSF; Sheila
Patenaude, FMM; Bernadette Raischl; Helen Budzik, OSF; and
Benedikt Mertens, OFM. We extend heartfelt gratitude to
Benedikt for letting us use his monograph to connect the chapters
of this anthology, and to Mary Catherine Gurley and Joseph
Antonelli, OFM, for sharing their writing expertise with us. We
give thanks to Margaret Carney, our good friend and teacher of
things Franciscan, for her contribution to this work and her
constant support and encouragement. We also extend this
gratitude to two sisters from Margaret's community, Barbara Ann
Zilch, OSF, who gave us the cassette tape of Ignatius Brady's
lecture on the "Rule for Hermitages," and Berenice Petrauskas,
OSF, who transcribed the lecture for us. We extend deep
gratitude to our computer consultant, Michael Cervone, for the
many painstaking hours spent refining our complicated text and
for rescuing us from some very difficult technical problems. We
are grateful to the Müller family of Eichstätt who gave us
hospitality in their home when we gave birth to this book. This
is the home of Colonel Valentin Müller (+1951), who, as
commander of Assisi during World War II, declared it a hospital
city, preserving it from the devastation of that war. We desire
as well to express our appreciation to Oktavian Schmucki, OFM
Cap, for his encouraging words about emphasizing the importance
of this original Franciscan ideal for the survival of the Order in
our time. We share his hope that this experience may touch

more than a small "spiritual" group within the Franciscan Order today. We thank Dacian Bluma, OFM, for his encouragement and suggestions.

With deep gratitude we wish to acknowledge the permissions received to translate from and publish the following authors:

Martino Conti, OFM, "Eremo ed evangelizzazione nella vita dei francescani," in G. Cardaropoli and Martino Conti, *Lettura Spirituale-Apostolica delle Fonti Francescani,* Pubblicazioni dell'Istituto Apostolico Pontificia Università Antonianum (Rome, 1980) 75-102.

Johannes Fleischacker, *Studien zu einer Eremitologie: Idee und Verwirklichung des Einsiedlergedankens im Kapuzinerorden von den Anfängen bis heute im deutschen Sprachraum* (Graz, 1988).

Benedikt Mertens, OFM, "In Eremi Vastitate Resedit," *Franziskanische Studien* (1992) 285-374, for all his contributions.

Cinzio Violante, "L' eremitismo in Occidente nei secoli XI e XII," Atti della seconda settimana di studio, *Miscellanea del Centro di Studi Medioevale IV,* (Milan, 1965) 9-23.

Eremitismo nel francescanismo medievale, Atti del XVII Convegno Internazionale della Società Internazionale di Studi Francescani, Assisi, 1991, for all of the following:
—. Edith Pasztor, "Ideali dell'eremitismo femminile In Europa tra i secoli XII-XV," 129-64;
—. Giovanna Casagrande, "Forme di vita religiosa femminili solitaria in Italia centrale," 51-94;
—. Grado G. Merlo, "Eremitismo nel francescanesimo medievale," 27-50.

Marcella Gatti, "Le Carceri di San Francesco" (Assisi, 1969), pages 15-29, authorized by the Lions Club, Assisi, Prof. Arcangelo Trovellesi, President.

Kajetan Esser, OFM, Latin text of the "Rule for Hermitages," *Opuscula Sancti Patris Francisci Assisiensis,* Editiones Collegii S. Bonaventurae Ad Claras Aquas (Grottaferrata, 1978) 296-98, authorized by Nazzareno Mariani, OFM.

Regis Armstrong, OFM Cap., "Rule for Hermitages," *St Francis of Assisi: Writings for a Gospel Life* (New York: Crossroads, 1994) 62–63.

Kajetan Esser, OFM, "Die *Regula pro eremitoriis data* Des Heiligen Franziskus von Assisi," *Franziskanische Studien* 44 (1962) 383-417.

Ignatius Brady, OFM, a recorded lecture on the "Rule for Hemitages" delivered in the summer of 1977 at the Franciscan Institute, St. Bonaventure University, St. Bonaventure, New York, authorized by Edward Coughlin, OFM, Director of The Franciscan Institute.

The Cord, at the Franciscan Institute, St. Bonaventure University, St. Bonaventure, New York, authorized by Joseph Doino, OFM, for the following articles:
—. André Cirino, OFM, "Hermitage in the City" (March, 1986) 89-96;
—. Sheila Patenaude, FMM, "Pink Magnolias or Assisi Revisited in the Bronx" (June, 1984) 162-66;
—. André Cirino, OFM, "Clare and the Rule for Hermitages" (July-August 1991) 195-202.

Costanso Cargnoni, OFM Cap., "Le case di preghiera nella storia dell'Ordine Francescano," in *Le case di preghiera nella storia e spiritualità francescana*, Studi Scelti di Francescanesimo 7 (1978) 55-112.

We wish to thank the Roderick Crispo, OFM, Provincial of the Friars Minor of the Immaculate Conception Province for his enthusiastic an generous support. We are very grateful to F. Edward Coughlin, OFM, Director of the Franciscan Institute, for publishing our work. And we remain indebted to Roberta McKelvie, OSF, our final critical reader; her technical editing assistance was the final piece which brought this work to completion.

Finally, for the creative work on our cover, we extend our gratitude to Marc Lisle for his artistic rendition of the Carceri banked in the solitude of nature.

Guidelines that will enrich the time you spend with our *child* are found in introductions to each of the five chapters. We urge you to look them over carefully for suggestions for reading the chapter and understanding our choice of material for this anthology. Ultimately, the only way for our *child* to grow and mature is through your use of this book. That would bring our *spiritual motherhood* to further fruition.

Eichstätt, December 1993
New York, April 1995
André Cirino, OFM, and Josef Raischl

Chapter One

Early Eremitical Elements
and
Movements Preceding and Contemporaneous
with the First Franciscans

Introduction

In this first section of our anthology we attempt to give the reader a survey of early eremiticism in order to better appreciate and understand Francis and Clare in their thrust for solitude. Having discovered a very rich tradition, we decided to include this material as historical background.

We begin with some biblical notions put forth by Martino Conti, OFM, scripture scholar and professor at the Antonianum in Rome. Then a few brief bridge notions about the postbiblical eremitical development are presented by the Austrian Johannes Fleischacker; Benedikt Mertens, OFM, from Mannheim, Germany, expands into the 11th century; Cinzio Violante builds on this foundation and brings the reader into the 12th century as well.

Because the Franciscan Movement has had a feminine component since its inception with the Lady Clare as well as lay people in the Order of Penitents (Secular Franciscans) joining Francis, we thought it would be appropriate to include research on the feminine hermit tradition. We conclude this section with a pair of articles by women on female hermits. Edith Pasztor, a colleague of Raoul Manselli, writes of the ideals of female eremitism in Europe from 1200 to 1500 while Giovanna Casagrande focuses on some forms of female solitary life in central Italy.

To preserve some chronological order, we spaced Mertens' and Conti's extensive research through more than one section of this anthology.

Hermitage and Evangelization
in the New Testament

by

Martino Conti, OFM[1]

Translated from the Italian
by
Nancy Celaschi, OSF

The first discussions behind the terms "hermitage and evangelization" require a suitable translation for the biblical term "desert" as well as the gospel expression "deserted place." Let us look at the two expressions in the context of the life of Christ and the Apostles, which is both the active and the contemplative life.

The "Desert" in Biblical Tradition

In Sacred Scripture the word "desert" (*midbar* in Hebrew, *eremos* in Greek) does not only mean a geographic region without water and vegetation, and therefore an uninhabited area (cf. Gn. 21:20; Ex. 3:1; Jos. 1:4; 2 Sm. 15:23; Jn. 11:54; 2 Cor. 11:26); it is also a theological concept. In its theological aspect the term "desert" can have a double meaning; it can be both positive and negative.[2]

In its negative sense the "desert" is a place not blessed by God, a place filled with mortal danger (cf. Dt. 8:15; Nm. 21:4-9; Is. 30:6) where the demons dwell (cf. Lv. 16:8,10,21,22; Lk. 8:29; 11:24), a place characterized by Israel's disobedience (cf. Ex. 14:11; Ps. 78:17, 40; Ez. 20:13). The "desert" is the opposite of inhabited land, as "curse" is to "blessing." As the opposite of the desert, inhabited land becomes the symbol of the difference between Canaan (the promised land) and Egypt (the land of slavery). In biblical language, Egypt was synonymous with the desert, understood as the dwelling place of demons (cf. Tb. 8:3) and of everything that is contrary to the people of God (cf. Ez. 20:36; Mt. 12:29, 43).

In its positive sense the "desert" recalls a privileged period in the history of salvation. In the Old Testament, it is under this aspect that the "desert" was always the desert of Sinai, site of salvation and revelation,[3] the place to which Moses repeatedly asked Pharaoh to let the people go so they could offer worship to God.[4] Their passage through the Sea of Reeds marked God's ultimate victory over Pharaoh's human arrogance and Israel's definitive liberation (cf. Ex. 13:17-15:21). In the desert of Sinai, God was revealed to Israel. Israel became God's own people; God gave them the code of the covenant and Israel was able to offer God fitting worship.[5] Hagiographers present the forty years in the desert as a time of Israel's particular intimacy with the God of its ancestors (cf. Hos. 9:10; 11:1; 12:20; 13:4-5).

The people of the covenant settle in the promised land and return to the disobedience of their ancestors (cf. Jgs.; 1-2 Kgs.); the prophets help the people to look longingly upon the generous years of their youth (cf. Hos. 2:17; Jer. 2:2) when they experienced divine salvation in the "desert" and God was revealed to Israel (cf. Ez. 16). From the special emphasis given to the salvific nature of the "desert" era comes the tendency to consider the "desert" as a time of grace and mercy: "The people that escaped the sword have found favor in the desert; . . . With age-old love I have loved you; so I have kept my mercy toward you" (Jer. 31:2-3).

Because the desert represents an ideal time, Israel expresses its desire to return to that experience again (cf. Is. 4:3; 41:18-20; 43:19-20; 42:21; 51:3). It is God who lures Israel into the desert to speak to her heart and convert her: "So I will allure her; I will lead her into the desert and speak to her heart. . . . She shall respond there as in the days of her youth, when she came up from the land of Egypt" (Hos. 2:16-17).

Israel extends in time the ideal of the "desert" whenever it turns away from whatever is contrary to the covenant, returns to its God with a sincere heart, listens to God's voice and is converted (cf. Jer. 3:6 - 4:4).

The same distinction is found in the New Testament. If, on the one hand, the period Israel spent in the desert is characterized by disobedience (cf. Heb. 3:8-9; Acts 7:41-43), so that that generation was vanquished and did not enter the promised land (cf. 1 Cor. 1:5; Heb. 3:17), on the other hand, the same period is a time of grace, and remains as such for the New Testament too; it is a time of revelation when God spoke to the people through Moses and handed on to them the "words of life" (Acts 7:38).[6]

Thus to experience the ideal of the "desert" as a time of grace means to experience the God who frees people from the power of darkness and transfers them into the kingdom of light (cf. Acts 26:17-18; Col. 1:12-13; 1 Pt. 1:9), and to listen to God who is revealed in Christ Jesus and continues to speak to human hearts in order to become known and loved.

What the "desert" was for the Hebrews, Christ is for Christians. It is in Christ's person, in fact, that the ideal of salvation and revelation connected with the "desert" theme is fulfilled: Jesus is our salvation (cf. Mt. 1:21; Lk. 1:69; 2:11,30; Acts 4:10-12; Rm. 3:21-26) and our revelation (cf. Mt. 11:27; Lk. 1:22; Jn. 1:18); in Christ we offer pleasing prayer to the heavenly Father (cf. Col. 3:17; 1 Thes. 5:18).

For today's man or woman, as in the past, returning to the desert means living the ideal, becoming detached from created things in order to meet Christ and to experience salvation, to accept revelation as the word of God, to have communion with God and the Church,[7] and to live in God's grace so as to give honor and glory to God (Eph. 1:6).

The "Deserted Place" in the Life of Christ and the Apostles

In the Gospels the expression "deserted place" is closely linked to the contemplative dimension of the life of Christ and the Apostles. For them the "deserted place" is the privileged place for prayer and encountering God.

After a day of intense activity at Capernaum (cf. Mk. 1:21-34), Jesus retired to a "deserted place"[8] to pray: "Rising very early before dawn, he left and went off to a deserted place, where he prayed" (cf. Mk. 1:35; Lk. 4:42).

The imperfect tense of the verb, *proseycheto* [prayed], tells us that Jesus' prayer lasted for some time.[9] In prolonged prayer Jesus found the quiet in which nothing separated him from God and the security of perfect adherence to the Father's will (cf. Lk. 22:41,44).[10]

The Gospels, especially the Gospel of Luke, frequently tell us about Christ's solitary prayer (cf. Mt. 14:13; Lk. 9:29; 11:1) after intense days of apostolic work. The greater Jesus' fame, and the larger the crowds flocking to listen to him and be healed of their infirmities, the more Jesus withdrew into solitary places to pray (cf. Lk 5:15-16; Mk 1:45).

Important moments in the life of Christ,[11] such as the choice of the Twelve, are also preceded by nights spent alone in prayer on the mountain: "In those days Jesus departed to the mountain to pray, and spent the night in prayer to God. When day came, Jesus called the disciples, and from them chose Twelve, whom Jesus also named apostles. . . " (Lk. 6:12-13).

Mark recalls how, after the first multiplication of loaves (cf. Mk. 6:33-44), Jesus ordered the disciples to get in the boat and go before him to the other shore, towards Bethsaida, while he sent the crowd away and, after taking leave, went alone to the mountain to pray (Mk. 6:45-46).

After days of intense work, Jesus invites the Twelve to draw away into "deserted places" to rest. Here, in calm and rest, they pray, and Christ speaks to them of the kingdom of heaven. When they return from their first missionary expedition (cf. Mk. 6:30), Jesus invites the Twelve to take a bit of rest in isolated places: "The Apostles gathered together with Jesus and reported all they had done and taught. He said to them, 'Come away by yourselves to a deserted place and rest awhile'" (Mk. 6:30-31). In fact, that was meant to be a period of quiet and recollection for them.[12]

Jesus chose the Twelve after a night spent in prayer (cf. Lk. 6:12-13); after an intense day of prayer in company with the Twelve (cf. Lk. 9:18), Jesus asks them about who he is, and tells them that he will die and rise again on the third day (cf. Lk.

9:18-22). The revelation of his glory took place on a mountain where Jesus had gone to be alone with Peter, James, and John to pray (cf. Lk. 9:28-36).

Commenting on the passage in Lk. 5:16, Valensin and Huby tell us:

> For centuries Jesus' prayer in the desert has been the object of the loving contemplation of Christian souls who saw in it both a mystery and a lesson. They admired the inner well from which the Master's activity sprang. Like Jesus, they joined the recollection of prayer to their labor in the apostolate. From the very beginning the Twelve remind us: prayer must be united to the ministry of the word (cf. Acts 6:4). Century after century this alliance of prayer and preaching prepared the Church's sanctifying activity throughout the world. Retiring to deserted places to pray while the crowd sought him, Jesus revealed the inspiration behind the Gospel and proclaimed the Good News by the power of the Holy Spirit.[13]

Taught by Christ, the Apostles were not content with daily prayer, but withdrew to "deserted places" to seek union with God, to know Christ and find the strength to fulfil the Father's will and obtain the gift of the Holy Spirit which makes them capable of proclaiming the Good News of the kingdom openly.

Combination of Contemplation and Action in the Apostolic Life

What characterizes the apostolic life is "being with Christ" and being "sent to preach" (Mk. 3:14). Mark's dyad gives the reason why the Apostles were named, for example, to live with Christ and participate in his mission.[14] "Being with Christ" is therefore the Apostles' first duty, and at the same time it is the foundation and purpose of going out to preach.[15] Their mission to evangelize cannot be separated from living in communion with Christ. In fact, it is from their intimacy with Christ that the apostolic life draws its content, coherence, and dynamism.

Accepting the invitation to "be with Christ," the Twelve share the type of life which the Son of God had chosen (cf. Mt. 8:20; Lk. 9:58; Jn. 4:34), his mission (cf. Jn. 20:21) and his fate (cf. Mt. 10:25).[16] To the Twelve and all those Jesus called from the crowd (cf. Lk. 6:13) and constituted (cf. 1 Kgs. 12:31) as disciples in the more limited sense of the word, Jesus is revealed in solitude[17] (cf. Mk. 9:2-8; Mt. 17:18), speaks about the fate awaiting Jerusalem (cf. Lk. 9:18-22), teaches them how to pray (cf. Lk. 11:1) and reveals the mystery of the kingdom of God (cf. Mk. 10:10-11; Acts 1:3).

Evangelization flows from and is prepared for by the experience of faith with Christ. Only those who live in communion with Christ can bear witness to Christ (cf. Acts 1:8), and can testify to the resurrection (cf. Lk. 24:46-48; Acts 2:32) and his glory (cf. 2 Pt. 1:18). "What we have heard, what we have seen with our eyes, what we looked upon and touched with our hands. . . . We have seen it and testify to it . . . to you" (1 Jn. 1:1-3).

Proclaiming Christ openly (cf. Acts 2:29; 4:29-31; 29:31) is typical of those who, like the Apostles (cf. Acts 10:39) and Paul (cf. Gal. 1:16), have a personal experience of him, a knowledge born of faith (cf. Jn. 6:35; *Sacrosanctum Concilium* 33; *Dei Verbum* 21), in the grace of the sacraments, and particularly in the Eucharist (cf. Jn. 6:51; *Sacrosanctum concilium* 47; *Dei Verbum* 21).

According to the Acts of the Apostles, too, prayer and evangelization are the primary, basic tasks of the Apostles.[18] As the number of disciples grew, the unity of the apostolic life was under threat of compromise; the Apostles knew that they were primarily responsible for presiding at prayer and serving the word, so they made the courageous decisions that were consistent with their vocation-mission. They called the disciples together and told them: "It is not right for us to neglect the word of God to serve at table. Select from among you seven reputable people, filled with the Spirit and wisdom, whom we shall appoint to this task, whereas we shall devote ourselves to prayer and to the ministry of the word" (Acts 6:2-4).

In fact, they had been given the specific task of taking care of divine worship and proclaiming the word.[19] Since it was not God's will that they neglect preaching the word and liturgical prayer in order to take care of other ministries, the Apostles free themselves from every other involvement which could compromise their ability to fulfil their specific vocation-mission perfectly.[20] This choice would be repeated throughout history by all those who are called to be with Christ that he might send them forth to preach" (cf. Mk. 3:14).

Evangelizers of all ages have the need and the duty to retire periodically to solitary places in order to experience personally once again the ideal of the "desert" as a moment of grace, that is, to experience the salvation of God and to allow Christ to speak to their hearts.

Endnotes

[1]M. Conti, "Contemplazione ed Evangelizzazione nella vita apostolica," G. Cardopoli and M. Conti, eds., *Lettura spirituale-apostolica delle Fonti Francescani* (Rome, 1980) 76-83.

[2]See C. Thomas and X. Leon-Dufour, "Deserto" in *Dizionario di teologia biblica,* (DCBNT) (Turin, 1968) 215-216; O. Bocher, "Deserto," DCBNT (Bologna,1976) 464-65; J. Plastaras, *Il Dio dell'Esodo* (Turin, 1977) 178-183.

[3]See E. Testa, "Il deserto come ideale" in LA 7 (1957):15.

[4]See Ex. 3:12,18; 4:23; 5:1, 3, 8, 17; 7:16, 26; 8:4, 16, 21, 23, 24, 25; 9:1,13; 10:3, 7, 8, 25, 26; 12:6, 11. Moses' request to Pharaoh to let Israel go to the desert to offer sacrifice to the God of their ancestors prepares for the constitution of the People of God with the Sinai covenant and the proclamation of its priestly prerogatives (cf. Ex 19:6; Dt 7:6; Is 61:6).

[5]See Plastaras, 138-191; G. Azou, *Dalla schiavitú al Servizio Il libro dell'Esodo* (Bologna,1975) 125-301.

[6]See G. Kittel, "Eremos" in GLNT, vol. 3, 893-94.

[7]see Testa, 15; Thomas and Leon-Dufour, 219.

[8]V. Taylor, *Marco* (Assisi, 1977) 175: "The 'deserted place' is not the desert, because the area around Capernaum was cultivated at that time; rather it refers to a solitary, remote place." See also M.J. Lagrange, Evangile selon Saint Marc, *Etudes Bibliques* (Paris, 1966) 27.

[9]G. Nolli, *Evangelio secondo Marco* (Rome, 1978) 22; A. Sisti, *Marco* (Rome,1974) 34:160.

[10]Kittel, 891-892; Sisti, 161.

[11]B. Rigaux, *Testimonianza di Luca* (Padua, 1973) 384-90.

[12]See J. Schmid, *L'evangelio secondo Marco* (Brescia, 1961) 170-71.

[13]A. Valensin, G. Huby, *Vangelo secondo san Luca,Verbum Salutis* (Rome, 1953) 107.

[14]R. Schnackenburg, *Vangelo di Marco*, vol. I (Rome, 1969) 89.

[15]G. Nolli, 59.

[16]See Schnackenburg, 89.

[17]In Mk. 4:10, as well as Lk 9:18, the Greek word means "alone," "in a solitary place," and therefore no longer in the boat or in the presence of the crowd. Cf. Nolli, 79.

[18]Cf. C. Ghidelli, *Atti degli Apostoli* (Turin, 1978) 69.

[19]Cf. A. Wirkenhauser, *Atti degli Apostoli* (Brescia, 1962) 107; J. Kürzinger, *Atti degli Apostoli*, vol. 1 (Rome, 1958) 155; C. M. Martini, *Atti degli Apostoli* (Rome, 1970), 37:118.

[20]Cf. J. Kürzinger, I: 156.

Hesychasm and Some

Hermits of the Desert

by

Johannes Fleischacker[1]

Translated from the German by

Josef Raischl and André Cirino, OFM

Hesychasm

A significant term stemming from eastern culture in eremitical spirituality is *quiet* (Latin *quies*—Greek *hesychia*). Solitary life in a cell or hermitage is the main means of attaining this *quiet*. To be totally free and able to provide inner space for God (*vacare Deo in solitudine*) requires solitary living as well as the quiet of the internal and external person.

The monk is a meditative person. If we are looking for a concept that is woven into the Rule of the Carthusians, it is *quiet, quies, hesychia*, with its synonyms—contemplation, peace, solitude.

Hesychia (*esthai* = sitting) refers to both an external and internal state of quiet, of silence, of peace, of equilibrium, and letting go. It is directed towards contemplation. *Hesychasm* looks for perfection in a loving union with God by constant prayer, reached by *hesychia*—quiet.

Since the *Justinian Code* the hesychast and the hermit have been interchangeable terms. The desert is the mother of *hesychia*.[2] *Hesychia is the first step, the proper disposition in the exercise of the spiritual life.*

In a letter to his friend Gregory Nazianzen, Basil recommends: "We have to try to keep our spirit in hesychia. An eye that constantly is moving around cannot apprehend an object. You have to fix your eyes intensely on the object in order to get a precise view. Thus the human spirit cannot penetrate the truth when loaded down by many secular cares."[3]

Eremitism is sometimes explained as an expression of the desire for the pneumatic depths of religious life and as one possible path to those depths.

Simeon, the new theologian, says:

Let me alone, sheltered in my cell.
Let me be with God who alone is good.
Stay away from me—even further away.
Let me die alone before my God who has created me.
No one should knock at my door. No one should raise their voice.
No one should visit me, neither friend nor relative.
No one should draw my spirit from meditation on the Lord.
I can see the King, I can see the true Light and the Creator of all light.
I can see the Fountain of all good, the Cause of all things.
I can see the Primordial Being,
I live in God from whom the whole universe came forth,
is nourished with energy, and also, by God's will, vanishes.
Why should I move out of my cell?
Back to that which I left? Let me be.
I want to cry and mourn over the days and nights I have wasted.[4]

Some Hermits of the Desert

Two hundred and fifty years after Christ large numbers of people moved into the desert to spend their entire lives there. The cradle of Christian eremitism is Egypt. "These Christian ascetics first lived with their families; afterwards they withdrew into solitude partly because they searched for a less distracted service of God or to avoid persecution. Other reasons stem from Egypt's social misery, taxes, military service, and the like."[5]

Historically, this is the start of a unique movement, namely that of the anchorites. The anchorites of Egypt, one of the first groups to flee from the world, developed as independent clusters.

The ascetical life of a Christian community developed into the monastic, ascetical model moving away from their own homes. In the deserts and steppes of Egypt, Palestine, Syria and Asia Minor many eremitical colonies arose.

Paul of Thebes (c. 228–341) is the first known hermit in the Christian sense of the word. His exodus into the desert is dated about 250 A.D. During the persecution by the emperor Decius (249–251), Paul fled to the desert of Thebes where he remained completely isolated for many decades. St. Antony, at age 90, met the 113 year-old hermit just before he died, and buried him.

Antony the Great (251–356) has been called the "Father of hermits and monks." About the year 370 Athanasius wrote his biography. Antony was born of rich parents. When he was 20 years' old, they died. At this time Jesus' words of invitation to the rich young man became his guide: "If you want to be perfect, go and sell what you have and give the money to the poor. Then follow me" (Mt. 19:21). He immediately put this gospel axiom into practice.

He became a model of a radical Christian life. He spent his entire life in solitude. Many followed, and Antony divided them into groups. "Soon they had disciples and had to organize them."[6] This development is the origin of Christian monasteries. However, these groups of hermits were so loosely organized that history has located them as living deep in the desert. Antony left his disciples and settled close to an oasis called Quolzonur where he lived for another 40 years and died at the age of 105. "Palestine, Cappadocia, Syria, Mesopotamia were populated by monks."[7]

Among the hermits we find very simple, illiterate people as well as theologians and mystics. Their experience is collected in the apophtegmata, which are sayings on the life-style of the desert and an account of their temptations.

In addition to these groups of hermits we find another type of eremitical life.

St. Pachomius (287–347) was the son of an Egyptian farmer. Baptized as an adult, he began to live as a hermit in Thebes. He went a step further: he founded the first real monasteries. There the monks lived together in one house, with a common rule and one leader. Thus he became the founder of the cenobitic monastic life. The first monastery was founded on the island of Tabenna in the Nile River about 330.

It is impotant to remember that "St. Benedict also began as a hermit. When disciples called him away from his cave, he organized their life into that which became a significant model for religious life in the monasteries of the West."[8] In the first chapter of his Rule, Benedict names four different types of monks:

> the Cenobites, who lived as a community of monks under the leadership of an abbot;
>
> the Anchorites, who lived a radical form of solitude and searched for a more exclusive relationship with God;
>
> the Sarabites, who lived with two or three others without a rule or superior [This term was applied to certain followers of the Franciscan Rule, namely, the Fraticelli. Eds.];
>
> the Gyrovagues, who never remained in one place, wandering from monastery to monastery according to their own desire.[9]

Endnotes

[1]J. Fleischacker, "Studien zu einer Eremitologie: Idee und Verwirklichung des Einsiedlergedankens im Kapuzineorden von den Anfängen bis heute im deutschen Sprachraum," unpublished dissertation at University of Graz, 1988, 13-15 and 47-50.

[2]J.M. Hollenstein, *Karthäuserspiritualität* (Ms. Pleterje, 1984) 30f.

[3]Anton Rotzetter, *Geist und Geistesgaben*, Seminar Spiritualität Vol. 2 (Zurich, 1980) 98.

[4]Kunkel 52 (No publication data available).

[5]K. Holtzgartner, *Chronik des Benefiziumbezirks, Zweite Chronik* (Haader, 1978) 22.

[6]S. Bonnet and B. Gouley, *Gelebte Einsamkeit:Eremiten heute* (Freiburg/ Basel/ Vienna, 1982) 142.

[7]Ibid. 143.

[8]Ibid.

[9]Cfr. ibid. 119 and the Rule of St. Benedict.

The Eremitical Movement

During the 11th Century

by

Benedikt Mertens, OFM[1]

Translated from the German by

Josef Raischl and André Cirino, OFM

1. The "New Hermits": Origins and Variety

The Historical and Geographical Outline

Analogous to the papacy and to monachism, eremitism also had its *saeculum obscurum*, its dark age. At the end of the 9th century and for parts of the 10th century, eremitical vestiges were lost. In Italy, especially, this time was marked by a loss of culture and dominion, a congruency that underlines a constant fact in the history of eremitism, namely, that a blossoming of the anchorites in the West goes hand in hand with a rich cultural and political era, with economic prosperity and social peace.[2]

Yet in the 10th century monachism did reach another peak. Centers such as Cluny, Gorze, Hirsau, Fruttuaria, Farfa, Monte Casino, and La Cava were characterized by an extension of monastic influence. Eventually abbey associations with their own customs organized monks to win independence from secular powers. A feudal system evolved within the abbey structure. The accumulation of donations and properties gave the abbeys powerful political and economic prestige.

Political and economic involvement caused this observance of monasticism to collapse. Moreover, clericalization and a one-sided emphasis on the divine office at the cost of handicraft (typical of Cluny, for example) provoked reforms. Many of these reform groups have eremitical offshoots.

The second wave of Western eremitism had already started in the 10th century with Romuald of Ravenna (952 – 1027) in whose footsteps followed the Camaldolese. The peak of the eremitical foundations is reached some fifty years later, with most of the foundations in France. Especially worthy of mention are Grandmont (Steven of Muret +1076), Fontevrault (founded by Robert of Arbrissel in 1099), Grande Chartreuse (founded by Bruno of Cologne in 1034) and Citeaux (founded by Robert of Molesmes in 1098).

Simultaneously, less influential communities with eremitical tendencies, as well as solitary hermits, were regionally concentrated all over Italy. These communities thrived in a different religious climate; some eventually united, as did the Hermits of St. Augustine in Tuscany in 1256.

The Components of Eremitism

The eremitical ideal touches all social classes as well as traditional expressions of religious life. One group of hermits or recluses from the monastic tradition remained within the borders of their abbey under the abbot's jurisdiction. This style, either limited or for a lifetime, was never common and did not cause tension within the community because "singles" were not a threat to general observance.[3]

The Cistercians, coming from a Benedictine reform, also had strong eremitical origins; their writers, however, preferred the term "solitary life."

The formation of the Camaldolese can also be traced to Benedict's *Rule*, though their form of organization as eremitical cenobites—that is, hermit colonies—is as unique as the Carthusians'.

Only the independent hermits looked for solitude outside the monastic experience. These included lay people or clerics as well as monks and canons who left their communities because they were not able to live their eremitical ideals within it.

Finally, the beginning and the development of the canons regular, especially from the Lateran Synod of 1059, was not independent of the eremitical movement.

Characteristics within the Variety

Traditionally the hermit contrasts with the cenobitic monk by reason of a more intense poverty and asceticism. The hermits looked for greater separation in order to face their "demons." In addition to this traditional monastic ideal, however, independent hermits were moderated by penitential practices, whereas the monks, by their vows, became part of the "triumphant Church and citizens of the heavenly Jerusalem." The hermits looked at themselves as penitents, anxious about their redemption. This stance was common among the voluntary penitents.[4]

The "new hermits" of the 11th and 12th centuries were not just a new wave of eremitism but also a different style of eremitism.

First, there was a different interpretation of solitude as an exterior condition for the *vacare Deo* [making space for God]. While the new hermits also looked for lonesome places, they did not reject certain forms of community life. There were different grades of personal solitude. Thus the new hermits opposed an emerging culture, and often situated their hermitages in forests, wilderness, or other remote places.

Despite the physical distance, however, hospitality as a Benedictine tradition was never questioned. In fact, numerous examples show an integration of care for the poor with the eremitical experience.

Radical poverty based on the gospel was another characteristic; the hermits were truly *pauperes Christi* [the poor ones of Christ]. They often separated themselves from the monastic practice of a personal poverty within a community that had considerable property. Biographies tell of these hermits who, when converted, distributed all their goods to the poor. Entire communities accepted the insecurity of gospel living over the comfort that comes from dependence on charity of others. Some were so negligent of their appearance and environment that they were considered miserable in the eyes of many. To be sure, their lack of personal hygiene permeated even their liturgies.

Their appreciation of manual labor and poverty grew together as different aspects of eremitism. Even though alms were accepted by some monks, others focused on manual labor to the degree that certain members of the community were designated as the workers (lay/*converse* brothers). Examples of this organization can be found in the Grande Chartreuse and the Hospice of Fontebono at Camaldoli.

Instability is a further distinguishing factor of eremitism in the High Middle Ages. Only a few hermits seemed to stay in one place. Though some hermits withdrew from curious people and disciples, many moved around due to their inner restlessness. This mobility was often combined with itinerant preaching. Permission to preach was a problem, however, especially for the lay people and was usually given only for the surrounding area. Clerics did not have general permission to preach everywhere. This entire problem can be seen as background for impending heresies.

A striking new element of eremitical life is a strong reference to the gospel and the Eastern monks and hermits. The best known example of this return to Scriptural sources is Canon Rainaldo's angry remark to Bishop Ivo of Chartres, who was trying to remove him from eremitical life. Having described the evangelical prescriptions of the primitive Church, he attacks the contemporary cenobites: "But this form of perfection, by their own witness, the cenobitic cloisters rarely or never embrace; because, as I see it, they happen to exclude as far as they can the poverty that the poor Christ preached."[5]

This last item is especially typical of the eremitical movement, namely, to pick up intensely traditional monastic and eremitical intentions and at the same time to oppose contemporary cenobitism. Since this move to the sources became radical, many different forms of itinerant preaching and inclusion were born. Often a single eremitical life contained all of those elements.[6]

We can conclude that in the 11th and 12th centuries there was a general tendency towards the institutionalization and clericalization of the independent eremitical movement. Very often this enormous growth demanded more organization than their various rules and customs offered.

The eremitical movement provided the possibility of living a religious life beyond social barriers known to traditional monasticism. Leyser says:

> The eremitical movement . . . had created institutions where a new spirituality was to flourish; it had broken the monopoly of the black monks. At the same time, it had come much closer to the traditional forms of monasticism than had originally been intended. It was a movement which had proved too popular, and if this made possible its successes, it was likewise the reason for its failures. . . .[7]

2. Eremitical Forms in France

The following representatives of the eremitical movement of the High Middle Ages are described here as examples of the variety of eremitical life forms.

Robert of Arbrissel and Fontevrault

One of the most exciting founders of religious orders in his time certainly was Robert of Arbrissel.[8] He was born about 1045 A.D. in the diocese of Rennes. As the illegitimate son of a priest, he probably took over his father's position as a canon. Only during his time in Paris from 1078 to 1088 did he begin theological studies. Realizing the low moral standards of the clerics, he underwent a deep conversion. In 1088-89 Bishop Silvester depended on him for the renewal of the diocese of Rennes. After the bishop's death in 1093 Robert was expelled by the clerics for his overzealousness, for they were unwilling to accept reform. Robert fled to Angiers where he attended the cathedral school under Marbod, who later became the bishop of Rennes. During these two years Robert underwent an even more radical conversion. In 1095 he finally realized his dream of living a hermit's life.[9]

Not far from the place of his failures, he began to live a life of the strictest penance. Soon many people followed his example and eloquent preaching. They joined him as companions. The status of this congregation of hermits changed in 1096 when Robert received permission to preach from Pope Urban II. His community was accepted at the same time as canons under St. Augustine's Rule.

For two years he traveled around preaching and guiding his canons. In 1098 he left Fontevrault for good to spend all of his time preaching. Though unsuccessful in reforming the clerics, his preaching touched the people. Soon many wanted to follow him—men and women of all ages, widows, lepers and prostitutes. He rejected no one.[10]

The bishop of Rennes, Marbod, reacted negatively to Robert's preaching, especially when it concerned clerical vices. For that reason, as well as for his unkempt appearance and suspicious relationships with women, Robert was summoned to appear at the Synod of Poitiers in 1100. His movement did not fit any already existing category. Since women, particularly noble women, evolved within Robert's monastic systems, the hierarchy, through the Synod, attempted to contain them within legal limits. In 1104 Robert left the leadership to a prioress when he journeyed through France on a preaching mission. It was at this time that he established various communities dependent on Fontevrault. His work was threatened with assimilation into regular cenobitism by Benedictine statutes, but he received papal approval of his Rule and foundation in 1115. According to Robert's Rule, the superior is called abbess and spiritual leader (shepherd) of male and female hermits/monks.

What did the organization at Fontevrault look like? To begin with, there was a strict separation of the women from the men. The women were assigned the contemplative role; the men did the manual work; the clerics did their own work. This division of labor and contemplative living was based on gender. The spiritual and organizational dimensions of their structure can be found in contemporary literature. The Martha/Mary paradigm (Lk. 10:38-42) began to emerge.

Robert of Arbrissel offered a religious life in common and in solitude to women and the marginalized of society, thus breaking the barriers of status. Even though the foundation of Fontevrault, which existed up to the French Revolution, never expanded beyond France and Spain, there is a striking similarity to the Franciscan movement in the 13th century. Francis of Assisi accepted all kinds of people in his movement. Thus Francis, inspired by God, organized his followers: the Friars Minor, the Poor Ladies, and the Brothers and Sisters of Penance.

Stephen of Muret and Grandmont

A contemporary of Robert was Stephen of Muret (c.1043-c.1124), founder of the eremitical order of Grandmont. His followers' writings tell us about his life and work.[11] We cannot rely much on the *Vita* for biographical details. In the *Liber sententiarum* [*Book of Sentences*] and the *Regula* [Rule] we find his spiritual testament.

Stephen was born in Thiers/Auvergne and as a child went with his father on pilgrimage to the sanctuary of St. Nicholas at Bari. Later he remained for twelve years with Bishop Milo at Benevento, where he was attracted to the severe and withdrawn life of the Calabrian hermits. After four years in Rome Stephen returned to France to seek out suitable places to serve God and do penance according to the style of the Calabrian hermits. Eventually Stephen settled in Muret, a wooded and mountainous area of Limousin. In 1078, at age thirty, Stephen established his own hermitage. Though only a few joined him in his severe, ascetical solitude, Stephen's preaching was received well.

A Roman legate became acquainted with Stephen's form of life in this cold place and inquired about his Rule. Not accepting the classification of monk, canon, or hermit, his simple answer was:: "My honor is nothing."[12] Stephen died in 1124.

Stephen's program is described in the introduction to the *Book of Sentences*: there is no Rule other than the gospel of Christ.[13] Again and again he emphasized his independence from following traditional Rules, yet they exerted an influence on the way he lived. Stephen's gospel way of life is characterized by a radical poverty and solitude as underlying themes in the Rule and the *Sentences*. Poverty is interpreted as the strict rejection of the possession of land, churches, or animals.[14] Begging for alms is only allowed if there is not enough for the day.[15] The hermits were instructed to give alms to the poor, and speaking to the poor was considered an honor.[16]

The Rule does not allow any preaching outside the dwelling and limits outside contacts only to visitors and guests. The same Rule restricted the hermit to his cell, because if he could not find God inside, he would not find God outside.[17]

According to Lk. 10:38-42, services are disposed accordingly: the clerics for contemplation and spiritual ministry; the lay brothers for the temporal care of the cells and outside contacts. Surprisingly, the Rule allows enough space for individual decisions according to each situation, and charity rules over all.[18]

When Stephen died in 1124, the congregation looked for another place because of difficulties with the Augustinians. Finally the congregation arrived at Grandmont/Limoges. From there the young Order expanded. In 1163 there were about 40 independent cells, and 130 by the year 1200.

Because of a growing clericalization, the order experienced a deep crisis at the end of the 12th century. Only by the intervention of Innocent III were the lay brothers, who felt their rights threatened, able to be reasssured of their rights.

The Carthusians

With the Carthusians there emerged the most original and steady expression of the eremitical movement of the High Middle Ages.[19]

After a carreer as cathedral scholar and episcopal chancellor at Reims, Bruno of Cologne, together with six companions, withdrew in 1084 to Chartreuse—near Grenoble—to live as strict hermits. This was the origin of the Carthusians. When he followed Urban II´s call to Rome, Bruno still kept in contact by letter with Chartreuse. He died in 1101 in his Calabrian foundation.

The eremitical colony of Chartreuse became stronger and cooperated with other foundations. In 1127 the Carthusian customs were published and sent to all Carthusians by Guigo I, the fifth prior of the mother-house.[20] These customs of Chartreuse were soon accepted by the others. Together with the statutes they form the legal code of the Order. Bruno had never written down his way of life, yet contemporary witnesses testify to the authenticity of the collection of the books of customs.

The Carthusians combined the cenobitic and eremitical elements in a form of life in its own setting completely attuned to their needs. The whole complex is split into two separate monasteries, the lower house for the lay brothers and the upper for the monks. Both groups were separated even at gatherings on feast days. Clear descriptions of the single rooms exist only for the upper house. Contrary to the traditional *coenobium*, or monastic community, not exceeding thirteen, each monk had his own cell with a garden. In the early years, the *coenobium* was a twig and clay hut. These cells were situated in a rectangle around the wooden and covered cloister connecting the cells. In the middle of the rectangle there is a graveyard. The church borders the cloister just by the choir. Alongside the church surrounding another small cloister are common rooms such as the kitchen, refectory, dormitory, and library. The cell guaranteed eremitical solitude for praying, cooking and individual daily living activity at least during the week. For work, the monk had books to copy and bind, and a garden to tend. They all gathered for community mass, matins and vespers. On Sundays they held chapter, engaged in conversation after lunch in the cloister, and enjoyed a weekly walk.

There are only vague texts written about the lay brothers, who numbered no more than sixteen. They worked to support the entire community. The total number of people in the monastery could not be more than they could care for themselves. The monks could not be dependent on benefactors.

With the Carthusians, the eremitical life, for the first time, had become both a steady and institutionalized alternative to the monastic, canonical, and individual offshoots of this movement.

In Francis's time the Carthusian Order had 32 houses in France, yet remained unknown in central Italy. The four Italian foundations dating from 1171 concentrated in the areas of Cuneo, Turin, and Frosinone.[21]

The Cistercians[22]

The Cistercians' way of life is summarized well by L.J. Lekai: "Their will is to live the Rule without compromise . . . and they preserved the absolute authority of St. Benedict and his Rule."[23] Most of the Cistercian abbeys reached their economical peak in the 12th century. Several hundred people could live in one place. Yet the partly eremitical impulse of the first generation of Cistercians never disappeared, at least not in their writing.

This return to the Fathers of the desert and eremitical ideas happened in the context of an apology against the Cluniac reform,[24] as well as by letters and personal friendships between leading writers of the young Order and their eremitical colleagues. In this context William of St.Thierry (+1148) wrote his famous letter to the Carthusians of Mont-Dieu;[25] Aelred of Rievaulx (+1167) gave the *Book of the Way of Life for Women Recluses* to his sister.[26]

The Carthusian eremitical idea is based on the typology of Mary and Martha.[27] Esser maintains that this is one of the influential elements of Francis's eremitical rule.[28] Yet this typology is very well known in the whole contemporary eremitical movement. So we cannot prove a direct influence. On the other hand, there is proof that there was contact of the first Friars Minor with the Cistercians. At Francis's death there was only one Cistercian abbey in Umbria. This is proven by a statute of Honorius III issued in 1223 stating that no member of either Order is allowed to join the other.[29] In fact, the mendicants were a threat to the Cistercians because they admitted laymen as potential candidates and full members of the order (with equal rights with the clerics!). The laymen's departure left the abbeys in ruin and materially impoverished.[30]

From 1216 on, there were two Cistercian abbots present at the chapters of the Friars Minor. This was ordered by the Fourth Lateran Council of 1215.[31] The Cistercians were favored by the Roman Curia. Because of that privileged position, Cardinal Hugolino appointed a Cistercian to be the first visitor of the Poor Clares.[32]

Although Francis's eremitism cannot be shown to have been influenced by the Cistercians, Francis lived during Bernard's time and was impressed by Cistercian spirituality which emphasized the imitation of the humanity of Jesus and paved the way for the poverty movement.[33]

3. The Eremitical Geography of Italy

In addition to France, Italy was a center of monastic reform and the blossoming of eremitism in the age of the Gregorian reform.

Romuald of Ravenna and the Camaldolese

One of the most stable and more important congregations of Italian hermits was the Camaldolese founded by Romuald of Ravenna (c. 952 - 1027). When he was about twenty years old, Romuald joined the abbey of St. Apollinare in Classe. After three years he left the abbey because of their poor discipline. In Venice Romuald entrusted himself to Marinus, a hermit, but he eventually left to join Abbot Guarino in the Pyrenees. From 978 to 982 Romuald lived in a hermitage in the shadow of the monastery and received his eremitical formation by reading Cassian and the lives of the Fathers of the Church. From his return to his native Italy until his death, Romuald's life can be described as a restless journey. Romuald's fantasy was to connect the entire world into a hermitage. [34] To support this dream, history shows that he had many disciples and founded hermitages and monasteries. Romuald's preaching,[35] as well as his silence, attracted the hearts of his listeners.

Secluded and unapproachable places, such as the woods of the Appenines and the Adriatic swamplands, were uppermost in Romuald's mind.[36] Yet this was not enough for him. At the request of Kings Borislav and Otto III, Romuald sent some brothers to the Slavonic people.[37] After their martyrdom Romuald received permission from Pope Sergius IV to go to Hungary, but because of illness he was unable to do so.[38]

The Camaldolese eremitical model (a small autonomous circle of shared or individual[39] hermitages around a church) can be found in Romuald's biography. When their numbers increased, they established a monastery next to their cells. An abbot was installed as superior of the entire compound. When Romuald died in 1027 at Val di Castro, this troublesome and self-willed reformer did not leave any writings. Many of his foundations ceased to exist at his death. Nevertheless, his work continued within the Camaldolese foundation in the diocese of Arezzo.

It was probably the intuition of the Bishops of Arezzo that preserved and protected the spiritual dimension of the strict eremitical life that led to the great expansion of Camaldoli, so that by the 12th century it was in the forefront of a huge federation of monasteries in central Italy and Sardinia.[40] During the 13th and 14th centuries many abbeys joined this federation.

The orally-collected customs of Camaldoli intended for all monasteries were written down under the fourth prior, Rudolf (1074-89). Additional sources were the *Life of Romuald* and the *Statutes* for the eremitical community of Fonte Avellana by Peter Damian. The Rule basically refers to the hermits at Camaldoli but also describes the eremitical life of Fontebono governed by Benedict's Rule.

A spirit of cooperation between hermitage and cenobium is clearly depicted in the earlier constitutions. The hospice Fontebono primarily took care of charitable functions, thus guaranteeing absolute solitude to the hermits.

According to Romuald's Rule, the cenobites served the hermits. The sick hermits were cared for in the hospice and the dead ones buried within the hermitage.[41] All material care was assumed by the monastery[42] to protect the contemplation of the hermits.[43] This practice is clear because of the demands of the eremitical life. To come to solitude was the highest perfection a hermit could live.[44]

Among the various regulations of the Rule regarding eremitical observance, the dominant features were fasting, the liturgical hours, and remaining in one´s cell. There were two periods of fasting with bread, water, and salt for the Camaldolese, except on Thursdays and Sundays. Outside of these times common meals were allowed. During Lent each hermit prayed two psalms in his cell in addition to the liturgical hours. Apart from the times of penance they gathered for the liturgical hours in the church. However, all hermits remained in their cells during Lent and on fast days. The Rule and the Constitutions acknowledge the recluse brothers who never left their cells.[45]

Romuald dedicated a major portion of his Rule to the spirituality of eremitical life. Chapters 2 through 9 offer eremitical models from the Old and New Testaments, the monastic tradition and the writings of philosophers. Of special importance is the motif of the imitation of Christ. Besides the allegorical interpretation of eremitical virtues (chapters 39-47), we note the instructions to practice meditation (chapter 44) as well as the biblical basis for the active and contemplative life from the models, Mary-Martha and Leah-Rachel (chapter 37 f.).

In the early 13th century the Camaldolese were in the Umbrian valley. There is the Abbey of San Silvestro on Monte Subasio near Spello, close to Assisi. Crosara speaks of the golden period of the Order between 1113 and 1299 with 21 hermitages and 86 abbeys.[46] Some historians claim that Francis and Cardinal Hugolino visited the hermitage of Camaldoli during the summer of 1220.

In 1188, the Camaldolese legal code of 1080-85, confirmed under the general prior Placidus II, added some interesting points such as forbidding possessions for individual hermits and enjoining complete silence.[47] Thus the Camaldolese Constitutions were a possible influence on the eremitical ideas of Francis.

Peter Damian and Fonte Avellana[48]

Romuald's concept of eremitism was adopted, explained, and defended by Peter Damian (1007-1072). In fact, it was Peter Damian who theologically arranged the eremitical ideals, separating them from traditional monasticism.

In 1035, Peter Damian, the well-educated man from Ravenna with no monastic formation, entered the hermitage of Fonte Avellana near Gubbio, Umbria. In the role of prior from 1043, Peter Damian attracted many to this foundation. The legal codes for Fonte Avellana are: *The Order of Hermits and Resources of the Hermitage at Fonte Avellana* (c.1045-1050) and the *Letter to Stephen the Monk* about the statutes of his congregation (1057).[49] The regulations were more or less the same as Romuald's, and included literal quotations from the Camaldolese texts. We have only to mention the architectonic structure of the setting.

Unlike the Camaldolese, Peter Damian does not mention dependent monasteries which are structurally separated. According to Peter Damian, the hermitage plan indicates a church in its center, with the usual monastic buildings: chapter hall, refectory, even a library situated in the compound. The entire hermitage had about 35 inhabitants. The cells of the monks were spread about but close to the church with one or two inhabitants in each cell, including novices. In addition to these there were the cellarer and other hermits living around the church who were responsible for certain duties.

As theologian among the hermits Peter Damian succeeded in describing the eremitical life not just as a prolongation of ceno-bitism but in its proper position within the church. Defending himself by quoting Benedict's Rule brought about a serious conflict with the cenobites. He calls Benedict "the cultivator of solitude."[50]

In 1057 Peter Damian was made Cardinal Bishop of Ostia and was involved in church politics and the work of reformation. Yet he still kept in touch with Fonte Avellana, to which he returned in 1066 upon resigning as bishop. He did not refuse further legacies.

Fonte Avellana never became the head of a larger congregation. From the 11th century up to the unification with Camaldoli in 1569, it could count only 8 hermitages and 30 monasteries, including Umbria as well. There is no evidence in the Franciscan sources of Francis having contact with the Avellanites. Nevertheless, Peter Damian's writings were spread far and wide. Francis's "Salutation to the Blessed Virgin Mary" seems to be influenced especially in vocabulary and ideas by the writing of Peter Damian.[51] And we should not forget that it was Peter Damian who composed the hymn "The Illustrious Goodness of Rufinus" for the people of Assisi in honor of their bishop-martyr and patron, St. Rufino.[52]

Southern Italy

An important contribution to the eremitical life of the High Middle Ages happened in southern Italy. Under the influence of Byzantine traditions, Nilus of Rossano (910-1004), Romuald's contemporary, spread the monasticism of Basil. In addition to that cenobitic presence, there has always been a steady eremitical presence.[53] In spite of the geographical limitation of southern Italy, there is no proof for any direct influence on Romuald and Peter Damian. There is some contact with the Latin monastic reform inspired by Greek models. It could be possible that Umbria was influenced by traveling monks coming from the south towards the Italian Byzantine center, Ravenna.[54]

John of Matera (1070-1139),[55] who first lived as a Basilian monk near Tarento, began a restless journey searching for a new place to live his ideals of solitude and severe penance. He bypassed Calabria and spent two years in Sicily. John later returned home to Matera where he did some preaching and gathered a small group of disciples for whom he founded his first monastery. Further stops on his journey were made at Capua, Monte Laceno, and Monte Gargano. John settled again in Pulsano and founded a monastery for the fifty disciples he gathered in a few months. The hermits' congregation used Benedict's Rule, but added some eremitical elements such as establishing cells in the caves of the monastery for individual solitude. Pulsano was not his only foundation. After John's death, and under the direction of Pulsano, his observance spread to Foggia. During the pontificate of Innocent III, the number of independent monasteries peaked not only in southern Italy but also in Tuscany. Because of his spirituality—itinerant preaching, solitude, penance, manual labor, and alms—John of Matera broke away from the contemporary feudal abbey, anticipating the mendicant ideals a century beforehand.[56]

William of Vercelli (1085-1142)[57] had a similar life. After returning from a pilgrimage to Santiago de Compostela, he became an itinerant in Apulia and Campania. William interrupted his itinerancy by periods of eremitical withdrawal. In 1124, together with some companions, William founded the monastery Montevergine near Avellino. It soon became a Marian shrine and the first of a loose association of monasteries in southern Italy and Sicily, which blossomed until the 14th century.

Upon returning from a visit to Salerno with the Norman King Roger II, William died in 1142 at Goleto. Like John he did not leave any writings to his followers. The starting point of William's religious constitution is Benedict's Rule, which interprets and clarifies contemporary customs of congregations like La Cava and Monte Cassino. However, he added an eremitical character to his foundation. Thus while William's eremitism was based on monastic tradition, his characteristic elements of radical poverty and a special closeness to the poor influenced the direction of mendicant spirituality.

"Thebes" in Central Italy

In addition to hermits living in large organized communities in Italy, we find a local and regional concentration of eremitical and individual penitents, a great percentage of whom were lay persons. Some mountainous regions and forests had such large concentrations of these hermits that they were called the "Italian Thebes." We will concentrate on those areas of importance at the beginning of the 13th century in relation to Francis's own Umbria.

First, let us consider Montagna dei Fiori near Ascoli in the Marches.[58] Depending on the region, different terminology is used —incarcerati, cellari, cellani, reclusi, murati, eremiti[59] —indicating people living close to churches in small communities. Thomas of Celano notes Francis's successful preaching in Ascoli. Thus, thirty clerics and lay people joined his order (1Cel 62).

Documents for this period are few in number, though there is one (1261) which testifies that female recluses predominated in the region of Fabriano in the Marches during the 12th century. So there is the possibility of local eremitism at the beginning of this century.[60]

The mountain range of Monte Pisano between Lucca and Pisa in Tuscany was called *mons eremiticus*, the hermits' mountain. There were individual hermits as well as eremitical communities of canonical origins, such as the hermitage of San Pantaleone

(1044) and the "Order of Hermits of the Church and Shrine of Rusticus" (1202).[61]

The most important example of an Italian "Thebes" was Monteluco, above Spoleto, about 30 miles from Assisi.[62] The founder of the eremitical life on Monteluco is Benedict's contemporary Isaac of Syria, who came to Spoleto under the Goths and died there around 532. On the site of Isaac's cell the hermits built the monastery of San Giuliano, where Syrian influences are still extant. Isaac was joined by other oriental monks. The neighboring hills were eremitically settled as well. According to the Syrian model, the hermits' huts or caves were grouped freely around the *asceterium*[63] where Isaac was teaching. After his death the monastery of San Giuliano became a cenobium, first a Cassianese and then a Cluniac abbey without ever extinguishing independent eremitism.

In the second half of the 13th century the encounter between the eremitical tradition of Monteluco and Franciscan spirituality inspired a widespread ascetical movement of women in cloistered and recluse communities. Francis certainly knew this eremitical center. Local Franciscan tradition links the foundation of a Friars Minor settlement of 1218 in Monteluco with the hermits of Monteluco.[64]

There seems to be a direct influence on Francis's eremitism by the eremitical tradition of Monte Subasio. This mountain, with its rough, wild view, and solitude, attracted monks and hermits from the time of the Barbarian invasions.[65] Besides the two abbeys of San Benedetto and San Silvestro, the anchoritic life was blossoming. Local witnesses note that two hills—Santa Maddalena and Colle Sant'Antonio—were eremitical from of old,[66] as well as the chapels of Santa Maddalena in Monte, San Giacomo, and Sant'Antonio, all named in a papal bull of Innocent III to Bishop Guido of Assisi.[67] Citing a papal bull, Fortini tells us the chapel of Santa Maddalena was used by hermits.[68] In the same document we find the sentence "the hermitage of Tenplus with the hill that is said to be royal" and Fortini shows that this means the hermitage or cave of the hermit Tenplus.[69]

In contemporary language *carcer* is used in this connection to stand for the voluntary separation from human surroundings. The word means "prison."[70] Thus Francis, by founding his hermitage of the Carceri on Mount Subasio, followed an old tradition of eremitical life.

Eremitical Groups Preceding the Great Union (1256) with the Order of the Hermits of St. Augustine

The eremitical movement of the High Middle Ages, begun in the 11th century, peaked in the second half of the 12th century in Tuscany, the Marches, and Romagna.

The beginning of the 13th century brought about a significant change. Almost all of those groups abandoned their original eremitical goal and chose begging and pastoral work instead. This tendency of trying to adapt to the new mendicant orders was recognizable within the eremitical communities. This adaptation is also due to the political interests of a very active Roman Curia. The Curia strictly enforced this adaptation and succeeded in unifying the eremitical groups and Orders of central Italy into the one Order of Hermits of St. Augustine. Having faced this political and religious chaos, the Roman Curia succeeded by ordering the hermits to fight for the papacy and for orthodoxy.[71] We will focus on two of the communities of the Great Union in the remaining section.

Extant sources for the life of the French nobleman and soldier, William of Malavalle (a founder of the Williamites), are poor and unreliable.[72] Before William came to Italy to become a hermit, he went on a pilgrimage of penance to Palestine. He lived as an anchorite. This stay is associated with his excommunication by Pope Eugene III because of an unknown serious crime.[73]

His biography claims William became a hermit in imitation of Christ. Thus, conversion for him meant to live in intimate communion with the suffering Savior, in penance and in solitude with the imprisoned Savior.[74] After attempting in vain to set up and reform the eremitical communities of Monte Pisano and Poggio al Pruno, William settled with two companions in the wilderness of Malavalle near Grosseto from September 1156 until his death on February 10, 1157. William's rigorous asceticism included constant fasting, prayer, hard manual labor, and strange practices of penance.[75]

William's first disciple, Albert, founded an eremitical community on the burial site of the saintly and venerated William. Shortly after the beginning of the 13th century the group was accepted by Rome as an Order and spread slowly throughout Tuscany, Latium, and the Marches. The approval of the Benedictine Rule, the Cistercian Constitutions, and pastoral ministries (1238) by Gregory IX terminated the "eremitical stagnation" of this period. These relaxations spread rapidly through Germany, Belgium, France, Hungary, and Bohemia before 1256 without ever eliminating the eremitical background completely.[76] The Williamites were the only group which refused the unification of 1256.[77]

History offers more information on the spirituality and life of John Bonus (1168-1249) from Mantua, founder of an Order lasting until 1256. All the documents and acts of his canonization process are still available (even though he was never canonized).[78]

The basic elements of his spirituality are strikingly close to Francis of Assisi. Not much is written about the time before his conversion. But we know that after it, John spent almost all of his time in the hermitage of Budriolo near Cesena, Romagna (1209-1249). He called himself *peccator eremita*, the sinner hermit.[79] [Trans. note: This is not the first time such a "phenomenon" occurs in these texts about eremitical life in the 11th to 13th centuries because of his life prior to his conversion.] Around 1217 John gathered his first companions at Budriolo. In 1225 they accepted the eremitical habit. About the same time they were allowed to live as regulars according to St. Augustine's Rule.

Among John's eremitical practices, we note his constant silence and fasting according to the liturgical calendar of the time.[80] Similar to the lay Friars Minor, John's prayer mainly was repeating the Lord's Prayer as well as other simple formulas. In his pastoral work John faced the political and religious dangers of the beginning of the 13th century.[81]

John's preaching records reveal him as a staunch defender of orthodoxy. Though he travels the annals of history as an uneducated man, his high respect for papal authority and his reverence for the eucharist and priesthood win for John a lasting reputation. We see similar themes in Francis's writings. (Cf. EpOrd 27 and the Testament 6. 8-10.)

The hermits of John Bonus traveled over northern Italy from the early 1230s. The Order embarked on a path of begging, preaching, and pastoral work. The number of priests increased in the community. Participation in parish work marked the turning point for a lay community living eremitically to becoming an Order providing ministry to the people of God.[82]

John himself seems to have rejected this dynamic of the growing order. Like Francis (who returned from Palestine in 1220 and removed himself from leadership in the Order), John stepped down from leadership, entrusting it to Fr. Andrew, a trustworthy friar. After the founder's death a schism broke out between the contrary poles of eremitism and urban pastoral work. Up to the Great Union this schism could not be breached.

4. Summary

1. Although the eremitical life of the 11th to 13th centuries is diverse and difficult to grasp, both in terminology and in content, we can still speak of an historical spiritual movement in those times. The phenomenon of eremitism was present in many geographic areas where it touched all social classes and expressions of religious life.

2. There was a very flexible element present wherein eremitical life and itinerant preaching were combined with stability as well. Eremitism, marked by order and a high degree of strict enclosure, was still able to serve the people.

3. The ongoing inspiration for this way of life was rooted in premonastic, Eastern eremitical traditions and in direct references to those Gospels that placed strong emphasis on poverty and penance. These sources of inspiration corre- lated to the sometimes radical break from the revived culture of the cities and contemporary religious groups (cenobitism). Thus, the practice of eremitism of the High Middle Ages, following the poverty movement, became a

base for ecclesiastical reform within the church and society.

4. As early as 1150, it should be noted, there was a strong tendency towards institutionalization and a return to monastic rules. When many eremitical groups accepted proven religious rules, these groups lost their specific eremitical character.

5. In Assisi, at the beginning of the 13th century, groups of hermits and recluses blossomed. Great tensions arose in Tuscany between those who wanted to shun the world as hermits and those who wanted to respond to the pastoral needs of the emerging cities. One group would later evolve as the Hermits of St. Augustine. These tensions spawned new directions for the mendicants and religious orders dedicated to serving the pastoral needs of the people.

Endnotes

[1] B. Mertens, "'In eremi vastitate resedit' Der Widerhall der eremitischen Bewegung des Hochmittelalters bei Franziskus von Assisi," *Franziskanische Studien* 74 (1992): 285-374; 288-319.

[2] Cfr. J. Sainsaulieu, "Ermites II Occident," *Dictionnaire d'Histoire et Géographie Ecclésiastique* (DHGE) XV, 773.

[3] H. Leyser, *Hermits and the New Monasticism: A Study of Religious Communities in Western Europe, 1000-1500* (London, 1984) 75: "This peaceful co-existence between monks and hermits was possible only because it had become the belief that the eremitical life was the way for the few."

[4] C. E. Delaruelle, "Les ermites et la spiritualité populaire," *L'Eremitismo in Occidente*, 221 ff.

[5] Quoted in G. Morin, "Rainaud l'ermite et Ives de Chartres: un épisode de la crise du cénobitisme aux XI et XII siècles," *RBen* 40 (1928): 99-115; 101.

[6] G. Constable remarks in his "Eremitical forms of Monastic Life" in *Monks, Hermits and Crusaders in Medieval Europe* (London, 1988), 249 writes: "While no one of these diverse tendencies in eremitism was in itself new—to a greater or lesser degree—they intensified in the twelfth century to a point where it is almost impossible to say exactly what it meant to be a hermit, and where people leading very different types of life were considered, by themselves and others, to be hermits."

[7] Leyser, 105.

[8] For the biographical notes see J. Delarun, *L'impossible sainteté; La vie retrouvée de Robert d'Arbrissel* (Paris, 1985) 1045-1116, as well as J.-M. Bienvenu, "Roberto d'Arbrissel" in: DIP III, 1865-68 and G. Oury, "Fontevrault" in: DIP IV, 127-29. There are also more bibliographic details to be found.

[9] Balderich von Dol, *Vita Roberti* II.11, in: PL 162, col. 1049 C.

[10] Cfr. ibid. III.16, col. 1051 C.

[11]Scriptores ordinis Grandmontensis in: CChrCM.

[12]*Vita Stephani* c. XXXII, "De Heremitis Calabriae" in: CCHrCM VIII, 121.

[13]"Liber de doctrinis vel liber sententiarum seu rationum Beati viri Stephani primi patris religionis grandmontensis," CChrCM VIII, 7.

[14]Cfr. Regula III *De terris non habendis*, 71 f.; V *De ecclesiis non habendis*, 73 f.; VI *De bestiis non habendis*, 74. Also, Francis in his earlier Rule (RegNB) forbids having animals.

[15]Regula IX *De questu vitando*, 75.

[16]Regula XXXVII *De beneficio pauperibus erogando*, 86.

[17]Regula LIV and XLVI, 93 and 89 f.

[18]The *conversi* should not dominate the others by organizing everything but love them. This thought is developed more in Regula LIX *De mutuo fratrum obsequio*, 95 f.; Cfr. also *Liber Sententiarum* XLVI *De caritate et excellentia caritatis*, 46 f.

[19]For the actual bibliography see the article by J. Hogg, "Kartäuser," in: TRE XVII, 666-73.

[20]Published by M. LaPorte, *Guigues Ier. Coutumes de Chartreuse* (SC 313), Paris, 1984.

[21]The Calabrian foundation of Bruno left the cooperation already in the middle of the 12th century.

[22]A voluminous commented bibliography up to 1977 is to be found in J. Lekai, *The Cistercians Ideals and Reality* (Ohio, 1977) 400-41.

[23]Lekai, 228.

[24]Writers like Stephen Harding (+1134) and Bernard of Clairvaux (+1153).

[25]J. Dechanet, *Guillaume de Saint-Thierry Lettre aux frères du Mont-Dieu* (Lettre d'Or) (SC 223) (Paris 1975).

[26]Book concerning the institution of recluses, cited by C.H. Talbot in work edited by A. Hoste, *Aelrede Rievallensis opera omnia* (CChrCM I) (Turmhout, 1971) 637-82.

[27]Cfr. ibid. 660 f. 667.

[28]Cfr. K. Esser, *Anfänge und ursprüngliche Zielsetzungen des Ordens der Minderbrüder* (Leiden, 1966) 243.

[29]Cfr. Esser, 23.

[30]Cfr. A. Schneider, *Die Cistercienser Geschichte, Geist, Kunst* (Cologne, 1986), 51.

[31]Cfr. Esser, 84.

[32]L. Oliger, "Documenta originis Clarissarum," AFH 15 (1922): 81. It was Fr. Ambrose (1218-1219/20 and 1220-1223).

[33]Cfr. W. DeParis, "Rapports de Saint François d'Assise avec le mouvement spirituel du XIIe siècle," EtFrNS 12 (1962):129-42. Mentioning parallels in Francis's writings and the mystical theology of the 12th century, the author shows that Francis has to be placed right into the mainstreams of spirituality of his age.

[34]*Vita Romualdi des Petrus Damiani*, G. Tabacco (Rome, 1957) 37, 78.

[35]Ibid. 52, 94.

[36]Cfr. G. Tabacco, "Romualdo di Ravenna e gli inizi dell'eremitismo camaldolese," *L'Eremitismo in Occidente*, 73-119.

[37]*Vita quinque fratrum* II, 719.

[38]Cfr. *Vita Romualdi*, 39; 79-82.

[39]In regard to Romuald himself, we are told (VR 31, 68): "But wherever the holy man would choose to settle, he first of all used to make an oratory with an altar within his small cell. Then on withdrawing into seclusion, he would close off the approach."

[40]Cfr. W. Kurze, "Zur Geschichte Camaldolis im Zeitalter der Reform," *Il monachesimo e la riforma ecclesiastica (1049-1122)* (Miscellanea del Centro di Studi Medievali VI) (Milan, 1971) 399-415.

[41]F. Crosara, *Le Constitutiones e le Regulae de vita eremitica del B. Rodolfo Prima legislazione camaldolese nella riforma gregoriana* (Rome, 1970) 19.

[42]Cfr. Regula, ch. 22-29.

[43]Cfr. ibid. ch. 28 and 59.

[44]Constitutiones 3, 39. According to that the cenobites in the hospice are preparing to be hermits as well (Cfr. 4, 40).

[45]Cfr. G. Cacciamani, "La Réclusion dans l'ordre camaldule," RAM 38 (1962): 37-54; 273-87.

[46]Cfr. Crosara, 19.

[47]Cfr. G.B. Mitarelli and A. Costadoni, *Annales Camaldulenses*, Vol 4 (Venice, 1759) 127- 29.

[48]Cfr. for bibliographical notes on Peter Damian, see H.P. Laqua, *Traditionen und Leitbilder bei dem Ravennater Reformer Petrus Damiani 1042-52* (MMS 30) (Munich, 1976): 344-76. For "Fonte Avellana" see Cacciamani, DIP IV, 124-26.

[49]PL 145, op. XIV (cols. 327-36) and op. XV (cols. 335-64).

[50]PL 144, col. 395.

[51]W. Lampen, "De S.P. Francisci cultu angelorum et sanctorum," AFH 20 (1927): 3-23, especially 13-15. Strengthening this viewpoint see L. Lehmann *Tiefe und Weite Der universale Grundzug in den Gebeten des Franziskus von Assisi* (FrFor 29), (Werl, 1984) 100 f. Lehmann also connects a prayer of Fonte Avellana with the RegNB 23, 6 quoting Elias and Henoch (Cfr. Lehmann, 205).

[52]Cfr. A. Fortini, *Nova Vita di S. Francesco*, vol. 1 (Assisi 1959) 64 f. Hereafter NVSF.

[53]Cfr. A. Guillou, "Il monachesimo greco in Italia meridionale e in Sicilia nel medioevo," *L'eremitismo in Occidente*, 355-79; and A. Pertusi, "Aspetti organizzativi e culturali dell' ambiente monacale greco dell' Italia meridionale," 382-420 in the same volume.

[54]Cfr. D. Gagnan, "François au Livre de la Nature 3:Le solitaire," EtFrNS 21 (1971):211.

[55]See bibliographical notes in G. Lunardi, "Pulsano," DIP VI, 1113 f. and A. Vuolo, "Monachesimo riformato e predicazione: la 'Vita' di San Giovanni da Matera (sec. XII)," NSMed 27 (1986):69-121.

[56]Translated from G. Lunardi, "Giovanni da Matera," DIP IV, 1233.

[57]Bibliography in G. Mongelli, "Guillaume de Verceil," DHGE XXII, 1038-42.

[58]Cfr. G. Fabiani, "Monaci, eremiti, incarcerati e reclusi in Ascoli nei secoli XIII e XIV," StPic 32 (1964):141-59.

[59]Respectively translated as "cloistered," "cell hermits," "cell dwellers," "recluses," "immured," and "hermits."

[60]Cfr. R. Sassi, "Incarcerati e incarcerate a Fabriano nei secoli XIII e XIV," StPic 25 (1957):67-85.

[61]Cfr. K. Elm, "Italienische Eremitengemeinschaften des 12. und 13. Jahrhunderts. Studien zur Vorgeschichte des Augustiner-Eremitenordens," *L'Eremitismo in Occidente*, 538-40.

[62]Here we follow the article by G. Chiaretti, "Eremiti del Monteluco," DIP III, 1167-75. See there the bibliography.

[63]Translator's Note: the word derives from a Greek verb, *askein*, which means "to exercise." Thus, the asceterium is the place where exercises of a religious nature occur.

[64]Cfr. L. Canonici., *L'Umbria con frate Francesco* (Assisi, 1979) 140: Allora ottenne dai monaci eremiti del Monteluco la capella di S. Caterina, attorno alla quale si svilupparono le prime cellette, nucleo del futuro ritiro francescano. The possible sources are mentioned by N. Cavanna, *L'Umbria francescana illustrata* (Perugia, 1910) 337.

[65]Translated from M. Gatti, *Le Carceri di San Francesco del Subasio* (Assisi, 1969) 24.

[66]Cfr. Fortini, NVSF III, 155.

[67]The *Bulla privilegii* dated May 26,1198 is reprinted in Fortini, NVSF III, 543 f.

[68]Ibid. 152.

[69]Ibid. 154.

[70]Cfr. Gatti 20.

[71]K. Elm, "Italienische," especially 549-59.

[72]Cfr. K. Elm, *Beiträge zur Entstehung des Wilhelmitenordens* (Münstersche Forschungen 14)) (Köln-Graz 1962), 11-16.

[73]Cfr. ibid. 24.

[74]Ibid. 25. Moreover, the author blames the political insecurity and growing commercialization of life in Tuscany for the rapid increase of eremitical foundations in Tuscany and other regions.

[75]Cfr. ibid. 21.

[76]Cfr. Elm, "Italienische" 531.

[77]Cfr. ibid., 555 f.

[78]Cfr. E. Carpentier, ActaSS Oct. IX (Brussels, 1858) 771-886 (reprinted in 1979). We follow Elm, 503-528.

[79]Francis was judged by his first biographers in a similar way. See 1 Cel 1 f., 5-7.

[80]Francis behaved similarly having spent Lent in solitude. Cfr. L. Profili, *Dizionario Francescano* (Padua, 1983) 1487-1500.

[81]Elm, "Italienische" 508. John's admonition to the ruler reminds one of the friars' encounter with Otto IV at Rivotorto (1 Cel 43). John's peacemaking between Ravenna and Cervaria has overtones of Francis's peacemaking attempts between Perugia and Arezzo (cfr. 2 Cel 37; 108).

[82]Cfr. Elm, "Italienische" 521.

Western Eremitism

in the 11th and 12th Centuries[1]

by

Cinzio Violante

Translated from the Italian by

Nancy Celaschi, OSF

1.   The canonical movement and the eremitical one seemed to merit a deeper, broader, and more thorough study because only in recent years has it been the object of renewed interest with scholars committing themselves to intense research into these two important aspects of the era of Church reform. Indeed, until now scholars have almost exclusively studied cenobitism. The disciplined and successful study and tradition, kept alive in the monastic orders, has produced a whole series of editions of source material, general works and studies of a particular nature. Among the monastic reform movements, the broadest area of ecclesiastical reform, the lion's share, has been given to the Cluny Order (to the credit or blame of Sackur[2] until the famous article of Sabbe, 1928)[3] and, a little later, the basic studies of Schreiber[4] and Grundmann[5] shed further light on the many forms of monastic reform centers and religious movements from the 10th to 13th centuries.

The canonical reform and the revival of the eremitical movement are perfectly situated in the 11th and 12th centuries. As early as the first decades of the 11th century, Romuald, John Gualbert, and Peter Damian especially showed an interest in the restoration and reform of the practice of the common life among the clergy.[6]

The reforming activity of Bishop Gerardo in the Diocese of Florence with his establishing fervent canonical communities, particularly in the outlying areas, preceded the Lateran Synod of 1059, in which the Burgundian prelate on the Chair of Peter published the first canons for the observance and spread of the common life among the clergy. The deacon Hildebrand was shouting his cry of alarm about the need for a radical reform with the imposition of individual poverty on the canons. Therefore, for a century and a half the movement for the reform of the canons was developing and spreading in various currents (sometimes with great internal differences) of varying degrees of severity in observing the common life and imitation of the *vita apostolica* [apostolic life]. From the end of the 11th century to the beginning of the 13th, the more tempestuous waves were calmed down. While the bitter condemnations of the monastic orders were becoming less so, the canonical communities became more secular within the juridical context first of the establishment of cathedral chapters, and then collegial bodies. Or they gradually assumed more monastic characteristics, eventually forming orders and congregations exercising ministry in offering hospitality to some degree.

The great flourishing of the eremitical movement takes place in roughly the same time frame; in the West it was the second flourishing, after that of the 5th-8th centuries. We can say that between the two periods, eremitism was rather rare, although there were isolated, independent eremitical movements, as well as the Benedictine tradition of the eremitical *ritiro* practiced by some monks in search of a higher degree of perfection. However, there are notable differences between the two periods and the various regions.

Flourishing once again at the end of the 10th century, Western eremitism developed to a great degree into the movements and mendicant orders at the beginning of the 13th century. The adoption of eremitical themes in the Flemish popular spiritual movements of the 13th-14th centuries and the English mysticism of the 14th paved the way for a new season of eremitism. In Italy it could be found during the Renaissance, assimilating some of its themes, although transforming them.

2. The first fundamental problem facing us is that of discovering the motives and the historical meaning of the above-mentioned second season of eremitic flowering in the 11th and 12th centuries. According to Sainsaulieu,[7] the eremitic movement died out in the 10th century because of civil and religious disorder, the long economic crisis and the social depression. It flourished once again around the year 1000 because of the reestablishment of political order and the increase in cultural activity. The hermitages' proximity to population centers, to major traffic areas and broad valleys, and the fact that they were often located on the best, most fertile land, would show the parallel growth between eremitism and economic, civil, and cultural life.

Similarly, Georges Duby[8] offered his hypothesis that the canons professing the regular life according to St. Augustine's model, renouncing personal property or even the vast community dominions out of love of poverty, came to a large extent from the new merchant classes of the cities. Their choice could be seen as a stance against a life that was ever more immersed in business and caught up with the concern for profit, such as they experienced in their own families. We know for certain that many of the hermits, particularly the independent ones, came from noble families, or at least from higher social classes and a more secure economic position, or from rich and powerful abbeys or chapter houses. However, Sainsaulieu's thesis is a very important one, which needs to be verified with thorough research.

However, in order to explain the reasons for eremitism's flourishing from the end of the 10th century to the beginning of the 13th, it is especially necessary to take into consideration its various aspects in this era and thus try to discover its essential characteristics. In my opinion, this cannot be done without setting the eremitic phenomenon against the background of the development of the ecclesiastical and political structures and institutions, considering the contemporary, closely-related evolution of the collective mentality, culture, and spirituality.

3. As we have seen, in the 11th and 12th centuries terms such as *eremus* [desert], *eremita* [hermit], *solitudo* [solitude], and *vita solitaria* [solitary life] can assume quite different meanings, indicating solitary hermitages with a single hermit, or sometimes a hermit accompanied by one, two, or more companions and additional disciples, with or without the bonds of a basic coenobium, or in groups of hermit cells (e.g., like at Fonte Avellana) or, finally, true *coenobia*, built in solitary areas far from city life. This distance from the busy centers, cities and towns alike, is a fundamental common demand of eremitism in the era we are looking at, both in relation to urban development and the flourishing of the economic and political life in the towns, as well as in the debate against the enormous wealth of the large monasteries, which often caused the development of large towns adjacent to their enormous holdings. The new or reform movements of hermits, who preferred the remote places and deserts, were the counterpoint of these powerful, rich communities of *monachi saeculares* [worldly monks]. The author of the *Liber de restauratione Sancti Martini Tornacensis* wrote quite clearly: "Later, (Odo) recognized it was impossible for the monks living just outside the city—whom folks thought of as well-liked, in touch with the times—to observe all the practices of the elders."[9]

A common characteristic of all hermits in the period under consideration is the commitment to poverty, not only individually, but also collectively for those who live in monastic or canonical communities. Going against the rich and powerful cenobitic groups such as Cluny, they reject the big, solemn buildings, repel ecclesiastical benefices and property (at least the large domains that need to be cultivated by "rustics"), wear poor, rough garments (*habitus pauper*), and even go so far as to reject magnificent vestments and liturgical furnishings and precious vessels. They pay great homage to manual labor, by which they earn a living. They turn against the ascetical practices of fasting, prolonged prayer, flagellation, and other forms of harsh corporal mortification.

This demand for absolute poverty, so strong in the hermits, is but one aspect, the strongest and most consistent one, of the whole vast poverty movement inspiring the popular, clerical, and monastic reforms at the beginning of the second millennium as a reaction to the moral and disciplinary ills caused by Church institutions' becoming involved in the court economy and the structures of feudal society. In eremitic spirituality, the desire for individual poverty developed into a desire for the absolute poverty of the community itself. The model of the "primitive apostolic life," holding property in common, was gradually replaced by the evangelical ideal of absolute poverty: "in poverty, following the poor Christ."

Only with difficulty can this ideal be achieved for a period of time within the structures of traditional monasticism, and only in reformed groups. However, it is more suited to the development of independent solitary forms of life. It was only with the mendicant orders that the problem of the observance of Gospel poverty in community could find an original solution.

Benedictine monasticism's traditional practice of a period of ascetical *ritiro* removed from the monastery, which was practiced by individual monks who sought a higher grade of personal perfection, could certainly not exhaust the greater spiritual demands of the new era, which required a reform of the communities themselves in regard to poverty and ascetical practices. On the other hand, as an attempt to renew and reform traditional cenobitism which was endangered by the new trends in spirituality, "monastic eremitism," as it was called, was but one aspect of the vast, complex eremitic movement flourishing in the 11th-12th centuries, and not one of the ones that would have greater, longer-lasting success.

Although Vallambrosian monasticism originated as an attempt to establish the strictest type of eremitical life in the well-closed circle of the cenobium, it ended up, towards the end of the 11th century, acquiring churches and priories in large numbers; it was far removed from the disdainful, drastic rejection of all property as practiced by its founder, John Gualbert.

Cistercian monasticism, which was a literal return to the sources of the Benedictine Rule, with its emphasis on passages taken from the desert writers, managed to preserve the commitment to total poverty for only about 50 years. By the middle of the 12th century Cistercian monasteries had already begun to request and obtain exemptions[10] and ecclesiastical benefices, and they began to form increasingly stronger attachments to the feudal nobility.

Outside the Benedictine tradition, the experiments attempting to practice the eremitic life as the desert fathers and mothers had done was begun by Odo in his cenobium in Tornay. Later attempts to establish it in the solitary form failed due to practical problems and the demands of the ever larger communities. The final outcome was the adoption of the practices of Cluny.

Towards 1145 many of the eremitic communities in France (especially in the western part) were changed into monasteries or affiliated to Citeaux, Prémontré, or even to Cluny.

One of the fundamental demands of eremitism, especially in the period under consideration, is to flee the world, to be freed from all worldly concerns and attachment to worldly goods. This desire is essential to the whole monastic movement. From the time of St. Basil, cenobitism held that this could be achieved most fully in the severely restricted community life of the cloister, where the individual is entirely separated from the world and freed from all concern because of the monastery's self-sufficiency and strong organization.

However, the desire for distance from the world and for total separation from temporal concerns first and foremost demands absolute poverty; this can be achieved in the monastery only with difficulty, and not in a lasting manner. The point of reference and the ideal is no longer the primitive Christian community of the Apostles, but the poor and naked Christ all alone.

Therefore the attempt to reconcile eremitism and cenobitism which precede (e.g., the Vallombrosian form) as well as follow the crisis in traditional monasticism does not meet all the spiritual demands of eremitism in the 11th and 12th centuries.

4. Eremitical spirituality is often in direct opposition to the cenobitic type (especially that of Cluny). By its rejection of community life with its perfect organization and total commitment to the common life, the cenobitic life keeps the individual safe from temptations and evil and does not accept the ideal of a perfect *societas* [society] removed from the temptations of the world, which is an earthly anticipation of the bliss of the *chorus angelorum* [choir of angels]. Isolated eremitism, and particularly the hermits who lived independently from any others, especially sought the mystical experience of intimacy with God. Solitude is sought through contemplation, that is, "continual application of the mind to knowing God," as William of Saint-Thierry wrote to his brother hermits. He added, "The responsibility of others is to serve God; yours is to cling to God[11]"—thus making a very clear distinction between hermits and canons. The hermit is docile to the inspiration of the Holy Spirit, who directly reveals God's will.

The hermit, then, is alone before God; however, the hermit is alone before the devil, too, *sine consolatione alterius* [without the support of any other], as the Benedictine Rule puts it with such great understanding.[12] The independent hermit is aware that there is a greater risk of trial and temptation in solitude. However, the hermit is ready to wage this battle with the Evil One, and does not reject the *militia diaboli*, the battle against the devil. The hermit's weapons are continuous private prayer, prolonged vigils, and the mortification of ascetical practice. The independent hermit rejects the monastery's community of life and prayer and the abbot's direct, absolute rule, accepting only the discreet guidance of a spiritual director.

Eremitical spirituality of the 11th and 12th centuries is the expression of a new, more individualistic mentality, one open to freer personal experiences, aimed at achieving a more intimate religious experience.

We have spoken of severe ascetical practices. This emphasis on the need for penance in the daily, individual struggle against the devil is another particular characteristic of independent eremitism, even more so than of monasticism.

The total renunciation of the world, the heroism of extreme penance and the harshest ascetical practices are the supreme demand of a life of witness that is intended to have the same value as martyrdom. At the beginning of the era under study, Bruno of Querfur declared that martyrdom was the supreme ideal of perfection, and a person achieves it after having passed through the highest levels of the contemplative and eremitical life.[13] These are extreme positions, but they reveal a mentality which aims to lead the solitary hermit to a total rejection of any openness to the world, to people.

5. By one of the none–too–rare paradoxes of Christian spirituality, the tendency towards a total separation from the world and from the problems of daily life is more pronounced in those perfect and circumscribed environments of the monastery, which tend towards material and spiritual self-sufficiency. The independent, solitary hermit, instead, does not want to be protected from the temptations of the world and the attacks of the devil. The hermit has rejected the safe refuge of the ordered cenobitic community and does not flee from the spiritual struggle, but rather seeks it. Since the hermit's material needs are not satisfied by providence through an organized monastery, the independent hermit is obliged to have recourse to the help of city dwellers and "rustics" in the nearby villages. Begging and the practice of manual labor require the hermit to ask for alms or to barter goods and thus come into frequent contact with people.

The hermit, not the monk, has an important place in popular literature of the Middle Ages. The hermit becomes a familiar figure in medieval society because the hermit has many more opportunities to mix with people than the monk does. Today we could say that a person who is so much a nonconformist by nature, often a bit eccentric, exceptional, and heroic in deed, could very possibly seem to be surrounded by a bit of the miraculous and elicit the most colorful tales from people's minds. Not only in Latin literature, but in the vernacular, too, including Boiard and Ariosto, the hermit often appears in the woods as the figure of a wise old counsellor surrounded by a magical aura.

The hermit strives to bear witness through the practice of asceticism and even through martyrdom, the crowning glory of the missionary vocation. In some cases the hermit is required to renounce martyrdom itself. These elements of eremitic spirituality are the exceptional expressions of a profound, general demand of the apostolate, which is made concretely possible by the mental attitude of the independent hermit who is open to the external world by material need for support and the spiritual demands of a direct, even frontal attack, against the devil.

Preaching about the perfection of the eremitic state of life, conversion of the infidels, reform of the corrupt monastic communities, correction of the behavior of the urban population, re-establishing peace between factions in civil strife, restoring heretics and excommunicated people to the ecclesial community, encouragement to make pilgrimages or joining the crusades — the reasons and occasions of the hermits' apostolate vary according to circumstances of time and place.

The hermits' apostolate does not have a systematic style, but is rather voluntary acceptance of opportunities as they arise. Theirs is an apostolate outside the context of traditional ecclesiastical institutions and the charismatic hierarchy, beyond all the limits of ecclesiastical jurisdictions (parishes, missions, archdiaconates, dioceses). Theirs is frequently an itinerant apostolate addressed to the faithful who come to them from various areas, near and far. It is a lively, effective moral preaching by people who had been monks or lay people, the *cura animorum* [the ministry to people] not canonically connected to a holy place which constitutes a true "hinge."

Not incardinated, not connected to monasteries nor set within colleges of canons fully organized in an unbroken common life, not subject to rigorous disciplinary obedience to the monarchical power of an abbot, the independent hermits are incredibly mobile because of their preaching, their missionary undertakings, or their long pilgrimages to the Holy Land, Compostela, or Rome. (Pilgrimage itself was once defined as an "ambulant eremitical life.")

It seems to me that apostolic involvement is rather characteristic of the second phase of Western eremitism (11-12th century). Is this not, perhaps, the ultimate reason why so many clerics, especially canons, transferred to the eremitic state? There are conversions of individuals and groups, sometimes even of entire communities of canons.

Involvement in the apostolate, which became typical of eremitism in the 11th and 12th centuries, attracted clerics to the eremitic life and also led many lay hermits to come together in groups of canons. It seems that in general the canonical communities that became hermits and the eremitical groups that became canons adopted the Augustinian Rule in its strictest ascetical form, the *Ordo Monasterii* [the Monastic Way of Life].

6. Because of the characteristics described above, as a whole the flourishing of eremitism around the year 1000 can be considered substantially a "novelty" in religious life and especially in the ecclesiastical institutions of Western Christianity, given the spiritual and structural conditions of the Church in the preceding age.

The political policy of the Carolingians, and later of the Ottoni, had always aimed at giving firm support to the religious life of the faithful, clerics and monks in the context of the traditional ecclesiastical structures and especially within the context of ecclesiastical and political jurisdictions. In reality, however, with the development of the institution of the private church and the monastic exemption, a type of particularism was strengthened, and this meant a greater articulation and fragmentation of ecclesiastical institutions within the traditional jurisdictions. Consonant with changes in the economy and society the ecclesiastical foundations more closely adhered to the local reality and became firmly rooted there, often gaining breadth and power. The rapidity and intensity of the spread of the private churches and monasteries and the exempt cenobiums was different in various regions. In the kingdom of Germany and also in Italy before the year 1000, monastic exemption was extremely rare or nonexistent. However, the Carolingian-Ottonian Church had a greater character of stability, as we can see from the decrees of the councils and the royal chapters of the lack of provisions against the "acephalous" [leaderless] clergy and the errant monks.

In the light of these considerations we can understand how the 9th-10th century lacked the strictly individual, independent type of eremitism extraneous to the Benedictine tradition or separate from the large monasteries; or at least we can find no important historic traces of it. The struggle against the independent hermits fought by the political authorities of the Carolingian era seems to have been victorious.

In the 9th and 10th centuries, however, there was certainly a monastic eremitism, as an experience of the solitary ascetical life lived by monks who move out from the cenobium but remain connected with it, particularly through a permanent bond of obedience to the abbot. This type of eremitism fit in quite well with the ecclesiastical structures of the Carolingian and Ottonian era which, as we have seen, were rigid and firm in their basis and closely bound up with the political institutions.

Therefore, in the two centuries before the year 1000, the eremitic phenomenon as an independent movement is not to be found, nor did it have much of an effect on religious life, and even less on the life of society.

Towards the beginning of the second millennium the flourishing of independent eremitism assumed the aspect of a "break" with ecclesiastical and social institutions in that it was the expression of a new demand for extreme moralism, of a spirituality of evangelical poverty, of a more intimate piety. But it also responded very well to the various mental attitudes of a society in which the process of development was rapidly accelerating, and the organizational structures were changing. The limits of the traditional ecclesiastical jurisdictions were surpassed and broken. People were being released from their old bonds with local institutions and had greater mobility, frequently leaving the isolated areas to move to the urban centres or villages. The instability of the independent hermits, their rejection of the traditional contexts of ecclesiastical organization, and their pilgrimages are elements corresponding to the new aspect of mobility of the society of that era, strongly marked by the resurgence of cities, the development of commercial trade and the circulation of money.

The practice of the independent eremitic life was immediately felt within traditional monasticism, especially as a violation of the obedience owed to the abbot and, even more, as a dangerous break with the bond of stability. On the threshold of the 11th century, Archbishop Leo of Ravenna, the former abbot of Nonantola, warned the monk Durand and his other companions who were given to living in hermitages that by leaving their monastic cloister and not observing stability in their congregation, they were betraying the Benedictine Rule.[14] Peter Damian himself, one of the masters of eremitism in the first half of the century, imposed the obligation of stability on his hermit disciples.

Although not condemning the eremitical ideal absolutely, Ivo of Chartres considered the cenobitic life spiritually much superior to the solitary life, since the latter did not guarantee the conditions for renouncing one's own will.[15] According to the severe canonist, the desire for independent solitude was often a diabolical temptation which could lead one to be separated from the Mystical Body.

Another "break" which would certainly meet with opposition in monastic circles was people passing directly from the clerical or lay state to the eremitic life. If at the end of the 9th century the Rule of life for solitaries of Grimlaicus said that the normal route to the hermitage was through the cenobium, Romuald and Peter Damian were now holding that it was necessary to have an experience of monastic life to lead the life of a hermit.

On the other hand, the clerics' change to the eremitic life meant they were no longer fixed in the church in which they were ordained, and thus they became "acephalous." In this case there was the hotly debated problem of the 11th and 12th centuries concerning the justification of breaking the bond of incardination or stability in order to change to a stricter way of life. Finally, the lay hermits' taking the initiative in preaching and the apostolate aroused concern, debate, and protests from the ecclesiastical hierarchy and all those who wanted to preserve the fine distinction among the various "orders" of the ecclesial body.

The spiritual demands and practical tendencies of the eremitic movement were interwoven with those of the canonical reform and the religious revival of the laity.

7. In the 11th and 12th centuries the experiences of the eremitic life not only enkindled the reform of monastic or canonical communities or attempts to find new forms of religious life, but they often led directly to new forms of monastic or canonical community institutions or the creation of mendicant orders in which the common life could be in agreement with the commitment to absolute individual and collective poverty.

Towards the end of the period under consideration, however, we see two very different trends in the eremitic movement. On the one hand, there is a process of clericalization, with clerics changing to the eremitic life and hermits becoming clerics and the formation of canonical communities of an eremitic origin, showing the tendency of some groups of hermits to form monastic communities or enter into the large monastic congregations. On the other hand, lay hermits emphasize the commitment to preaching and the vocation of the apostolate which resist the increasingly concerned interventions, limitations, and prohibitions of the ecclesiastical hierarchy to the point that these groups are often confused with the heretical types, such as the followers of Arnaldo or the Waldensians.

Converging with the popular religious movements and the reform of canonical life, the eremitical movement was the catalyst for many changes or new creations which occurred in the ecclesiastical structures or institutions during the 11th and 12th centuries under the impulse of new, varied, and even contrasting spiritual demands. This was another, and not the least, of the reasons that the eremitic flourishing after the year 1000 takes on a certain "newness" and the idea of a "break" in religious life and ecclesiastical institutions.

Endnotes

[1]C. Violante, "Western Eremitism in the 11th and 12th centuries," *Eremitismo* (1965) 19-23.

[2]E. Sakur, *Die Kluniacense in ihrer kirchlichen und allgemeingeschichtlichen Wirksamkeit bis zur Mitte des XI Jahrhunderts*, 2 vols. (Halle, 1892-1894).

[3]E. Sabbe, "Notes sur la réforme de Richard de Saint-Vannes dans les Pays-Bas," *Revue belge de philologie et d'histoire*, 7 (1928) 551-70.

[4]See the articles contained in the volume *Gemeinschaften des Mittelalters Recht und Verfassung, Kult und Frömmigkeit* (Münster, 1948), especially "Cluny und die Eigenkirche" (pp. 81-138); "Zur cluniacensischen Reform" (pp. 139-49); "Gregor VII, Cluny, Citeaux, Prémontré zu Eigenkirchen, Parochie, Seelsorge" (pp. 283-370).

[5]H. Grundmann, "*Religiöse Bewegungen in Mittelalter,*" Berlin 1935; "Neue Beiträge zur Geschichte der religiösen Bewegungen in Mittelalter" in *Archiv für Kulturgeschichte*, 37(1955) 129-92.

[6]There are ample references in the two volumes *La vita comune del clero nei secoli XI e XII* (Milan, 1962), especially pages 186-211; 228-35.

[7]Sainsaulieu, DHGE XV, cols. 771-87; 772.

[8]G. Duby,"Les chanoines réguliers et la vie économique des Xieme et XIIeme siècles," *La vita comune del clero*, vol. 1, 72-81.

[9]*Liber de restauratione Sancti Martini Tornacensis*, ed. G. Waitz, *MGH, SS*, 14, 306.

[10]Concerning the problem of *exemptio* in general, see J.B. Mann, *L'ordre cistercien et son gouvernment des origines au milieu du XIIIeme siècle*, 2nd ed. (Paris, 1951) 71-169.

[11]"*Epistula seu tractatus ad fratres de Monte Dei,*" *Etudes de philosophie médiévale*, ed. M.M. Davy , 19(Paris, 1940) 74.

[12]*Regula*, I, 12.

[13]"*Passio sanctorum Benedicti et Iohannes ac sociorum eorundem*" MGH. SS, 15, (Hanover 1888) 719. [*Passio* is often a technical term in early Christian Latin documents and I chose to render it *The Suffering and Death*, E.Kahn, trans.]

[14]"Here begins the admonition of Archbishop Leo of Ravenna to the monk Durandus and his fellow hermits," *Italia sacra II*, 2nd ed., 355-59.

[15]Ep. 192 *Monachis Columbensibus*, PL, 162, cols. 196-202.

Ideals of the Women's Hermitage Movement

in Europe during the 12th-15th Centuries

by

Edith Pásztor[1]

Translated from the Italian by

Nancy Celaschi, OSF

1. The incluse is "one who, renouncing the world, chooses the solitary life, desiring to be hidden, never to be seen and, dead to the world as it were, to be buried in Christ": thus the Cistercian Aelred of Rievaulx, described them when, upon the repeated request of his sister who had chosen this form of life, he wrote his *De institutione inclusarum* [Recommendations for Incluses], about 1160.[2]

Here we find an idea of the essence of the life of reclusion and its position in the world of religious movements: total abandonment of the world in order to live in solitude with Christ.[3] As such, it is one of the most radical expressions of the women's religious model in the Middle Ages. The main theme of this state of life in sources from that time is not penance but the mystical espousal, the desire to serve the Lord, "yearning more freely for Christ, with deep sighs," as Aelred of Rievaulx observes.[4] This is almost always concretely expressed also in visions and conversations with God which reinforce the relationship.

The Church did not allow women to live alone in a true hermitage, contrary to the position of Philibert Schmitz, who rather attributes their inability to face the difficulties of the eremitical life to a lack of courage.[5] If women who want to remain "orthodox" do not manage to free themselves most of the time from that other ban, the one forbidding them from leading an itinerant life,[6] by living a mendicant life in the cell of a recluse, on the contrary, they rediscover the solitude of the hermitage. This lifestyle, however, was also condemned by some churchmen. Thus, in a letter probably written before the schism in 1130, St. Bernard writes to a nun of the community of Saint-Marie in Troyes, who had expressed the desire to withdraw to a life of solitude; with unexpected, almost vehement words, he advises her against it. According to Bernard, in fact, "the desert offers" evil an "abundance of opportunities, . . . the woods, solitude, . . . silence. Where there are no accusers to fear, the tempter can draw near in security, an evil act can be committed more freely. . . ."[7] In this perspective the hermitage offers an opportunity for meeting God, but the devil lives there, too, and the young woman who wants to withdraw there with the desire of "pleasing the one to whom alone" she has dedicated her life, "fleeing affluence, the crowd of the city, ease and comfort," finds there "the serpent's venom, the trickery of the deceiver, the cleverness of the werewolf." Then he adds: "The wolf lives in the woods," and "the lone lamb" who enters "the shadow of the woods" can become "the wolf's prey."[8]

There is no hint, then, of the value of contemplation in solitude, of the most authentic motive of the mystical experience. Bernard simply treats the incluse from his preconceptions and attributes to them the weakness with which the medieval mentality generally credits women and the supposed ease with which they fall into temptation. He is a convinced supporter of the opportuneness of making them live under the control of someone in their own families or in a monastery. He praises the choice of the state of life of the prudent virgins, rejecting that of the foolish ones, without analyzing the meaning of the gospel parable in the context of the life of solitude.[9]

On the other hand, we can see from the sources that Bernard was not the only one to follow this train of thought. Thus in 12th century England, ecclesiastical authorities systematically try to lead the incluse into monastic communities.[10] For example, the

Archbishop of York offered the incluse Christine of Markyate the position of superior in the monastery of York. When she refused, he advised her to enter the community of Marcigny or Fontevrault.[11] Holdsworth writes that in England the episcopate "considered the recluses as a somewhat disturbing element in the Church," and therefore they first "sought to use every means possible to gain close control over them" and then later sought to eliminate them by having them absorbed by a monastic community.[12] This phenomenon does not seem to be limited only to England.

The Cistercian, Caesar of Heisterbach,[13] a native of Cologne who was favorable to incluses[14] and even attributes special supernatural favors to their prayer,[15] equates their way of living in holiness with that of nuns. Yet in writing of the incluses' resistance to trial, he never attributes the victory to them but to the intervention of a vision of God, Mary, the saints or angels, or to the advice of priests serving as their confessors.[16]

It seems that many authors were impressed by external aspects, such as the lugubriousness of the cell, without managing to understand those who live there in mortification, unable to accept the idea that a great degree of spirituality is the first requirement for undergoing such sacrifices. They see the incluse as the biblical Eve, now protected by the clergy and supernatural world. However, they do not understand that she has this protection because this Eve is already living according to a different set of values than her ancestor did, and tends to behave differently than had been usual for women in previous centuries. These authors suppose that the incluse brings to her cell all the qualities of her state in the Church and all its negative implications. It is not without purpose that canon 26 of the Second Lateran Council (1139) forbids women from building *receptacula et privata domicilia* [places of retreat and private dwellings] and living alone there. The only possibility open to women is to live in monastic communities under the Rule of St. Augustine.[17]

Rather than "eremitic holiness," the incluses also have their own contribution to make, which certainly deserves our examination because there is a whole range of interwoven sentiments and manifestations of devotion and piety in which women see the mystical union with God in different, original ways. This in turn gives rise to new manners of expression. We could say that the incluse's manner of living enclosed in a very small space makes it even more possible for her to explore her spiritual creativity, with its wealth of religious themes, unravelling the individual threads. It is the earthly space opening up to the supernatural, freeing the incluse's imagination.

2. In the studies of the world of women in Western medievalism, including scholarly works, the incluse is often portrayed in an unclear, confused manner. Frequently the term incluse is attributed to women who were obviously nuns or those who lived in community with a *reclusorium* [a hermitage] (therefore, not in solitude), or who did not choose the hidden life for their religious experience. Anyone who wants to be certain in understanding the religious choices involved or reconstructing the hagiographical models related to these choices must necessarily return to the sources: canonization processes where these have been preserved; biographies (although this writer prefers the Latin term *vitae*) which are more or less contemporary with the person's life, although keeping in mind the limits of these sources, which aim more at giving example than at reporting historical fact.

There is a wealth of historical studies related to the incluses of Western Europe. Among them we should point out the work of Gougaud,[18] Dörr[19] and Marie Christine Chartier;[20] André Vauchez's beautiful work on the Eucharistic devotion of two of them, Jeanne-Marie de Maillé and Dorothea von Montau.[21] This relieves this author of the need to analyze all aspects of the topic. I would like to mention only two descriptions which shed light on the type of problem caused by the phenomenon.

Le Bras lists three groups of what he calls the fringes of religious life for women:[22] recluses, beguines, and women who serve in the leprosaria or hospitals in charitable activity. As examples, we may cite the recluse Eve de St.Martin of Liège,[23] the beguines such as Marie d'Oignies,[24] and hospital workers such as Yvette d'Huy[25] at a certain period of her life. We hold that they are in a position somewhere between the lay status and the regular one, in some kind of a hybrid formation. In other words, according to Le Bras, they are the ones living on the fringes. This expression has nothing to do with Turner or Holdsworth's "sacred marginalization."[26]

With greater historical sensitivity, Kaspar Elm speaks of

> men and women who, with the blessing and consent of their pastors and bishops, have abandoned the world in order to live the eremitic life, without an approved Rule, with no constitutions, under their own responsibility and personal freedom. This lifestyle offers several possibilities: from that of the most complete separation from the world, sealed off like the incluses, to those who help pilgrims and travelers on the roads or near the rivers.[27]

The data that emerge from these descriptions: the preventive measure of the incluse's need for the permission of the ecclesiastical authority; the absence of a Rule and, therefore, absolute freedom in organizing their spiritual life within the cell; the distinction between cells built next to a church and others which were built at the city gates or on the bridges.

3. This data can be developed further. From the 12th century on, however, the incluse's cell could not only be attached to the churches administered by the secular clergy, but also to those cared for by the religious orders—generally male orders, but in a few cases women's orders too. Sometimes the incluses themselves ask for norms for organizing their own life. Here we can cite the above-mentioned institutions of Aelred of Rievaulx,[28] the Ancren Riwle,[29] or other texts which Philippe Rouillard has included under the entry of "Regole per reclusi" in the *Dizionario degli Istituti della Perfezione*.[30]

It should be emphasized, however, that this is completely extraneous to what is normal for the culture of reclusion, which is understood as a solitary life in which each person establishes a personal relationship with God, and every regulation coming from external sources is a foreign element. These rules, however, are important sources of information because they show how the life of the incluse is understood and described by authors who are, without exception, men, and usually monks or bishops. We find one common element: this phenomenon has an effect on general religious sentiment. In her *Hortus deliciarum,* which was written in the second half of the 12th century, the abbess Herrad of Landsberg puts the incluses in second place on the scale of values of religious behavior, preceded only by the real, true eremitic life which, as has been noted, the Church permitted to men alone.[31]

In the centuries under consideration, the incluses' cells are many. There is a great movement from the suburbs to the city, although in 1126 Bishop Guy of Le Mans, the successor of Hildebert of Lavardin, is still giving food and clothing to the incluses living "in suburbio civitatis" [in the suburb of the city].[32] We find them not only living in cells adjacent to the churches— "sub paretis ecclesiae" [close to the walls of the church]—but, for example, also in the Cemetery of the Innocents in Paris[33] or in a cell in Bonn with windows opening onto the cemetery,[34] at the city gates of Toulouse, on a bridge in Garonne,[35] and in the Auvergne region, in the ancient capital of Saint-Flour, on the bridge of Saint Christine;[36] in Hungary, on an island in the Danube.[37]

While the cells adjacent to the churches served to satisfy the spiritual needs of individual women, the others were frequently built and maintained by the city in order to ensure their prayers for the defense of the city's inhabitants, pilgrims, and buildings, too. In the former case it is primarily a matter of individual piety; in the latter, the incluse is somehow fulfilling the role of protectress of the city, which was not usually a woman's job in the Middle Ages. It is important to emphasize this connotation because the incluse was required to do very little, or nothing at all, for the civil society, not even participating directly in helping the poor, because she was destined, body and soul, to serve the Lord alone.

In addition to the rules, we should take into consideration other literary genres which offer us valuable information about the incluses. First of all, there are the rituals for reclusion,[38] and the advice given by secular priests, monks, or nuns to women who have already chosen the solitary life or are about to make such a choice.[39] Finally, there are last wills and testaments which, through the bequests they make, give us information about the existence of incluse's cells which would otherwise be unknown to us.[40]

The rituals for reclusion are based on the liturgical rites for the deceased.[41] The counsels contained in them show us the image evoked by this state of life, which the person enters as into a tomb to wait there until the angels come to draw the soul to Abraham's bosom. However, it is a wait that can last for decades, and which is to be spent in devotion and asceticism, in regard to which the spiritual directors offer suggestions.

One of the oldest bits of advice which has come down to us can be dated to the end of the 11th century. It is the *Liber Confortatorius* of the English Benedictine Goscelin of St. Bertin.[42] The work, which is certainly later than 1078 but earlier than 1098, the supposed date of the author's death, is addressed to the incluse Eve, herself an Anglo-Saxon, but the daughter of a Danish man and of a woman from Lorraine, who is living in a cell near Angers.[43] We must establish a brief premise before continuing.

Sources from the early Middle Ages indicate individual cases of incluses: for example, the nun in the monastery of Sainte-Croix in Poitiers mentioned by Gregory of Tours;[44] Liutberg, an incluse near the church of Wendhausen in the Diocese of Halberstadt, known as "the first recluse of Christian Saxony," who died in 880;[45] or St. Wiborada of Thurgau, a victim of the Hungarian invasion of Sant Gallen in 926.[46] However, the phenomenon did not have such great historical relevance until the second millennium. It achieved its true golden age in the renewal of piety which characterized the 12th century, in which the world of women sought by various means to participate.[47] It is the result of the effect of the new religious orders which grew and bore fruit on the old Benedictine stock; a new spirituality whose most marked values were poverty, asceticism, prayer vigils, fasting, prayer in continual prostration, flight from the world, the search for solitude, and a sensitivity lived more intimately with Christ.

At the turn of the 11th-12th century there are two particularly important incluses found in the sources: the Anglo-Saxon, Eve[48] and Herluca, a Swede, whose *vita* was passed on to us by an eye-witness, Paul of Bernried,[49] who also wrote the biography of Gregory VII.[50] The former is important because she helps us see a special way of living. The author describes her as an incluse—"she lives alone in her cell"—but, in reality, she is surrounded by various companions, virgins and widows, and her spirituality reflects an interpretation of Christ's passion which will undergo great change in later devotional practices. In reality, Herluca represents a period of transition in women's piety from the High Middle Ages to the Low Middle Ages. As such, she deserves our attention, while Eve is typically the daughter of the new age. The events of her life are in perfect chronological conformity with the founding of the Cistercian Order, and even reflect some of its main characteristics.

Eve was given over to the monastic life by her parents and settled at Wilton, where she became the spiritual daughter of Goscelin. After some years, however, she left the monastery and crossed the Channel, settling as an incluse, first at St. Laurent, and later at St. Eutrope, in the area around Angers, "in a solitary place." Here the hermit Hervé already had his cell. Through the wall of adjoining cells he served as her spiritual director.[51] Geoffrey of Vendome wrote a letter to the two incluses in 1102.[52]

Eve left her monastery to retire to solitude, like Robert of Molesme seeking the "desert." Like the founder of the Cistercians, she is also impelled by a desire for poverty. The "luxury" of the community in Wilton does not satisfy her religious aspirations, just as that of Molesme in turn was not to Robert's liking. She wanted to retire to live like "a little poor maid of Christ,"[53] day after day facing difficulty in finding something to eat or, more often, practicing fasting.

Here she discovers *"The Book of Encouragement* by Goscelin the monk of England, to Eve, enclosed at S. Laurence, for the name of Christ"[54] which, besides giving her some useful advice, affords her an image of life in the cell in a way that merits our attention, always keeping in mind that this is a source from the last decades of the 11th century.

First let us look at the advice. Perhaps the most important is that which recalls the necessity of reading in addition to prayer. Goscelin mentions that on Eve's "mensa scripturarum" [writing table], which should be placed in front of the window of the cell, symbolically creating a barrier against the outside world and thus maintaining the incluse's solitude, she should have a series of works: the *Vitae* of the Fathers, especially the life of Antony, and the writings of Eusebius, Augustine, Orosius, Cassiodorus, and Boetius.[55] This clearly shows, on the one hand, the broad education which Eve must have had, contrary to the situation of the majority of the women of her day; on the other hand, it shows how little Goscelin really knew of an incluse's life. In fact, it would have been very difficult for Eve to have such a library because of her poverty, her isolation from the world, and even her educational status.

Goscelin sees the cell under two particular aspects: a place of martyrdom,[56] and a tomb.[57] According to him, like the martyrs of old, Eve must fight against wild animals, which were symbolic of demons. However, he considers that the woman is capable of overcoming temptations, defeating the animals, holding a cross in her hand. He sees the presence of the Lord and his angels as witnesses at the woman's victory.[58]

The cell, which Goscelin calls the "portiuncula, casula, domuncula" [little portion, cottage, small cabin][59] is the tomb for waiting, but it is also the pledge of the resurrection.[60] Thus inclusion becomes a sign of the future meeting of those who lived on earth desiring God.

The cell must contain a crucifix.[61] However, for Goscelin, Christ on the cross does not represent the passion, sadness, and suffering. He is the Redeemer who opens wide his arms, kindly and affectionately inviting the people he has redeemed from sin to embrace the cross.[62] According to "The Book," the cross has a two-fold symbolic value: it is the instrument by which Eve conquers the devil, but it is also the means by which Jesus has saved humanity. Only a few decades separate this interpretation from the heresy of Peter of Bruys,[63] but during this period the meaning of the cross will undergo a notable change.

Eve died in 1115 surrounded by an aura of holiness so great that monks and priests even came from distant areas for her funeral.[64]

A century later the aforementioned work of Aelred of Rievaulx[65] recommends manual labor in addition to prayer, without specifying any particular type of work.[66] Other sources, such as the Ancren Riwle, speak of making vestments and altar linens or repairing the clothes of the poor.[67] Aelred is more interested in another problem: how to dispose of the profit from this work while maintaining poverty.[68] He finds the answer, introducing the figure of the trusted liaison (the precursor of the "spiritual friend" found in the Franciscan rule[69]), who then has the duty of distributing it to the poor. The incluse receives a supernatural reward.[70]

Aelred first and foremost emphasizes the cell's aspect of enclosure: total separation from the world. The sister should use the window for no other purpose but assisting at the liturgical activities held in the church. Most of all, she should not teach young people.[71] This separation should be emphasized because it contradicts the practice in other regions. Hildegard of Bingen, for example, received her first schooling from the incluse Jutta, who lived *"in monte* S. Disibodi" until 1136.[72]

According to Aelred, the incluse must meditate on the life of Christ, from the annunciation to the resurrection. She must recite the psalms even while working and interrupt her work several times for prostration.[73] Her life should be like the preparation of linen.[74] It must first of all be cleansed of its earthen color in order to become dazzling white, the image of purity. "Everyone is born bearing the color of the earth," but the incluse must become particularly white, snow white, in order to be worthy, like linen, to adorn the altar, to cover the Body of Christ. Being washed in water corresponds to baptism; drying to abstinence. Its combing is similar to undergoing temptation. Finally it is subjected to a more thorough washing, which symbolizes liberation, first from the more serious sins, and then from the venial ones as well. Spinning is a sign of perseverance. Finally, treatment with fire and water corresponds to the tribulations through which she is perfected.[75]

We could elaborate more on this source, but I would like to touch briefly on another rather special bit of advice which we find in the process of canonization (art. 19) of Dorothea von Montau.[76] This counsel comes directly from Christ, the one who leads Dorothea, after many years of marriage during which she bore several children, "into the solitude of the cell" in the church of Marienwerder. These are the words attributed to Christ: "When you enter into the cell, you must live a holy life. You will have a glass window in front of you; you must never even stick your hand out of it without the permission of your spiritual director. If you do, you must confess this and do penance. Do not accept any gifts from anyone: 'I myself will be your reward.'"

With Dorothea von Montau we meet a new problem deserving our attention: the spiritual journey of the woman before deciding to become an incluse.

4. As we have seen, Dorothea was married, though not the only incluse to have been so. If a woman is to live in her cell in a mystical marriage with Christ, keeping all her thoughts, affection, sentiments, and being for Jesus, virginity is not necessarily the starting point.

In fact, in comparison with the *vitae* of nuns, the only comparison possible since these were the only two expressions allowed women in the Church, the sources telling us about the incluses put much greater emphasis on the daughter's duty to obey her parents, who more often than not have her married off as soon as she comes of age. The future nun can flee from home and enter a preexisting community, immediately undergoing the "rites of passage" such as cutting her hair and changing her dress. Thus if her family tries to take her back, they are faced with a *fait accompli*. The woman who has chosen the life of the incluse, however, has no place to flee. She must first build her cell, obtain ecclesiastical approval, and undergo the liturgical rite of reclusion. Therefore, she is often forced to submit to her parents' will, a prisoner of so many obstacles.

Hagiographical sources, however, often see a model of supernatural aid and protection for the incluse, emphasizing that, despite her marriage, reclusion and all its values can be achieved, creating a picture rather different than the monastic one.[77]

Unlike Dorothea, the future incluse will often succeed in convincing her husband to live by mutual agreement in a chaste marriage, in virginity. One of the many examples is the case of Jeanne-Marie de Maillé of the diocese of Tours, who succeeds in convincing her husband, Robert de Silléle-Guillaume, to preserve his own virginity. Both of them devote their lives to serving the victims of the plague. It is only after her husband's death that Jeanne-Marie retires into inclusion, living at Planche-de-Vaux.[78]

Virginal marriage as a hagiographical theme deserves our attention from various points of view. Even if the young woman shows some weakness in regard to her family, she remains faithful to her mystical spouse, Christ, for whom marriage does not mean breaking her religious promises. Furthermore, the young woman's "helpmate" is a layman, her husband, who enables her to overcome the impediment created by her parents. Last of all, inclusion appears as a commitment which is won by sacrifice.

Sometimes, however, the sources tell of difficult variations. For example, despite her parents' forceful intervention, Christine of Markyate at first succeeds in getting her husband to live in chastity. After some time, however, he changes his mind and she is forced to leave home.[79] According to what we are told by an anonymous monk, an account contained in the *Gesta abbatum S. Albani* [Deeds of the abbots of S. Alban's],[80] the hermit Roger came to Markyate and enclosed her in a cell next to his hermitage.[81] According to the sources, she lived in her own cell for 16 years without being seen by anyone.[82]

There are obviously also women who are virgins when, with their parents' consent, they become incluses. Thus Caesar of Heisterbach writes about a beautiful, rich girl in the diocese of Würzburg who rejected the marriage offers arranged by her parents because she wanted to remain faithful to her heavenly spouse, Christ.[83] She then received their permission to fulfil her desire, left home, and "had a cell built for herself," which she entered "velata et reclusa" [veiled as a recluse], led by the bishop, to live in solitude with Christ.[84] The bishop entrusted her to the care of the abbot of the Cistercian monastery of Brombach.[85]

The sources tell us very clearly about the beginning of the inclusion of Eve of Saint Martin of Liège.[86] She was "in the bloom of her youth" when she was attracted by that manner of living "under the inspiration of Christ." At the same time, however, human weakness tempered her desire and made her experience anguish along with her religious fervor.[87] Throughout her life she had a particular bond of friendship with Julianne of Cornillon, who visited her once a year, during which brief time they shared many of their experiences. Urged on by her friend, Eve succeeded in overcoming herself and she withdrew into that way of life which had at first attracted her: the hidden life of the cell.[88] Hers is a victory which the biographer describes as Eve overcoming Eve.[89] This is not just a play on words, but it shows the distinction between our Eve and the biblical one. It is an affirmation that the spirit has managed to make the flesh submissive.

5. Events in the incluse's life in the cell take place amid sorrow and pain, just like those of any other person. However, the content of the sentiments involved has a different meaning. Suffering can be the result of physical ailment as well as spiritual dryness; joy is closely tied to the mystical experience. It is the sweetness of feeling Christ's closeness, of experiencing particularly fruitful prayer and meditation, of having supernatural visions, experiences or conversations which are an anticipation of heavenly joy.

A recluse receives an apple, a fruit which she has never tasted. She likes it very much, but she is convinced that the flavor does not come from the apple but that Christ's presence in her cell is what gives the fruit its taste or the flower its perfume. The incluse's spirituality is centered on feeling an immediacy in everything concerning the divine. We can explain this by the twofold conviction that she experiences God everywhere and her certainty that, removed from all earthly realities, she is sure of living with God.

Renunciation of all earthly property, the austerity of life in the cell, silence, prayer vigils, fasting, flagellation or wearing a hair shirt, far removed from all of life's adversities, are certainly a contributing factor in this sentiment. The incluse has her own vocabulary with words and signs that are different than those used by others. She is even exposed to different temptations: lust,[90] the pleasures of eating, and dominion over others are almost non-existent. Rather, there is the impression of having been abandoned by Christ, or even "doubting in God and the Christian faith."[91] Religious fervor, which was so strong at the beginning, gradually weakens, and the sense of being with the mystical spouse disappears.[92]

An incluse complains about losing God in an account given us by Caesar of Heisterbach, an account which is a gem of popular piety. It involves a woman who is obviously not learned, and who tends to interpret whatever she hears literally. To console her an abbot tells her to seek God in the cracks in the wall of her cell, and the incluse obeys immediately, without wasting any time.[93]

Another incluse was rebuked by some people who were looking into the window of her cell while she was apparently shouting harsh words at them. In reality, however, the woman was speaking to the devils whom she saw with the eyes of her soul, standing there in front of the window, ready to enter her cell.[94]

Living in the world but removed from its reality, seeing people but at the same time also seeing their future fate, are, on the one hand, some of the facts that their contemporaries admire in the incluses. On the other hand, these gifts create a problem for them because many people came to the incluses, who saw through them, including their virtues and vices.[95] They speak with priest and prelate and see all the faults these have committed in the past or will commit in the future, without being able to intervene except by promising to pray for them. The supernatural gift of being able to see beyond the body and into souls adds anguish to their solicitude. The clergy's guilt makes their earthly security uncertain.

They often predict the future, which is a source of embarrassment and pain, especially when they foretell a death, such as happened to Haydewig, an incluse near Liège.[96] They are especially sensitive in regard to the Eucharist.[97] Looking into the church through the window of their cell, they can tell when there are no consecrated hosts left after Mass or whenever, since the clergy were generally opposed to the incluse's frequent communion, they would give them an unconsecrated host to silence their complaints. All the incluses show a great desire to receive the Eucharist more often, even daily if possible. A "girl enclosed in a small cell" in the village of Vernon in Lombardy was aided by a dove who brought her communion on Saturday, while she received from the priest on Sunday.[98] In his *Historia occidentalis* Jacques de Vitry tells how on those two days fire seemed to come down from heaven and fill the cell and the incluse heard beautiful angelic choirs.[99] These motifs return in the *vitae* of Italian women, giving us valuable material for comparative studies.[100]

A separate study could be dedicated to interpreting the incluses' visions, and these could be analyzed and read in different ways. Yvette d'Huy, who lived about 1230, led a very exciting life. Forced to accept marriage, she also experienced motherhood and widowhood. She then went on to care for lepers, and then became an incluse in a cell near the monastery of Orval, where her son was a monk. There she had a vision of herself before the judgment seat of God.[101] She knows she must be condemned for having desired her husband's death and for hating marriage. However, the Blessed Virgin intercedes for her and then, following the usual iconographical scene of the crucifixion which is now transferred to the judgment scene, Christ entrusts her to Mary. "'Mother,' he said, 'this is your daughter.'"[102] This iconographical component returns in diverse applications in the *vitae* of Italian mystics, giving their visions a twofold importance.

6. I have left for last the study of the incluses' Christocentric experience, which is also the aspect closest to Franciscanism.

While in the 12th century *vitae* we really do not find meditations on the passion of Christ, after the spirituality of St. Francis penetrated into the feminine expression of religious life, we find in the incluses, too, expressions of the desire to imitate and physically experience Christ's human suffering during the crucifixion.

First of all, let us see how Christ is presented in the 11th and 12th centuries. Herluca, an incluse at Epfach, whom we learn about from Paul von Bernried, sees Christ enter her cell and show her his bleeding wounds. Herluca's only reaction is horror.[103] She says she never wants to see them again although she claims that she is ready to suffer martyrdom for Christ.[104] We have already seen that Goscelin of St. Bertin does not speak to the Anglo-Saxon Eve about the wounds caused by the nails on the cross, but only about the extended arms which, in this perspective, are not a sign of suffering, but rather are an affectionate invitation. They do not represent the suffering of Christ the human but the triumph of Christ as God, calling to mind the joy of redemption.[105] Eve of St. Martin shows her friend Julianne de Cornillon "her genuine icon." The woman, recalling Christ's passion, falls to the earth in a faint. The incluse embraces her, helps revive her, puts her head in her lap and consoles her, saying: Calm down, "my lady, because the anguish of Christ's passion has by now vanished."[106] It is something that happened in the past. It is over and done with, a closed case. It should be known about and its consequences should be drawn, but it never has to stir up compassion.

I find a curious difference between the behavior of these women and the image of Christ who shows his bleeding wounds.[107] These wounds and this blood, however, will speak to St. Francis who will recognize them in their human dimension of suffering and receive them in his own body. Following him women also begin to put Christ crucified at the center of their religious experience but it will take a long time until they, like Francis, discover the joy and happiness present in suffering.

Alpais of Cudot[108] contemplates Christ's passion by observing the actions of a dove.[109] On Holy Thursday a beautiful white dove enters her room and stays in front of her, its wings fluttering, with a happy look on its face. On Good Friday the dove lowers its eyes, inclines its head and seems to tremble. It finds no place to settle down, nor is it capable of lifting its wings. It seems to be suffering from some inner pain. With a sad look on its face, it continues in a mournful plaint. The dove stays like that all day and all night and into Saturday "until the ninth hour." It is only when the bells are rung in church announcing the resurrection that the dove stops its lament and resumes its joyful behavior. Thus Alpais participates indirectly, through the dove, in the suffering of Christ's passion.

Jeanne-Marie de Maillé, whose *vita* was written by her Franciscan confessor, Martin de Bois-Gaultier,[110] was only 11 years old when Mary appeared to her during Christmas Mass, holding the infant Jesus in her arms. She was also bearing a thurible containing drops of Christ's blood with which she seemed to incense the future incluse.[111] Thus in the *vitae* of this woman (whose life certainly cannot be compared with that of her contemporaries), blood, the symbol of the passion, appears in combination with the newborn Jesus during Christmas Mass. Thus we have a union of Christ's initial moments and his final suffering in the redemption. Still but a child, Jeanne-Marie wants to imprint Christ's sufferings in her heart but finds no better way to do so than by taking a picture of Christ crucified "painted on parchment" and carrying it always next to her heart.[112] Dressed in rough garments, so much so that people mockingly called her the "hermitess,"[113] she goes out to beg. Her biographer writes: "according to apostolic custom,"[114] a term rarely used for a woman. She begs for food, not from the rich, but from the poor.[115] She sleeps beneath the window of a half-ruined barn.[116] She performs a type of social work, trying to save women of ill-repute,[117] and pleads to God for the salvation of those who died without making a deathbed confession because there was no priest available.[118] She retired to Planche-de-Vaux to live as an incluse, leading a "very strict life,"[119] but then she went to Tours and settled into a chapel from which she was later cast out.[120] Finally she finds a home in a hovel at the Franciscan convent.[121] She lives on the alms of the faithful among the poor, abandoning herself to Christ's sufferings.[122] She finally leaves the

Franciscans and returns to her cell in Planche-de-Vaux, walking "with a staff, carrying around her neck the knapsack of the poor, as a little poor woman, a stranger, a pilgrim."[123] Here we have a repetition of the words used to describe the first Franciscans.[124] Hers is the story of a life begun with the gift of a few drops of Christ's blood. Although they are not the stigmata, they are also signs of the passion.

I have left for last the story of the woman who wanted to bear Christ's wounds in her own flesh: Julian of Norwich.[125] We are in eastern England,[126] between the 13th and 14th century when we treat of this incluse[127] whose name we do not even know; all we know is that she lived as an incluse next to the church of St. Julian in Norwich, and she was the author of a very important work: "The Revelations of Divine Love."[128]

Julian asks Christ for three gifts: participation in his passion, illness, and three "wounds," that is, contrition, piety, and a longing for God.[129] She receives all three, experiencing all the phases of the passion with Christ. She writes: "At this point I realized that Christ loved me so deeply that in all the universe there would be no suffering comparable to that which I felt in assisting in the unimaginable sufferings of the passion."[130] Thus she comes to understand that human life is nothing other than being with Christ on the cross until the person is together with Christ in paradise. It is only from the state of suffering, she writes, that one can pass over to that of joy.[131]

7. It is obvious that there are many more personages involved than the few I have mentioned; it is also obvious that the topic of the incluses' mystical experiences requires various levels of interpretation. The incluses' ideal certainly is a topic needing a great deal more research and analysis to learn its role in feminine spirituality, in the piety of learned women as well as in popular devotion.

Endnotes

[1]E. Pasztor; "Ideals of the women´s hermitage movement in Europe during the 12th-15th centuries," *Eremitismo Francescano*, 29-164.

[2]Cf. Aelred de Rievaulx, *La vie de recluse. . .*, ed. C. Dumont, Sources Chrétiennes, 76 (Paris, 1961)): "For a number of years, now, my sister, you've been asking me to provide you with a guide for the way of life you have adopted for Christ. You want to model your behavior according to this guide, as well as to arrange exercises necessary for expressing religious conviction"(42). And: "But now, let anyone who renounces the world in choosing the solitary life with the desire to remain hidden, never to be seen, and to be buried with Christ as though dead to the world, let such a one pay attention to my words and assimilate them" (80). Regarding the work itself, see C.H. Talbot, The "De Institutis Inclusarum of Aelred of Rievaulx," *Analecta Sacri Ordinis Cisterciensis* 7 (1951): 167-217.

[3]"There are those for whom it is detrimental to live in community. There are others for whom it is not detrimental, but costly. And there are some who need not fear either prospect, but who consider it more advantageous to live in seclusion. Thus the elders . . . chose to live as solitaries. Hence, it turns out that many used to dwell alone in the desert, supporting themselves by the work of their hands. Still others used to believe this is not safe for them because of the solitary's freedom and the opportunity for wandering about. They considered it safer to be enclosed in a cell with passage to the outside blocked. And so it has seemed good to you; you have devoted yourself to a covenant of this type," Aelred de Rievaulx, 44.

[4]". . . that they yearn, sigh, in fact, more freely for Christ's embrace," ibid.

[5]Cf. P. Schmitz, *Histoire de l'Ordre de Saint-Benoit*, VII (Maredsous, 1956) 53-58.

[6]We need only recall the story of Robert d'Arbrissel concerning itinerant preaching and the foundation of Fontevrault. Cf. J. Von Walter, *Die ersten Wanderprediger Frankreichs Studien zur Geschichte des Mönchtums*, I (Leipzig, 1903); R. Niederst, *Robert d'Arbrissel et les origines de l'Ordre de Fontevrault* (Rodez, 1952); J. M. Bienvenu, *L'étonnant fondateur de Fontevraud, Robert d'Arbrissel* (Paris, 1981); J. Dalarun, *L'impossible sainteté: La vie retrouvée de Robert d'Arbrissel* (Paris, 1985); and *Robert d'Arbrissel fondateur de Fontevraud* (Paris, 1986), also by Dalarun.

[7]Cf. Epistola CXV: "Ad sanctimonialem quamdam de monasterio S. Marie trecensis," *Sancti Bernardi Opera* VII, edited by J. Leclercq and H. Rochais (Rome, 1974) 294-95.

[8]"Will not my virtue be safer in the desert where I may live in peace with a few companions or even alone, and where I may please him with whom I have won favor? By no means. To a person who wants to behave sinfully, the desert offers abundant opportunity, the woods their shadows, solitude its silence. The evil that no one witnesses, no one denounces. Besides, when one need not fear an accuser, the tempter has easier access, the evil deed freer execution. In the convent, on the other hand, should you do something good, no one objects. But if you want to do something sinful, it's not permitted. I recognize, daughter, I recognize and would that you'd recognize it too, the serpent's venom, the deceiver's trickery, the werewolf's cleverness. In the woods lives the wolf. Were you to enter the shadow of the woods as a lone little lamb, you would be prey for the wolf. But listen to me, daughter; pay attention to sound advice. Be you sinner or saint, do not separate yourself from the flock, lest he carry you off and there be none to rescue you. Are you a saint? Make sure, through your example, to win companions for your sanctity. Are you a sinner? Do not pile up sin upon sin. Rather, do penance right where you are, without withdrawing, to your own peril in fact, as it has been demonstrated. You would leave behind a scandal for your sisters, and egg on the tongues of numerous backbiters besides." Ibid.

[9]See the opinion advanced by J. Leclercq in *La femme et les femmes dans l'oeuvre de Saint Bernard* (Paris, 1983).

[10]See L. M. Clay, *The Hermits and Anchorites of England* (London, 1914); A.K. Warren, *Anchorites and their Patrons in Medieval England* (Berkeley-Los Angeles-London, 1984).

[11]See G. Holdsworth, "Christina of Markyate," *Medieval Women*, ed. D. Baker (Oxford, 1978) 224-48.

[12]Holdsworth 230.

[13]See *Caesari Heisterbacensis monachi Ordinis Cisterciensis Dialogus miraculorum* I-II [Ceasar of Heisterbach, Monk of the Cistercian Order: Treatise on Miracles I-II.] (Cologne, Bonn, and Brussels, 1851). For information on the author, see the article by F. Wagner in *Lexikon des Mittelalters* II, 1363-66.

[14]He describes them as holy, religious, devout, venerable (the *Dialogus* consists of distinctio [henceforth d.] and capitulum [henceforth c.]; the examples referred to can be found in d. V, cc. XLVII, L; d. VI, cc. V, XVIII; d. IX, cc. XXXI, XLVI or "propter Christum inclusae" [incluses for Christ] (d. V, c. XLVI); "propter revelationes Dei, quibus illustratur, notissima" [renowned for revelations from God, for which she was distinguished] (d. V, c. XLVII); "divinis revelationibus assuefacta" [accustomed to divine revelations] (d. VI, c. XVIII).

[15]An abbot turned to an incluse specifically to ask her a question and receive an answer from God: "'Sister, please ask God for me to tell you whether it pleases him and is also profitable for me to remain in office in this abbey.' She rose, left to pray, soon returned, and told the abbot what had been revealed to her" (d. VI, c. XVIII). Even more interesting is the case contained in d. XII, c. 27, which includes a conversation between an incluse and a dead person who was condemned to purgatory for having practiced magic. A *miles* [soldier] asks Bertrada about the fate of his wife who died a short time before. "As she prayed, the wife appeared, complaining to her that she endured great suffering. Bertrada inquired about the cause of her suffering; for she had been held in high regard as an honorable woman. 'For practicing magic,' the wife replied. 'I was afraid he would sin with other women if he should come to dislike me. Then I would be the cause of his adulteries. So, with a few skills which I had acquired, I meant to stir the embers of his love for me. Because lust was not my purpose but a pious intention, I thought I could find welcome assistance.' All this was reported to the soldier. Whereupon, out of deep compassion for his wife, he endeavored to help her with prayer, fasting and almsgiving; he commended her soul to as many people as he could." The wife of the *miles* [soldier] is one of the best described women in the Dialogus. For more on females in medieval literature see L. Pellegrini, *Specchio di donna L'immagine femminile nel XIII secolo: gli "exempla" di Stefano Borbone* (Rome, 1989).

[16]In the account found in d. IV c. XXXIX a monastic community is praying for a "contristata vel desparata" [depressed, desperate] incluse who lost her faith. The question is: "Who knows whether there is a God; whether there are angels and souls with him; whether there is a kingdom of heaven?" Because of prayer the incluse has a vision which is narrated: "My soul was escorted from my body and I saw the holy angels, I saw the souls of good people, I saw the rewards of the just." Thus she regains her faith, and feels "highly comforted and consoled." A "vir religiosus" [devout man] helps another incluse who senses the devil's presence and his disturbances in her cell (d. V c. XLVI): the magic word for casting him out is "benedicite" [Blessed be God]. The next account, found in d. V c. XLVII, is more complex: the male incluse who helps the female one identify the "angelum tenebrarum" [angel of darkness] as the "angelo lucis"[angel of light] is not satisfied with a word, but suggests a magical action in which Christian elements (the cross) are mixed with magical elements (gesticulating with a candle): "Use blest wax to mark with a cross the window through which it usually enters. If on entry it does not shun the cross, it is an angel of the Lord. Otherwise, it is an angel of darkness." We will return to this episode later (note 94). In d. VI c. XXXI once again it is an abbot who intervenes to counsel an incluse; this episode will be considered again later (note 53). There is an identical case but a different suggestion which a confessor gives a happy incluse who believes she has been the recipient of angelic visitations. Here we see evidence of another aspect

of women's piety in Caesar's opinion: extreme gullibility. The loss of the earthly dimension: the woman, alone in her cell and immersed in continuous meditation on eternal things, seems oblivious to the visit of supernatural beings. It is the confessor who, in Caesar's view, has a different piety and recognizes the illusory nature of the heavenly visitation, not because it is the result of imagination, as someone of a more pragmatic piety might suggest, but because he is more inclined to identify it as the action of the devil, which he finds plausible. Therefore he tells the incluse to act as follows: "When the angel visits you again, say: 'My lord, please show me my Lady.' If he does so, when you see her, kneel down and say: 'Hail Mary, full of grace, and so on.' Then, if she stays, she is not a hallucination. If she does not stay, you'll know you're being deceived by the devil. She acted on this advice. And the devil said: 'Why do you want to see the Lady? My presence ought to be good enough for you.' But she resolutely insisted. So, through diabolic intervention, a virgin of marvelous beauty presented herself. At the sight, the incluse fell at her feet. When she had recited the angelic greeting in the presence of the fantasm, it dissolved in a whirlwind. As the enemy vanished, he so greatly frightened her that she lost her mind. Only half a year later did she regain her senses through the prayers of many friends." (d. VII c. XXVI). For the topics dealt with here, see H. Haag, *Teufelsglaube* (Tübingen, 1974); R. Manselli, *La religiosità popolare nel Medio Evo* (Bologna, 1983); E. Pásztor, "Gli angeli nelle visioni medioevali," *Prospettive nel mondo* 14 (1989): 69-70.

[17]See J. Alberigo, J.A. Dossetti, et al., *Conciliorum oecumenicorum decreta* (Bologna, 1973) 203.

[18]See L. Gougaud, *Ermites et reclus* (Ligugé, 1928).

[19]O. Dörr, *Des Institut der Inclusen in Süddeutschland Beiträge zur Geschichte des alten Mönchtums und des Benediktinerordens* (Münster, 1934).

[20]See "Reclus en Occident" in *Dictionnaire de la Spiritualité*, with its rich bibliography.

[21]A. Vauchez, *Les laics au Moyen Age Pratiques et expériences religieuses* (Paris, 1987). The book treats various aspects of the incluse problem.

[22]See G. Le Bras, *Institutions ecclésiastiques de la étienté médiévale Préliminaires et Ière partie, Livre I*, Histoire de l'Eglise 12 (Tournai, 1959) 196.

[23]See endnote 86 below.

[24]See the *Vita b. Mariae Oigniacensis* [Life of Blessed Marie d'Oignies] by Jacques de Vitry in Acta Sanctorum (hereafter referred to as AA. SS) Iuni V, 547-72.

[25]See note 101 below.

[26]See V.W. Turner, *The Ritual Process* (London, 1974) 103; Holdsworth, "Christina," 247.

[27]Cf. K. Elm, "Die Stellung der Frau in Ordenswesen. Semireligiosentum und Häresie zur Zeit des heiligen Elisabeth," *Sankt Elisabeth, Fürstin, Dienerin, Heilige* (Sigmaringen, 1981) 17.

[28]See endnote 2 above.

[29]A 13th century Anglo-Saxon text hypothetically attributed to Richard the Poor (1217-1229), who supposedly wrote it for the incluses of Tarrent; G. Meuner, *La règle des Recluses, dite aussi le livre de la vie solitaire* (Ancren Riwle) (Tours, 1928); C. P. Rouillard "Regole per reclusi, 5. 'Ancren Riwle' or 'Ancrene Wisse'" in DIP, VII (Rome, 1983), 1535 . Includes bibliography.

[30]Ibid., 1535-36.

[31]See Herrad of Hohenbourg, *Hortus deliciarum [Garden of Delights]: A Reconstruction. . .* ed. R. Green, I-II, Studies of the Warbourg Institute (London-Leiden, 1979) 36. Herrad was abbess of Hohenburg, near Strassburg. See also J. Autenrieth, "Einige Bemerkungen zu den Gedichten im Hortus deliciarum Herrads von Landsberg," *Festschrift B. Bischoff* (Stuttgart, 1971) 307-21.

[32]Cf. G. Busson and A. Ledru, "Actus pontificum Cenomannis in urbe degentium," *Archives Historiques du Maine* 2 (1901) c. XXXVI: "Deeds of Bishop Guido:

with food and clothing he cared for the recluses who stayed in the suburb of the city."

[33]Alice la Bourgotte lived for more than 46 years as an incluse at Paris in the Cemetery of the Innocents in a cell near the church (+1466). See J. Hubert, "L'eremitisme et l'archéologie," L'eremitismo in Occidente 486. See J. Huizinga, Herfsttij der Middeleeuwen (Haarlem, 1928) 210: the cemetery of the Holy Innocents, that "horrible celebration of death with piles of bones exposed to public view. Who can imagine anything more frightening than living as a hermit enclosed next to the church in that place of horror?" This opinion expressed by a 20th-century historian should be compared with a passage from a 12th century source which does not see the cemetery as a "horrible celebration of death" but rather as the place where the sacred meets the profane (see note 34).

[34]Cf. Caesar of Heisterbach, Dialogus, d. XII, c. XLVI, in which he narrates a Marian apparition in a cemetery within the context of the vision of a recluse: An incluse "quite godly and devout" one night saw her cell filled with light. So "she rose and opened the window facing the cemetery. There, at the head of the tomb of a scholar recently buried, she saw a woman of extraordinary beauty. The radiance of her body had caused the illumination. Also there was a snow-white dove hovering over the tomb. The woman took hold of the dove, placing it in her bosom. Although the recluse already understood the meaning, she reverently inquired what it could be. The woman replied: 'I am the Mother of Christ and I have come to raise up the soul of this scholar who is a true martyr...,'" which also includes the idea that a dead student was considered a martyr: "in truth, scholars who live blameless lives and learn cheerfully, are martyrs."

[35]See J. Hubert, 485-87.

[36]See P Rouillard, 1234: "In Saint-Flour (France) the city government had a home for a recluse built on one of the bridges leading to the city and guaranteed the support of the recluse and the person who was to serve her." The cell's presence in the city fostered the religious sense of the people and, as Huizinga said, increased "religious emotion and imagination," (259) reminding people of the existence of a manner of existence which considers all earthly ties as nothing, in order to be absorbed in God.

[37]See Vita latina, ed. K. Böle, O.P. "The cause of the canonization of B. Margherita of the Arpad dynasty and her oldest Latin biography" (Budapest, 1937) 17-73, republished in Sacra Rituum Congregatio, Positio super aequipollente canonizatione b. Margaritae ab Hungaria, sanctimonialis Ordinis Praedicatorum (Rome, 1943) 173.

[38]See E. Marténe, De antiquis ecclesiae ritibus libri, II (Antwerp, 1736) 496-99.

[39]See, among others, the counsels of Goscelin of St Bertin (note 42) and that of Aelred de Rievaulx (note 2); however, this is a frequent topic in the whole of medieval sources which would deserve a separate treatment.

[40]An important contribution is given in this regard in Warren's work (see note 10) which, besides the inheritances, mentions other gifts, dividing the data into categories based on the donor's status: royal support; aristocratic and gentry support; merchant and other lay group support; clerical support (127-29).

[41]See the work cited in note 37 above and the passage by Gregory of Tours in note 44 below.

[42]See C.H. Talbot, The "Liber Confortatorius" of Goscelin of St. Bertin, Studia Anselmiana (Rome, 1955) 37.

[43]Ibid.

[44]See Gregorii Episcopi Turonensis Libri Historiarum X, ed. B. Krusch and W. Levison (MGH Scriptores rerum merovingicarum I/I) (Hanover, 1951) 29 (ad a. 582). The nun acts following a vision in which she was led to a stream of living water (the myth of the sacredness of water) and a man advises her to drink in order to be assured of eternal life. At that time her abbess appears and removes her habit and

replaces it with regal robes, a gift from her bridegroom. (The importance of the dress code is very interesting here because the young woman is a nun and is not wearing a dress worthy of the bride of Christ, which she is; she receives it only after having drunk of the living waters, an act which here symbolizes a rite of passage!) Gregory also describes the rite with which she becomes an incluse: the whole community gathers, the nuns have burning lamps in their hand and come forward in procession, with Queen Radegonda herself leading, reciting psalms. Before closing the cell forever, they each offer the incluse the kiss of peace. From that moment on, Gregory notes, the nun devoted her whole life to prayer and meditation.

[45]See "*Vita* Liutbirgae," in MGH SS IV, 158-64; see also O. Menzel, "Die 'heilige' Liutbirg," *Deutsches Archiv* 2 (1938): 189-93.

[46]See E. Irblich, *Die "Vitae s. Wiboradae" Ein Heiligen-Leben des 10 Jahrhunderts als Zeitbild* (Constance, 1970). See also "Viborada," *Bibliotheca Sanctorum* XII, 1062-63. Wiborada had her cell next to the church of St. Magnus in St. Gallen: she was introduced there by the Bishop-Abbot Solomon (890-920), and spent her life in prayer and ascetical practice; she was also known for the advice which she gave to the abbots who turned to her. See also J. Duft, "Die Ungarn in Sankt Gallen," *Bibliotheca Sangallensis* I (Zürich-Constance, 1957).

[47]Cf. R. Manselli, Il *secolo XII: religione popolare ed eresia* (Rome, 1983).

[48]See note 42.

[49]Cf. AA. SS. Aprilis II, 549-54; the author, who describes himself as an eye-witness (549), writes three years after Herluca's death. See also J. Leclercq, *La Spiritualité du Moyen Age* (Paris, 1966) 269-70.

[50]See J. M. Watterich, *Pontificum Romanorum. . . Vitae I* (Leipzig, 1962) 474-546; H. Fuhrmann, "Zur Benützung des Registers Gregors VII durch Paul von Bernried," *Studi Gregoriani* V, 299-312. The author also mentions Herluca in his *vita* of Gregory VII.

[51]See C.H. Talbot, *Goscelin* 22-23. See also G. Constable, "Aelredo de Rievaulx e la monaca di Watton Un episodio agli inizi della storia dell'Ordine Gilbertino," *Sante, regine e aventuriere nell'Occidente medievale*, D. Baker, ed., 266-67 (see note 11).

[52]See Migne PL 157, 184-86; it is ep. 48 of book IV of his epistolarium: "To the servant of God, Herve, and to the maidservant of God, Eve, incluses" that expresses the wish that the two can "bring to conclusion in even finer fashion what they have so auspiciously begun." Letters 49 and 50 are addressed to "Herveo incluso" alone.

[53]See C.H. Talbot, Goscelin 23; A. Wilmart, "Eve et Goscelin," I-II, *Revue Bénédictine* 46 (1934): 414-38; 50 (1938): 42-83.

[54]See note 42 above.

[55]Talbot, "Liber Confortatorius," 70.

[56]Ibid., 64.

[57]Ibid., 70.

[58]Ibid., 64.

[59]Ibid., 68.

[60]Ibid., 70.

[61]Ibid., 79. Aelred of Rievaulx says the same (see note 2), 104: "Let an image of the Savior hanging on the cross suffice for your altar. This makes his passion present to you for your imitation. With widespread arms it invites to his embraces, within which you may surrender yourself. From his bare breast flows the milk of sweetness by which you may be refreshed." The idea of breast-feeding is repeated in St. Clare's vision; however in her case the figure of Christ becomes that of St. Francis. See M. Bartoli, "Analisi storica e interpretazione psicanalitica di una visione di S. Chiara d'Assisi," AFH 73 (1980): 449-72; or *Chiara d'Assisi* (Rome, 1989) 194-98.

[62]See C.H. Talbot, *Goscelin* 79.

[63]See R. Manselli, "Pietro de Bruys," R. Manselli, ed. Il *secolo XII*, cited in note 46, 87-100.

[64]Cf. C.H. Talbot, *Goscelin* 79.

[65]See note 2.

[66]Ibid., 48: "Let the incluse see to it that as far as possible she live by the work of her hands."

[67]Cf. G. Meunier, *La règle des recluses, dite aussi le livre de la vie solitare* (Ancren Riwle); see also note 29.

[68]Cf. Aelred de Rievaulx, 46-50.

[69]Cf. K. Esser, *Opuscula sancti patris Francisci Assisiensis, Bibliotheca franciscana ascetica Medi Aevi,* XII (Grottaferrata, 1978) 230-31, "Regula bullata" chap. IV: "I firmly command all the brothers that they in no way receive coins or money, either personally or through an intermediary. Nonetheless, let the ministers and custodians alone take special care to provide for the needs of the sick and the clothing of the other brothers through spiritual friends according to places and seasons and cold climates, as they may judge the demands of necessity; excepting always, as stated above, they do not receive coins or money."

[70]Cf. Aelred de Rievaulx, 50: "The incluse is bound to turn over from the work of her hands, that which is superfluous for livelihood, to one of the faithful, who then may distribute it to the poor." Thus, it is true, the incluse is deprived of any opportunity to care for the poor, but she is also freed from the continual pressure to have recourse to alms. This is the only way the incluse can freely fulfil her vocation to be "poor among the poor. . . . It would be a sign of serious infidelity for an incluse to be anxious about the morrow." Aelred adds, 48, another idea that we shall see again in early Franciscanism.

[71]Ibid., 52. "Do not make yourself accessible to boys and girls. Some incluses busy themselves with teaching children and turn their cell into a schoolroom. The incluse sits at the window, the children on the porch. She attends to each one and in accord with their youthful responses, now becomes angry, now laughs, now makes threats, now coaxes, now slaps, now kisses, now calls closer for a slap one who weeps, strokes one's face, caresses another's neck, and hastening to embrace calls her daughter, friend. Amid all this, what can mindfulness of God be like when such worldly, yes sensual, things though they may not be so flagrant, are nonetheless an irritant, occuring as publicly as they do."

[72]Cf. AA. SS. Septembris V, 679-680; AA.SS. Octobris XIII, 97; see also F. Baumann, "Jutta di Disibodenberg," *Bibliotheca Sanctorum* VII, 1032-33.

[73]Cf. Aelred de Rievaulx, 66, 116-145.

[74]Ibid., 102.

[75]"Let sparkling white linen adorn your altar to symbolize chastity with its gloss and to illustrate simplicity. Consider what exertion, what blows are required for linen to discard the earthen hue it first bears, and to come to such radiance that it may adorn the altar, mantle the body of Christ. Why, we are all born bearing the color of earth; for I have been conceived in iniquity, and in my sins my mother has conceived me. First, linen is immersed in water; we, in the waters of baptism, are buried with Christ. There inquity is overcome, though weakness is not yet healed. Some splendor we receive in the forgiveness of sins; but not yet do we fully put off the earthen color because of the deep-rooted corruption that remains. After immersion, linen is dried. So is it necessary, after the water of baptism, for the body, dried out through abstinence, to be emptied of illicit leanings. Next, as linen is beaten with mallets, so our flesh is wearied with many temptations. After this, linen is combed with iron needles to put aside all superfluity. And we, scoured by the hooks of discipline, scarcely retain what is necessary. Next, for linen comes a more thorough cleansing from lesser imperfections. And we, with our worst faults overcome by generous toil, are cleansed in simple confession and penance, of our lesser, more habitual sins. Then spinners stretch out the linen; we are stretched toward the future in patient perseverance. Indeed, to ensure a more ideal attractiveness, fire and water are

applied. So must we pass through the fire of tribulation and the water of compunction, to arrive at the repose of chastity. Let ideas like these shed light on the decor in your oratory; do not gratify your eyes with silly diversions." Ibid., 104.

[76]See Johannes Marienwerder's *vita* of Dorothea in AA. SS. Octobris XIII, 493-498 and the modern biography of her by H. Westpfahl, *Dorothea von Montau* (Meitingen, 1949). The process for her canonization (1404-1406) was published by R. Stachnik-A. Triller-H. Westpfahl, *Die Akten des Kanonisationsprozesses Dorotheas von Montau* (Cologne-Vienna, 1978); for article 19 in canonization test, see page 21. See the listing for "Dorothea von Montau" in the index of A. Vauchez, *La sainteté en Occident aux derniers siècles du Moyen Age d'après les procès de canonisation et les documents hagiographiques* (Rome, 1981), as well as his other work already cited in note 21, pages. 273-300.

[77]See A. Vauchez, *I laici*, 207-63: "La donna fra matrimonio e nozze spirituali."

[78]See AA.SS. Martii III, 734-762; A. Vauchez, *I laici*, 250-263: "Una 'santa donna' della valle della Loira al tempo della guerra dei Cent'anni: Giovanna Maria di Maillé."

[79]See G. Holdsworth, note 11, 228-37. See also C.H. Talbot, *The Life of Christina of Markyate, a Twelfth Century Recluse* (Oxford, 1959).

[80]See *Gesta abbatum monasterii S. Albani a Thoma Walsingham. . . compilata, Rerum Britannicarum Medii Aevi Scriptores*, 28/4, ed. H. T. Riley (London, 1867) 98-105.

[81]See G. Holdsworth, "Christina," 226-27. Concerning Christina's ascetical life in the hermitage, see *Gesta*, note 80 above, 98: "she sat on a cold, hard stone, wasting away in fasting, hunger and thirst in a narrow space, having nothing to cover herself when she felt cold."

[82]See Holdsworth, "Christina," 226-27.

[83]See *Dialogus*, d. IV, c. XXXIX: "In our province there lived a beautiful girl of marriageable age, the daughter of wealthy parents. When the parents wanted to present her to her prospective husband, she refused with the words: 'No man shall I marry other than my heavenly spouse, the Lord Jesus.' At last, wearied with her persistence, her parents left her to her own pleasure."

[84]Ibid.

[85]Ibid.

[86]AA. SS. Aprilis I, 437-477: it is the life of Julianne of Cornillon which also includes events in Eve's life, 452-460, 464-65. Both of these had a significant part to play in the institution of the feast of Corpus Christi. See Clotilde de Sainte Julienne, *Histoire d'un glorieux passé Sainte Julienne de Cornillon, Sainte Eve de Saint-Martin et la Fete de Dieu* (Brussels-Paris, 1924); A. Lazzarini, *Il miracolo di Bolsena* (Rome, 1952) 783-86.

[87]See A. Mens, *Oorsprong en Betekenis van de Nederlandse Begijnen Begardenbeweging* (Antwerp, 1947) 244-45.

[88]AA. SS. Aprilis I, 452: "Eve was in the bloom of her youth. At the inspiration of Christ, she felt a strong attraction for an enclosed cell. Nonetheless, given her human weakness, she felt daunted in the face of such an exalted proposition. Juliana, coming to know of this dilemma, drove the foolish concern from Eve's heart with forceful assurances. In addition, with skillful counsel, she encouraged Eve to carry out her proposal."

[89]Ibid. "As a result, Eve entered the poverty of a recluse's cell, in order to subordinate her own Eve-nature (that is, her flesh) more freely to her spirit. Likewise, in order to embrace more daringly the fruits of spiritual goodness. . . ."

[90]There is an interesting case in this regard found in Caesar of Heisterbach's *Dialogus miraculorum* in d. VIII c. XLII: The "angel of the Lord" offers a certain incluse a terrible choice; since it is not possible to live without temptations, he asks her after having her first experience both, whether she would prefer these temptations to be carnal in nature or doubts in faith ("spiritus fornicationis" or "spiritus blasphemie") [the spirit of fornication or the spirit of blasphemy]. She chooses the former: "Even though it will have proven base, at least it was human . . . to doubt concerning God

and christian faith . . . is, in short, diabolic." This is one of the few instances in which the incluse decides for herself, without receiving advice from anyone (see note 16).

[91] Ibid.

[92]This is the case of the young woman mentioned in note 83. She entered into her cell voluntarily and enthusiastically, and found herself tempted by the devil, who was jealous of "such virtue . . . by inserting the venom of sadness into the maiden's heart, he caused her to become sick. Soon she began to be disturbed by all sorts of imaginings, to waver in faith, to despair of persevering." The abbot of Brombach visited her and asked "how she was doing, how she was getting along," and she replied: "I'm in bad shape. I'm not doing well. Why I've been shut up in this place, for what purpose, I have no idea." Dialog., 207.

[93]Ibid., d. VI, c. XXXI: "Master John, now Abbot of St. Trudo, was once visiting an incluse-friend of his in Saxony. She was weeeping. He said: 'Dear lady, what is the matter? Why these tears?' Her response: 'I have lost my Lord.' Noting the fervor of her devotion, and aware that she was a saintly woman, he added by way of jest: 'Go around to the corners of your cell and say, "Lord, where are you? Answer me." Perhaps you'll find him in a crack of the wall.' She accepted these simple words at face value. After his departure, she made the circuit of the cell's walls as she had been advised, calling on her beloved. She found the one she sought; she recovered what she had lost." Concerning popular piety, see R. Manselli, Il soprannaturale e la religione popolare nel Medio Evo (Rome, 1985).

[94]This case is narrated in the Dialogus, d. V c. XLVII (see also note 16). When the incluse realizes that she has been tricked by the devil "she spit at him, broke into insults and, for fear of presuming too much, commanded him in the name of the most holy Trinity."

[95]Ibid., d. IX c. XXXXI: an incluse named Uda, "to whom God used to reveal many things" while she was assisting at the Mass of a priest, " saw a fiery globe above his head," a sign of his holiness of life. See also d. V c. L: a young woman of Aachen, "before being enclosed, while still dressing as a laywoman, though quite saintly, . . . saw demons in the shape of monkeys and cats sitting on the shoulders and scapulars of monks from Porceto as they were walking in the oratory. . . . She noticed something even more horrible. Large, repulsive looking dogs were walking along in front of some of the monks, so that the chains visible on their necks encircled also the necks of the monks. By means of these chains, the dogs pulled the monks along as objects of derision."

[96]See AA. SS. Aprilis I, 455: Julianne of Cornillon tells the incluse of the death of her mother and sister.

[97]A. Vauchez, see note 21, 280-94.

[98]See J. F. Hinnebusch, The Historia Occidentalis of Jacques de Vitry: A Critical Edition (Fribourg, 1972)) 88.

[99]Ibid.

[100]See E. Pásztor, "Chiara da Montefalco nella religiosità femminile del suo tempo," S. Chiara da Montefalco e il suo tempo, eds. C. Leonardi and E. Mentesò (Perugia-Florence, 1985) 183-267.

[101]See AA.SS. Ianuarii I, 86-87: it is a vita compiled by Hugh, canon of Floreffe: "The biography and way of life of the servant of Christ, Yvette, incluse at the lepers' house near Huy." L. Laurent, Yvette, le sainte recluse (Paris, 1980).

[102]See AA. SS. Ianuarii I, 87.

[103]Cf. AA. SS. Aprilis II (see note 48) 554 and 555 of the vita of Gregory VII: "while she had withdrawn in solitude to her cell" she saw Christ enter and he showed her his wounds.

[104]Ibid.

[105]See note 62 above.

[106]Cf. AA. SS. Aprilis I (see note 86), 453-54: "When the recluse (Eve) had revealed her true icon, the maid of Christ (Julianne) fixed her gaze on the image of the Savior. Forthwith, overcome with extreme distress from recalling Christ's passion, she collapsed in a faint on the floor. The recluse took her into her arms and laid her on the bed. Intending then to dispel her distress, or at least to lessen it, she remarked: 'Calm down, my lady; for by now the anguish of Christ's passion has passed away.'"

[107]This is a hagiographical theme which we find not only in the *vitae* of the incluses, but also in that of the monks; it is tied up either to the passion or the Eucharist. ("This is my body," Christ says, for example, to Adele Langmann [+1375], entering into her monastic cell.) See P. Ariès, G. Duby, *Histoire de la vie privée II De l'Europe féodale à la Renaissance* (Paris, 1985) 522.

[108]See AA. SS. Novembris II, 166-209; see also J. Hinnebusch, 87, 257 (with bibliography). Her *vita* was written after 1180 by a Cistercian who knew her personally. Jacques de Vitry recalls her as a model for those who reject penitential practices: "In the kingdom of France, in a diocese in the region of the Seine, the Lord offered to everybody, as a paradigm of abstinence, a poor young girl of the hamlet of Cudot. For many days she suffered from a severe illness. But after the Blessed Virgin had appeared to her in person, she lived for some forty years or so neither eating nor drinking. However, to moisten her parched palate and throat, she occasionally used to suck a bit of fish or something similar; but she never allowed anything into her stomach. On Saturday nights and on Sundays, the peace of God that surpasses and buries every sensation, used to render her totally quiet and immobile. For she was so transported in spirit that she could neither speak nor feel; nor did she seem even to breathe." Alpais' fasting was not something miraculous, but rather an act of penance "in propitiation for those who neglect to do penance for their sins." As a reward Alpais receives a visit from the Blessed Virgin in her cell and the sense of total peace in a spiritual rapture during the night between Saturday and Sunday. It seems it is not necessary to stop to consider the female mystic's sense of peace following the suffering borne with Christ on the cross. For more on the central position of Christ's passion in feminine mystical experiences, see E. Pásztor (note 100), particularly pages 218-20, 260-61. The prologue of the *vita* of Alpais (AA. SS. Novembris II) contains the following comment on the young woman's fasting: "Not in a hundred years has it been heard that a young maid of such fragile condition did not need bodily nourishment, was not sustained with earthly foods. Constantly she lay prone in bed as all who were privileged to see her testify, never eating, never drinking, as other folks do" 174-75. In regard to refusing to take food, the most famous example from the Middle Ages is that of Catherine of Siena who, according to Raymond of Capua, her biographer, at a certain point in her life began to refuse to eat, deriving the strength to exist only from daily communion. Alpais's *vita* is significant also because it shows how the experience of inclusion was spread throughout the whole of society in the Middle Ages, including rich and poor, simple people and nobility. Alpais of Cudot is the daughter of farmers who send her to tend the "cows and other cattle" on Sundays and holy days too, as her biographer tells us (175), while the other girls go to dance. She has to do hard work while Jeanne-Marie de Maillé, for example, is related to the royal family of France through her mother (cf. A. Vauchez, *I laici*, 251).

[109]Cf. AA. SS. Novembris II, 182: a dove "transfiguring itself in her presence." In reality, it seems as if she is watching a mystery play of some sort.

[110]Cf. AA. SS. Martii III, 737-47; See also A. Vauchez, *Una "santa donna."*

[111]See AA. SS. Martii III, 738.

[112]Ibid. This is a typical expression of popular piety. In the same *vita*, 740, there is another example of this type of practice, which is also valuable for the relationship it shows between devotion and art, which should be pointed out. According to her biographer, Jeanne-Marie is reflecting on how she can spread devotion to our Lady, and "to give her heart peace," the only solution she can come up with is to have

three statues of Mary made: "she had three statues of the Virgin made." She designates them for three different places: the first is to be placed in the upper part of the choir of the canons of St. Martin in Tours; the second is to be placed in the choir, but at the western exit "over the altar of the Slothful Ones, as it is popularly called"; the third is to be placed in the hermitage dedicated to our Lady at Planche-de-Vaux. Only the second of the three statues is described in the *vita*: "she wanted that statue to be called 'the Virgin of Sweet Consolation' and so she requested." The statue destined for Planche-de-Vaux was entrusted to a "certain pious gentleman," but Jeanne-Marie accompanied it herself: "With herself as bearer, they walked along with bare feet, not heeding gutters full of water, muddy streets, thorns or thistles. They passed along easily just like a ship on the sea. Thus they seem not to have walked, but to have fairly flown." Her ordering three statutes shows what a prominent position popular culture gave to iconographical language, to things that could be seen by the human eye, things which can be understood by the unlettered, by those who cannot follow sermons on doctrine. One need only think of Giotto's "Bibbia pauperum" [Bible of the poor] in Padua. For more on this topic, see E. Male's analysis of the medieval period in *L'art religieux en France* (Paris, 1898-1908) and J. Huizinga's *L'Autuno del Medio Evo*, particularly the chapter on "Il pensiero religioso e le sue rappresentazione figurate," 232-37. See also G. Duby, *L'arte e la società medioevale* (compilation containing three works in French: Adolescene de la chrétienté occidentale (980-1140); L'Europe des cathédrales (1140-1280); Fondements d'un nouvel humanisme, 1280-1440 (Bari, 1977); R. Delort, *La vie au Moyen Age* (Lausanne, 1972), particularly the chapter on "Signs and Symbols."

[113]See AA. SS. Martii III, 740: "For that reason, many people with their trivial racket, often used to call her "hermitess" by way of ridicule."

[114]Ibid., "Just like an apostle, she followed the Lord Jesus Christ, the Redeemer."

[115]Ibid., 741. Many of them refuse to help her, however, because they fear her parents.

[116]Ibid.

[117]Ibid. "On the streets and squares, she reclaimed women of ill repute from the clutches of young men. She used to give them a good scolding with enthusiasm and spirit."

[118]Ibid. Lack of clergy was a very concrete problem at that time. A situation of this type is recounted as a miracle in the hagiographical literature. Jeanne-Marie's prayer is credited with keeping a dying woman alive until a priest could come to hear her confession.

[119]Ibid., 742.

[120]Ibid.

[121]Ibid.

[122]Ibid; she changes her seal "into another form . . . fashioned after the instruments of Christ and sealed with the marks of the Lord's passion."

[123]Ibid.

[124]See K. Esser, 231: *The Later Rule*, VI: "As pilgrims and strangers in this world who serve the Lord in poverty and humility, let them go begging for alms with full trust." It should not be forgotten that Jeanne-Marie's biographer is a Franciscan.

[125]See E. College, J. Walsh, *A Book of Showings to the Anchoress Julian of Norwich* (Toronto, 1978).

[126]Norwich is in East Anglia, not far from the coast; it is the capital of County Norfolk and was an episcopal see in the Middle Ages.

[127]We do not know the date of her birth (perhaps 1342) nor of her death. There are only two certain facts: in 1373 she experienced the revelations, which were transcribed around 1393; in 1413 Julian received a visit from Margery Kempe (see the introduction of the work in note 125); P. Molinari, *Julian of Norwich, the Teaching of a 14th century Mystic* (London, 1958); J. Stéphan, in *Bibliotheca Sanctorum* VI, 1177-81.

Concerning Margery Kempe, see *The Book of Margery Kempe*, ed. S. Brown Meech and H.E. Allen (London, 1940); R. Brentano, "Catherine of Siena, Margery Kempe and a 'caterva virginum'" in *Atti del Simposio internazionale Cateriniano-Bernardiniano*, ed. by D. Maffei and P. Nardi (Siena, 1982) 45-55.

[128]See note 125. Hers is a very important mystical work; God makes his revelations to Julian one day in May 1373 (there is a debate if it is the eighth or 13th), after the incluse has asked for three gifts.

[129]*Revelations*, chapter IV.

[130]Ibid., chapter XVII.

[131]Ibid., chapter XXI.

Forms of Solitary Religious Life

for Women in Central Italy

by

Giovanna Casagrande[1]

Translated from the Italian by

Nancy Celaschi, OSF

The idea of "for women" in the title of this work should be placed in parentheses, so as to say that it does not preclude from the world of males. However, I have given pride of place to this idea, drawing on a historical method which has seen and continues to see the flourishing of a great expanse of literature on the topic of women in the Middle Ages.

I draw on a historical method, as I said, but also am encouraged by evidence of a more significant feminine presence to be found in the 13th and 14th century sources. These are, in fact, the chronological terms assigned to me, perhaps not casually, because they do correspond with the spread of new orders, and they allow the use of more documentary material capable of attesting to more than just a few solitary forms of religious life (for women and for men).

Having said this, I must note that this report is not the climax of a synthesis, the final outcome of a series of thorough, complete studies, but rather a moment open to investigation, an attempt to put many ideas out in the open.

This field of study, however, is rather sophisticated and subtle, and in some ways we must be satisfied with finding information from gauges, clues, or suggestions in the midst of a quantity of information which is sometimes larger than it seems.

The choice of central Italy was motivated by the fact that this vast area presents a great deal of data on the solitary forms of religious life. This does not mean, however, that central Italy is a special case. Similar forms of the solitary life can be found, for example, in northern Italy. Perhaps this aspect should be given further study.[2] Nor should it be assumed that central Italy is an isolated case, or particularly exceptional in the whole European context,[3] although the particulars in comparison with more distant situations should be pointed out.[4]

More recent or more or less specific references and studies have made central Italy a privileged area for this type of study. Even though it is premature to attempt a synthesis, it is at least possible to begin some articulated considerations.

The better-known documentation regarding central Italy offers us a number of personages living generally in immediately sub-urban areas or in "strategic" locations in urban areas; they are generally called *reclusi* [recluses], *carcerati* [enclosed], *incarcerati* [incarcerated]; but also *heremitae* [hermitesses] or the simple name of *fratres et sorores* [brothers and sisters], letting others know that their life involves some kind of religious connotation.

To put these people into context, to restore them to what I believe is a more precise historical connotation, to make them "exit" from the generic, all-inclusive context of the penitential (*bizzocale*) movement, I think it is opportune to begin further back in the attempt to show the evolution of an ancient type of religious life which was susceptible to new development.

Eremitism between Endurance and Evolution

The search for the solitary life has its deepest roots in the ideal of separation and detachment from the world which is part of the Christian vocation.[5]

It is a separation from the world which is not necessarily effective, but rather moral and affective. It does not exclude the possibility of a "physical" separation. "Christian perfection," Turbessi writes, "is in direct proportion to separation from the world and . . . it finds its concrete, culminating expression in the vocation of the ascetic, the hermit."[6]

The hermit, then, is the concrete personification of separation from the earthly world in order to devote oneself to a constant, direct relationship with God. The desire to be separated from and extraneous to the world is expressed in a physical, logistical choice to live in deserted, uncultivated places[7] or in closed, confined places (cells).[8]

It is also common knowledge that Western monasticism evolved in the direction of the cenobitic community.[9] In reality, however, the life of solitude and hermitage never died out. It remained constant, developing parallel to the cenobitic life.[10]

Hermits, and especially hermit-recluses, can be found in the works of Gregory of Tours[11] and in the *Dialogi* of Gregory the Great.[12]

At the end of the eighth century the search for the solitary life, with reclusion as a specific response to that quest, entered into the Church's norms in canon 12 of the Council of Frankfurt-am-Main (A.D. 794): "that none become recluses except those whom the bishop of the province and the abbot shall have approved and who enter a place of reclusion in accord with their decision."[13]

The passage of time tended to have a regularizing and stabilizing effect on the development of the solitary life manifested in reclusion. A key moment in this trend, however, can be found in the *Regula solitariorum* [Rule of life for solitaries] of the recluse Grimlaico. The text was edited in the first half of the 11th century,[14] that is, in the Carolingian age, perhaps as an attempt to codify the phenomenon and bring it back into the ranks of the monastic-cenobitic institution:

> There are two kinds of solitaries. One is anchorites, that is, hermits; the other, cenobites, that is to say, monastic (these would be the recluses). Neither of these kinds ought to be undertaken by a novice in the fervor of conversion. Rather, they must first be tested, in the daily discipline of the monastery, to what degree they are able, with God's mercy, to mount toward the summit of perfection.[15]

In perfect line with the tradition of the Rule of St. Benedict and the canons of the councils (see endnote 9), Grimlaico's Rule clearly says that one cannot begin to live any type of solitary life, which is seen as the summit of perfection, without first having experienced life in the monastery: "must first be tested in the daily discipline of the monastery." One cannot enter it directly as a result of conversion, that is, in the novice's fervor of conversion. The solitary life is more perfect and can therefore be embraced only by a person who has been tried by the cenobitic life.

In sixty-nine chapters, the Rule dictates norms on various aspects of the life of a recluse (e.g., how the cell should be made).[16] Everything is marked by moderation, *discretio*, the mother of all virtues.[17] It tells us that the recluse's day is to be divided among prayer, reading, and manual labor, with no room for laziness.[18] The recluses are advised, among other things, to live in small groups of two or three in order to challenge one another and not to feel more perfect than others.[19]

Chapter 15 treats of regulations for entering the state of reclusion,[20] clearly confirming the close ties between reclusion as an institution and the monastic, cenobitic life.

Grimlaico does not view the solitary life in an isolated perspective, but rather as conditioned by the cenobitic institution in line with the Benedictine and conciliar tradition.

People speak of a "monastic crisis" in the 11th and 12th centuries, but it is also a "cenobitic crisis." Because of the ensuing prosperity which on the whole is seen as proof of its vitality, during this period the two souls of monasticism—the cenobitic and eremitic aspects—are both renewed to the point where they can offer solutions which are not totally unoriginal.[21]

The desire for the solitary life and flight from the world, which was never dormant and always persistent, was given new life in this period and in turn gave rise to a great variety of hermits.[22]

With Romuald of Ravenna and his biographer, Peter Damian, eremitism acquires full dignity and autonomy in relation to cenobitism. With them the eremitic-cenobitic formula is offered in two centers of power in central Italy (Camaldoli and

Fonte Avellana). We know that from Romuald's viewpoint, the cenobium should ideally and really be subordinate to the hermitage and their common abbot should live in his own cell in the hermitage.[23]

Historians have pointed out how the Damians gave autonomous dignity to the eremitical institute to the degree that it was not necessary for a person who wanted to enter it first to enter the cenobium. The Damians' Rule gave everyone the possibility of a *conversatio eremitica*, an eremitical way of life, putting itself in the position for an eventual break with the tradition expressed by Benedict, Grimlaico, and the councils.[24]

In the context of Camaldoli and Avellana, the hermitage-cenobium word pair was joined by a third element, reclusion. This was related to the figure of Romuald himself who, although only for a period of time, practiced this specific style of solitary life,[25] which was also embraced by others: "Indeed, some were so hemmed in by the gates of their sentence that they seemed dead to the world, as though they had already been entombed."[26]

With their diverse solutions of institutionalized eremitism combined with cenobitism, Camaldoli in Italy and Grand-Chartreuse in France[27] gave strong momentum to the spirituality of the solitary life lived in the cell.[28]

If Camaldoli and Chartres represent the two points of reference for an organized eremitical life, this does not mean that they drew the whole vast, diverse eremitical movement towards their solutions. Recently Penco emphasized the persistence of an irregular eremitism, that is, one extraneous to the institutional contexts and outside those eremitical movements which in turn became constituted into approved orders (Camaldolese and Carthusians). It is probable that the "cenobitic crisis" fostered the development of eremitical streams "outside the bodies which had sprung up to channel these same streams."[29] It is also probable that there was a certain diffidence and the impossibility of "entering into an established organism, of adapting to an ordo, of submitting to a Rule or a set of customs."[30]

The tendency towards a contemplative, solitary, eremitic life which had developed in the 11th and 12th centuries, giving life to institutionalized forms of eremitism, to an eremitism lived in common, to individual phases of the solitary life, will not end in the course of the 13th century and beyond.

If eremitism is an enduring phenomenon, evolving and being transformed as time passes, it will go into decline and then rise up once again, taking on new and different expressions.

What was Francis of Assisi in the first days of his conversion if not an irregular, independent lay-penitent hermit? One of those hermits (not a recluse) seeking solitude, but who does not cut himself off from contact with the world of the faithful.[31]

Thanks to Francis we have one of the few Rules for hermits,[32] while the Rules for recluses are considerably more numerous. This is a sign of the complex personality of the saint who passed through many of the experiences of religious life of the time.[33] This complexity would later be projected onto the Friars Minor, in whom, it is general knowledge, there has been a persistent attraction for the solitary life and for the *ritiro*.

We also know that groups of hermits were formed in central Italy in the 12th and 13th centuries:[34]the Guglielmiti who gathered around William [Guglielmo] of Malavalle in the Grosseto area; the Brettinesi, who were involved in apostolic activity and had a more structured organization.[35] In Cesena another movement with an eremitical matrix began, the one headed by Giovanni Bono, whose penitential life spent in the cell makes us think of a type of hermit-recluse; like the Brettinesi, the Giambonini were given permission to hear confessions and preach.[36]

Another sizable group was the Hermits of Tuscia, whose eremitical foundations were called "cells." They may have been rural canons (with priests, clerics, and laity) or lay foundations evolving towards the clerical life.

These eremitical groups began to be regularized, following the guidelines of the Fourth Lateran Council, taking a precise Rule, usually either the Augustinian or Benedictine Rule.

These groups born from an eremitical matrix were evolving towards the common-life "solution" and, to some degree, taking on pastoral ministry. From them a new Order arose, the Hermits of St. Augustine, which would assume an entirely different connotation than the eremitical one: from the hermitage to the city, we could say.[37]

This Order is significant because of its transition from eremitism, and in certain areas, I would say, even went beyond it. This is also seen to be true when considering the history of the Carmelites and the Servants of Mary.[38]

The eremitical thrust of the 11th and 12th centuries lasted into later centuries, but the evolution into institutionalized religious groups, including the mendicant Orders which were the complete antithesis of eremitism itself, is entirely evident.

The attraction to the solitary life will persist within Orders such as the Franciscans, Servites, Carmelites, and Augustinians, and will be taken up anew (Capuchins, Paolo Giustiniani). The mendicant Orders in the 13th and 14th centuries (except perhaps for the Dominicans) were not insensitive to the eremitical calling, but sooner or later tended towards the cities and an active apostolate, the *cura animarum* [the ministry to people] and a life of fraternity/community.[39] This development shows the dynamic tension between objectively necessary forces and ideals and the opportunity they provide for integration into the changing socio-political context. It shows as well the desire to face new religious demands and challenges.

If 11th and 12th century eremitism flees the city and seeks the "desert,"[40] in the case of the new Orders this orientation is inverted as it is overcome by an increasingly urban-centered context.

A Strange Development: Reclusion

A clear distinction is not always made when speaking of hermits and recluses. It is obvious that a recluse is also a hermit, but a hermit is not necessarily a recluse.

While Leclercq indicates that the words "hermit" and "anchorite" are equivalent for the English–speaking world,[41] it has been noted that "hermit" usually remained the more generic term, while "anchorite" took on the narrower meaning of recluse.[42]

In regard to the geographical area involved in this study, I did not find the term *anchorite*. Recluses are indicated as such or by the term *incarcerati* [incarcerated] (and variations of it), *cellani* [those in cells] or *eremitae* [hermits] (Pisa).

In the 11th and 12th centuries *eremus* [desert] and *eremita* [hermit] indicate diverse realities: solitary hermitages with a sole hermit or one accompanied by a disciple or companion, with or without bonds to a cenobium, groups of hermits living in cells, as well as cenobia built in isolated areas.[43]

Among these realities the type of eremitic life most closely related to the life of the recluses in central Italy is that of groups of hermits living in separate cells, following the model given greater popularity because of the set-up used by Romuald's and Peter Damian's followers. Peter Damian describes the life:

> The order of hermits is twofold: namely, some dwell in small cells; others wander at random through the uninhabited desert, considering fixed abodes of little value. But those who wander about through the desert are called anchorites; while those who are content with cells are referred to with the customary term hermit.[44]

Thus the hermit is one who lives in a cell. In this perspective the prominence given to reclusion in the Romuald-Damian stream can be well understood.

The recluse is a hermit who for any reason whatsoever never leaves his cell in a more strict stance of separation and isolation from the world.

The style of the solitary life lived in reclusion in a cell is an ancient, well-established one. The Camaldolese movement prob-ably played a role in its adoption and rebirth, at least in central Italy.

The phenomenon of reclusion, however, is not tied to any particular religious order, even though there is naturally place for it in the Camaldolese eremitical stream.[45] This is true, so much so that in the 12th century, for example, we find communications addressed to recluses—both male and female—from all over Europe by personages belonging to different orders: Peter the Venerable, Abbot of Cluny; the Cistercian, Aelred of Rievaulx; the Carthusian, Bernard of Portes.

It is Peter the Venerable who, writing to the recluse Gisleberto, recommends the cell.[46]

Taking into consideration the prominence of the cell in Carthusian circles or that of their "sympathizers" (e.g., William of Saint Thierry), we can say that in the 11th-12th centuries there is a real exaltation of solitude lived in the cell,[47] which in turn provides strong direct or indirect spiritual motivation for reclusion itself.

If eremitism is on the fringe of monastic life,[48] reclusion is on the extreme edge of the eremitic fringe.[49]

There are two spiritual themes characteristic of the life of reclusion. The first one is more of a penitential nature. It is the theme of self-incarceration, that is, taking on a state of penance and punishment for one's own sins, as is clearly expressed in the Rule of Grimlaicus.[50] The second motif is that of death to the world. The recluse is not only separated from the world, as all monks and hermits are; even more so, he or she is dead to the world, already buried,[51] one who is buried with Christ, as Peter the Venerable and Aelred of Rievaulx write.[52]

As early as the *Vita Romualdi*, Peter Damian had described those who chose the enclosed life as "dead to the world" and already placed in the tomb (see endnote 26). In praise of the eremitic life, exalting the cell, the proper place of a hermit/recluse, he writes: "O cell that almost rivals the Lord's tomb, you receive those who are dead to sin and make them live again for God by the inspiration of the Holy Spirit! You are a burial place apart from the troubling harassment of this life, but you open wide the entrance to heavenly life."[53]

If, therefore, reclusion can be seen as a special aspect of eremitism, it should be said immediately that the latter retains a primarily male connotation, while the former develops a predominantly, but not exclusively, female connotation.[54]

Hagiography and documentary sources, the two types more commonly used, will be combed for more information on the phenomenon.

Saintly Women Hermits/Recluses

It is not easy to name women hermits, as opposed to the case for males. Proof of this is seen in Omaechevarría's very short entry under the title of "Eremitismo femminile" in the *Dizionario degli Istituti di Perfezione*.[55] It mentions only one of the very few cases, and a very late one at that (15th century); it tells of a pious virgin who dressed as a Friar Minor and lived at the convent of the Carceri near Assisi.[56]

A thorough search of Iacobilli's *Vite*[57] yields a group of saintly men called "hermits," but not one holy woman from that category.

Anna Benvenuti Papi has the merit of having sketched a view of holy women hermit/recluses[58] which allows us to discern immediately the important figures from central Italy.

To tell the truth, there are few women hermits because the distinction between hermit and recluse is such a subtle one, especially if one is trying to avoid "a fantasy world with stories that are hard to believe."

According to Benvenuti's study, we need only mention Chelidonia (11th-12th century), who led a solitary life "among some rocks" and later became a hermit dependent on Subiaco.[59] Then there is Brigid of Fiesole, of Irish origin.[60] In addition to them there is a hermit/recluse known only as Santa Franca found in the area of the Marches (11th century). In order to flee the insidiousness of unworthy priests, she retired to a hermitage to lead a life of solitude.[61]

We could say that others were temporary hermits, like St. Bona of Pisa (c.1165-1207), whose life of pilgrimage included a period as a hermit in the Holy Land.[62] Then too in the area of Umbria and the Marches there is Sperandea (1216-c.1276), whom Benvenuti calls a "case of existential confusion," that is, a sign of that almost uncontrollable flux of lifestyles proper to the late Middle Ages. She is a periodic hermit. During Lent, for example, she would retire to a cell or a cave.[63]

In the area of Rome we need to take a new look at Margherita Colonna (+1280), who is claimed by both the Poor Clares and the Order of Penitents. Certainly it was the eremitical life which she embraced from 1273 on, when she withdrew into a cave on the Prenestine Hill and then attracted other companions. Giacomo Colonna is said to have given them an anchoritic Rule of life. The "eremitic community" remained on the hill until after Margherita's death, when it evolved in the direction of Poor Clare monasticism.[64]

This group's whole development fits into a none too unusual pattern. To the degree in which it takes on a community aspect— also of necessity because of the regulations of Lateran IV and Lyons II —it must evolve from a spontaneous state to a more regular, institutionalized existence.

Earlier, Filippa Mareri (+1236) lived first as a recluse in her own home. Then, with some followers she moved to a dormitory not far from her castle, and finally entered into the movement of St. Clare and the Poor Ladies of San Damiano.[65] Recluse-hermit-Poor Clare: Filippa represents a figure in transition, joined into that new order of San Damiano which per se represented the first organic attempt to give a common expression to the spontaneous phenomena of women's groups.

These women's living conditions are not always clear and easily defined. I believe that if this is not a sign of a restlessness, it is certainly a mark of a search for a sufficiently satisfying and acceptable state of affairs; a sign that there was no immediately available answer or that the familiar forms were no longer adequate. It was also a sign of various inclinations existing together in a single person, attracted by many existing religious experiences. In that regard Margherita Colonna is an extremely important example.

There is a much broader range of holy women than of hermits who can be classified as recluses. I will not enter into the argument since Benvenuti described the biographies of eleven recluses (from central Italy and elsewhere), two of whom are affiliated with the Camaldolese and are from the same city, Pisa.[66] One has a Vallombrosian bent and moves from the life of an individual recluse to the cenobitic life.[67] Three of them are from three different "minor" centers in Tuscany, having in common a modest social background, which led to a strong civic sense, typical examples of local holy women.[68] One is an example of a person alternating between strict individual reclusion and a community life.[69] Another is an example of temporary, periodic reclusion;[70] another is typical of the "superimposition" of religious states in the minorite context.[71] Still another is aggregated to the Order of Preachers.[72] The last is from the Abruzzi region, and is an isolated example from the 15th century.[73]

Although there is no great number of recluses, they come in a rather varied range. We could also add Umiliana Cerchi because of her desire to spend her life in a cell and Clare of Montefalco as a typical example of "reclusion in a community."

These figures certainly do not represent a linear development. Take for example, Umiltà of Faenza and Margherita of Cortona. The majority, but not all of them, came from the laity. They led complex lives, never easy ones. They were of modest or wealthy social extraction. Sometimes they show how a person can live in several religious states. Their common denominator is never that of living as recluses in an urban complex, in a broad sense.

Hagiographical sources proposing this form of life as a model to be followed are, Benvenuti complains, very rare in comparison to the many incarcerated/recluses referred to in documentary sources.[74]

Why is such a small list given the honors of hagiography? Is there a lack of exceptional piety? Even though it was rather widespread in a certain period, this solitary form of religious life is rather "marginal" compared to the institutional forms and the organized structures of the religious orders which by their very nature require functional figures for their affirmation. The tendency will be to skip over this irregular, independent form in order to propose models of holy women who are more firmly situated in the Orders (the mendicant Orders first of all) and thus, also taking into consideration what Benvenuti calls a certain "lack of hagiographical concern on the part of the secular clergy,"[75] a Tertiary spirituality will develop.

The documentary presence of the incarcerated recluses will also tend to work to the advantage of the ever more numerous and imposing presence of the Tertiaries. Women saints and blesseds are but the tip of the iceberg of a much broader and more widespread phenomenon than the documentary sources allow us to discover, but only superficially, in such a way that it leaves open a whole range of questions that is probably too broad.

Urban Recluses

We have already mentioned eremitism's evolution into a community lifestyle and its transformation into forms that are its direct opposite (Hermits of St. Augustine). Reclusion also takes on a new dimension.

Leclercq points out two principal periods of the phenomenon. The first, which includes the 12th century, is that of a predominantly monastic style of reclusion where men and women live in the area of the monasteries and/or are connected to them. From the 13th to late 15th century there is a growing urbanization: the recluses, both men and women, tend to move to the urban areas.[76]

Society's ever more urban-centered context polarizes every manifestation. Consequently, an "archaic" religious form of life such as reclusion adapts to the changing times, thus experiencing new momentum and a development that was previously unthinkable.

Looking at hagiographical sources, I would like to pause on two of them in particular in which it seems we can see how the strictly eremitical-solitary model was overcome.

The first is the biography of Umiliana Cerchi,[77] which was written by the Friar Minor, Vito of Cortona.

Umiliana withdrew to live in the tower of her family's palace without wanting to settle there as a recluse: "She was even hoping to be enclosed in her tower and said: 'Would that my father would enclose me in this tower for the name of Christ in such a way that there would not be in it either a door or a window.'"[78]

She could ideally be considered as a person living in a cell. This, however, was not her only desire: "She wanted to live in lofty mountains and in deserts and wildernesses, in inaccessible places, where for her nourishment she would have only herbs; and where, according to her desire, she would freely meditate on God, and break out in praises and devout cries out of love for her beloved Jesus Christ."[79]

However, everything remained only a desire. Gisla, too, one of the holy women who appear in Umiliana's life, wanted to be alone "in uninhabited places," but "since solitude is dangerous for women, she recommended herself to B. Umiliana."[80]

But there is more. At a certain point the biographer has Umiliana herself say that "she encouraged some to reconciliation, others to penance; to still others she recommended the lives of Saints, . . . for others, again, she advised the solitary life, saying: 'Think of your home as a hermitage in a grove, your family as the animals of the forest, and among them you will be as though in the grove, observing silence and applying yourself to continual prayer.'"[81]

The hagiographer's desire to offer a model of a holy penitent living in the world is also obvious when, after having said that Umiliana had taken the habit of the Franciscan Third Order,[82] he writes:

> What less than the holy hermits did she have, she who in the middle of the city found solitude for herself, and transformed her sleeping room into a retreat? . . . Others have done battle for the Lord after they have abandoned the world and their ancestral homes and fled to a hermitage; she achieved solitude in the home of her father, and in noble struggle, conquered both the world and vice in the midst of worldly affairs.[83]

Solitude, therefore, can be lived in one's own home, and in the midst of the city.

Giunta Bevegnati, Margaret of Cortona's biographer, puts the following words addressed to the saint in the mouth of Christ himself: "You asked me to be able to live in the same condition of solitude as Magdalene did. However, I have not destined you to live in a desert (the deserts are not appropriate for our time); however, you can be as solitary in your city as if you were living in an endless desert."[84]

The idea of solitude and separation from the world ("flee the world and seek solitude," Christ repeatedly tells Margaret)[85] remains, but it is the context in which it can be lived that changes. The growing urban dynamism tends to change the very context of solitude, because this is not necessarily to be sought in remote, inaccessible places, but can be lived in urban areas, and it is even advisable for women to do so.

Thus Francesco of Barberino wrote in the 10th part of his *Reggimento e costumi di donna* when treating of the woman who withdraws into a cell: "I praise whoever makes one's hermitage where there are people rather than those solitaries who shy away from people."[86]

In the biography of Verdiana of Castelfiorentino we find:

He established that type of life in the Thebaid, with that celebrated community in Egypt, having assembled eremitical cells. This maid of ours in Italy, though she was not living in a desert, nonetheless led a solitary life, just like the hermits—a life approved by God through miracles.[87]

Although the biographer exaggerates the similarity between St. Antony and Verdiana, it seems that this brief text at least gives us an understanding that the solitary life is no longer necessarily to be lived in the hermitage.

Spread and Characteristics of the Phenomenon

"If the institute of recluses, both of men and women," Penco wrote, "were to become more accentuated towards the late Middle Ages to the point of becoming a typical manifestation of that era's piety, it is between the 11th and 12th centuries that the earliest examples of the phenomenon appear in Italy."[88]

It is, however, the 13th century documentation which gives us increasing amounts of information, although here the term *information* is used in the sense of scattered items of single and isolated appearances, information lacking any systematic organization.

Without claiming to have compiled all the statistics, let us take a quick look at the spread of the phenomenon, remembering that we are dealing with "partial results" which are open to the most varied interpretation.[89]

In fact, the presence of recluses in a given place is attested to by simply a statement, or little more. It is a hopeless task to try to reconstruct its history. However, the fact remains that the phenomenon is recorded in indirect documentation, that is, the recluses themselves do not do the writing. There are some testaments bequeathing property, or some arrangements made by a commune or bishop which help us see immediately that we are looking at something that is not institutionally concrete. This, if you will, is the phenomenon's strength and weakness. It is its strength because it is an independent form, one not necessarily linked to the control of an Order. The recluses are free to live their life with no obligation to follow common regulations. Its weakness, however, consists in the fact that it has no organized structure capable of guaranteeing them a more secure existence.

Documentary evidence shows that the phenomenon is found in Umbria,[90] the Marches (and in the area of Massa Trabaria),[91] in Tuscany,[92] Emilia Romagna,[93] and Lazio.[94] It seems to indicate a religious lifestyle that is marginal and hidden in the underbrush, as it were.

Proof of this can be found in last wills and testaments, the sources in which recluses are most frequently mentioned. The amounts left to them personally are modest (the smallest is 2 denarii, and the largest 50 soldi).[95] A testament from Città di Castello in 1284 seems to establish a kind of scale with a part of the funds left to "the churches, the brothers and the incarcerated."[96] A 1320 will from Rieti puts priests and recluses (incarcerati) on the same level, with a bequest of 12 denarii each.[97] However, another will from Città di Castello (1350) provides 12 denarii "to every recluse and to every leper."[98] At Bettona at times we find wills lumping "every fraticello and recluse"[99] together and at Gubbio "every abode of ladies or incarcerated women and of the fraticelli of Plano, on the mountains."[100]

This irregular, noninstitutional form of religious life is recognized by those making their wills, but perhaps in a secondary way, almost as if to let us see that they have a vague awareness of these persons, who are worthy of being remembered in their will. They are in some way a part of the devotional circuit, but are in a type of subordinate position because they are individuals, and therefore do not need enormous sums to provide them with some margin of survival.

The civic documentation seems to reflect the same consciousness. Wherever we find evidence of decisions made about the distribution of alms (Perugia, Rimini) it is a question of 10 or 20 soldi per capita (maybe per annum).[101]

The bequests are often rather generic in form [as seen in the terms extracted from ancient records]:

> to each hermitage; to each hermit and hermitess; to the enclosed; to each hermitess; to each hermit; to each man or woman in a cell; to recluses; to hermits and the incarcerated; to recluses and hermits; to each male and female hermit enclosed in a cell; to each hermit in a cell; to each recluse and incluse; to each hermit . . . to male and female incluses.

Then there is a list of places, these too mentioned rather generally:

> of the city and outside it; of the city and outside it for one mile; within the city and outside for one mile; of the city . . . and from outside the city . . . for two miles; outside the city and inside it; inside the city and near it; near the city; in the district; outside and near the region. . . .

Others are mentioned more precisely:

> under the bridge; in the vicinity of the mountain . . .; on the mountain . . .; on the mountain and the plain; at the bridge . . .; near the the church . . .; outside the gate; next to the gate; on the highway; on the road. . . .

All the data are generic, because neither the names nor the number of the recluses are given. What we are told about their location suggests that they can be found throughout the city and its immediate surroundings in strategic locations. The most isolated position is on the mountain, but even these are not generally far from inhabited areas.

When the documents are more generous in providing information, for example, testaments and the distribution of alms, we are able to determine the network of the distribution of recluses almost to the point of discovering another image of a medieval city and the cells or hermitages located about it.

In such a variegated context anything is possible, and it seems that there was room for everyone, expressed, as it were, in an endless creativity of forms and religious states. Incarcerated and recluses are also a world of laity and religious who are hidden, perhaps because for the greater part they are not linked to any Order or perhaps because they are a freer, less stable form, and therefore more subject to a transitory nature and, by their very nature, do not need a complex structure.

Three documents, for example, coming from three different cities in central Italy, allow us to see different expressions of the phenomenon.

In 1290 in Perugia there were 56 sisters and 12 brothers found in twenty-one zones spread throughout the five areas of the city.[102] It is not clear how these recluses lived. Were they together in one hermitage? Were they in separate cells which were close to one another? Nevertheless, it seems there is a whole range of owners: laity and institutions of various types (the hospital of Colle, the canon's house of St. Laurence, churches). We also learn of three "sisters in cells belonging to the Friar Preachers." They are found alongside churches, monasteries, along the roads, in vineyards or in suburban or semirural areas.

In Pisa in 1302 we have a will probated[103] that gives us the names of 30 hermits, 28 female and 2 male. Their cells are for the most part located along Via San Pietro a Grado, the road leading to the sea. San Pietro a Grado, a Romanesque Basilica, was also a pilgrimage shrine, and there was a cell right in front of the church. We also know of a certain concentration of cells opposite the Poor Clare Monastery of All Saints, which was also on Via di San Pietro a Grado. There are other cells in Kinzica: one in front of the Vallombrosian monastery of St. Paul, one near the church of St. Andrew and another "along the path that leads to St. Mary Magdalen's." The cells are sometimes designated with names of specific persons or churches (the cell named after Leopard, the cell named after the sons and nephews of the deceased Datus, the cell named after Saint John of Gaitani, the cell named after Saint Martin of Vectula).

While the document from Perugia does not give us any personal data about individual recluses, the one from Pisa gives their names and that of their fathers, and even some idea of where they came from. Can we make a thorough study? From the document we discover the widow of a maker of armor, the daughter of an inn-keeper, the widow of a master carpenter, the daughter of a sailor and a broker's daughter, too.

In the list we find Checcha di Giacomo, openly called a *soror de penitentia* [a sister of penance], on a hagiographical level similar to Margaret of Cortona or Sibyllina of Pavia. Her story is confirmation of that superimposition of religious states so frequently found at Pisa. We can consider the case of Giovanni Cini, a soldier who became a *conversus* [a lay brother], then a brother of penance, and ultimately a hermit in a cell near the oratory of the Disciplinati of St. John the Evangelist.[104] Then there is also the priest Alexius, a brother of penance "who lived in a cell belonging to the Oratory."[105] The document mentions six widows and three cases of sisters living in the same cell.

A will from 1367 in Fabriano[106] helps us locate 12 hermitages with a total of 15 recluses, 12 of whom are women. The hermitages are found next to or near the city gates, close to churches or monasteries. The recluses seem to live separately or two to a hermitage. It seems that the owners are lay people or the recluses themselves, or some organization or institution of a religious nature (in one specific case it is a confraternity).

Some documents are rather generous in providing information. From them we have a rather good idea of how the cells or hermitages were located: along the roads; near city gates and bridges; next to churches in urban, suburban, semirural or rural areas;[107] near monasteries; in vineyards; in areas of urban expansion which were not totally urbanized, but neither truly rural; in areas of "transit." From these documents we sometimes learn the number of recluses.[108] We have some idea of the identity of the owners of these cells and hermitages: lay people, various institutions, the recluses themselves. We learn about their existence in larger or smaller centers. In my opinion there is still much to be learned, many areas to be explored and many questions that remain open. To understand how much remains to be done, we need only mention the case of Rome.

The year is somewhere around 1320, and we find in the city a total of 260 women recluses and 470 nuns,[109] a truly phenomenal number compared to the number of *moniales*, contemplative women religious!

Testaments from the late 13th century indicating inheritances left to recluses[110] tell us the phenomenon was certainly present there. However, there is a big difference if we want to learn anything more than the indications given us by Oliger. The Roman situation is all the more interesting because of its connection with the life of St. Francis and St. Dominic.

Relative to St. Francis himself there is the well-known case of Praxedes, the image of the "perfect" recluse who does not want to violate her state of complete isolation, not even in very serious situations.[111]

Among the miracles of St. Dominic recounted by Sister Cecilia, two of them were performed on behalf of recluses. One of them lived in a tower near the Lateran gate, the other behind the church of St. Anastasius.[112]

In regard to the areas still unexplored, I would point out the area of Abruzzi, and cities such as Ferrara[113] and Bologna,[114] for example. There are so many questions still to be solved.

We can see that these hermit/recluses are independent and for the most part do not have any precise bonds with the Orders. If their cells are situated near a monastery, for example, it does not mean that we can automatically say they have some kind of "dependence" or connection with it, or even less so that these are then instances of a type of oblate.[115]

The phenomenon seems to attract the piety of the faithful and is not without some form of protection. Did it escape the control of the ecclesiastical authorities? According to ancient norms, in order to become a recluse a person had to have the permission of the bishop, or the abbot in cases of monastic reclusion.

A recent study concerning England has examined the role of the bishops and their responsibility in regard to recluses.[116] In central Italy we do not find evidence of much interest on the part of bishops in this type of religious life. A search of diocesan archives has found information on the topic in Gubbio and Nocera Umbra.[117] Other examples of interventions by the bishop found in Città di Castello, Sansepolcro and Camerino[118] give us an idea of the bishops' marginal interest.

In order to be so widespread and protected by the civil authorities, would not the phenomenon need some source of legitimacy? Was the consent of civil authority or the owners of the cells enough?[119]

We have not found the information we would like to have telling us about relations between the bishops and recluses. Who authorized a person to become a recluse? Who celebrated the liturgy of reclusion?[120] Was it the bishop, his delegate, or some other ecclesiastical authority?

What relationships were there, if any, with the church, the monastery, the settlement, the confraternity, the hospital, or the canons' house near which (or on whose property) the recluses lived? Who was responsible for the care and spiritual guidance of this lay religious?

The first hermitage mentioned on the bridge of Graces (at Rubaconte) in Florence in 1326 is that of "Giana, wife of the late Vannus Braccus from Montelupo, a tertiary of the Holy Cross at Florence, judging from her garb, who undertook religious life, as one may see, in a hermitage located in the neighborhood of St. Remigius at the bridge of Rubaconte." Its pastoral care was handed over by the friars of Santa Croce to the rector of St. Remigius parish.[121] It should be noted that the phrase "entered religious life" (which seems to have escaped Benvenuti's attention[122]) seems to emphasize her passage from the secular status of *pinzochera* [tertiary] to that of *religious* according to the canonical tradition of reclusion.

In 1400 the bishop ordered the spiritual care of the small community of Blessed Apollonia (on the Bridge of Graces) to be entrusted to the parish priest of St. Romeo, who brought communion to the recluses every Sunday.[123] Might this be an example of a bishop intervening on behalf of the recluses? Hagiographical sources suggest some kind of spiral effect.

Maria and Gherardesca of Pisa, especially the latter, were aggregated to the Camaldolese (Cf. endnote 66); Umiltà of Faenza to the Vallombrosians. It was at the church of St. Apollinarius, a dependency of the abbot of Crespino, where Umiltà's cell was built.[124] The abbot received her into obedience to the order and he himself gave her the habit (Cf. endnote 67).

Verdiana of Castelfiorentino has some kind of bond with the secular clergy. In the liturgy of reclusion Verdiana had promised obedience to the parson, and not to the bishop (Cf. endnote 121).

Once she moved into the cell near St. Basil, Margaret of Cortona left the sphere of influence of the Friars Minor, and her spiritual care was taken over by a priest of the secular clergy (*see* Badia).[125]

In the *reclusorium* [hermitage] of Sibyllina of Pavia, a Dominican penitent, there was an altar where "devout religious and secular priests" celebrated Mass for her.[126]

Even though there are privileged relations, the overall picture of the spiritual care of these holy women recluses seems to be a not too rigid one, and the traditional clergy is anything but extraneous.

However, studies of this type do not tell us everything about the various types of reclusion which documentation offers. Who, for example, was responsible for the spiritual care of a recluse living in a certain vineyard?

Was the state of reclusion permanent or temporary, rigid or rather flexible? This is to say nothing of the problem of a Rule, if, indeed, they followed one. It has been claimed that the Umbrian synods of Gubbio and Nocera Umbra[127] must have been inspired by the Rule of Grimlaicus, but it is an open question as to just how much influence this Rule exercised over time,[128] although perhaps we cannot rule out the fact that it was a reference point on which the life of reclusion was modelled. Could living in very small groups (two–four persons) have been a "heritage" of the Rule of Life for solitaries which, in chapter seventeen (Cf. endnote 19), advised the solitaries to live in groups of at least two or three?

Was the Rule of Grimlaicus addressed exclusively to men? We have already noted that in the English-speaking area,

Aelred of Rievaulx wrote a Rule for the sister recluses, but how can we infer that this Rule's influence reached all the way into Italy?

It is, however, surprising that for the English language area there are 13 known texts including letters, Rules, and spiritual guides; while on the other hand, no similar text has been found concerning central Italy, although the phenomenon of reclusion certainly had a following.[129]

What did these recluses do to pass the day? Did they pray, that is, recite the psalms? Did they work? What level of education did they have? Did they know some of the texts of the desert fathers? Did they, for example, know the *vita* of St. Mary of Egypt?

The Italian recluses do not have their Julian of Norwich, unless Angela of Foligno is thought to have been a *cellana* [woman in a cell].[130]

Were they entirely dependent on public support or did they have some resources of their own?

Despite this whole tangle of questions, from the sources at our disposal we have a good idea, at least a "marginal" one, of the extent of this solitary life, of this attempt to isolate one's self from the world in the urban context.

Who embraced this lifestyle? Was it a "choice" made because it was impossible for the person involved to enter the preexisting institutions or found new ones; that is, was it a type of "rebound" solution, or was there some margin of free choice?

Was the life of reclusion in the cell or hermitage an obligatory part of the process for joining less well-off or marginal groups? Hagiographical sources studied by Benvenuti shed light on the cases of Verdiana of Castelfiorentino, Giovanna of Signa, and Giulia of Certaldo, who came from socially marginal groups (two former servants and a farmhand). By choosing the life of a recluse they changed in some way their social status by becoming "public property, mediatrixes of divine graces from heaven to the world which accepts them."[131] However, can we learn anything from the documentary sources? Probably too little to build a valid argument.

We have evidence of recluses who own their own hermitage at Fabriano.[132] However, in this city, as in other places, much more frequently others (lay people or various institutions) are the owners. Known cases include a servant girl in Assisi,[133] a woman with some ties to the artisans in Pisa,[134] and an *incarcerata* [incarcerated woman] who takes out a perpetual lease on a plot of land in Massa Trabaria (Cf. endnote 91). Can we automatically connect the phenomenon of reclusion to a marginal situation or one of social solitude?

Is it a case of people who could not embrace other, more structured and organized forms of religious life and therefore chose some possible alternative, the life of a recluse in a cell or hermitage, alone or in small groups which were destined to become communities themselves and thus, with the passing of time, take on a monastic structure? Since we lack more concrete data, we must leave the question aside in order not to make hasty conclusions.

Embracing the recluse's way of life could gain a respect which should not be overlooked[135] and guarantee a *modus vivendi* of some dignity, attracting the piety of the faithful with a penitential life conducted in an exemplary solution of separation from the world, thus transforming the hermit's cell into an urban *carceri* visible to all, a model of detachment from earthly things. Recluses were devout figures on whose prayer people knew they could depend. Why were so many lay people the owners of cells or *carceri*? It is probable that "tolerating" or promoting their existence could be to their advantage (prayer, presence of a somewhat sacred figure). The establishment, maintenance, and endurance of a hermitage could also somewhat help save one's soul.[136]

I do not believe there is a single key for interpreting the "success" of urban reclusion in the 13th and 14th centuries. Several factors must have merged together for the life of reclusion to develop in urban areas: social, economic, or demographic changes (more women looking for space), causes which are often more open to intuition than proof; religious and spiritual motives which, perhaps, are all too hidden, that is, an unappeased desire for solitude for contemplation's sake

(Margaret of Cortona) and a demand for prayer and meditation on the part of the faithful. One writer has even mentioned an apotropaic role because of the logistically strategic locations they occupied.[137] One of their functions was probably to incarnate the ancient Christian demand for separation from the world and perhaps something more, a symbolic death to the world, gaining credibility not by placing themselves in a remote, less visible, eremitic setting, but in the concrete setting of daily life in populated areas, thus finding for themselves a religious and social position.

Do we hear the distant echoes of the words of Peter Damian, that great proponent of the solitary life lived in a cell, but within the context of a hermitage? These words were addressed to the woman hermit Teuzone who was enclosed in a cell near the Florentine Abbey:

> To this point it happens that you have decided to lead an eremitical life not in the desert, but within the walls of a populous city. . . . But, pray tell, if you are a monk, what have you in common with cities? If a hermit, what is there in common between you and hordes of citizens? What benefit do cells confer, or, for that matter, bustling marketplaces, or turreted defence-works? Indeed, what is to be thought of those who seek solitude in the cities—as though the forests had all disappeared—except that they are not the perfection of solitary life, but are hankering after applause and recognition.[138]

In all probability the recluses, both men and women, whom we find in the cities of central Italy were seeking neither advantage nor glory, but the possibility of survival guaranteed by a religious state.

A Few Notes on Communal Reclusion

The terms *reclusa/inclusa* become all-embracing. They include the primitive Poor Clare communities; the Camaldolese; the *dominae* [ladies] of San Jacopo di Ripoli (Florence), who eventually enter into the ambit of the Friar Preachers;[139] individual forms or even the microgroups. The term almost always seems to indicate any type of woman who lives a life separated from the world, alone or in a community.

The term begins to take on various meanings. Was this a result of the phenomenon's natural evolution towards the community form, just as eremitism will take on the connotation of a community experience; or was it rather a widespread semantic application of the word?

I myself am not convinced that the term "recluse" could also be used to indicate the *bizzoche*; a *bizzoco*, or the feminine *bizzoca* (the name is derived from the rough wooden shoes they wore), indicates penitents or tertiaries. However greatly the religious states in this period were superimposed on one another or blended together, the words "recluse," "incarcerata" and "cellana" retain their own special meaning, as we have seen, indicating persons living in cells or *carceri* in a lifestyle that is somehow separated from others even though, given the phenomenon's integration into the urban context, it is probably not purely solitary.

To the best of my knowledge, it seems that in the 13th and 14th centuries the documentary sources do not use the term *bizzoco* to indicate recluses. The latter, as such, are leading a lifestyle rooted in past eras, and therefore their very name has a firm, ancient tradition.

Pauperes moniales recluse/incluse ordinis S. Damiani [poor enclosed nuns/incluses of the order at S. Damiano] is one of the recurring terms used to indicate the new monastic reality begun by St. Clare.

Did Clare have an experience of reclusion at Sant'Angelo di Panzo?[140] Did Filippa Mareri perhaps not go through a period of domestic reclusion and then, in the crypt on the mountain a period of community eremitic reclusion?[141] However, it is also true that the two experiences are parallel and distinct. Given the total silence of the sources about St. Clare, every hypothesis is only a hypothesis.

It is certain that the above-mentioned phrase indicates a community of women living in a cloister, that is, women who were in some manner recluses, separated from the world, but in a cloistered, regular community in some way devised to give cover to an entirely new feminine religious movement.

The term, which has an ancient tradition, as we have shown, eventually comes to indicate various developments whose common denominator is a certain attitude of separation from the world now lived in various modes and formulas.

The variety of forms of religious life in the area did not lack groups of recluses living in *carceri* or *reclusoria* who, after assuming a number of members, became monasteries with an approved Rule (Augustinian, Benedictine, and perhaps even that of St. Clare). This was especially true in the second half of the 13th century and beyond, when even the new orders, including that of St. Clare, do not absorb or intend to place limits on their absorption to the request to enter a regular religious life when it was not possible for everyone to enter the regular monastic life (limited numbers, dowry, etc.).[142]

All this could have been a spontaneous development, but it is more probable that it was a necessary part of the process for leaving behind the irregular generic types of religious, following the guidelines of the Fourth Lateran Council and the Second Council of Lyon, and even the Council of Vienna (1311) and the *Sancta Romana* (1317).

The case of the hermitage where Clare of Montefalco lived with her sister Giovanna is typical. We would not need to insist on this except to emphasize that it must have already been too crowded if Clare asked to transfer in order to lead an eremitic-penitential life with a holy woman on Monte Cucco.[143]

Is this a literary clue or even a gauge that in an inhabited area such as Montefalco, the hermitage was no longer suited to an authentic solitary life? Clare, an urban recluse, wants to live a more isolated life. Is this a sign of the evolution of the phenomenon of reclusion which, having taken the road of common life, no longer guaranteed the desired solitude?

Even in the mid-13th century the solitary life was not fully accepted. We find reference to this in the *Summa* of St. Thomas, who questions "whether the religious lifestyle of those who live in community is more perfect than that of those who lead a solitary life."

Thomas recognizes the validity of the solitary life, but warns of its dangers,[144] and the very fact that such a question is brought up again at such a high level is indication of a certain tension. Embracing the solitary life without adequate preparation can be dangerous.

It is rather probable that our recluses knew little or nothing about such lofty debates. The needs which triggered the evolution towards the monastic community were perhaps less than ideal, but real and concrete: the need for organization; to find space amid the growing demand for religious life, especially among women; to have a guaranteed status which was not dependent on occasional or provisional sources, and the like.

It is good to note, however, that to the very same degree that the women's groups living in carceri or reclusoria in community groups become monasteries, assuming an approved rule, the phenomenon of reclusion in the literal sense of the word begins to fade away.

In the early years of the 14th century the preacher Jordan of Pisa, looks suspiciously upon those "mad men and women who close themselves up in cells" without the spiritual guidance of preachers and confessors.[145] Francesco of Barberino says that the state of individual reclusion is "very, very dangerous."[146] In the early years of the 15th century Giovanni Dominici recommends that those who want to become hermits should choose a site "so well located that at least on the holy days of obligation they can assist at Mass and receive communion when it pleases God. I would be suspicious of too much ignorance because a recluse cannot go to hear the preachers; and being too long without hearing about God can give rise to dangerous opinions."[147]

There is a certain wariness about the recluse's form of life, a sign of a progressive dying out of the phenomenon.

In Conclusion

The lifestyle of the recluse existed from the very first centuries of eremitism itself. It had very close ties to the monastic-cenobitic institution and, it would seem, assumes a more irregular, independent aspect during a phase of vitality and growth in the 13th and 14th centuries, at the same time that the urban-communal civilization was developing. In my opinion, its decline can be found either in what was mentioned above (evolution into a monastic community; no lack of suspicion about this type of life) or in the growing and crushing development of the Third Order seculars and regulars destined to give a more legitimate appearance to the various types of religious life.[148]

Endnotes

[1]G. Casagrande, "Forme di vita religiosa femminile solitaria in Italia centrale," *Eremitismo francescano*, 51-94.

[2]References to forms of reclusion, for example, in M. P. Alberzoni, "Penitenti e terziari a Milano fino agli inizi del XIV secolo," *Prime manifestazioni di vita comunitaria maschile e femminile nel movimento francescano della Penitenza* (1215-1447) (Rome, 1982) 214, notes 31 and 32; D. Rando, "Il Convento di S. Maria Mater Domini di Conegliano nel Duecento: condizionamenti politici ed esperienza religiosa," in *Le Venezie francescane* II, 1/2 (1985): 55; 62, note 93; P. G. Molmenti, *La storia di Venezia nella vita privata Dalle origini alla caduta della Repubblica*, I, La grandezza (Bergamo, 1927); 2nd edition (Trieste, 1973) 125-26.

[3]The spread of the phenomenon in East and West is well-known. Therefore, I limit myself to referring to the following recent dictionary sources: T. Spidlik, P. Rouillard, M. Sensi, "Reclusione" in DIP 7 (1983): 1229-45; M. Ch. Chartier, "Reclus," in *Dictionnaire de Spiritualité* 13 (1987): 217-228. See also E. Pásztor's article in this volume.

[4]For a comparison between Italy and England, see my work "Il fenomeno della reclusione volontaria nei secoli del Basso Medioevo," *Benedictina* 35 (1988): 504-507.

[5]Cf. G. Turbessi, "La solitudine dell'asceta come espressione ideale della vocazione cristiana," *Benedictina* 8 (1954): 43-55. See also Z. Alszeghy, "Fuite du monde," *Dictionnaire de Spiritualité* 5 (1964): 1575-1605.

[6]Turbessi 55.

[7]*Eremus* is equivalent to *desertum* [uninhabited] or to *incultum* [uncultivated], according to J. Leclercq, "'Eremus' et 'eremia' Pour l'histoire du vocabulare de la vie solitaire," *Collectanea ordinis Cistercensium Reformatorum* 25 (1963): 8-30.

[8]L. Gougaud, "Cellule" in *Dictionnaire de Spiritualité* II (1953): 396-400. For general ideas of the eremitical phenomenon, see J. Besse, "Anachorets," *Dictionnaire de Théologie Catholique* I/1 (1909): 1134-41; P. Doyère, "Ermites," *Dictionnaire de droit canonique* V (1953): 412-29; See also P. Doyère, "Erémitisme en Occident," *Dictionnaire de Spiritualité* IV (1960): 953-82; T Spidlik, J. Sainsaulieu, "Ermites," *Dictionnaire d'histoire et de géographie ecclésiastiques* XV (1963): 766-87; J. Gribomont, P. Rouillard, I. Omaechevarria, "Eremitismo," DIP 3 (1976): 1224-44.

[9]That is, with the imprint of John Cassian (5th century). Cf. C. Leonardi, *Alle origini della cristianità medievale: Giovanni Cassiano e Salviano di Marsiglia* (Spoleto, 1978). The Rule of St. Benedict, which was approved during the Carolingian age, subordinates the eremitical life to the cenobitical. (There are some references of a general nature in *Dall'eremo al cenobio* [Milan, 1987], particularly the contributions of Picasso and Leonardi.) Councils such as those of Vannes (465), Agde (506) and Toledo (646) make a connection between the solitary life (*in cellulae*) and the monastic community life because the solitaries first had to have lived in community and because once they become hermits they still remain under the authority of the abbot (cf. H. Leclercq, "Reclus," in *Dictionnaire d'archéologie chrétienne et de liturgie* XIV/2 [1948]: 2150; Gribomot, 1239).

[10]Cf. G. Tabacco, "Eremo e cenobio," *Spiritualità clumniacense* (Todi, 1960): 326-35; G. Constable, "Eremitical forms of monastic life" in *Istituzione monastiche e istituzioni canonicali in Occidente (1123-1215)* (Milan, 1980) 254 ff.

[11]PL 71, 827-910, 1009-96. Cf. H. Leclercq, "Reclus," cited above, 2154-58; J. Hubert, "L'érémitisme et l'archéologie," *L'eremitismo in Occidente nei secoli XI e XII* (Milan , 1965) 467, 469 ff.

[12]See U. Moricca, ed., on Gregory the Great, *Dialogi* (Rome, 1924) 175-77.

[13]Mansi, XIII, 908. See J. Heuclin, *Aux origines monastiques de la Gaule du Nord: Ermites et reclus du V au XI s* (Lille, 1988) 245.

[14]See M. Chartier, both "Regula solitariorum," DIP 7 (1983): 1598-1600; and "Reclus," 221-28.

[15]Grimlaico, "Regula solitariorum," ch. I, PL 103, 578.

[16]Ibid., chapter XVI, PL 103, 594.

[17]Ibid., chapter LX, PL 103, 651-52.

[18]Ibid., chapter XXXII, PL 103, 621-22; chapter XXXIX, 629-31; chapter XL, 631.

[19]Ibid., chapter XVII, PL 103, 595-596.

[20]"Moreover, without the permission and consent of the bishop, or of one's own abbot and all the brothers of the monastery in which the aforesaid brother has been formed, let nothing whatsoever be done concerning this matter [that is, access to the state of reclusion]. Furthermore, it is absolutely forbidden for anyone to pursue this aspiration of religious living in any other place except only in congregations of cenobites." Ibid., chapter XV, PL 103, 593.

[21]J. Leclercq, "La crise du monachisme aux XI e XII siècles," *Bulletino dell'Istituto storico italiano per il Medio Evo* 70 (1958): 19-45. For a general study giving a synthesis of the situation, see J. Leclercq, *La spiritualité du Moyen Age* (Ligugé, 1961) 161 ff.; F.A. Dal Pino, *I frati Servi di S. Maria dalle origini all'approvazione, I* (Louvain, 1972) 454 ff.; A. Vauchez, *La spiritualità dell'Occidente medievale* (Milan, 1978) 101-106; and *L'eremitismo in Occidente nei secoli XI e XII.*

[22]Dal Pino, *I frati Servi*, 462-63. Concerning the variety of eremitical solutions, see J. Leclercq, "L'érémitisme en Occident jusqu'á l'an mil," *L'érémitismo in Occidente*, 31-36; Constable, "Eremitical forms," 239-64.

[23]G. Tabacco, "Romualdo di Ravenna e gli inizi dell'eremitismo camaldolese," *L'eremitismo in Occidente*, 73-119. Concerning Peter Damian's position on eremitism, see J. Leclercq, *Saint Pierre Damien ermite et homme d'Eglise* (Rome, 1960).

[24]As a result of chapter 29 of the famous Opuscolo XV (PL 145, 361). See Leclercq, *Saint Pierre Damien* 55-59; O. Capitani, "San Pier Damiani e l'istituto eremitico," *L'eremitismo in Occidente*, 122-163; C. Pierucci, "La vita eremitica secondo s. Pier Damiano," *San Pier Damiano nel IX centenario della morte*, IV (Cesena , 1978) 67 ff.

[25]Pier Damiani, *Vita Romualdi*, edited by G. Tabacco (Rome, 1957) chapter 31, 67; chapter 52, 94; chapter 69, 111-12.

[26]Ibid., chapter 64, 105. For the whole eremitical movement traceable to Romuald in general, see the entry under "Camaldolesi" in DIP 1 (1974): 1718-28; G. Penco, *Storia del monachesimo in Italia* (Milan, 1983) 197-204; Leclercq, *Moyen Age*, 142-58. For reclusion in particular see G. Cacciamani, *Le reclusione presso l'ordine camaldolese*, (Camaldoli, 1960). Examples of recluses can be found in the Opuscolo LI of Peter Damian (PL 145, 753-54, 756). References are found in the "Costituzioni of S. Rodolfo" in *Annales Camaldulenses*, III (Venice, 1758) 544, 546.

[27]See in general "Certosini," DIP 2 (1975): 782-821; Leclercq, *Moyen Age*, 189-202; B. Bugny, "L'érémitisme et les Chartreux," *L'eremitismo in Occidente*, 248-63; Vauchez, *La spiritualità*, 104-05.

[28]See C. Leonardi on Guillaume de Saint-Thierry, *La lettera d'oro* (Florence, 1983); A.M. Piazzoni, *Guglilemo di Saint-Thierry: il decline dell'ideale monastico nel secolo XII* (Rome, 1988).

[29]G. Penco, "L'eremitismo irregolare in Italia nei secoli XI-XII," *Benedictina* 32 (1985): 204.

[30]Ibid., 206.

[31]See G. G. Merlo, *Tensioni religiose agli inizi del Duecento* (Torre Pellice, 1984) 50-55. The hermit, a familiar figure in the Middle Ages, had more opportunity for mixing with common folk than the cenobite did (C. Violante, "L'eremitismo," *Studi sulla cristianità medievale* [Milan, 1972] 136-37.)

[32]See "Regole per eremiti,"DIP 7 (1983): 1517 ff.; "Regole per reclusi," ibid., 1533 ff.

[33]See A. Rigon, "Dalla regola di S. Agostino alla regola di Niccolò IV," *La "Supra montem" di Niccolò IV (1289): genesi e diffusione di una regola*, R. Pazzelli and L. Temperini, eds. (Rome, 1988) 43 (with bibliography).

[34]K. Elm "Italienische," 491-559; B. Van Luijk, *Gli eremiti neri nel Dugento con particolare riguardo al territorio pisano e toscano Origine, sviluppo ed unione* (Pisa, 1968) Dal Pino, *I frati Servi*, 632-61.

[35]In 1243 Innocent IV granted permission for the Order's *fratres sacerdotes* to hear confessions and preach with the consent of the bishops and the rectors of the churches (see Dal Pino, *I frati Servi*, 637-38).

[36]In 1246; see Dal Pino, 638 ff.

[37]"urbaniti, non eremiti" — see K. A. Fink, *Chiesa e papato nel Medioevo* (Bologna, 1987) 103.

[38]In regard to the latter, "the eremitism embraced by the seven founders on Mount Sinai . . . is not the solitary type which can easily admit of the presence of a disciple or two; rather it is that type of 'communal' solitude which became increasingly widespread beginning in the 12th century in which the only element of anchoritism maintained was the search for contemplative solitude and austerity, which was then situated in the context of a rule of fraternity" (Dal Pino, *I frati Servi*, 804).

[39]Thus abandoning the eremitic-cenobitic manifestation. See Tabacco, "Eremo e cenobio," 334.

[40]In the 11th and 12th centuries hermits preferred rural environments (Penco, "L'eremitismo irregolare," 208). In the *Liber de diversis ordinibus* [The Book of various orders], which dates from the first half of the 12th century, the hermits, who often lived alone or with a few companions, were listed first; among the examples of this type of life listed was that of Christ who, "in withdrawing to the mountain or the desert, which is distinctive of hermits, he consecrated their way of life in himself." (PL 213, 812).

[41]Leclercq, "Eremus" et "eremita," 24-25.

[42]A. K. Warren, *Anchorites and their Patrons in Medieval England* (Berkeley-Los Angeles-London 1985) 8.

[43]See Violante, "L'eremitismo," 131, who follows Leclercq, "Eremus" and "eremita."

[44]Pier Damiani, Opuscolo XV, PL 145, 338.

[45]See "Reclusione,"DIP, 1233-34.

[46]PL 189, 90.

[47]See "Cellule" in *Dictionnaire de Spiritualité*, 397-98.

[48]Leclercq, *L'érémitisme en Occident*, 37.

[49]See "Ermites," *Dictionnaire de droit canonique*, 420.

[50]PL 103, 592. See "Reclus," *Dictionnaire de Spiritualité*, 222. See also Warren, *Anchorites*, 93 ff.

[51]The liturgical ceremony for reclusion was inspired by rites for the deceased; see P. Schmitz, *Histoire de l'Ordre de Saint Benoit*, 7 (Maresdous, 1956) 55; "Reclusione," DIP 7, 1243; Warren, *Anchorites*, 97 ff.

[52]"Thus, enclosed in the cell of your reclusion by a life-giving interment, may you be buried with Christ. . . . In this tomb . . . your life will be hidden with Christ in God." Thus Peter the Venerable writes (PL 189, 91, 100). Aelred of Rievaulx writes in his rule for the woman recluse: "buried in the cave with Christ as though dead to the world" (PL 32, 1458). See "Reclus," *Dictionnaire de Spiritualité*, 222.

[53]PL 145, 249. It has been pointed out that this glorification of the life of solitude in the cells must have influenced Pietro da Morrone (Pope Celestine V) who went off several times to retire to one (cf. S. Sticca, "S. Pietro Celestino e la tradizione eremitica," *Bullettino della Deputazione abruzzese di storia patria* 70 [1980]: 235-84).

[54]See Schmitz, *Histoire de l'Ordre de Saint Benoit*, 54; A. Vauchez, *La sainteté*, 490-91.

[55]DIP 3 (1976) 1236-37.

[56]*Martyrologium Franciscanum* (Rome, 1938) 442.

[57]L. Iacobilli, *Vite dei Santi e beati dell'Umbria*, 3 vols. (Foligno, 1647, 1656, 1661).

[58]A. Benvenuti-Papi, "'Velut in sepulchro': Cellane e recluse nella tradizione agiografica italiana," *Culto dei santi, istituzioni e classi sociali in età preindustriale*, ed. S. Boesch Gajano and L. Sebastiani (L'Aquila-Rome, 1984) 365-455. Henceforth "Velut."

[59]Ibid., 376-79.

[60]Ibid., 381-82.

[61]B. De Gaiffier, "Hagiographie du Picenum Vie de S. Elpidius, Passion de Ste. Franca," *Analecta Bollandiana* 75 (1957): 288-89, 294-98; Penco, "L'eremitismo irregolare," 217.

[62]Benvenuti Papi, "Velut," 443, note 108; Penco, "L'eremitismo irregolare," 217.

[63]Benvenuti Papi, "Velut," 383-84.

[64]L. Temperini, "Fenomini di vita comunitaria tra i penitenti francescani in Roma e dintorni," *Prime manifestazioni*, 606-14; A. Cadderi, "La beata Margherita Colonna (Clarissa) (Rome, 1984). For the editions of her *vitae* see L. Oliger, *B. Margherita Colonna* (Rome, 1935). For the rule assumed by the group which was transferred to S. Silvestro in Capite in Rome, see BF III, 544.

[65]A. Chiappini, "S. Filippa Mareri e il suo monastero di Borgo S. Pietro de Molito nel Cicolano," *Miscellanea Francescana* 22 (1921): 65-119; E. Cerafogli, *La Baronessa santa Filippa Mareri* (Vatican City, 1979); *Santa Filippa Mareri e il monastero di Borgo S. Pietro nella storia del Cicolano* (Borgo San Pietro, 1989). See especially the articles by Brentano and Pásztor.

[66]Maria of Pisa (+1200) and Gherardesca (mid-13th century), see Benvenuti Papi, "Velut," 388-94.

[67]Umiltà of Faenza (1226-1310), ibid., 395-400.

[68]Verdiana of Castelfiorentino (+1242), Giovanna of Signa (+1307), Giulia of Certaldo (14th century). Benvenuti Papi, "Velut," 401-409; "Santità femminile nel territorio fiorentino e lucchese; considerazioni intorno al caso di Verdiana da Castelfiorentino," *Religiosità e società in Valdelsa nel basso Medioevo* (Società Storica della Valdelsa, 1980), 113-44; J. Delarun "Jeanne de Signa, ermite toscane du XIVème siècle, ou la sainteté ordinare," *Mélanges de l'Ecole francaise de Rome* 98 (1986): 161-99.

[69]Justine of Arezzo (+1310); Benvenuti Papi, "Velut," 410-12.

[70]Clare of Rimini (1280-1326), ibid., 412-13.

[71]Margaret of Cortona (+1297), ibid., 414-27.

[72]Sybillina of Pavia (1287-1367), ibid., 427-29.

[73]Gemma of Goriano Sicoli (L'Aquila), ibid., 431; 454, note 280.

[74]Ibid., 431.

[75]Ibid., 409.

[76]J. Leclercq, "Solitude and Solidarity: Medieval Women Recluses," *Medieval Religious Women II Peaceweavers*, ed. L. Thomas Shank and J. A. Nichols (Kalamazoo, 1987) 69-70.

[77]AA. SS., Maii IV, 385-418; see A. Benvenuti Papi, "Umiliana dei Cerchi Nascita di un culto nella Firenze del Dugento," *Studi francescani* 77 (1980): 87-117; A. Vauchez, "L'ideal de sainteté," *Movimento religioso femminile e francescanesimo nel secolo XIII* (Assisi, 1980) 329 ff.

[78]AA.SS., Maii IV, 395.

[79]Ibid.

[80]Ibid., 392.

[81]Ibid. See Vauchez, "L'idéal de sainteté," 334.

[82]Concerning the Franciscan Third Order, the "antiquity" of this hagiographical statement should be noted; see Benvenuti Papi, "Umiliana dei Cerchi," 111.

[83]AASS, Maii IV, 389.

[84]Giunta Bevegnati, *Leggenda della vita e dei miracoli di Santa Margherita da Cortona*, trans. E. Mariani (Vicenza, 1978) 39.

[85]Ibid., 27.

[86]Francesco da Barberino, *Regimento e costumi di donne*, ed. G. Sansone (Turin, 1957) 173. Cf. Papi, "Devocroni private" 573ff.

[87]AA. SS., Februarii I, 261.

[88]Penco, "L'eremitismo irregolare," 218. Near the church of St. Clement in Novara, a woman recluse lived in the first half of the 11th century; a woman from Parma, Mabilia by name, lived from 1189 to 1237 (the recluse of S. Eusebius) in the basilica of that name in Vercella.

[89]In preparing this I have used the most noted current works. A thorough search has been made not only of archival material, but also of various bibliographical material (periodicals, local histories, and editions of the early sources) in order to find hints and documentary evidence. Similar attempts were made in L. Pellegrini, "A proposito di eremiti laici d'ispirazione francescana," *I frati Minori e il Terzo Ordine Problemi e discussioni storiografiche*, Acts of the 23rd Study Congress of Medieval Spirituality (Todi, 1985) 115-42; Casagrande, "Il fenomeno della reclusione volontaria," previously treating only the Umbrian area, under the title of "Note su manifestazioni di vita comunitaria femminile nel movimento penitenziale in Umbria nei secc. XIII, XIV, XV," in *Prime manifestazioni*, 461 ff.

[90]Perugia, Gubbio, Città di Castello, Assisi, Deruta, Bettona, Foligno, Nocera Umbra, Spello, Trevi, Todi, Spoleto, Gualdo Tadino, Bachi (Orvieto), Norcia. References to the phenomenon's presence in Umbria are scattered in various studies and published works (notary and communal documents, statutes, etc.) and are also included in some works of a more general nature: Casagrande, "Note su maniestazione," 460 ff.; Casagrande, "Il fenomeno della reclusione volontaria"; Pellegrini, "A proposito di eremiti laici." In regard to Basch, see M. Rossi Caponeri, "Nota su alcuni testamenti della fine del secolo XIV relativi alla zona di Orvieto," *Nolens intestatus decedere* (Perugia, 1985) 106, note 3. For Città di Castello, see "Chiese e conventi degli ordini mendicanti in Umbria nei secoli XIII-XIV. Gli archivi ecclesiastici di Città di Castello," ed. G. Casagrande (Perugia, 1990), with related references to documentary information. For Norcia, see G. Garampi, *Memorie ecclesiastiche appartenenti all'istoria e al culto della B. Chiara da Rimini* (Rome, 1755) 101 and note.

[91]Fabriano, Ascoli Piceno, S. Ginesio, Camerino, Esanatoglia (Macerata). See R. Sassi "Incarcerati e incarcerate a Fabriano nei secoli XIV," *Studia Picena* 25 (1957): 67-85; G. Fabiani "Monaci, eremiti, incarcerati e reclusi in Ascoli nei secoli XII e XIV," *Studia Picena* 32 (1964): 147-50, 157-58; M. Sensi "Incarcerate e penitenti a Foligno nella prima metà del Trecento," *I frati Penitenti di San Francesco nella società del Due e Trecento*, ed. Mariano d'Alatri (Rome, 1977) 302, note 32; M. Sensi, *Vita di pietà e vita civile di un altopiano tra Umbria e Marche (secc. XI-XIV)* (Rome, 1984) 65, 221; F. Allevi "Francescani e penitenti a San Ginesio nei secoli XIII e XIV," *Prime manifestazione*, 601, note 120. References in Pellegrini, "A proposito di eremiti laici"; Casagrande "Il fenomeno della reclusione volontaria." For Massa Trabaria the documentation is

found in Città di Castello, Diocesan Archive, Register of the Diocesan Chancery, 7, f. 131 v.

[92]Florence, Pisa, Sansepolcro. (There is also documentary evidence in regard to other locales in hagiographical sources: Signa, Castelfiorentino, Certaldo, Cortona.) See Benvenuti Papi, "Velut," Benvenuti Papi, "Donne religiose nella Firenze del Due-Trecento; appunti per una ricerca in corso," *Le mouvement confraternal au Moyen Age: France, Italie, Suisse* (Rome, 1987) 41 ff.; S. Barsotti, *Un nuovo fiore serafico: il beato Giovanni Cimi, confessore pisano, soldato ed eremita, fondatore dei fratelli della penitenza ed uno dei fondatori della Pia Casa della Misericordia* (Quaracchi, 1906) (chapter IX and documents II, V, VIII, IX); A. Battistoni, "La Compagnia dei Disciplinati di S. Giovanni Evangelista di Porta della Pace in Pisa e la sua devozione verso frate Giovanni soldato," *Bollettino della Deputazione di storia patria per l'Umbria* 65 (1968): 205, 207-209, 220-21; M. Ronzani, "Penitenti e ordini Mendicanti a Pisa sina all'inizio del Trecento," *Mélanges de l'Ecole française de Rome* 89 (1977): 741. I am also indebted to Ronzani for some of his unpublished notes. G. Casagrande, "Forme di vita religiosa femminile nell'area di Città di Castello nel sec. XIII," *Il movimento religioso femminile in Umbria nei secoli XIII-XIV*, ed. R. Rusconi (Perugia-Florence, 1984) 149-50. References in Pellegrini, "A proposito di eremiti laici," Casagrande, "Il fenomeno" cited above.

[93]Area of Rimini, Montefiore, Ferrara. See Garampi *Memorie ecclesiastiche*, 99-102. Samaritani offers documents of the 13th, 14th and 15th century relative to the presence of hermits in Ferrara, but it is not clear when and if they are dealing with hermit-recluses, although sometimes a certain type of bequests would seem to support this. See A. Samaritani, "Conventualizzazione di eremiti e pinzocchere a Ferrara tra Medioevo e Umanesimo (metà sec. XIII-metà sec. XV). Contributo documentari," *Prime manifestazioni*, 347 ff.) References in Casagrande, "Il fenomeno della reclusione volontaria."

[94]R. Brentano, "Il movimento religioso femminile a Rieti nei secoli XIII-XIV," in *Il movimento religioso femminile*, 67-83; Brentano, "Death in Gualdo Tadino and in Rome (1340, 1296)" in *Studia Gratiana* 19 (1976): 98; L. Oliger, "Regula Reclusorum Angliae et Questiones tres de vita solitaria saec. XIII-XIV," *Antonianum* (1934): 265-68. References in Casagrande, "Il fenomeno della reclusione volontaria."

[95]Ibid., 489. Sometimes the sums left to the recluses of a certain area as a whole are greater than what was left to the Mendicant Orders themselves. See "Chiese e conventi . . ." 2.15.15.

[96]Ibid., LXXVI.

[97]Brentano, "Il movimento," 74.

[98]"Chiese e conventi . . ." 2.15.11.

[99]G. Casagrande, "Presenza di Fraticelli nell'area di Bettona," AFH 74 (1981): 323, 325, 327.

[100]Garampi, *Memoire ecclesiastiche*, 100.

[101]Casagrande, "Il fenomeno," 490. If there was a large number of recluses the commune could end up giving out tens of lire. In 1290 each recluse in Perugia was to be given 10 soldi, for a total of 56 lire (Casagrande, "Note su manifestazione," 463-64, note 14), whereas the large convents were given 100 lire.

[102]Ibid.

[103]Barsotti, "Un nuovo fiore," 155-160. Thanks to Mauro Ronzani for having told me about this and provided me with the text.

[104]Ibid. Battistoni, "Disciplinati," 205 ff.

[105]Ibid, 165, note 1. Marianus of Florence, for example, tells us of a Franciscan tertiary woman who became a recluse in Ancona. M.D. Papi, *Il Trattato del Terz'Ordine o vero "Libro come Santo Francesco istituì et ordinò el Tertio Ordine de Frati et Sore di Penitentia et della dignità et perfectione o vero Sanctità Sua" di Mariano da Firenze* (Rome, 1985) 383.

[106]Sassi, "Incarcerati e incarcerate," 81.

[107]In 1247 Juliana, daughter of William, became an "incarcerated recluse" near the church of S. Angelo di Sterpete (Sensi, "Incarcerate et penitenti a Foligno," 294, note 12); in 1280 Cecilia, daughter of Guido Uliveri is an "incluse or one enclosed" in the parish of St. Andrea "Vallis Casole" in Massa Trabaria (see note 90); in 1298 Lapa is inclusa near the church of Santa Maria in Soffiano (Benvenuti Papi, "Donne religiose," 44).

[108]Pellegrini, "A proposito di eremiti laici", 128-130; Casagrande, "Il fenomeno," 488-89; here we should add the data concerning Pisa, where from 1302 we have a list of 30 women hermits (see note 102); in 1305 16 recluses (15 females, 1 male) name a Brother of Penance their procurator to collect an inheritance (Barsotti, "Un nuovo fiore," 158-59, note 2); in 1345 we have 19 recluses located in 10 areas of the city (Pisa Archdiocesan Archives, "Atti Straordinari," n. 4, f. 235v); in 1348 11 sorores name a procurator (Pisa State Archives, Dipl. Spedali [Trovatelli] 1340, July 7). I am indebted to Mauro Ronzani for this information. In Città di Castello in 1350 there must be more than 15 recluses ("Chiese e conventi . . ." 2.15.15).

[109]Oliger, "Regula Reclusorum Angliae," 265 ff.

[110]Brentano, "Death in Gualdo Tadino," 98.

[111]Thomas of Celano, *Tractatus de Miraculibus*, sometimes called Third Celano; since this work has not been totally translated into English as yet, we are providing our own translation of the passage.

Praxedes was rather well-known among the women religious of Rome and the whole Roman area. Out of love for her eternal Spouse, at a very tender age she enclosed herself in a small cell and remained there for almost 40 years. She had a special friendship with St. Francis. In fact, the saint received her into obedience, as he had done for no other woman, devoutly granting her the habit of religion, that is, the tunic and cord. One day she went to the loft in her cell and, overcome by dizziness, fell down to the ground, fracturing a foot and leg and dislocating a shoulder, too. For many years this virgin had wanted to avoid anyone entering her cell, and she continued to remain firm in this commitment; however, lying on the ground like a log and not wanting to accept help from anyone, she did not know to whom she could turn. By order of a cardinal and his council of religious, she was urged to break this enclosure in order to have the help of some pious woman and thus escape the danger of death which was possible in that situation if it was neglected and not treated. She, however, refused to make concession to their demands and resisted with all her might because she did not want to violate her vow in even the smallest matter. Therefore she turned in supplication, throwing herself at the feet of divine mercy; toward evening she cried out with pious lamentation to the blessed father Francis: "O most holy father, who always comes to the aid of the many people who did not even know you when you were alive; why don't you help me, this unfortunate one; unworthy as I am, I enjoyed your most tender friendship when you were alive. In fact, as you can see quite well, O father, I must either change my vow or die!"

While her heart and lips were saying these things and she implored mercy with repeated pleas, she was suddenly overcome by sleepiness and fell into a trance. Dressed in his white robes of glory, the most holy father came down into her dark cell and began to speak to her ever so gently: "Get up, O blessed daughter! Arise and do not be afraid! Receive the gift of complete healing and keep your promise inviolate!" He took her by the hand, raised her up and disappeared. She began to walk all about her cell; she did not understand what had happened to her through the action of the servant of God. She thought she was still seeing a vision. Finally, going to the window, she made the usual sign. A monk came running to her, all concerned and full of wonder, and asked her: "What has happened to you, O mother, that you are able to stand up?" But she thought she was still dreaming and, not knowing that it was he, asked him to light a fire. When the light was brought to her, she came to her senses and felt no more pain. Under orders, she told them everything that had happened to her.

[112]A. Walz, "Die Miracula Beati Dominici der Schwester Cäcilia," *Archivum Fratrum Praedicatorum* 37 (1967): 40-41.

[113]See note 93. In 1507, a recluse walled herself up in a small cell in the cathedral (cf. "Reclusione" in DIP 7, 1239).

[114]Who are the 21 *sorores* mentioned in a testament written in 1269? (B. Giordani Acta franciscana e tabulariis bononiensibus deprompta, *Analecta franciscana* IX (Quaracchi, 1927):113*, 771.

[115]Sassi, "Incarcerati e incarcerate," 75, 83; Sensi, "Incarcerate e penitenti a Foligno," 301-302.

[116]Warren, *Anchorites*, 53 ff.

[117]A. Bartola, "Sinodi diocesani e movimenti laicali agli inizi del '300," *La "Supra montem,"* 1199-1217.

[118]Casagrande, "Il fenomeno," 491-92. Among the hagiographical sources we can recall the bishop of Florence's devotion to Verdiana of Castelfiorentino (a devotion which perhaps was not totally lacking in control). See Benvenuti Papi, "Santità femminile," 125; Benvenuti Papi, "Velut," 403-404.

[119]At Pisa, for example, in 1315 the elders of the people established "that the hermitage or cell, which is at the foot of the wall of the Pisa commune at the Gate of Peace, be given to Ghino of Pisa, son of the former Consul, who is a man of Penance and plans to serve God in the cell." Battistoni, "Disciplinati," 220-21.

[120]For example, we read in the *Vita* of Verdiana of Castelfiorentino that she promised obedience to the parson and not to the bishop. See Benvenuti Papi, "Velut," 402-403.

[121]Benvenuti Papi, "Donne religiose," 44.

[122]Ibid.

[123]A. Benvenuti Papi, "Le forme comunitarie della penitenza femminile francescana. Schede per un censimento toscano," *Prime manifestazioni*, 434.

[124]A small cell with two windows; see Benvenuti Papi, "Velut," 397.

[125]Giunta Bevegnati, "Legenda della vita e dei miracoli," XXX-XXXI, 195, 197-98.

[126]Benvenuti Papi, "Velut, "429.

[127]See "Reclusione," DIP 7, 1235.

[128]"Regula solitariorum," in DIP 7, 1600.

[129]Casagrande, "Il fenomeno della reclusione volontaria," 506.

[130]See M. Sensi "La Beata Angela nel contesto religioso folignate," in *Vita e spiritualità della beata Angela da Foligno* (Perugia, 1987) 72-73.

[131]Benvenuti Papi, "Santità femminile," 124.

[132]Sassi, "Incarcerati e incarcerate," 75, 81.

[133]C. Cenci, *Documentazione di vita assisana 1300-1530*, I, (Grottaferrata, 1974) 57.

[134]Barsotti, "Un nuovo fiore," 157.

[135]"In many of the more feminine things believe a woman enclosed in a cell rather than a master in theology." See Francesco da Barberino, "Reggimento," 216. Cf. Benvenuti Papi, "Devozioni private," 575.

[136]One woman left her *carceri* in Assisi to Cicia, her servant, and asked that after the servant's death it should go to the poor or to servants of Christ "to stay in it in order to praise and bless God and his saints" (a. 1311) (see note 132). In 1228, in Città di Castello, Guido of Orlandino Magaltti, to repair his sins and save souls, gave to"Bona and Bontadosa, sisters in Christ, and to all persons who desire to imitate or lead your way of life a plot of land so that you may set up a house on the land, with two cells, and in them pursue your way of life, you and everyone who wishes to be in them and live in them after your death." See Casagrande, "Forme di vita religiosa," 147. In 1328 a man in Fabriano leaves for five years to the recluses who live in his *carceri* a salma of wine and a salma of water for his soul; he wants the carceri to

continue "and if any of the aforesaid sisters should depart [?] I direct that my heirs choose another, one or more, in place of the one or more who has departed and arrange it so that the house or hermitage and its progress be perpetually dedicated and devoted to the good of my soul for the honor of God." See Sassi, "Incarcerati e incarcerate," 76-77. In the 1370's a pious Florentine woman decided to destine a little house on the bridge at Rubaconte "as a retreat for a few good women . . . recluses or hermitesses . . . who would stay there as recluses" and entrusts to them, in exchange for their works and prayers, "the alms of passersby." See Benvenuti Papi, "Donne religiose," 42.

[137]Chartier, "Reclus," 223.

[138]Peter Damian, Opusculo LI, PL 145, 753.

[139]Benvenuti Papi, "Donne religiose," 43.

[140]Sensi, "Incarcerate e penitenti a Foligno," 305, note 41; Sensi, "Incarcerate e recluse in Umbria nei secoli XIII e XIV: un bizzocaggio centro-italiano," *Il movimento religioso femminile*, 93, note 23.

[141]E. Pásztor, "Filippa Mareri e Chiara d'Assisi," *Santa Filippa Mareri*, 67 ff.

[142]Casagrande, "Il fenomeno," 477 ff.

[143]*Vita Sanctae Clarae de Cruce*, ed. A. Semenza (Vatican City, 1944) 10; E. Menestó, *Il processo di canonizzazione di Chiara di Montefalco* (Perugia-Florence, 1984) 5.

[144]Oliger, "Regula Reclusorum Angliae," 243-47; see also "Erémitisme en Occident," *Dictionnaire de Spiritualité*, 966.

[145]C. Del Corno, *Giordano da Pisa e l'antica predicazione volgare* (Florence, 1975) 51-52; see Benvenuti Papi, "Devozioni private," 591-92.

[146]Ibid., 573-74.

[147]G. Dominici, *Regola del governo di cura familiare*, ed. D. Salvi (Florence, 1860) 100; see Benvenuti Papi, "Devozioni private," 598-99, note 101.

[148]Bibliographic postscript: A. Benvenuti Papi, *In castro poenitentiae Santità e società femminile nell'Italia medievale* (Rome, 1990), which includes various studies mentioned above, and some others. The phenomenon of reclusion is also mentioned in *Storia delle donne Il Medioevo*, ed. C. Klapisch-Zuber (Bari, 1990).

Chapter Two

The Eremitical Experience of Francis and the First Franciscans

Introduction

Our interest in Franciscan eremitism was deepened while we heard Lazaro Iriarte, OFM Cap., speak on the subject at the Capuchin Franciscan Institute in Rome. It was there he made the startling statement that Francis had founded no hermitages but had rather sought out solitary places for prayer. It was later Franciscan generations which called Francis's places of prayer "hermitages." Focusing on Francis's desire for solitude, we now take a look at the eremitical experience of Francis and the first Franciscans.

We realize that an anthology such as this must take a critical look at the eremitical life of Francis at this point. Consequently, the following are basic works already published in English that the reader will find helpful:

Kajetan Esser, *Origins of the Franciscan Order*

Oktavian Schmucki, *A Place of Solitude: An Essay on the External Circumstances of the Prayer Life of St. Francis of Assisi* and

—. *Mentis Silentium: Contemplation in the Early Franciscan Order*

In this chapter Benedikt Mertens, OFM, provides a glimpse into *"Solitude In Francis's Life."* Then Martino Conti, OFM, takes a look at Francis's primitive hermitage experience and apostolic choice. With clarity, Conti notes the balance Francis sought between the active and contemplative stances. Marcella Gatti, through her historical profile of the Carceri, gives a descriptive background of one of the places where Francis sought not so much to establish a hermitage as to find solitude among hermits. Finally, Mertens offers a concluding summary to this section.

Solitude in Francis's Life

by

Benedikt Mertens, OFM[1]

Translated from the German by

Josef Raischl and André Cirino, OFM

Francis of Assisi was not a hermit. His intuitive grasp of gospel life surpassed the choice offered him and his companions by Cardinal John of St. Paul in 1210. Though the latter advised him to choose the life of a monk or a hermit, Francis desired a totally different way of life (1Cel 33). Although geographically close to some eremitical groups—the Camaldolese, the hermits on Mount Subasio, or the hermits of Monteluco near Spoleto—Francis did not want to join them.

Nevertheless, none of the biographies could ignore the eremitical signs in his life, namely the first places of solitude, the hermitages in central Italy, and Francis's "Rule for Hermitages."

While rejected as an exclusive choice, after 1210 the eremitical life remained an issue of fraternal discussion as well as part of the life of the first Friars Minor. Francis's serious doubts, described in 1Cel 35 and LM XII.1f.,[2] were not resolved in the next few years. He did not move completely into the itinerant life but integrated a strong contemplative and eremitical combination with his radical gospel-oriented life. Thomas of Celano brings it down to a simple formula. It was Francis's custom to use the time God had given him to earn grace in two ways: first for the benefit of people and then for the solitude of contemplation.[3]

This is confirmed by Jacques de Vitry who, in 1216, wrote that in the daytime the "lesser brothers" visited villages and houses in order to convince people of their gospel life. And in the evening they returned to hermitages or other lonely places for contemplation.[4]

If one tries to find some order for Francis's periodical withdrawal into solitude, the sources offer us the liturgical year. The fact that Francis appreciated the liturgical hours is not just a prominent aspect of his spirituality but also reveals the key to his balance between the life of itinerant preacher and the life of a hermit. Looking at the entire year, the sources mention five eremitical times of penance. One example of Bonaventure shows how staying in a hermitage is to be understood in a Christocentric way and under the guise of following Christ:

> Jesus Christ crucified always *rested like a bundle of myrrh in the bosom* of Francis' soul (Cant.1:12), and he longed to be totally transformed into him by the fire of ecstatic love. As a sign of his special devotion to him, Francis spent the time from the feast of the Epiphany through forty successive days—that period when Christ was hidden in the desert—secluded in a lonely place, shut up in a cell, with as little food and drink as possible, fasting, praying and praising God without interruption.[5]

Moreover, Francis perceived no barriers between action and contemplation, an indication of the contemplative growth that happened when the eremitical ideal became a part of the itinerant life. The Founder's Order sounds like this: "In the name of the Lord go out two by two . . . wherever we are, or wherever we go, we always take our cell with us; for Brother Body is our cell, and our soul is the hermit who lives in it, constantly praying to God. . . . If the soul cannot remain quiet in its cell, then a cell made with hands is of little value" (*CompAss* 108).

Nonetheless, this motif of the body as the cell appears in the spiritual literature before Francis and in him reaches a stage of integration. Esser describes eremitism as the leitmotif of Francis's interior life.[6]

Endnotes

[1]B. Mertens, "Eremitica Francescana Ein historischer Streifzug," *Thuringia Franciscana* NF 47 (1992): 355-85, 355-59.

[2]E.Cousins, Legenda Maior XII , 1 f., *Bonaventure,* The Classics of Western Spirituality (New York, 1978) 291f.
[3]1 Cel 91.
[4]R.B.C. Huygens, *Lettres de Jacques de Vitry* (Leyden, 1960) 75f.
[5]Cousins, LM IX.2, (page 263).
[6]Esser, Regula, 383-417.

Hermitage and Evangelization in the Life of Francis

by

Martino Conti, OFM[1]

Translated from the Italian by

Nancy Celaschi, OSF

Just as in Sacred Scripture, for St. Francis "hermitage and evangelization" are an inseparable pair. Led by God's word on the path of evangelization, he embraces the itinerant apostolic life in stages. An important part of this spiritual, vocational process was his early temporary experience of the eremitic life.

St. Francis's Primitive Hermitage Experience

Recalling the beginnings of his conversion in his Testament, St. Francis makes no explicit reference to his primitive hermitage experience. However, he includes it in the phrase "I left the world." After the Lord granted him to begin to do penance (*incipere faciendi poenitentiam*), he lingered a little and then left the world,[2] that is, he began to live as a monk/ religious.[3]

St. Francis's first experience of the eremitic life dates to the beginning of his conversion when, still wearing his secular dress, he already had a "religious" soul and sought out solitary places.[4] He sought solitary places (*solitaria loca*)[5] and often went to secret places (*loca abscondita*) because he felt they were more conducive to prayer.[6]

In the years marking the various phases of his conversion and vocational maturation, St. Francis felt a strong attraction to the eremitic ideal.[7] Once he had restored San Damiano, he put aside his worldly dress and began dressing like a hermit.[8] In this way he declared to the ecclesial community his determination to dedicate himself entirely to the service of God[9] and was recognized by everyone as a religious.

For St. Francis, too, as we find in the Old Testament, the hermitage/desert is a place of salvation and revelation. Having left the world, Francis withdrew to solitary places. Here he experienced God's salvation; God's self-revelation unfolded, and gradually God's plans for Francis were made known to him. Francis left the hermitage/desert experience as a converted person,[10] ready to assume the mission which God would entrust to him.

Francis's Apostolic Option

St. Francis becomes aware of the divine call in 1205 during an illness. His dream of the castle and arms[11] takes place after the vision in Spoleto where a voice asks him who can be of more use, the servant or the master.[12] Docile to God's voice, Francis lets himself be led by the divine message which reveals God's plan for him and the work to which he has been called:

> He was already changed in heart and close to being changed physically too, when one day, passing by San Damiano, the Spirit led him inside to pray. Calling him by name, the image of the crucified spoke to him and entrusted him with a mission: "Francis, go and repair my house which, as you see, is in ruins."[13]

St. Bonaventure notes that later the Holy Spirit will teach Francis that the divine words referred mainly to the Church which Christ had ransomed with his blood.[14]

However, Francis's vocation becomes clear only when he hears the Gospel passage of the the mission of the Apostles (Mt. 10:7-13).[15] On that occasion, with the priest's help, he understands that the Lord is sending him, like the Apostles, to preach the kingdom of God, conversion and peace.[16] His reaction to the impact of the Gospel is immediate: "This is what I want, this is what I seek, this is what I long to do with all my heart." Without delay he hurries to put into practice faithfully what he had heard: he takes off his shoes, abandons his walking stick, is satisfied with a single tunic, changes his cincture for a cord and begins to preach penance to all.

In this detailed description of Francis's new habit, modeled on the Gospel passage he hears at the Portiuncula, the biographers want to affirm that here we are looking at a decisive choice in Francis's life. By changing his habit he abandons the eremitic life and chooses the apostolic life, beginning by preaching the kingdom, conversion, and peace to all. In all his preaching he wished everyone peace, saying "May the Lord give you peace."[17]

Francis will always see that Gospel passage which had a decisive influence on his life as an explicit divine revelation.[18] When he was near death, he asked the friars to take him in a hurry to the Portiuncula because he wanted to give his soul back to God "where for the first time he had clearly understood the way of truth."[19]

Having been sent by God to proclaim the truth to the whole world following the example of the Apostles,[20] Francis wanders between cities and castles proclaiming the kingdom of heaven, peace, the way of salvation, and penance for the remission of sins.[21] Committed to sowing the seed of the divine word, he fills the earth with the gospel of Christ. In a single day he was able to go through four or five villages, and cities too, proclaiming to everyone the kingdom of God. He edified his audiences no less by his example than his teaching. It could be said of him that he had made his whole body a tongue.[22]

Like one of the rivers of Paradise (cf. Gn. 2:10), Francis, the new evangelist, flooded the whole world with the waters of the gospel and with his works he brought the life and true doctrine of the Son of God.[23] Conscious of having been sent by God to win the souls which the devil wanted to snatch away,[24] he felt that he was no friend of Christ unless he loved the souls which Christ had loved. In fact, he said that nothing is more important than saving souls. Hence his commitment to prayer,[25] his moving from one place to another in order to preach and his great concern to give good example.[26]

Led along the path of evangelization by the word of God, like Christ and the Apostles, St. Francis did not see apostolic activity as alien to the ideal of the hermitage. After intense periods of apostolic involvement, he felt the need to withdraw to a "hermitage" in order to devote himself more freely to contemplation.[27] Franciscan sources mention some of the hermitages to which Francis would go.[28] There, in prayer and fasting, he pre–pared to celebrate certain feasts, such as St. Michael the Archangel,[29] the Assumption,[30] and Saints Peter and Paul,[31] in addition to Christmas and Easter.[32] He also fasted during the time following Epiphany, which Jesus consecrated by his fasting,[33] and on Fridays during the year in memory of Jesus' passion.[34]

In line with Scripture (cf. Mt. 6:1-18) and the Fathers of the Church,[35] St. Francis joins fasting and almsgiving to prayer. Since it is a component of gospel piety, fasting is one with prayer and cannot be separated from it (cf. Tb. 12:8; Lk. 2:37).[36] Withdrawing to hermitages or solitary places and fasting, Francis humbled himself before God (cf. Lv. 16:29, 31). He placed himself in God's presence in an attitude of humble dependence and total submission (cf. Dn. 9:3; Ex. 8:21),[37] was open to the action of grace and to understanding of the word of God (cf. Dn. 10:3, 12).[38] Renewed in spirit, he was able to set off again on the path of evangelization in order to give everyone the gift of the word that saves.

Francis's "Hermitage" Temptation

St. Francis felt a strong attraction to the hermitage, despite his hearing the Gospel passage on the mission of the Apostles (Mt. 10:7-13), the pope's mandate to preach penance, and the assurance he received in prayer that he had been sent by the Lord to teach the gospel[39] in order to win for Christ the souls which the devil was trying to snatch away. There was risk of his giving in to it.

His usual custom was to divide the time given him to merit grace, and, as seemed best to him, to devote part of it to working for the good of his neighbor and the rest to solitary contemplation.[40] Once he was really troubled by doubts about choosing between the apostolic and contemplative life, and so he turned to his brothers and asked them to help him solve the problem. Reflecting on the pros and cons of prayer and apostolic activity, he expressed his ideas in the following way:

> Little and simple, not an expert in speaking (cf. Ws. 7:24, 27), I received the grace of prayer more than preaching. In prayer, besides, one acquires or accumulates graces; in preaching one distributes the gifts received from heaven. In prayer we purify our sentiments and unite them with the one, true, supreme Good and give new strength to virtue; in preaching, however, the spirit becomes sullied and drawn in many directions and loses some discipline. Finally, in prayer we talk to God, listen to God and converse in the midst of the angels; in preaching, however, we must very often descend to people, living as people in their midst, thinking, seeing, talking and listening in human ways. However, there is one thing in preaching's favor, and it seems that in God's eyes it outweighs everything else, and that is that, for the salvation of souls, God's only-begotten Son, infinite Wisdom, left the Father's bosom (cf. Jn. 1:18), renewed the world with His example, speaking to people the Word of salvation and gave His blood as the price of their ransom, the bowl for washing them (cf. Ep. 5:26), drink to fortify them, keeping absolutely nothing for Himself, but offering everything generously for our salvation. Now we must do everything, following the model which we see shining in Him, as on a mountaintop (cf. Ex. 25:40). Therefore, it seems more pleasing to God that I put aside my rest and go into the world to work.[41]

Unable to resolve his doubt, Francis sends two friars to Sylvester and Clare to ask for their prayer and a response from God. Their answer was unanimous: it was God's will that the herald[42] of Christ should "go out to preach."[43] Having learned God's will, he immediately got up, girded his loins (cf. Jn. 21:7) and, without delaying for an instant, set off on the road.[44]

In his overcoming the anguish caused by doubt, we see that St. Francis is once again an example of Christ who traveled the roads of Palestine proclaiming the gospel of salvation to everyone, and who gave his life as a ransom for many.[45]

Endnotes

[1]M. Conti, "Contemplazione ed Evangelizzazione nella vita di San Francesco," G. Cardiapoli and M. Conti, eds. *Lettura spirituale-apostolica delle Fonti Francescane* (Rome, 1980) 83-89.

[2]St. Francis of Assisi, Test 1.4 (FF, 110), C. Esser, *Opuscula Sancti Patris Francisci Assiensis* (Bibliotheca Franciscana Ascetica Medii Aevi, tom. XII), Ed. Collegii S. Bonaventurae ad Claras Aquas (Grottoferrata, 1978) 307-08; in *Francis and Clare, The Complete Works*, R. Amstrong and I. Brady, trans. (New York, 1982) 154.

[3]See K. Esser, *Il Testamento di S. Francesco d'Assisi* (Milan, 1978) 115.

[4]2 Celano 9 in AF X, 135: "Thus already beneath his secular garb he wore a religious spirit and, withdrawing from public to solitary places, he was often admonished by a visitation of the Holy Spirit." M. Habig, *Omnibus of Sources* (Chicago, 1973) 369.

[5]St. Bonaventure, *Legenda maior*, ch. 1, 5 in AF, X, 562: "After that he began to seek out solitary places, well suited for sorrow; and there he prayed incessantly with unutterable groanings (Rom.8:26)." Cousins, *Bonaventure* 189.

[6]Cf. 2 Celano 9.

[7]Cf. G. Paludet, "Vita comunitaria e contemplazione," in *La comunità Esperienze dello Spirito* 2 (Vicenza, 1978) 147.

[8]1 Celano 21: "At this time he wore a kind of hermit's dress, with a leather girdle about his waist; he carried a staff in his hands and wore shoes on his feet." *Omnibus of Sources*, 246. Cf. Julian of Speyer, "Vita S. Francisci," 14.15 in AF, X: 341-342; "Legenda Trium Sociorum," 25 , AFH 67 (1974): 109.

[9]Legend of the Three Companions, 21: "Francis the servant of God . . . held his life of no account and dedicated himself to the service of God in every possible way." *Omnibus of Sources*, 911. The fraternity which began is recognized as a religious institute. See James of Vitry, *Historia occidentalis*, lib. 2, cap. 32, 1 in Lemmens, "Thirteenth Century Testimonies," *Omnibus of Sources* 1609.

[10]Cf. C. Thomas-X. Leon-Dufour, "Deserto," *Dizionario di teologia biblica*, 217.

[11]Cf. 1 Celano 5; Julian of Speyer 3; Legend of the Three Companions 5; Anonymous of Perugia 5.

[12]Cf. 2 Celano 6; Legenda maior 1.3; Legend of the Three Companions 6; Anonymous of Perugia 6.

[13]2 Celano 10; Legenda maior 2.1; Legend of the Three Companions 13.

[14]Legenda maior 2,1.

[15]According to some writers, the Gospel passage Francis heard was not from Matthew but from Luke 10. Cf. M. Conti, "La Sacra Scrittura nell'esperienza e negli Scritti di san Francesco—Criteri ermeneutici," *Lettura biblico-teologica delle Fonti Francescane* (Rome, 1979) 27. As per the goals of this study, there is no problem on the vocational level or the exegetical, whether it is the Gospel of Matthew or Luke.

[16]Cf. M. Conti, "La Sacra Scrittura," 27-29; *Lettura biblica della Regola*, 85-89.

[17]Cf. 1 Celano 22-23; Julian of Speyer 15-17; Legenda maior 3,1-2; Legend of the Three Companions 25-26.

[18]Testament 14.

[19]1 Celano 108; cf. Julian of Speyer 68; Legenda maior, 14,3; 1 Celano 206.

[20]1 Celano 39.

[21]1 Celano 36.

[22]1 Celano 97.

[23]1 Celano 89.

[24]1 Celano 35.

[25]For a treatment of prayer seen as "struggle," see M. Conti, *La missione degli Apostoli nella Regola Francescana* (Genoa, 1972) 245-54.

[26]2 Celano 172; Legenda maior, 9,4.

[27]Cf. 2 Celano 46; Treatise on Miracles, 15; Legenda maior, 7,12.

[28]Borgo san Sepolcro (Legend of Perugia, 90), Fonte Colombo (cf. Legenda Maior, 7,11), Greccio (cf. 2 Celano 167), Poggio Bustone (2 Celano 131), Rocca di Brizio (Legend of Perugia, 89), Sant'Eleuterio near Rieti (Legend of Perugia, 85), Sant'Urbano (Legenda maior, 5,10), Sarteano (2 Celano, 59), La Verna (1 Celano, 94), a poor hermitage in Spain (2 Celano 178).

To these we should add some others alluded to but which are identifiable: one "near Assisi" (the Carceri) mentioned in Legend of the Three Companions 12, and another "near the lake of Perugia," that is Isola Maggiore in Lake Trasimeno (Fioretti, ch. 7). Other hermitages are mentioned rather vaguely (e.g., *in quodam eremitorio* in Legend of Perugia 72) while still others, such as le Celle in Cortona (1 Celano 105), are not called hermitages, but in reality they truly are.

[29]Cf. 2 Celano 197; Legenda Maior 9,3.

[30]Legenda Maior 9,2.

[31]Legenda Maior 9,3.

[32]cf. Later Rule, ch. 3.

[33]Legenda Maior, 9,3.

[34]cf. Later Rule, ch. 3; Earlier Rule, ch. 3; Legend of the Three Companions 14.

[35]St. Peter Chrysologus, Sermo 43.

[36]Cf. M. Conti, *Lettura biblica della Regola*, 211-14.

[37]Cf. Fioretti, Third Consideration on the Stigmata.

[38]Cf. 2 Celano 209; Legenda Maior 4,11.

[39]Legenda Maior 4,1-2; 1 Celano 35; Julian of Speyer 23.

[40]1 Celano 91.

[41]*Lettura spirituale-apostolica delle Fonti Francescane* (Rome, 1980) 75.

[42]At the beginning of his conversion Francis called himself the "herald of the great king." See 1 Celano 16; Julian of Speyer, Vita 10; Legenda Maior 2,5.

[43]Legenda Maior 12,2; Fioretti 16.

[44]Legenda Maior 12,1-2.

[45]1 Celano 35; Julian of Speyer, Vita 23; Legenda Maior 4,2.

A Historical Look at the Carceri

in the Pre-Franciscan and Early Franciscan Period

by

Marcella Gatti[1]

Translated from the Italian by

Nancy Celaschi, OSF

Not much research has been done on the Carceri, and the few known sources are all in agreement that the place was a gift to Francis and his early companions, given to them some time between 1210 and 1216 by the abbey of St. Benedict on Mount Subasio, by an abbot named Pietro or Teobaldo or Maccabeo. An oratory already existed there, but Francis named it in honor of Our Lady, according to the 14th century Gothic inscription in the chapel: SANTO FRANCESCHO PUOSE A Q[U]ESTA CHAPELLA EL NOME DI SANTA MARIA. The name "Carceri" was supposedly given it because of its sparseness. There was a spring of water which St. Bernardine of Siena channeled into the well in the courtyard. Other than identifying the various caves frequented by St. Francis and the early companions, the sources are rather silent about the place until the Fioretti narrates events related to the beginnings of the Observant reform.[2]

Thanks to the work of scholars, we now have access to some documents which, although not numerous and rather remote in time, are sufficient to shed some light on the Carceri's pre-Franciscan period and the early years of the Franciscan era. Let us just summarize a few of them.

The first document is Pope Innocent III's *Bulla privilegii* sent to Bishop Guido II of Assisi in 1198. A listing of diocesan property mentions a "hermitage belonging to the Temple, together with the entire area known as the Royal Hill."[3]

Not letting ourselves be carried away by interesting but futile debates on how to interpret the "Collis Regalis" and the "Templo,"[4] we cannot fail to point out that this is the first Assisian document mentioning the word "carceri," and this is in a context not related to the commune of Assisi.

Taking into consideration the meaning that the word would take on in later documents,[5] we can assume that even before the time of St. Francis the word "carceri" somehow referred to the "locus" of a hermitage on Mount Subasio.

Local usage already shows the precise meaning of the term which would eventually pass from a generic designation to become the name of the Franciscan hermitage on Subasio. In the language of the time it indicated the eremitical life's external aspect of breaking away and separation from the world, that which is most obvious to the popular mentality. It would be a "separation" or an "incarceration" and thus the site where this took place became a *carcer* or *carceres*, as is clearly shown in the following documents.

Let us consider the so-called "Praise of Brother Elias" which was probably written by Friar Bona of Ferrara. It was read and published in the bishop's palace in Assisi on August 28, 1237, and defines the controversy over some land on Mt. Subasio claimed in a dispute by both the town and the chapter of San Rufino Cathedral.

The cathedral chapter is given clear title to the land above the road which begins at "Saxa Malloci," passing above the hermitage or *carcere* of St. Francis and ending at Fossa Luparia. "I grant to the prior and chapter and to the venerable church, from the aforesaid property on Mount Subasio, the path that passes near the Saxa Malloci and leads directly above the desert, that is, hermitage, of St. Francis and comes out at the Luparian Ravine. . . . The rest of the property on the Mount I grant to the honorable commune." Since the site of the Carceri is above "Saxa Malloci" and below the road which, turning right, leads above the hermitage, it is unequivocally recognized as the property of the town, and not of the canons; there is no mention of the Benedictines at all.

More important yet, for the first time—and this in a very important document dated only 11 years after the death of St. Francis—the place is called *heremus sive carcer Sancti Francisci,* thus giving authoritative confirmation to the meaning of *carcer,* which Franciscan sources have traditionally affirmed as St. Francis's dwelling in the Carceri.

The third document is rubric 34 of Book III of the *Statutorum magnifica civitatis Asisii* [Statutes of the glorious commune of Assisi] which, although printed in 1543, contains material which "is certainly a compendium of other, more ancient statutes, some of which date back to 1242."[6] This rubric clearly shows, first of all, the public veneration which the town of Assisi had for St. Francis at the Carceri: "to the honor of blessed Francis, and so that the very site of the Carceri on Mount Subasio be treated with greater respect"; this is a veneration which is too strong, too eloquent, not to be based on a sure fact that the saint frequently stayed there.

This is followed by an equally solemn, public commitment to defend and promote, for the present and the future, the dwelling and way of life which the friars want to lead in that same place, continuing to follow the example of St. Francis: "In addition, so that the brothers who wish to live there for their ministry and for keeping alive the memory of blessed Francis more authentically, may dwell there in a more fitting and reclusive manner." This makes it the first explicit testimony about the practice and continuity of the Franciscan contemplative life at the Carceri. The presence of devout friars does not merely touch on the past history of the founding period, but especially the present.

In regard to these goals, let it suffice to say that in the document they are given priority, and the town of Assisi enacts generous measures to provide for the "Carceri of St. Francis" and the life of the friars.

A part of the woods (four modules) surrounding the Carceri is reserved for the exclusive use of the friars. Not only is no one else allowed there, but the town is also forbidden to sell it, clear it, or use it as pasture land. Thus no one, for any reason whatsoever, could dare disturb the friars in the place which had been granted to them:

> They decreed and ordained that the common woods surrounding the Carceri be neither sold nor felled by the commune of Assisi, nor by anyone else, including any persons who might purchase the same woods from the aforesaid commune; nor sold for pasture rights; nor may pasturing of cattle be permitted for the space of four modules, to be calculated around the Carceri according to the mandate of the former owners.[7]

However, the friars' use and freedom over the place is not based on any right, but has an important limitation: the town retains ownership of the Carceri. The friars cannot be chased out by anyone but the town. However, neither can they cede or sell the property to others: "Nevertheless, let the ownership of the same four modules pertain to the commune; and by the authority of this chapter no right be granted to the Carceri, nor may the Carceri initiate any contrary judgment against the commune."

As already noted in a partial citation above, another observation can be made based on rubric 34 of the Statutes, namely, that the "Carceri of St. Francis" was not the only hermitage on Mount Subasio. Actually, not only was it not the only one, it was not even the oldest:

> and that all the hermitages and dwellings on Mount Subasio in the territory of the commune of Assisi have, and should have, at their own site, one module for each of the dwellings. Let a parcel be measured out from the common woods for each: for living quarters, cloister area and a portion of the woods. Furthermore, that when the common woods are sold, the sale not include woods adjacent to the dwellings nor the dwellings themselves; but let them be treated as reserved and set apart. . . . Again, that all the aforesaid hermitages and land and woods belong to the commune

of Assisi; and, that possession and ownership remain with the same commune. Again, that all the brothers and fraticelli in these dwellings are strictly bound to acknowledge that they occupy these same hermitages in tenancy to the Assisi commune . . . .

Thus we see that there were other "carceri" called by the same name, which was obviously a generic term. Because of the same religious concern and subject to the same conditions, each of them was given a "module" of land, substantially less than the amount given to the "Carceri of St. Francis."

These same statutes give us the name of the inhabitants or owners of some of these "carceri": "Carceres Angeli Bruni," "Carcerem Millutie."[8]

Contrary to what some people claim,[9] Assisi documents mention hermitages on Subasio even much later than the end of the 14th century: "Many hermits lived on the Mount in pursuit of holiness," we find in a passage of the epitome of the life of St. Vitalis.[10] In all probability this referred to "carceri" or individual hermitages where the eremitical life was to be practiced in the anchoritic tradition or close to it, and which was up to the free initiative of individuals who, as we find in the life of St. Vitalis, seemed to have a common bond with "their elder" who was the minister of all the hermits. The religious care of a large part of them was probably provided by the monks of the abbey of St. Benedict whose abbot, according to Di Costanzo, "was responsible for all the hermits." Proof of this can be seen in the fact that after the abbey's violent destruction in 1399 this way of life gradually waned and disappeared entirely. If today's Carceri is the only one to have lasted and even won out over all the others, it can be attributed to an obvious reason: it was "the desert or Hermitage of St. Francis" and it was in a certain sense the gauge and encouragement behind the ascetical-contemplative movement of one of the Church's largest and most energetic religious orders, the Order of St. Francis.

This gives us a look into the pre-Franciscan period of Mount Subasio. With its woods and lonely peaks, Assisi's mountain at the lower edge of the Spoleto valley, like its sister mountain of Monteluco at the other end,[11] had a strong attraction for hermits and monks since the period of the barbarian invasions.[12]

There is much evidence supporting this eremitical tradition. First of all there are the remains of the famous Abbey of St. Benedict on Mount Subasio, halfway up the mountain's south-western flank. These were the monks who frequently gave St. Francis protection and friendship.[13] Then, also, two parts of the mountain had always been dedicated by the hermits of the area to two saints who were models of the penitential and eremitical life: the western area was known as St. Anthony's hill, and to the south there was "La Maddalena." We also have documentary and architectural evidence of chapels in which hermits from the various zones gathered: "the chapel located at the top of the hill of St. Rufinus (or St. Mary Magdelene on the Mountain), of St. James, St. Anthony, St. Thomas," we find in the *Bulla privilegii* [Bull of entitlement] of 1198. In the above-mentioned epitome of St. Vitalis we find mention of "the dwelling of St. Mary of Violis, not far from the retreat of Blessed Savinus, St. Angelus and St. Potens of Carnucio," where at that time their "maggiore" was to be found, the minister of all the hermits scattered throughout the whole wooded area of the mountain: "where their elder was minister for all the hermits living on that thickly wooded mountain." We could right away add other hermitages: the hermitage of St. Honophrius and the Benedictine women's hermitage of Sant' Angelo di Panzo. Then, in the valley we have the monastery of San Masseo near San Damiano. Higher up, near the Carceri, there is the hermitage of the Carcerelle with its chapel dedicated to Our Lady of the Snows. Closer to Spello there is the monastery of St. Sylvester, to name but a few.[14]

It was this vigorous tradition and Subasio's appeal to the thirstiest of souls, those who were more restless in their search for God, combined with particular local and Franciscan historical motives, which would draw passionate, argumentative heretical groups to this mountain in search of a secure refuge or spiritual stronghold, as we shall see.

Again it is Rubric 34 of the Statutes that tells us about it. In fact, along with the brothers who occupied the "Carceri of St. Francis" and the four "modules" of woodland belonging to the town, the rubric speaks of the "brothers and the *fraticelli*" of the other mountain hermitages to whom the town grants a "module" of land:

> And no one may plant or cut trees in the woods contrary to the will of the brothers and the fraticelli and their companions . . . again, that all the brothers and fraticelli in those dwellings are bound . . . not to disturb or trouble the other brothers and fraticelli in any way . . . again, that the brothers and fraticelli may not sell the hermitages . . . again, if one of the brothers or fraticelli should leave . . . none of the brothers or fraticelli living in the hermitages and dwellings may be removed or expelled . . . except by the Assisi commune . . . since the aforementioned hermitages are meant for the brothers and fraticelli . . . .

Taking into account the textual distinctions to which we will return later, Rubric 34 refers to a time in which on Mount Subasio there were the "fratres" at the Carceri of St. Francis, that is, the Franciscans; in the other carceri there were the "fratres et fraticelli" (mentioned five times in the text) or the "fratres seu fraticelli" (mentioned twice). These terms are obviously distinct and show that some hermitages were occupied by hermit friars and others by "fraticelli." "Fraticelli" no doubt refers to those heretics who sprang up among the "spiritual" extremists, separated from them and, passing themselves off as Franciscans, rebelled violently, agitating for the "spiritual" ideals.

With the apparent poverty of their lifestyle, which appealed to popular sentiment, and the bitterness of their anti-papal ideas, they came from other places to Assisi and, to their own advantage became involved in the religious battles shaking the Order of Friars Minor[15] at the time, becoming embroiled in local political battles too.[16]

No one can say with certainty when the hermits referred to in Rubric 34 came to Subasio. Tracing backwards, however, from a few definite dates we can see that it was certainly at the beginning of the 14th century, the period in which the rubric in question was drawn up.

What interests us particularly, however, is a new fact which is not only unexpected, but habitually ignored by the written tradition of the Carceri, and which can only be traced by historians of the Order. And that is the fact that at a certain point the "fraticelli" moved from the nameless hermitages and places of Subasio to the "Carceri of St. Francis" itself. We know for certain that they seized it "violenter"[17] against the Franciscans' will, and lived there for many years, making it their most important center in the whole area.[18]

There is no universal agreement on the dates of the period of the Carceri's "profanation." Cristofani puts it between 1307 and 1340, while Fortini, based on Papini, claims that it began in 1318. Documents do not substantiate either claim, however. We find yet another date in Wadding's history where, under the year 1331, he makes note of the resolute act of the Minister General Gerardo Oddone (1329-1342), who asked the citizens of Assisi to chase the fraticelli from the Carceri and restore it to the Franciscan order:

> He urged the citizens of Assisi to expel from the convent of the Carceri on Mount Subasio the Fraticelli who had resorted to violence in seizing the place. . . . Once they had been expelled, he remained there a few days along with some God-fearing, most upright men whom he had chosen and called together to that place from various localities.

Cristofani, however, claims that the fraticelli's eviction from the Carceri took place "no earlier than 1340." On the other hand, we have a 1341 will of a certain Laetitia, the widow of Hugolino di Leto, who leaves 25 pounds of denari "for the needs of the brothers and fraticelli who will live here for a time (sic) at the Carceri of blessed Francis on Mount Subasio." Since the two dates are both prior to 1342, the last year of Gerardo Oddone's term of office, perhaps we can assume that his action took place in 1341, not in 1331 as Wadding claims. In a will dated 1346, Master Andrea di Giacobuzzo di Ottaviano from Porta San Giacomo shows us clearly that the restoration of the Carceri to the Franciscans is now an accomplished fact: "Likewise, he bequeathed and consigned a share of his property to the brothers dwelling at the Carceri of Blessed Francis on Mount Subasio, out of love for God and to benefit the poor."

Doubtless the chronology of this obscure period of the Carceri's history is not very clear. However, it seems that we can safely say that the period of the fraticelli's stay in the Carceri of St. Francis was not a brief one, but rather lasted for several decades.

On the one hand, it was a humiliating affront to the Franciscan Order, while for the fratricelli it was a cause for boasting and gave weight to their claims.[19]

Summarizing what we have learned up to this point, we have to correct and integrate some of the data which the Franciscan sources commonly tell about the Carceri. The contemplative eremitical life was lived there for centuries prior to St. Francis, and thus the experience of the Saint and his companions was simply inserted into the mountain's eremitical tradition, although with some originality. We should probably give more consideration to the part which hermitages in general and, perhaps, even the hermits of Subasio, played in the first years of Francis's conversion and religious formation.

Although Franciscan tradition has always claimed that the Carceri was given to St. Francis by the Benedictines at the Abbey of St. Benedict on Subasio, there is no further need to discuss this. It was never true for the simple reason that the place never belonged to the Benedictines.

In fact, it was never given to St. Francis nor to his friars. The town, which owned the property at least since 1237, never gave the place to anyone. The town merely established generous terms placing it at the friars' disposal, always retaining ownership.

The idea of the Benedictines' giving the property can probably be explained by a pious story similar to what occurred with the Portiuncula, supported perhaps by the proximity of the Benedictine Abbey and the desire to give greater weight to the little hermitage chapel among the rocks.

The silence (not of historians, obviously) which passes over the whole period from Franciscan origins until Paoluccio Trinci and his reform movement can be filled in partially, but with great weight, by the story of the fraticelli.

Endnotes

[1]M. Gatti, "Profilo storico delle Carceri nel peréodo prefrancescano e francescano," *Le Carceri di San Francesco del Subasio* (Assisi, 1969) 15-29.

[2]This first section of the book's first chapter was summarized by the translator.

[3]Cf. A. Fortini, NVSF III, 149, 543.

[4]Cf. A. Fortini, NVSF III, 154.

[5]We can cite a document from 1311 (Archives of the Sacro Convento in Assisi, Str. VI, 15) in which a certain Giovanna wills to Cicicia di Francesco "one of his cells located in the hills above Assisi, including all the goods and supplies in the cell . . . for this purpose that the aforementioned cell, after the death of said Cicicia, be given to the poor, or to servants of Christ who would live there to praise and bless God."

[6]*Statuta magnificae civitatis Asisii* (Perusiae per Hieronumum Francisci Baldasarris de Carthulariis, 1543, die XI Augusti) fol. 7; cf. T. Locatelli Paolucci, "Santuario di Santa Maria delle Carceri presso Assisi," MF 13, 65 a.

[7]See also foglio 20 of book five of the same statutes: "Likewise, they decreed and ordained that no one cut down or burn the trees of the forest at the Carceri of St. Francis on Mount Subasio, from the designated spot up to the hermitages themselves, an area staked out by wooden crosses. The penalty for each offense is 25 pounds of denarii."

[8]Statute, book V, rubric 65.

[9]L. Brancaloni, "Il Monte Subasio e le Carceri di S. Francesco," *Frate Francesco* I (1924): 174.

[10]G. Di Costanzo, *Disanima degli scrittori e dei monumenti resguardanti S. Rufino, Vescovo e martire di Assisi* (Assisi, 1797) 432.

[11]Concerning the famous Italian "Tebaid" of Monteluco, see J. Leclercq, "L'Erémitisme en Occident jusqu'à l'an mil" in *L'Eremitismo*, 34-35.

[12]L. Brancaloni, 172-73.

[13]See Edouard D'Alençon, *L'abbaye de Saint-Benoit su Mont Soubase près d'Assise* (Couvin, 1909) 20; A. Pantoni, "San Benedetto al Subasio," *Benedictina* 2 (1948): 47-48; M. Bachea, "La cripta triastila di San Benedetto al Subasio," Atti dell'Accademia Properziana del Subasio (1956, series V) n. 4.

[14]L. Bracaloni; A. Fortini, NVSF III, 152-55; 163-69; A. Fortini, 1 *Fioretti delle Carcerelle* (Venice, 1956) 11-19.

[15]The General Chapter which discussed the burning issues concerning the Order in regard to Pope John XXII was held in Perugia in 1322. Cf. H. Holzapfel, *Manuale Historiae Ordinis Fratrum Minorum* 60.

[16]At the side of the Ghibelline Muzio di Francesco in Assisi's political struggles we find the fraticelli who, given their position in regard to the Pontiff, we can realistically assume sided with Muzio and the Ghibellines out of hatred for the pope.

[17]AM VII, 1331, 126, XXI; "Agostino da Stroncone," MF 3, 157.

[18]Cf. "Agostino da Stroncone." See also L. Fumi, "Eretici e ribelli dell'Umbria," *Bollettino della Deputazione di Storia Patria per l'Umbria*, 5 (1899): 218 f.

[19]However, we do not intend to discuss the question of the popularity the fraticelli enjoyed among the simple folk who left money to "fratribus et fraticellis" without distinction, but also the ecclesiastical authorities' regard for them. For

example, in Perugia in 1361 the inquisitor tried the fraticello Liberato of Borgo San Sepolcro while in 1363 Bishop Andrea Bontempi of Perugia confirmed Fra Liberato's election as prior of Santa Maria del Sasso di Montemalbe.

Eremitism:

An Authentic Element of Franciscanism

by

Benedikt Mertens, OFM[1]

Translated from the German by

Josef Raischl and André Cirino, OFM

(By way of concluding this chapter, we offer the following considerations from Mertens. Eds.)

1. After examining all possible sources of the life of St. Francis, one notices the existence, importance, and practice of the eremitical dimension in Francis's life and in the first generation of the Friars Minor. Eremitism is not just one episode in Francis's life: it encompasses his whole life.

2. Franciscan eremitism is as authentic an expression of the way of life of the Friars Minor as is the preaching apostolate that was motivated by following the poor Christ.

3. There are three proofs of the harmonious integration of eremitism in the Franciscan way of life:

   First, biographers describe Francis's life as a mixed life with sojourns of eremitical withdrawal and periods of journeying and preaching. The liturgical times of penance offer an idea of when and for how long Francis remained in hermitages. The inner connection of the two extreme poles of hermitage life and public preaching illustrate his desire to know God's will and to follow Christ.

Secondly, eremitism in Francis is a dynamic concept similar to his unsteady wandering life. The Franciscan hermitage, with its temporary and provisional character, was part of the Order's insecure existence, relying on Divine Providence. It was integrated into the mission and self-concept of the Friars Minor by its elements of extreme poverty in housing, openness to the poor, emphasis on brotherhood, sporadic preaching, and service of prayer for the kingdom of God.

Finally, the eremitical element influenced the primitive itinerant and preaching expressions of the early Friars Minor by its own spirituality. Eremitism as a Franciscan characteristic was particularly influential in forming a religious attitude—especially in Francis himself.

4. In the writings of Francis the eremitical life is presented as a possible way of living in the Order. The "Rule for Hermitages" corresponds to passages of the biographies and, moreover, has overtones similar to the "Letter to a Minister" and the *Earlier Rule*.

Endnote

[1]B. Mertens, "Der Eremitismus als authentisches Element der franziskanischen Lebensweise," part of the same author's "'In eremi vastitate resedit' Der Widerhall der eremitischen Bewegung des Hochmittelalters bei Franziskus von Assisi," *Franziskanische Studien* 74 (1992): 285-374.

Chapter Three

THE "RULE FOR HERMITAGES"

by Francis of Assisi

Critical Text and Commentary

Introduction

Guiding the reader through this third section—the "heart" of our anthology—we would like to make some suggestions by way of mapping out a possible route for both a casual and a more scholarly approach to the text.

Both the casual and the scholarly reader can begin the journey by taking a look at the critical text of Kajetan Esser, OFM, offered in the Latin version of the manuscript tradition alongside the most recent English translation by Regis Armstrong, OFM Cap. Readers can continue the journey guided by Benedikt Mertens' introductory comments. But after this point, we recommend two routes.

The casual reader may want to begin with the introduction and then read Part Two of Esser's commentary. A route for the scholarly reader might be the introduction, followed by Part One and then Part Two of Esser's commentary.

Both readers can travel together through the readable lecture of Ignatius Brady, OFM, on the "Rule for Hermitages." Having come upon this lecture in the form of a cassette tape, we chose to transcribe it in its colloquial form so as to be faithful to the lecturer and offer it as a tribute to him for his contribution to Franciscan research and studies.

Finally, both types of readers can end their journey with Mertens' conclusions concerning the eremitical experience of Francis and its connection with the eremitical tradition.

Regula Pro Eremitoriis Data

A Rule For Hermitages

Original Latin Text edited
by Cajetan Esser, OFM (column I)[1]

English Translation
by
R. Armstrong, OFM Cap (column II)[2]

Illi, qui volunt religiose stare[3] in eremis[4] sint tres fratres[5] vel quattuor ad plus; duo ex ipsis sint matres[6] et habeant duos filios vel unum ad minus.

1. Those who wish to dwell in a religious way in hermitages may be three brothers or, at the most, four; let two of these be the 'mother' and have two 'sons' or at least one.

Isti duo, qui sunt matres,[7] teneant vitam Marthae et[8] duo filii teneant[9] vitam Mariae[10] (cf.Lc 10:38-42) et habeant unum claustrum, in quo[11] unusquisque habeat cellulam suam, in qua oret et dormiat.[12]

2. Let the two who are 'mothers' keep the life of Martha and the two 'sons' keep the life of Mary (Cf.Lk 10:38-42) and have one enclosure in which each one may have his cell in which he may pray and sleep.

Et semper dicant completorium de die statim post occasum solis;[13] et studeant retinere[14] silentium; et dicant horas suas; et in matutinis surgant[15] et primum quaerant

3. And let them always recite Compline of the day immediately after sundown; and strive to maintain silence, recite their Hours, rise for Matins; and seek

regnum Dei et iustitiam eius (Mt 6:33).

first the Kingdom of God and His justice (Mt 6:33).

Et dicant primam hora(sic), qua convenit et post tertiam[16] absolvant silentium; et possint loqui et ire ad matres suas.

4. And let them recite Prime at the proper hour and, after Terce, they may end their silence, speak with and go to their mothers.

Et, quando placuerit, possint petere ab eis eleemosynam sicut parvuli pauperes propter amorem Domini Dei.

5. And, when it pleases them, they can beg alms from them as poor little ones out of love of the Lord God.

Et postea dicant sextam et nonam; et vesperas dicant[17] hora qua convenit.

6. And afterwards let them recite Sext, None and, at the proper hour, Vespers.

Et in claustro, ubi morantur, non permittant aliquam[18] personam introire et[19] neque ibi comedant.

7. And they may not permit anyone to enter or eat in the enclosure where they dwell.

Isti[20] fratres, qui sunt matres, studeant manere remote ab omni persona; et per obedientiam sui ministri[21] custodiant filios suos ab omni persona, ut nemo possit loqui cum eis.

8. Let those brothers who are the 'mothers' strive to stay far from everyone and, because of obedience to their minister, protect their 'sons' from everyone so that no one can speak with them.

Et isti filii non loquantur cum aliqua persona nisi cum matribus suis et cum ministro et[22] custode suo, quando placuerit[23] eos visitare cum benedictione Domini[24] Dei.

9. And those 'sons' may not talk with anyone except with their 'mothers' and with the minister and his custodian when it pleases them to visit with the Lord's blessing.

Filii[25] vero quandoque officium matrum assumant, sicut vicissitudinaliter eis pro tempore visum fuerit disponendum; quod[26] omnia supradicta sollicite et studiose[27] studeant observare.

10. The 'sons,' however, may periodically assume the role of the 'mothers,' taking turns for a time as they have mutually decided. Let them strive to observe conscientiously and eagerly everything mentioned above.

Endnotes

[1] C. Esser, *Opuscula Sancti Patris Francisci Assisiensis*, Grottaferrata (Rome) 1978, 296-298.

[2] "Rule For Hermitages," *Gospel Living* 62–63.

[3] *vivere*: i, habitare: Lt.

[4] *eremitoriis*: a, c, i.

[5] om Bc, BP, Lt.

[6] *patres*: hic et semper BU.

[7] *qui sunt matres*: om a, i.

[8] *om* Bc; alii add a, c, i; alii vero: add Bc.

[9] filii teneant: om a, c, i; *duo vel unus vitam Mariae*: Lt.

[10] Magdalenae: add a; Illi qui tenebunt vitam Mariae (Marthae: Ax, Wa; Magdalenae: add Lt): add a; Illi qui tenuerint (tenent: BU; tenuerunt: Bu, Is3, Ma) vitam Mariae: add c, i; postea om et: a, c, i.

[11] *in quo*: om, sed add et: a, c, i.

[12] cellulam...dormiat: om, sed add locum suum, ita quod non habitent simul nec cubent: a, c, i.

[13] *statim...solis*: om, sed add quando sol revertitur ad occasum: a.

[14] tenere: MS2, a, c, i.

[15] in...surgant: om, sed add *surgant ad matutinum*: a.

[16] *Et hora congrua dicant primam et tertiam et post horam tertiam:a; Et dicant primam et tertiam et* (om BU) *hora qua convenit post horam tertiam: c; Et dicant primam et tertiam et post horam tertiam*: i.

[17] *om* a, c, i; hora qua convenit: om, sed add tempore debito: a.

[18] *mulierem sive* (aut: FO) quamcumque: add Bc, FO, Wa.

[19] *om* Fg, Is1; sed: a (praeter Fg, Is1), c, i.

[20] *Et illi*: a, c, i.

[21] *custodis*: a, c, i.

[22] *ministro et*: om a, c, i.

[23] *eis*: add c (praeter FU, Ko); sibi: add Is3; ei: BU, Ko, a.

[24] *om* a, c, i.

[25] *Filii vero... observare*: om k.

[26] qui: a (praeter Ax), i; quod... observare: om S.

[27] *studiose et sollicite*: trsp a.

Introduction to Critical Considerations

of the *Regula Pro Eremitoriis Data*

by

Benedikt Mertens, OFM[1]

Translated from the German
by
Josef Raischl and André Cirino, OFM

There is no scholarly doubt about the authenticity of this work of Francis. Kajetan Esser's critical studies of Codex 338 of the library of Assisi have proved its existence as early as the middle of the thirteenth century. Moreover, there are 24 other manuscripts from the next two centuries.[2] The variations of the text stem not so much from content but rather from linguistic corrections, additions or omissions made when copied. The text tradition is significantly homogenous. The only problem seems to rest with the title.

Relying on the manuscript (Codex 338, Assisi Library, no title), Esser's critical edition entitles the text "The Rule Given for Hermitages." Esser's title breaks with the traditional title of this century, namely, *De religiosa habitatione in eremo* [The abiding of religious persons in hermitages]. Following Esser, Boccali uses the same text but the latter title.[3]

Both titles can be accepted as conveying the sense of the work. The word "rule" must not be understood as a technical term because it was never used the way the word "rule" is used in the legal sense for the *Earlier Rule* or the *Later Rule*.

The Franciscan sources do not explicitly refer to Francis's authorship. Yet there are enough references with Francis's biographies that support the "Rule for Hermitages" or even rely on it. It is noteworthy that the language and style of writing is similar to Francis's other writings. Thus there is no doubt regarding the authenticity of this writing.

There is no evidence of an exact date for this writing, yet we are able to find some leads. The earliest possible date when the young fraternity met for the Pentecost Chapter and was divided into provinces presided over by provincial ministers is 1217. The "Rule for Hermitages" uses the terms minister and custodian. The latest possible date of writing is 1224, because the bull *Quia populares tumultus* of December 1224, allowed the celebration of Mass in oratories. The "Rule for Hermitages" does not mention either the oratory or Mass. Thus, this text would have been composed before the end of 1224 or even before March 1222, when the bull *Devotionis vestrae* allowed possession of an oratory. However, the earlier date is more probable because of stylistic closeness to the *Regula non Bullata* (1221) and the *Letter to a Minister* (1217/1218-21). In conclusion, we can date the "Rule for Hermitages" between 1217 and 1221.

There is no way to tell where it was composed. Yet there is a probable clue in the *Considerations of the Sacred Stigmata* of Saint Francis found in the *Fioretti* (not a very reliable source),[4] which points to La Verna.

Endnotes

[1] B. Mertens, "In eremi vastitate resedit" 285-374; 347-49. This title translates as "He dwelt in desert emptiness."

[2] Cfr. K. Esser, Die "Regula pro eremitoriis data," 383-89.

[3] I. Boccali, *Concordantiae verbales opusculorum S. Francisci et S. Clarae Assisiensium* (Assisi ,1976) 73.

[4] Seconda Considerazione, *Omnibus of Sources* (FF) 1586.

The *Regula Pro Eremitoriis Data*

of St. Francis of Assisi

by

Kajetan Esser, OFM[1]

Translated from the German
by
Berard Doerger, OFM

Among the *Opuscula* [Writings] of St. Francis, the instruction for those friars who wish to lead a contemplative life in solitude occupies only a small space. For that reason it also has received hardly any special consideration in modern Franciscan research. Generally, just a few short notes are found regarding this instruction, and they do not tell us very much. Thus, for example, N. Papini, in his critical treatment of the Wadding edition of the *Opuscula*,[2] considers this instruction only briefly, and then only in regard to textual criticism, in as much as he compares the text of the Wadding edition with a manuscript form in the Sacro Convento at Assisi, which text is apparently the present-day Codex 338 of the public library in Assisi.[3]

On the question of hermitages, which was vehemently debated between the Spirituals and the Community in the Order of Friars Minor at the beginning of the 14th century, Fr. Ehrle, SJ, proposes that consideration be given to the regulations "which Francis is supposed to have written for those brothers living in

---

[1]K. Esser, "Die Regula pro eremitoriis data des heiligen Franziskus v. Assisi," *FranzStud* 44 (1962) 383-417. Reprinted in *Studien zu den Opuscula des hl. Franziskus von Assisi* (Rome, 1973) 137-79.
[2]L. Wadding, *B.P. Francisci Assisiatis Opuscula*, (Antwerp, 1623).
[3]N. Papini, *Storia di s. Francesco d´Assisi, II* (Foligno, 1827) 148.

hermitages."[4] Referring to the above-mentioned Codex 338 of Assisi, which, according to his view, stems from the 13th century, Ehrle concedes the possibility "that these regulations originate from the manuscript tradition which reaches back to the first years of the foundation of the Order."[5] He never gives, however, a more thorough evaluation of this short work.

In a similar vein, Paul Sabatier works this "precious memento" in a positive way into his presentation of the life of Francis. He considers the possibility "that in it there is preserved for us a fragment of the *Rule* which was compiled about the year 1217."[6] In the various editions of his "Mirror of Perfection," Sabatier also attempts an explanation of the text of this "Rule of the Hermitage Friars."[7] All this is done, however, in a rather "by-the-way" fashion.

W. Goetz, in his critical investigation of the "Sources for the History of St. Francis of Assisi,"[8] lists this *opusculum*, without any hesitation, among the genuine works of the Saint. As Ehrle and Sabatier before him, he does not include it, however, in the corpus of the *Admonitions*, as many manuscripts would demand, nor even in the *Collationes monasticae* as Wadding had done. He inclines rather to the view "that this instruction about the life in the hermitages originated as a preliminary work, or as a supplement to the *Rule* of the Order." Perhaps he considered it as one of the doubtless "genuine, but insignificant works for the historical evaluation of the Saint."[9] Otherwise he would certainly have given it more attention.

It is probably thanks to Goetz's opinion, however, that this "Rule for Hermitages" was admitted without any difficulty into

---

[4]Fr. Ehrle SJ, "Die Spiritualen, ihr Verhältnis zum Franciscanerorden und zu den Fraticellen," *ArchLitKirchGesch* III, 604. Apparently, behind his wording "haben soll" ("is supposed to have") there is no doubt concerning the authenticity of this work when this wording is considered in the whole context.

[5]Ibid., 604f.

[6]P. Sabatier, *Vie de S. François* 125; *ColEtDoc* I, CLXXI and I; P. 26 n. 1; II, CXXV, CXLVII.

[7]*Speculum perfectionis*, ed. P. Sabatier, *CollEtDoc* I, (Paris, 1898), CLXXI, note I; CLXXXII; CLXXXV and other places. *Le Speculum perfectionis*, ed. P. Sabatier, A.G. Little, British Society of Franciscan Studies, vol XIII, I (Manchester, 1928) 150, 182, 213, loc. cit.; II, (Manchester, 1931) 100f.

[8]W. Goetz, *Die Quellen zur Geschichte des hl. Franz von Assisi: eine kritische Untersuchung* (Gotha 1904) 45, 49, 55.

[9]Ibid., 48, footnote 1.

the critical editions of the *Opuscula* of St. Francis which appeared at the beginning of this century.[10] Boehmer includes it among the Saint's shorter works "in which Francis alone speaks; which works are thus all the more valuable, if one wishes to get to know Francis." Lemmens, like Boehmer, separates the "Rule for Hermitages" from the *Admonitions* and merely remarks that in "style and content, it is consistent with St. Francis." As might well be expected, after these preliminary studies, this "Rule for Hermitages" was admitted into all the translations of the writings of St. Francis.

In a very critical review of the edition of Lemmens, the scholarly Bollandist, Fr. Van Ortroy, SJ, expresses doubts about the authenticity of this writing: "The recommendations for religious living in hermitages hardly inspire me with confidence." He therefore considers it necessary that this work, like every piece of manuscript tradition, be carefully examined in detail, at least in terms of the chronology and textual criticism.[11] However, he does not give any further reasons for his doubt.

Without taking up what Van Ortroy suggests, J. Cambell, OFM, in what is probably the most extensive critical study of the *Opuscula* of St. Francis, includes the "Directives pour les Ermitages" among the genuine works of St. Francis. But he too is opposed to an association with the *Admonitions*. As proofs of au-

---

[10]H. Boehmer, *Analekten zur Geschichte des Franciscus von Assisi* (Tübingen, 1904). This small publication brought out in the "Sammlung ausgewählter kirchen-und dogmengeschichtlicher Quellenschriften" appeared in 1930 in a second edition provided by Fr. Wiegand, and in 1961 in a third edition containing an instructive supplement by C. Andresen. L. Lemmens, *Opuscula sancti patris Francisci Assisiensis* (Quaracchi, 1904). Abbreviated in the following: *Analekten* and *Opuscula*. It should be noted, however, that many critical observations and justified expectations have been voiced by E. Lempp concerning the publication of Boehmer in: *TheolLitZeit* 29 (1904) 710f. and by Fr. Van Ortroy, SJ concerning the publication of Lemmens in *Anal Boll* 24 (1905) 411ff., to name only the most important critics.

[11]Ibid., 413. O. Bonmann, OFM, also represents his position when he desires that the definitive publication of the *Opuscula* be prepared "gradatim tantum, passu pro passu singillatim plene stabilito," *Antonianum* 33 (1955): 337. In this connection the judgment of L. Hardick, OFM, should also be noted: "The texts for example of the writings of St. Francis are indeed in the most part reliable according to the present editions, however, in many details a definitive edition would be desired," *FranzStud* 44 (1962): 125.

thenticity, the evidence of the manscripts and the style suffice for him.[12]

However, since precisely this work of St. Francis is of great significance for the early history of his Order for various reasons, it seems to be time to devote a distinct investigation to it. In the following pages, therefore, the questions of its authenticity and its significance will be asked anew and treated in detail.

Part One

The Authenticity of the Rule for Hermitages

To establish the authenticity of a work, one must begin by investigating the manuscript tradition before relying on internal criteria. In regard to this, we are fortunate that this work of St. Francis, in spite of its small size, is attested to very early and very frequently. It is found in the following manuscripts:[13]

As = Codex 338 of the public library at Assisi, folio 43r-v, originating from the middle of the 13th century.[14] The copyist included it separately in the *Opuscula* after he had left blank many pages, which space he had apparently provided for the *Office of the Passion*, but never copied, so that we are left with only a fragment of this work (i.e., the *Office of the Passion*). Why he placed our work completely at the end remains to be explained.[15]

---

[12]J. Cambell OFM, *Les écrits de saint François d'Assise devant la critique* (Werl/Westf, 1954) 39f. This study is published again in *FranzStud* 36 (1954): 82-109; 205-264.

[13]In the following pages, the logograms will be retained which were used in our research on the Testament of St. Francis; new logograms will be so selected that they offer no cause for confusions. See K. Esser, OFM, *Das Testament des heiligen Franziskus von Assisi Eine Untersuchung über seine Echtheit und seine Bedeutung, Vorreformationsgeschichtliche Forschungen*, vol. 15 (Münster i.W., 1949) 17ff.

[14]K. Esser OFM, *Die älteste Handschrift der Opuscula des hl. Franziskus von Assisi (cod. 338 von Assisi), FranzStud* 26 (1939) 129-142. See also Cambell, *Les ecrits*, 4.

[15]Cambell, 39f., thinks it should be accepted without doubt that this happened because the work became known to the copyist only toward the end of his work. Against this spirited conjecture certainly stands the fact that the copyist of As calculated exactly how much space he had to leave open in his manuscript for the *Officium passionis* (he wrote only the beginning of it in order to supply the rest later!),

Ax = Codex 1310 (1445) of the Bibliothèque Publique at Aix, folio 5r-v, from the 15th century. This manuscript is probably of Italian origin and belonged earlier to the Friars Minor at Chiusi in Tuscany.[16] Our *opusculum* comes immediately after the *Admonitions.*

B_1 = Codex theol. lat. qu. 196 of the former Prussian State Library at Berlin, folio 104. Stemming from the second half of the 14th century, it belonged earlier to the Friars Minor at Thorn on the Weichsel.[17] In this codex also, our *opusculum* follows the *Admonitions.*

Bc = Codex 665 of the Biblioteca Central at Barcelona, folio 47v, from the 14th/15th century. It is apparently related to the Italian manuscript, and our *opusculum* is likewise placed after the *Admonitions.*[18]

BM_5 = Codex addit. Mss 16567 of the British Museum in London, folio 181r-v, likewise of Italian origin. It, however, places our "Rule for Hermitages" after the "Letter to a Minister" of St. Francis.[19]

BP = Bartholomew of Pisa, *De conformitate vitae beati Francisci ad vitam Domini Jesu* [The Conformity of the Life of Blessed Francis to the Life of the Lord Jesus], lib.I, fruct.XII, p. 2, Chapter 30 (*Anal Franc* IV, 623), written between 1385-1390. He includes the complete text, and although the work is by itself, he adds to the Incipit: *"Franciscus in suis admonitionibus."* Thus the manuscript he copies from had this order.

Bs = Codex I.F. 271 of the University Library of Breslau, folio 303vb, written after 1468 and probably of Franciscan origin; likewise, after the *Admonitions.* [20]

---

before he wrote our *Opusculum*. So he had this work in front of him with the layout of his work from the very beginning.

[16]Ibid., 19f. contains a detailed description of this noteworthy manuscript.

[17]Ibid., 10. In spite of exhaustive investigation, nothing has been discovered of the remains of this manuscript since the last war. It must be considered as disappeared. Fortunately a photocopy is found in the archives of the College at Quaracchi, of which we thankfully were permitted to avail ourselves.

[18]Ibid., 7. Cambell classifies this manuscript with the southern group of the *Speculum perfectionis*, which includes manuscripts of the Italian Province.

[19]See Catalogue of Additions to the Manuscripts in the British Museum in the years 1846-1847, London 1864, 280. The manuscript has an old and a new numbering; here the new was considered. Cambell doesn´t mention it in his research.

[20]This manuscript was described in great detail by Cambell, page 10, footnote 36; still he had to confess himself that he could only present in a summary fashion the

Bu = Codex Med. Aevi lat. 77 of the library of the Hungarian National Museum at Budapest, folio 70rb-va, from the first half of the 15th century; again after *Admonitions.* The manuscript probably originated in Germany.[21]

FO = Codex F. 19 of the Cloister Ognissante at Florence, folio 6v; after the *Admonitions.* Written about 1370, it belonged

---

pages which contain the *Opuscula* of St. Francis. This part, therefore, should be more exactly described:

folio 297va: *Hic incipiunt psalmi, quos beatus franciscus ordinavit ad reverentiam et memoriam passionis dominicae . . . Officium passionis .*

fol 300ra: Hic incipiunt canticum beati francisci quod dicitur canticum solis: Altissimo omnipotente bon signore . . . de te altissimo porta significatione (first strophe of the *Canticle of the Sun*).

fol 300ra: Quomodo fuit certificatus per christum de vita eterna: Unde quadam nocte considerans . . . usque ad diem mortis sue (Delormé, *Legenda* 43).

fol 300va: Quomodo per laudes quas fecit episcopum et potestatem assisi concordat: Eodem tempore cum iaceret infirmus . . . Unde nos qui fuimus cum beato francisco testimonium perhibuimus quod semper cum aliquid prediceret ad litteram fiebat (Delormé, *Legenda* 44).

fol 300vb: Exhortatio ad sorores oridinis sancte Clare. Similiter illis diebus . . . existerent patientes (Delormé,*Legenda* 45).

fol 301ra: Incipit testamentum beati francisci.

fol 301vb: Hic incipiunt ammoniciones beati francisci. Et primo de sacramento corporis et sanguinis domini (*Admonitiones*).

fol 303vb: De religiosa conversatione in hermitorijs admonicio et doctrina quam beatus franciscus edocuit (our text).

fol 303vb-304ra: Has laudes ordinavit sanctus franciscus et dixit ad omnes horas diei ac noctis ante officium beate virginis. Sic incipiens: Sanctissime pater noster cum gloria patri. deinde dicuntur laudes. Sanctus . . . (*Laudes ad omnes horas*).

fol 304ra: Laudes de virtutibus.

fol 304rb: Salutacio beate virginis.

fol 304rb: Item alia luas quam sanctus franciscus edocuit. Deus sanctus dominus deus tu es deus deorum qui solus facis . . . misericors salvator. Amen (*Laudes dei altissimi*).

fol 304rb: Benedictio fr. Leoni data.

fol 304rb: Incipit epistola beati francisci missa universis christianis (*Epistola ad aomnes fideles*).

fol 305vb: Incipit epistola beati francisci ad capitulum generale missa cum esset infirmus (*Epistola ad capitulum*).

fol 307ra-rb: De reverencia corporis domini et munditia altaris ad omnes clericos debet poni ante passum de virtutibus regine sapientia (!). Attendamus omnes clerici . . . se benedictos a domino jhesu christo (*Epistola ad clericos*).

The order of the individual pieces is exactly that of the codex 12 of the Petropaulina at Liegnitz (see Op.CritHist I, 55-58). Certainly the references stated here by Sabatier from his publication of the *Speculum perfectionis* are not correct; the three pieces agree, as stated above, with the text of Delormé's *Legenda.* Since the Codex of Liegnitz is considered lost since the war, Bs thus becomes even more valuable. A photocopy of the *Opuscula* from Bs can be found in the Archives *Wissenschaft und Weisheit* at Mönchengladbach/ Germany.

[21]Cambell, page 14, footnote 41. This manuscript can be found with whatever concerns the *Opuscula* in the above-mentioned archives, likewise photocopied.

formerly to the Magister Gabriel, the Provincial Minister of the Tuscan Province of the Order of Friars Minor.[22]

Fg = an undesignated codex, which was formerly in the Capuchin monastery at Foligno. Today it is still preserved in the Provincial archives of this Order in Assisi; folio 23rb-va; after the *Admonitions*. It originated in the 15th century.[23]

Is_1 = Codex 1/25 of the College Library of St. Isidore in Rome, folio 16v-17r; after the *Admonitions*; written in the 14th century. It belonged formerly to the monastery of the Friars Minor of S. Francesco al Monte in Perugia. Cambell proposes the years 1318-1350 as its date of origin.[24]

Is_2 = Codex 1/73 of the same library, folio 18v-19r; likewise written in the 14th century and certainly in Franciscan possession at the beginning of the 15th century. Our *opusculum* comes after the "Letter to the Faithful" of St. Francis, although the codex also contains the *Admonitions*.[25]

Lb= Codex I.G. 17 of the University Library in Lemburg (Levow), folio 338v; after the *Admonitions*. It was written in the 15th century and probably belonged formerly to the Polish Franciscans, likely originating in the Lemberger Monastery.[26]

Li = Codex 12 of the library of Peter and Paul's Church in Liegnitz, folio 135ra; after the *Admonitions*; written in the year 1480 in the Carthusian House of that place.[27]

Lt = Codex lat. theol. d. 23 (Philipps Ms 12290) of the Bodleian Library at Oxford, which formerly belonged to the library of A.G. Little and became known as such; folio 141r-v; after the *Admonitions*; written about 1400.[28]

Ma = codex XII.2. 154 of the public library in Magdeburg, folio 86va; from the first half of the 15th century and probably

---

[22]Esser, *Testament* 20.

[23]Cambell, op. cit. 7. Since the manuscript has become known in the research as the Manuscript of Foligno, we list it here so that all confusion is eliminated.

[24]Ibid., 7.

[25]Cf. Lemmens in: *DocAntFranc* III, 60-69.

[26]Cambell with good reasons conjectures this. He also offers a very exact description of this manuscript (*Les écrits*, 11, footnote 39). We give thanks here also to the Archives of Quaracchi for being able to use the photocopy found there.

[27]Esser, *Testament* 22. According to all accounts, this manuscript would also have to be considered lost since the last war. Unfortunately, in the photocopy of Quaracchi, precisely that section is missing which contains the *Opuscula* of St. Francis; see, however, above: footnote 20.

[28]Esser, *Testament* 22; Cambell, *Les écrits* 7.

of German origin. Here also the "Rule for Hermitages" is found after the *Admonitions.*[29]

MS$_2$ = Codex lat. 11354 of the Bavarian State Library in Munich, folio 42v-43r; from the 15th century. This manuscript, earlier mentioned by Boehmer and Lemmens, has not yet been given the consideration it deserves.[30]

---

[29]Cambell offers a useful description of the photocopy found in Quaracchi, *Les écrits* 13, footnote 40. The manuscript has disappeared since the war, but here also the photocopies of Quaracchi are at our disposal, for which we are once again grateful.

[30]The Clm 11354 (Polling 53), membr., saec. XV, came from the Choir-masters Monastery Polling (Upper Bavaria) in the Munich State Library. It still bears, however, an older notification of possession: "Codex fuit Coelestinorum prope Offemontem"; according to that, it stems from the Kloster Ste-Croix-sous-Offemont, Diocese of Soissons; cfr. Catholicisme, t. II, s.v. Celestins). How it came from there to Bavaria is not able to be established. The description in *Catalogus codicum latinorum bibliothecae regiae Monacensis*, II (Munich, 1876), is likewise not complete with what concerns the Franciscan part. This section might therefore be as exactly described as possible:

fol 25r: In nomine patris et filii et spiritus sancti. Amen. Haec sunt verba sacrae admonitionis venerabilis patris nostri francisci ad omnes fratres (*Admonitiones*).

fol 31v: Incipit *Opusculum* venerabilis patris nostri sancti francisci commonitorium et exhortatorium (*Epistola ad fideles*).

fol 35v: De littera et admonitione beatissimi patris nostri francisci quam misit fratribus ad capitulum quando erat infirmus (*Epistola ad capitulum*).

fol 40r: Oratio beati Francisci: Omnipotens eterne iuste . . .

fol 40v: De reverentia corporis domini et de munditia altaris ad omnes clericos (*Epistola ad clericos*).

fol 41v: De virtutibus de quibus fuit decorata sancta virgo et debet esse sancta anima (*Laudes de virtutibus*).

fol 42r: Sequuntur laudes quas ordinavit sanctissimus pater noster franciscus et dicebat ipsas ad omnes horas dici et noctis et ante officium beatae marie virginis sic incipiens Sanctissime pater noster qui es in caelis etc. cum gloria patri, deinde laudes: Sanctus, sanctus, sanctus . . . (*Laudes ad omnes horas*).

fol 42v: (Without Incipit!) Illi qui volunt religiose stare . . . (our text).

fol 43r: De custodia oris et penitentia fratribus imponenda . . . (Delormé, *Legenda* 78; cfr. Sabatier, *Speculum* 82, 4-12, Lemmens, *Speculum* 35).

fol 44 v: Epistola Bonaventure ad abbaissam et sorores S. Clare.

fol 47r: Incipiunt collationes sancti fratris Aegidii (not like in the catalogue: Francisci!), quas habebat eum fatribus (*Verba aurea fratris Aegidii*).

The headings are almost word for word those of the codex As, with which the order of the *Opuscula* also corresponds. Only MS$_2$ passes over the *Regula bullata* and the *Testamentum*, which are found in As before the *Admonitiones*, as likewise the *Canticle of the Sun* and the *Office of the Passion*, which are found there before our text. This manuscript is not found in Cambell. But precisely this manuscript is a prime valuable witness for the fact that As does not exist alone, as Cambell presents it, *Les écrits* 4f. Manuscript As also stands in a family, which is even represented outside of Italy, and in the Ms$_2$ manuscript, perhaps forms the bridge to those manuscripts which are found in the group of the *Speculum perfectionis*, named the "groupe septlentrional" by Sabatier. They also exhibit an obvious relationship with the text of As. Unfortunately, our text is not found in the above-mentioned collection,

SFl = Codex 148 of the Monastery Library of St. Florian, Upper Austria, folio 41ra-rb; after the *Admonitions*; written between 1343-1348. In it the *Opuscula* of St. Francis and many other Franciscan works are interwoven in an explanation of the *Rule* of the Friars Minor.[31]

Si = Codex F.XI.15 of the municipal library at Siena, folio 4ra-rb; after the *Admonitions*; from the 14th century. It belonged formerly to the Observant friary there.[32]

V_1 = Codex lat. 4345 of the Vatican Apostolic Library, folio 42r-v; after the *Admonitions*; written after 1340 by a German copyist.[33]

V_2 = Codex lat. 7650 of the same library, folio 13va-vb; after the *Admonitions*. Written in the 15th century, the manuscript came to the Vatican from the Generalate of the Friars Minor at Aracoeli.[34]

Wa = Codex 9 of the Library of the Holy Name College in Washington, folio 33r-34r, after the *Admonitions*; written in Italy in the 15th century.[35]

iFR_1 = Codex 1407 of the Riccardiana at Florence, folio 102v-103r; it has our *opusculum* in an Italian translation after the *Admonitions*. It was copied by a Brother Anthony Bruni of Florence, who finished this work on October 25, 1503. His translation is also contained in several other manuscripts in his handwriting.[36]

W = under this designation should be considered the text which Luke Wadding includes in his first publication of the *Opuscula*, [37] and for which Wadding depended on BP as well as on two other manuscripts.[38] In spite of the brevity of this piece of

---

wherefore we cannot discuss the question here any further. Already Cambell indicated that the *Opuscula* are produced in it in the order of codex As: op. cit. 5; cfr. also under footnote 38!

[31]K. Esser, OFM, "Eine Expositio regulae Ordinis fratrum minorum aus dem 14. Jahrhundert," *FranzStud* 37 (1955): 18-52.

[32]*Speculum perfectionis*, ed. Sabatier and Little, II, 23-28.

[33]Numerous literary allusions in Cambell, *Les écrits* 11.

[34]Esser, *Testament* 24.

[35]S. de Ricci, *Census of Medieval and Renaissance Manuscripts in the United States and Canada* I (New York, 1935,) 471; Cambell, *Les écrits* 7.

[36]Esser, *Testament* 25f.

[37]Wadding, *Opuscula* 290, especially "Adnotationes" on p. 291f.

[38]The manuscript of Assisi used by Wadding is hardly, as Papini supposes (cfr. above at footnote 3), the modern 388 of Assisi, of which not a single characteristic

writing, and in spite of its obviously temporary contents, it is attested to very well in the manuscripts. Analyzed according to centuries, it presents the following picture:

from the 13th century:

As (about mid-century);

from the 14th century:

Is_1 (1318-1350), V_1 (after 1340),
SFl (1343-1348), FO (about 1370),
BP (1385-1390), B_1 (the second half century),
Is_2, Si, Bc (14th/15th century);

from the 15th century:

Lt (c.1400), Bu and Ma (first half century),
Bs (after 1468), Li (1480), Ax, BM_5,
Fg, Lb, MS_2, V_2, and Wa;

from the 16th century:

iFR_1 and its related manuscripts.

If the readings of the individual manuscripts are compared with one another, then the following groups can be distinguished:[39]

a = As and MS_2; yet this latter manuscript in one passage, along with all the other manuscripts, disagrees with As. In a second passage it coincides with SFl and Lb, and in five passages it is alone with its own variations. In all other readings As and MS_2 agree. There exists, therefore, a very close relationship, yet

---

reading can be found in the text of Wadding. The Codex of Fano, which was used much by Wadding, has not been able to be verified up to this time. Since the text of Wadding has no special variants in common with the two manuscripts of the Library of San Isidoro, none of these can be identified with the MS Farense. Consequently, the text of Wadding is also based on manuscripts which are no longer known to us today; thus it deserves consideration.

[39]Certainly the groups of the manuscripts are better comprehended here than with those of the *Testament* 27-36, precisely because the oral tradition, which played an important role with the *Testament*, does not need to be taken into consideration here. Also, individual families of the *Testament* drop out completely, because the manuscripts do not contain our *Opusculum*. This is particularly true of group "d" below, which includes manuscripts from the territory of the medieval province of the Order in Cologne. Although the *Admonitions* are richly passed down in it, our piece is completely lacking. This might lie partly in the fact that most of the manuscripts preserved for us in this group have not originated in the monasteries of the Order of Lesser Brothers, but in other religious orders, for which this small rule was not of interest.

no direct dependency. Unfortunately the connecting links are unknown.[40]

b = V_1, SFl, B_1, Bu, Ma, Bs, and Lb. Here we are dealing with that group which we have labeled as "c" in the filiation of the manuscripts of the *Testament* of St. Francis.[41] This group agrees with (a) in decisive places, but in some other places it disagrees with (a) along with all the other manuscripts. A closer relationship exists within this group between Bu and Ma, which in three places offers unique readings against the five others, and in one place agrees with Lb against the four others. Occasionally Ma and Bs also agree. However, all the manuscripts of this group also exhibit characteristic peculiarities, which exclude a direct dependency. Within this group, manuscripts B_1 and Bs are very independent, but each in its own way. As with the *Testament*, so also here it must be stated that already the three oldest witnesses of this group (V, SFl and B_1), in spite of all their conformity, indicate three independent forms.[42] This clearly shows that in the course of transmission our text was worked on, although it cannot be established when and where this occurred in the individual manuscripts.

c = Is_3 and BM_5. Both are of Italian origin, although in many places they depart very decidedly from the other Italian manuscripts and coincide with (a) and (b). They have individual readings in common with (b) against (a), but also individual readings along with the rest of the manuscripts against (a) and (b). Thus they form a very independent group of transmission, which, with Is_3, reaches back likewise into the 14th century. However, they also contrast in such an independent way with each other that it cannot be proven that the more recent ones were copied from the older ones. In both (c) and (a), our

---

[40]Now the question naturally arises whether it is objectively founded to designate the families of manuscripts of the *Opuscula* according to those of the *Speculum perfectionis* as Cambell has done. In order to be able to establish genuine filiation, one must still proceed from the texts themselves.

[41]As far as can be established, these manuscripts stem from the region of the medieval Saxony Province of the Order of Lesser Brothers, and almost all of them offer the text or excerpts of the Legend "Fac secundum exemplar," which unfortunately has not been edited up till now. This legend is related more to Delormé's *Legenda* than, as Sabatier would like us to admit, to his *Speculum perfectionis*.

[42]Cfr. Esser, *Testament* 33.

opusculum has no association with the *Admonitions,* although Is$_3$, as well as (a), does present the texts of the *Admonitions.*[43]

d = FO, Bc, Wa, and iFr$_1$. These agree to a great extent with the group of Italian manuscripts yet to be characterized. They have, however, many common traits peculiar to themselves alone. This is so for FO and Wa, even more than for Bc. Here and there we also find an agreement with Fg and other manuscripts of the next group. Occasionally Lb from the group (b) is reckoned in this family.

e = Is$_1$, Fg, BP, Si, Lt, Ax, and V$_2$. In this group characteristic similarities are shown by Is$_1$ and Fg, and likewise by Is$_1$ and V$_2$, as also by Si and Lt. The codex Ax offers repeatedly readings which are characteristic for group (b) (above all Lb) and (d). On the whole this group disagrees just as much with (d), as it agrees with (d) against (a), (b), and (c), while at other times it maintains a common line with (b), (c), and (d) against (a).

With our present knowledge of the manuscript transmission, it is impossible to prove a strong filiation running within these groups. The individual lines of the transmission separate themselves in such a way that we have to work with too many unknowns, if we wish to establish exact stems. At any rate, the following can be asserted: group (a) stands out very independently within the whole manuscript transmission. In many places it is supported by (b) and (c); (d) and (e) vary the most from it. However, the (b)-(e) groups all together form a more tightly bound unity among themselves.

In what follows, first the text of the oldest witness (Codex As) will be compared with that of the other manuscripts. Also, as was the case repeatedly with the *Testament,* by doing this a definite text will emerge, which will allow many readings to be rejected as not belonging to the original text. Only obvious copying mistakes and isolated occurring transpositions will not be taken into consideration. Likewise no attention will be paid to the different kinds of writing.

---

[43]In this sense, Cambell, *Les écrits* 39, must be improved. Really only a few manuscript groups place our *Opusculum* at the conclusion of the *Admonitions.*

To begin with, it is striking that As and MS_2 do not have any heading, but begin immediately with the text. The original manuscript of group (b), of which we do not have knowledge, evidently found our *opusculum* already joined with the *Admonitions* (at the beginning of the 14th century!). Indeed the copyist considered this connection noteworthy, for which reason the copyist formulated a heading, which was then retained as a characteristic mark of this group: *"De religiosa conversatione in eremitoriis admonitio et doctrina, quam sanctus (beatus: V_1, SFl, Bs) Franciscus (pater eos: SFl) docuit"* (*edocuit*: B_1, Bu, Ma, Bs). Group (c) has likewise a heading, which is found nowhere else: *"Qualiter fratres debeant vivere in eremitoriis."* FO is the only manuscript which offers the heading which Boehmer and Lemmens have selected for their critical editions: *"De religiosa habitatione in eremitoriis."*

Already in this heading, something of the grouping of the manuscripts becomes evident. At the same time, however, the difficulty arises as to which reading should be given preference, since all emerge already in manuscripts of the 14th century.

Text of *Codex As*:

1. *Illi, qui volunt religiose stare[44] in eremis[45] sint[46] tres fratres[47] vel[48] quattuor[49] ad plus[50]; duo ex ipsis sint matres[51] et habeant[52] duos filios vel[53] unum ad minus.*

---

[44]vivere: c; habitare: Lt.

In the following, *add* indicates additions to the word marked with the number; *om* indicates the omission of the given words; *trsp* indicates a deviation of the word order. If one of these marks are present, then the text of codex As presented in the apparatus is to be read instead of that of the text indicated by the number. Unfortunately, the division into sentences introduced for the text of Lemmens by D. Vorreux, OFM, *Les opuscules de saint François d'Assisi* (Paris, 1955), is not able to be retained, since in many instances a different picture results.

[45]eremitoriis: b, c, d, e, w.

[46]sicut: V_1, Lb.

[47]*om*: BP, Lt, Bc, w.

[48]et: Bu, Ma, Bs; ac: BM_5; aut: V_1, SF1, B_1, Lb, Is_3, d, e, w.

[49]fratres: *add*. Bc.

[50]aut plurimi: Lb.

[51]patres: Bs (also in the following always instead of matres!).

[52]habent: V_2.

[53]aut: BP; vel ad unum ad minus: SF1.

2. Isti[54] *duo, qui sunt matres teneant vitam Marthae, et*[55] *duo filii teneant*[56] *vitam Mariae*[57] *et*[58] *habeant unum claustrum, in quo*[59] *unusquisque*[60] *habeat cellulam*[61] *suam, in qua oret et dormiat.*

3. *Et semper dicant completorium de die*[62] *statim*[63] *post occasum solis et*[64] *studeant retinere*[65] *silentium; et dicant horas suas et*[66] *in*[67] *matutinis surgant et primum*[68] *quaerant regnum Dei et iustitiam*[69] *eius.*

4. *Et*[70] *dicant primam*[71] *hora,*[72] *qua convenit,*[73] *et*[74] *post*[75] *tertiam*[76] *absolvant*[77] *silentium et possint*[78] *loqui et ire ad matres suas,*[79] *et,*

---

[54]Illi: b; Isti duo . . . vitam Mariae; *om:* c, d, e, w.

[55]alii: *add* b.

[56]filii teneant: *om* b.

[57]Illi (autem; add Is$_1$, Fg, BP, Lt,, V$_2$) qui tenuerint (tenuerunt): B$_1$, Bu, Ma, Is$_3$; tenebunt: d, e) vitam (locum: Bc) Mariae (Martae: Wa, Ax: Mariae Magdalenae: Lt): *add* b, c, d, e.

[58]*om* b, c, d, e.

[59]in quo et: b, c, d, e.

[60]quilibet: d, e. w.

[61]cellulam . . . dormiat locum suum ita quod nec (non: SF1, B$_1$, Ma, Lb, Bs, c, d, V$_2$; neque: BP, w) habitent (habitant: Lb) simul nec (neque: BP, w) cubent: all except a.

[62]de dic: *om* V$_1$, Si.

[63]statim . . . solis] quando sol revertitur ad occasum: d, e, w.

[64]*om* : w.

[65]tenere: MS$_2$, b, c, d, e, w.

[66]*om:* w.

[67]in . . . surgant] surgant ad matutinum: d, e, w.

[68]primo: V$_2$.

[69]vitam: Lt.

[70]hora congrua: *add* d, c, w; Et . . . convenit: *om* Is$_1$, Fg.

[71]et tertiam et: *add* b (except for Bs); et tertiam: *add* Bs, c, d, e, w.

[72] hora qua convenit: *om* c, d, e, w.

[73] ipsis: *add* Lb.

[74]*om* : b.

[75]horam: *add* b, c, d, e, w.

[76]tertiae: FO, Wa.

[77]sovant: BP, Si, w.

[78]possunt: Ma, Bs.

[79]patres suos: Bs; Et postea dicant sextam et nonam et vesperas tempore: *add* Fg.

quando[80] placuerit,[81] possint[82] petere ab eis[83] eleemosynam sicut[84] parvuli pauperes propter amorem Domini Dei. Et[85] postea dicant sextam[86] et nonam et vesperas[87] dicant[88] hora[89] qua convenit.

5. Et[90] in claustro,[91] ubi[92] morantur, non[93] permittant[94] aliquam[95] personam introire[96] et[97] neque ibi comedant.

6. Isti[98] fratres, qui sunt matres, studeant manere[99] remote[100] ab omni persona et[101] per obedientiam sui ministri[102] custodiant filios[103] suos ab omni persona, ut nemo possit loqui[104] cum eis. Et isti filii[105] non loquantur[106] cum aliqua persona nisi cum

---

[80]cis: *add* Is[1,] Fg.

[81]placuerint: MS[2].

[82]possunt: MS[2], SF1, Lb; possint *om* Wa.

[83]ab eis petere: *trsp* Lb, Bs, Ax; ab eis: *om* Si; eleemosynam ab eis: *trsp* MS[2].

[84]propter amorem Domini Dei (amore Domini Dei: Bu, Ma) sui (*om:* V[1], SF1) sicut parvuli pauperes: *trsp* b, c; propter amorem Domini (*om:* Fg) Dei sicut pauperes et (*om:* e) pauperculi: *trsp* d, e, w.

[85]*om:* w; Et . . . convenit: *om* Fg.

[86]sextam dicant: *trsp* V[1], SF1, B[1], Bu, Ma, c; dicant: *om* Lb, Bc.

[87]vesperos: Is[1], V[2].

[88]*om:* b, c, d, e, w.

[89]hora . . . convenit] tempore debito: d, e, w.

[90]*om:* w.

[91]claustrum: Si, Lt.

[92]in quo: MS[2].

[93]nec: Bs.

[94]permittunt: Is[3].

[95]mulierem sive quamcumque: *add* d.

[96]intrare: b (except for SF1, B[1]).

[97]sed neque ibi: b (except for SF1), c, BP, Si, Lt; sed nec ibi SF1, d, Ax; neque ibi: Is[1], Fg; sed nec ibi: V[2]; sed neque ullus ibi comedat: w.

[98]Et illi: b, c, d, e; Illi: w.

[99]remanere: Is[1], Fg.

[100]remoti: FO, Wa, Fg, Si, Lt; remote manere: *trsp* V[1].

[101]et . . . persona: *om* Ax, w.

[102]custodis: b, c, d, e, w.

[103]fratres: V[1], Lb.

[104]loqui possit: *trsp* MS[2]; possit eis loqui: BP, w; ita quod non loquantur cum eis: Lt.

[105]filii isti: *trsp* Bu, Ma; illi filii: Wa.

[106]loquentur: MS[2].

matribus suis[107] *et cum*[108] *ministro*[109] *et custode suo, quando placuerit*[110] *eos visitare*[111] *cum benedictione Domini*[112] *Dei.*

7. (*Filii*[113] *vero quandoque*[114] *officium matrum*[115] *assumant,*[116] *sicut vicissitudinaliter*[117] *eis pro tempore visum fuerit*[118] *disponendum,*[119] *quod*[120] *omnia supradicta*[121] *sollicite et studiose*[122] *studeant observare).*[123]

Commentary

Apart from the addition at the end (sentence 7), which will be treated separately, the many readings offer no *essential* variations, but only *grammatical* alterations. Mostly these variations are directed to the improvement of the Latin wording[124] or to the clarification of the often obscure text of the group of manuscripts. Apparently the set-up of the first hermitages in the Order was later on unfamiliar, with the result that the "obscure" text was deciphered by assimilating to it the circumstances of the later hermitages, which hermitages already bore a more cloistered character. Just this fact, however, to allude to it already here,

---

[107]*om:* Lb.

[108]cum ministro et: *om:* Is₃, Is₁, Fg, BP, V₂, w.

[109]ministro et: *om* b, BM₅, d, Si, Lt, Ax.

[110]placebit: d, e; eis: *add* b (except for Bs), BM₅; ei: *add* Bs, d, e, w; sibi: *add* Is₃.

[111]visitare ipsos (*om:* Fg): d, e, w.

[112]*om:* b, c, d, e, w.

[113]Filii . . . observare: *om* a.

[114]aliquando: Bu, Ma; quandocumque: Is₁, Fg, V₂.; quandoque: *om* Lb, d.

[115]quandoque: *add* Lb, d.

[116]sumant: c; assumunt: Is₁, V₂.

[117]sicut: *add* Is₃.

[118]pro tempore visum fuerit eis: *trsp* d, e, w.

[119]dispensandum: Lt.

[120]qui: B₁, c, d, e (except for Ax), w; quod . . . observare: *om* Si, Bs; Omnia quae supra dicta sunt studeant sollicite observare: *add* Bs.

[121]praedicta: Bu, Ma; sua dicta: Lb.

[122]studiose et sollicite: *trsp* d, e, w.

[123]For this final sentence, which is not found in the group (a) manuscripts, we take the text from V₁ as a starting point of comparison. A separate Excipit is not found in any of the manuscripts; also not as an Excipit to the *Admonitions.*

[124]This tendency is most strongly exhibited by Wadding, who, for example, cancels out as far as possible the "et" with which Francis so typically begins a sentence. He also refines the former ruggedness in contrast to the whole manuscript tradition. In many places, one cannot resist the impression that even Boehmer and Lemmens followed this tendency, when they selected the smoothest reading from the material at their disposal.

speaks for the authenticity and originality of the text which is found in the (a) group of manuscripts. This affirmation will now be pursued in detail.

In sentence 3 the expression of Codex As: *studeant retinere silentium,* which is indeed unusual, is improved in all the other manuscripts by *studeant tenere silentium.* We find the first formulation, however, word for word in the *Regula non bullata.*[125] Hence, it seems that Francis was accustomed to use this expression.

Also worthy of note is the wording *et in matutinis surgant* of the same sentence, which—literally taken—appears to oppose the custom of the midnight choir-prayer.[126] Thus the reading from (d) and (e) offers as grammatically more polished and sense-wise more precise: *et surgant ad matutinum.* But precisely by that alteration it shows that it is the more recent manuscript.

Also grammatically offensive is the *et neque ibi comedant* of group (a) manuscripts in sentence 5. Here the correction, *sed neque (nec) ibi comedant,* which is found in the other groups, is also still not the best. This phrase is expressed first *neque ibi comedant* by the reading in Is$_1$ and the closely related Fg manuscripts. This alteration, however, was apparently unknown by the manuscript W, so the writer produces the best correction of all: *sed neque ullus ibi comedant.*

To be considered as a grammatical correction is likewise the *manere remoti* instead of *manere remote* found in sentence 6 of some of the Italian manuscripts. Certainly the whole remaining tradition is opposed to it. Here belong also the changes in sentence 4 from *absolvant silentium* to *solvant silentium,* in sentence 5 from *in claustro* to *in claustrum,* and in sentence 6 from *possint loqui cum eis* to *possint eis loqui.* Also we should note in this connection that the *et* at the beginning of the sentences is frequently crossed out in later text witnesses.[127]

---

[125]Chapter 11: "immo studeant retinere silentium"; *Analekten* 12, *Opuscula* 40.

[126]Cfr. 2 Celano 168: "in quadam eremo . . . horam nocturno tempore in qua sanctus ad divina obsequia surgere solitus erat"; Three Companions §41: "Surgebant in media nocte soliciti et orabant devotissime. . . . " For both, the expression "surgant ad matutinum" fits better than "in matutinis surgant."

[127]Cfr. Esser, *Testament* 86-91.

As the last example of this type, we cite two readings from the final sentence (sentence 7). Here the *quod* of group (b) is apparently linguistically harsher than the *qui* of other manuscript groups, and also the transposition *tudiose et sollicite studeant* sounds better than *sollicite et studiose studeant* with the two almost similar sounding words in succession. The most radical resolution in both cases is that of Bs: *Omnia quae supra dicta studeant sollicite observare.*

As brief as our text is, it too exhibits quite clearly in its transmission that law of improving the Latin wording of St. Francis, which trait is even more noticeable in the text-history of his *Testament.* We can see exactly in that a proof for the more authentic text-form of Codex As,[128] which comes closest to the Latin style of St. Francis, which we know to have been clumsy and often incorrect.

Another law of transmission, which likewise had been observed in the text-history of the *Testament,*[129] is also clearly discernible in our text, at least in one instance: namely, the influence of the later texts by similar formulations in better known writings of St. Francis. In the *Regula bullata* (chapter 2) and in the *Testament* (chapter 8) we find: *cum benedictione Dei.*[130] Therefore it does not surprise us when the later manuscripts have the short form of the *Rule,* or of the *Testament,* respectively against As (*cum benedictione Domini Dei*).

What prompts the other amendments in the text can many times be easily discerned. In certain cases, however, the resolution will certainly be more difficult. In the first sentence we immediately run into one of these latter cases.

In sentence 1, (a) reads: *stare in eremis,* while all the other manuscripts proffer *stare in eremitoriis.* That originally *eremis* could have stood here is shown perhaps by the heading of Fo, Wa, and Fg, which manuscripts have in the heading *in eremo,* or *in eremis,* respectively, although they offer in the text itself the

---

[128]The MS2 manuscript related to it has for its part already linguistic improvements, which are, however, peculiar only to it: "possunt" instead of "possint" (sentence 4); "in quo" instead of "ubi" (sentence 5); "loquentur" instead of "loquantur." In all these instances, As probably offers the unimproved, and because the poorer, therefore also the older, reading.

[129]Cfr. Esser, *Testament* 78-85.

[130]*Analekten* 31 or 38 respectively; *Opuscula* 65 or 80 respectively.

second reading *in eremitoriis*. Here it would seem that probably an old traditional wording has been preserved, for this title or heading can only have originated from a text which took its reading from (a). An interesting transitional solution in this connection is that offered by iFr$_1$, which places side by side for a choice *heremo* and *heremitorii*. A conclusive clarification in this case also cannot be found in the other writings of St. Francis. In the *Regula non bullata* (chapter 7), the manuscripts have a great diversity between *in eremis* or *in eremitoriis* respectively,[131] while in the "Letter to a Minister" we find *eremitorium*.[132] Judging from that, we can say that both expressions appear to have been synonymous for Francis himself. Probably we ought to decide in favor of *eremis* with As, since this is the older and more unusual manner of expression.

Still more difficult at first glance is the solution to the divergent readings in sentence 2. Here we are confronted actually with three grammatically unlike traditions, which hardly are derived from a common source. For the sake of clarity, they are presented here side by side:

As	V$_1$	Is$_1$
Isti duo qui sunt matres, teneant vitam Marthae, et duo filii teneant vitam Mariae, et habeant unum claustrum, in quo unusquisque habeat cellulam suam, in qua oret et dormiat.	*Illi duo qui sunt matres, teneant vitam Marthae et alii duo vitam Mariae. Illi duo qui tenuerint vitam Mariae habeant unum claustrum et unusquisque habeat locum suum ita quod non habitent simul nec cubent.*	*Illi duo teneant vitam Marthae et alii duo vitam Mariae Magdalenae. Illi autem qui tenebunt vitam Mariae habeant unum claustrum et quilibet habeat locum suum, ita quod nec habitent simul nec cubent.*

Apparently the mode of expression of Codex As is not clear enough as to whether the *claustrum* is for the mothers or only for

---

[131]*Analekten* 8: "in eremitoriis"; *Opuscula* 34: "in eremis." Boehmer presents the second reading in the critical apparatus.

[132]*Analekten* 28; *Opuscula* 108.

the sons or for all. From the longer text it follows now that the enclosed area of the *claustrum* is only for the sons: for these leave it in order to go to their mothers and to eat there, which it is forbidden to do in the *claustrum* itself. The texts of groups (c), (d), and (e) follow that opinion for this situation. All ambiguity is removed. Only the two manuscripts Wa and Ax contest that opinion. According to them, the mothers live in the *claustrum*. Clearly we cannot be dealing here with a copying mistake, because these two manuscripts belong to different groups. In any case, they prove there exists here an obscure passage. Perhaps they also had in mind the later hermitages, in which separate hollows or cells lay scattered around a small enclosed area, as it still can be shown today in the Carceri at Assisi.

That the cells in the hermitages had been established for prayer, as As alone indicates, is proven from the unanimous finding of the Legends.[133] If the subsequent manuscripts since the 14th century suppress this, they do so deliberately. Apparently there exists behind their formulation the concept of the hermitage (*eremitorium*) as the small cloister in which there was an oratory or a chapel,[134] and probably also a dormitory (*dormitorium*) in which each one had his own sleeping place, but no cell.[135] In such hermitages the precept of the "cloister of

---

[133]1 Celano 50; Julian of Speyer, *Vita* 31; 2 Celano 35, 45, 100, 169, 171, 178; LM V, 5; XI, 11 etc. Also the *Specula perfectionis* very clearly make this distinction. According to them, on Mount Alverna, separated from the dwelling of the other Brothers, Francis had a "cella ubi orabat et iacebat" (cfr. the text of codex As!) and a "cella ubi comedabat." Both expressions emphatically attest to the conditions in which our *opusculum* originated, but, along with that, to the originality of the reading which the group (a) offers (cfr. *Speculum Sabatier* 117, 1-6; Delormé, *Legenda* 50).

[134]Cfr. the bull of Pope Honorius III from 3.12.1224 (*Quia populares tumultus*), "quia populares tumultus . . . fugientes secretos recessus libenter appetitis, ut in sancta quiete liberius orationi vacare possitis . . . indulgemus, ut in locis et oratoriis vestris cum viatico altari possitis Missarum sollemnia et alia officia celebrare" (*Bull Franc* I,20). The introduction of this privilege attests to the move to the contemplative-solitary life, which was peculiar to the Lesser Brothers. Besides the right to have hermitages, they obtained also the privilege of having their own oratories. Both appear to be worthy of note for the early history of the Order.

[135]Cfr. the *Statuta Narbonensia* of St. Bonaventure (1260) in: *Opera omnia* VII, 454a and 455b. For a complete treatment, cfr. also the marginal notes to a report of the Delormé, *Legenda* (12), according to which a house was built near the Portiuncula because the many Brothers there "non habebant locum ubi possent quiescere et dicere horas suas, ita quod oportebat dare illis loca sua ubi iacebant. . . ." From this foundation, there developed in the later hermitages those conditions as they are somewhat graphically portrayed by Salimbene in his *Chronicle* (MGSS XXXII, 225, 289,

cells," expressed in the manuscripts of group (b)-(e) would make sense. At any rate, the statements of group (a) coincide with the witness of all the old Franciscan sources.

Also of interest is the deviation of group (d) and (e) against (a), (b), and (c) with reference to the time assigned for Compline. While the latter assigned the time "immediately after sunset," the others write: "when the sun nears its setting." It may have been that this corresponded to the later Ceremonial of the Order, according to which Compline was to follow immediately upon the evening collation.[136] However, this collation certainly took place still in daylight.

In a certain sense, the prescriptions in (a) for the praying of the small hours are also not clear. Since it is only mentioned here that the silence which began with Compline is to be broken after Terce, it is not surprising, if in later manuscripts, it is expressly noted that Terce is to be prayed. This occurs in group (b) still rather awkwardly,[137] whereas the rest of the manuscript groups (c) through (e) have a smoothflowing text. Then, together with the above change, the *hora, qua convenit* is replaced by *hora congrua*. This is probably an assimilation to the terminology of the statutes of the Order.[138] For the inconsequential transposition at the end of sentence 4, it suffices to say that the formulation *sicut parvuli pauperes* (a), (b), (c), corresponds more to the language used by St. Francis. The *pauperculi* of many manuscripts can be traced to a copying mistake, which is also found in the tradition of the *Testament* (chapter 12).[139]

569, etc.), and as they are expressed in the variations of later manuscripts; however, they still did not pertain to the original life in the hermitages.

[136]H. Golubovich, OFM, *Caeremoniale Ord. Minorum vetustissimam*, §8; in: *ArchFrancHist* 3 (1910): 65. The formulation of the groups (d) and (e) fits better with the hymn of Compline already existing at that time: "Te lucis ante terminum . . ."; cf. G. Abbate, OFMConv, "Il primitivo breviario francescano (1224-1227)," *MiscFranc* 60 (1960): 98.

[137]The copyist of Bs seeks to circumvent this awkwardness when he formulates: "Et dicant primam et tertiam hora qua convenit. Post tertiam horam absolvant. . . ." That is for this level of tradition a similar smooth formulation, as, on their part, the groups (d) and (e) present.

[138]Cfr. for example *Statua Narbonensia*, op. cit. 453b.

[139]Cfr. the *Regula non bullata* 23 (*Analekten* 24, *Opuscula* 59); *Ultima voluntas* (35, 76); *Testamentum* 11 and 13 (39f, 81f); *Epistola ad capitulum*, Prol. (57, 99); *Epistola ad populorum rectores* (70, 111); cfr. Esser, *Testament* 47.

The change from *hora qua convenit* to *tempore debito* in the same section, which signifies no essential change, is probably to be settled only on the basis of the age of the manuscripts. Now most of the old manuscripts have the first mentioned reading; that reading therefore should be retained.

In sentence 5 we find the addition in group (d) manuscripts: *aliquam mulierem sive quamcumque personam,* which likewise lies as the basis for the translation in iFR₁. This addition, in so far as it shows that there was an attempt to later clarify the text, should be considered here in light of the cloister regulations in force at that time.[140] It is particularly this obvious addition or insertion that fills one with a certain mistrust against codex FO, in which Boehmer and above all Lemmens put great confidence, even if not in this particular passage. (Compare the title!)[141]

A somewhat difficult problem is presented in Section 6 by the statements about the higher superior of the friars in the hermitages. In all the manuscripts, with the exception of group (a), he is called "custos." Group (a) reads first "minister" and, a little further on, "minister et custos."[142] Here the visitation of the friars in the hermitages appears as the chief task of this superior. However, already by the *Statutes of Narbonne* (1260), the usual visitation of the friars had been transferred to the custos as the leader of a small administrative unit within the province, as he generally appears in these statutes as the one responsible for the life of the Order in his custody.[143] Concerning this judicial status, it was natural to correct our text to correspond

---

[140]Cfr. 3 Celano 37.

[141]In that same connection, compare also in sentence 4: "post horam tertiae," as also in sentence 6: "remoti."

[142]One should not be led astray here by the text of Boehmer. He combines the "cum ministro et custode suo" of group (a) with the "quando placuerit eis eos visitare" of group (b) and (d); a combination which has no foundation in the manuscripts (cfr. above footnote 44).

[143]Rubr. VIII; op. cit. 458b. For visitation, custos and custody, cfr. Esser, *Ordo fratrum minorum. Über seine Anfänge und ursprünglichen Zielsetzungen,* in: *FranzStud* 42 (1960): 95-129 and 297-355; 43 (1961) 171-215 and 309-347. Since this investigation was printed in two different volumes of the *FranzStud* and the page numbers are therefore overlapping, we will cite them in the following pages by reference to them first by the chapter number, then by the page numbering.

with it, which text still retained the duty of visitation by the minister, which was stipulated by the *Rules* of the Order.[144]

A correction concerning the later conditions in the Order also underlies the second instance. Here we find according to (a): "minister et custos." Apparently this is the older reading; for (b) and BM5 present the following text: *cum custode suo, quando placuerit* eis *eos visitare*.[145] These manuscripts present us with an unfamiliar text, which expanded the text of As with an *eis*, because it considered *minister et custos* in the sense of the later development as two separate officials. The manuscript As, as so often, has preserved here the oldest tradition, according to which *minister et custos* is a similar synonymous expression like *minister et servus*.[146] Then the *quando placuerit*, just as in sentence 4, does not need any completion by an *eis, sibi* or *ei*.[147] This expression could be translated suitably by *ad libitum* (at will).

Finally, there is still the question of the authenticity of Section 7, which is missing in the group (a) manuscripts. Apparently it was also missing already in the text-copy which the copyist of Codex As used. For on folio 43v there would have been enough space to include the sentence if it had existed in the original copy. Why it was missing in this original copy cannot be surmised, since we are left only with conjectures. On the other hand, this passage is attested to uniformly in all the rest of the manuscript tradition, disregarding the three transpositions and the isolated, inconsequential variations.

A statement from 2 Cel 178 speaks for the authenticity of this passage. According to Celano, a Spanish cleric related to St. Francis:

---

[144]*Regula non bullata* 4, *Regula bullata* 10 (*Analekten* 4f and 34, *Opuscula* 29f. and 71f.). For the duty of the visitation of the Minister, cfr. Esser, ibid. III, 326ff. If in the *Speculum Sabatier* our *Opusculum* is applied to the Brothers leading a contemplative life at the Portiuncula, it would say exactly as in As: "Et ipsi non loquantur cum aliqua persona, nisi . . . cum ministro, quando visitaret eos" (55, 36); of the same tenor: Delormé, *Legenda* 10. Thus the text of our codex As stands behind this tradition!

[145]This "eis" cannot refer to the "Mothers" since the right of visitation belongs only to the Minister and later the custos. Therefore the copyists of Bs and Is3 seek to avoid this difficulty by replacing the "eis"with "ei" or with "sibi," respectively.

[146]Cfr. Esser, *Ordo fratrum minorum III*, 312.

[147]One notices that also here the groups (d) and (e) already early offer a refined text: "quando placebit ei visitare ipsos."

> Your friars are living in our land in a small hermitage.
> They have so arranged their way of living that half
> of them take care of domestic needs and the other half
> spend their time in contemplation. In this way, each
> week those that lead the active life exchange with
> those who lead the contemplative life, and the quiet
> of those giving themselves to contemplation is changed
> for the business of work.

This alternating between the life of Martha and that of
Mary corresponds exactly with this last sentence of the "Rule for
Hermitages," which was followed also in other details by the
friars in the Spanish hermitage. Since the regular alternating of
the "Rule for Hermitages" was left to the judgment of the friars,
the weekly rotation, which was observed here, would be a living
explanation of our sentence. Francis, therefore, praised these
brothers, "who by their good example cause their profession to
give off a fragrant odor." Thus Francis approved their way of
living in all its details. We could also conclude that what was
said about their regular alternating of tasks was likewise in
agreement with his will. Therfore, in spite of its absence in
Codex As, our final sentence can be considered in accord with the
mind of St. Francis for the life of the friars in the hermitages.

Another indication of the authenticity of this sentence is the
use of the pronoun *quod*, which is typical of St. Francis. This
quod is attested to by five manuscripts of group (b) and by the
Codex Ax, while all the others substitute for *quod* the more
correctly sounding word *qui*. This was done because the later
copyists did not take into consideration that here the *quod* took
the place of the common *per que*, which can mean just as well *ut*
as *quod* and *quia*, and therefore also require the subjunctive
studeant after it. This misunderstanding is likewise familiar from
the text-history of the *Testament*. [148]

Not last of all, we might ask who—after the introduction of
the house superior in the Order and after the clericalization of
the Order (since 1239), which also was accepted by the later
Spirituals[149]—who could have had any interest in inventing such

---

[148]Cfr. Esser, *Testament* 90.

[149]Sabatier, *Speculum* 55, 33-36; Delormé, *Legenda* 10. Perhaps we ought to refer
also yet in this connection to the use of the word "studeant," which is used not only

an "impossible" regulation for this later age, if there did not exist a genuine piece of tradition? Everything considered then, we should recognize this sentence, from the standpoint of its wording and its content, as going back to Francis.

In conclusion we can say that it is certainly not possible—as with the *Testament* of St. Francis—to arrive in any way at the original text of our *opusculum*, because even any mention of it is lacking in documents that are older than our manuscripts.[150] But it can be shown that the text of Codex As has preserved, throughout the manuscript, the older reading, which corresponds to the original conditions in the Order. Priority, therefore, belongs to it for (a) text-edition. Only for the last sentence must the text be completed according to the testimony of the other manuscripts.[151] In any case, in a critical edition the most important readings of the later groups cannot be neglected.

We must now further consider the question whether the manuscripts present this "Rule for Hermitages" as the work of St. Francis. This is the case very definitely in the *incipit* (the introduction) of group (b) manuscripts, likewise in the group (d) and (e) manuscripts, which have this work at the conclusion of

---

in this rule twice in the same sense, but also in the other writings of St. Francis; cfr. *Regula non bullata* 2, 6, 7, 9, 11, and 17 (three times!); *Regula bullata* 2; *Admonitiones* 3; cfr. also *Epistola ad capitulum* 6: "operentur et studiose reponant." At the same time it is striking that this word appears only in such writings in which Francis is speaking to his Brothers in the Order.

[150]To be sure, the *Specula perfectionis* (cfr. above footnote 64) give reports of a testament which Francis "circa mortem suam" published for the "locus sanctae Mariae de Portiuncula" (as to the formal and substantive misgivings against this oft-reported mandate, cfr. Esser, *Testament* 14-16); behind these reports which are authenticated since the beginning of the 14th century, there exists apparently the knowledge of what our *Opusculum* describes. These witnesses are worthwhile for our question, in so far as they show precisely that in the Franciscan tradition the knowledge of this small work of St. Francis was alive, even if it is applied in the *Specula* reports also somewhat clumsily to a "Testament" for the Portiuncula. In the second part of our investigation, we will come back to individual statements of the report. In 2 Celano 19, in a similar report, there are gathered together, by the expression "ceteris regularibus institutis," the characteristics which later are found in the *Specula* reports. We are tempted by a comparison of these reports to see in this expression of the Celano report a proof for our *Opusculum*.

[151]We have referred to a similar procedure with the "Laudes Dei altissimi", which Francis wrote on the cartula for Brother Leo, which is still preserved. Here the conclusion is no longer legible on the original and can be completed only according to old manuscripts. Thus the copyist of As could have been provided with the original of our small rule in which the conclusion was no longer legible, while the other groups go back to older copies which still presented the complete text. Still this remains only a conjecture, which should be advanced with the proffered caution.

the *Admonitions* and state these expressly as coming from Francis.[152] Is₃ in group (e) begins: "Certain sayings of our blessed Father Francis." Then follow the *Admonitions*, "Letter to the Faithful," our "Rule for Hermitages" and excerpts from the *"De legenda antiqua."* BM₅ has our "Rule for Hermitages" with the above given *incipit* proper to group (e) after the *Opusculum* which has the *incipit* "Letter of St. Francis to a certain minister." Finally in group (a) manuscripts, it is also found, although without a heading, in a collection of the works of St. Francis. Therefore, we can conclude with Lemmens: "The manuscripts know no other author."[153]

Along with these *external* criteria for the authenticity of this small work of St. Francis, various authors suggest also *internal* criteria, especially the contents and style. How very much the contents of this "Rule for Hermitages" coincide with the earliest conditions in the Order of Friars Minor has already been shown in individual instances. This, however, will be proven with still greater clarity in the second part of this research. That many elements of style are typical of St. Francis is shown, if only briefly, by much that has been already stated.

First of all, here, just as in the *Testament*,[154] the connecting *et* is used very frequently. Thus the various regulations in sentence 3 and 4 are connected by a nine-fold *et*. This method of connecting so simply leads even in sentence 5 to the incorrectly formulated *et neque*, which caused so much grief to later copyists.

Typical also is the use of the pronouns *ille* and *iste* as a substitute for the definite article, as also *suus* instead of *ejus*. Again, as in the *Testament*, all quotations are missing, except for the original application of the word of the Lord in Lk 12:31.[155] Therefore, Boehmer could correctly state that this "Rule for Hermitages" belongs to the shorter *Opuscula*, "in which Francis alone speaks; which works are thus all the more valuable, if one wishes to get to know Francis."[156]

---

[152]Only the codex Lt begins the *Admonitions* without Incipit. Ax gives to the whole collection the inscription: "Incipit speculum fratrum minorum de mirabilibus dictis et factis beati Francisci et sociorum ejus."

[153]*Opuscula* 177.

[154]Cf. for the following: Esser, *Testament*, 86-91.

[155]Ibid. 114f.

[156]*Analekten* XLVII.

For a definitive edition of the *Opuscula* of St. Francis, we would like, as the result of our investigation, to propose the following text, which is based on codex 338, taking the last sentence from the oldest manuscripts of group (b). In the critical format there will be cited only the variations of the groups and specific other variations which are of special importance for the history of the text. From that it will become evident on what grounds the editions of Boehmer and Lemmens arrived at their text. That is important, because these editions, with some precaution, still continue to be useful. For all further questions of the history of the text, the complete presentation of all the variations which have been presented in this section will have to be consulted.

Part Two

The Significance of the "Rule for Hermitages"

In the first part of our investigation we were able to show that our "Rule" must be considered as belonging to the genuine works of St. Francis, whose original form can at least be approximately restored. Now we shall consider some general questions which can aid in a better understanding of this work. An interpretation of the individual sections will then follow these considerations.

1. The Name

The assignment of a name to this piece of writing has always been a problem, in the Middle Ages as well as in the more recent research about Francis. While Wadding had still retained the title of many manuscripts,[157] Papini believed that he had to correct him in this, whereas he formulated the title, probably in conjunction with the introductory sentence of Codex As: *Regula pro fratribus volentibus stare in eremis.*[158] Ehrle also speaks of "the regulation which Francis is supposed to have drawn up for the brothers living in hermitages."[159] Sabatier favors the expression

---

[157]*Opuscula* 290: "De religiosa habitatione in eremitoriis."
[158]*Storia di s. Francesco II*, 148.
[159]*ArchLitKirGesch III*, 604.

"règlement," but uses likewise in other places "règle des frères ermites."[160] Boehmer writes in a very general way: "the note on the religious life in the hermitage,"[161] and Van Ortroy just as cautiously uses these words: "les recommandations *De religiosa habitatione in eremo.*"[162] Both critical editions at the beginning of this century had selected the Latin title *De religiosa habitatione in eremo* in preference to all the other manuscripts, although it is found only in Codex PO.[163] W. von den Steinen lists our work among the "scattered regulatory fragments" and he gives it the title "Of Pious Living in Hermitages."[164] The title of Esser-Hardick, "The Life of the Brothers in Hermitages," stays away from any detailed characterization.[165] A similar uncertainty is found also in the best known French translations: "La vie religieuse dans les ermitages,"[166] "Du séjour dans les ermitages,"[167] and "Règle pour les ermitages."[168]

Already this title shows then that most of the authors, even though they shun the word "Rule," still are inclined to see in this work a regulatory document. But, if it contains, as Goetz already correctly observed, "precise stipulations for the life and the division of the day of the Brothers staying in the hermitages,"[169] it is in fact a rule!

---

[160]*Vie de s. Francois* 125; *ColEtDoc* I, CLXXI u. 1; p. 26 n.1; II, CXXV, CXLVII.

[161]*Analekten* XVII and XXVI.

[162]*AnalBoll* 24 (1905) 413.

[163]*Analekten* 68, *Opuscula* 83. In accord with that, M. Rederstorff, OFM, *Die Schriften des hl. Franziskus von Assisi*, translates: "Vom religiösen Leben in der Einsiedelei" (Of the Religious Life in the Hermitage) (93); similarly O. Bonmann, OFM, *Die Schriften des hl. Franziskus von Assisi* (Freiburg im Br., 1940) 54. Unfortunately the German word used "religiös" does not have the double meaning of the Latin "religiosus" and doesn't imply "ordensmässig" (belonging to an Order).

[164]W. von den Steinen, *Franziskus und Dominikus. Leben und Schriften* (Breslau, 1926), 81f; most recently again in: *Franziskus von Assisi Die Werke Die Blümlein* (Hamburg, 1958) 29.

[165]K. Esser and L. Hardick, *Die Schriften des hl. Franziskus von Assisi, Franziskanische Quellenschriften I* (Werl i.W., 1956) 90.

[166]D. Vorreux, OFM, *Les opuscules de s. François d'Assise* (Paris, 1955) 159.

[167]A. Masseron, *Saint François d'Assise Oeuvres latines et Cantique de frère soleil* (Paris, 1959) 109.

[168]Willibrord de Paris, OFMCap, *Les écrits de saint François d' Assise* (Paris, 1959) 179; *Le message spirituel de s. François d'Assise dans ses écrits* (Blois, 1960) 19 and 347.

W. Perquin, *St. Franciscus' Word* (Antwerp, no date), translates: "Over het verblijf in de kluizen" (73); nevertheless, the question remains whether the Franciscan hermitages are to be considered cloisters in the genuine sense.

[169]*Quellen* 45.

Since a title is missing in the manuscripts of group (a), and since in the rest of the groups no uniform title has been handed down,[170] we might, with the same right as with the other Writings of St. Francis,[171] give this small work a title that is meaningful. Therefore we select for the Latin text: *Regula pro eremitoriis data.*

By that title we furnish this work with a name, which name indicates at the same time the essential contents.

2. General Character

Since this "Rule for Hermitages" is transmitted in many manuscripts in close association with the collection of the *Admonitions,* the question might justly be raised whether this association is based on objective grounds. Considered purely externally, it might be recognized as quite significant that only the four manuscripts of group (a) and (c) do not have this association. On the other hand, however, we must also consider that there are known to exist today still twenty-six other manuscripts for the *Admonitions,* which do not contain our "Rule for Hermitages" at all. To these belong above all the codex X, Plut. XIX dextr. of the Laurentiana at Florence, which was copied toward the end of the 13th century,[172] as well as several manuscripts from the first half of the 14th century. Even some manuscripts of the beginning of the 16th century are not acquainted with the "Rule for Hermitages" as a permanent part of the *Admonitions.* Thus we would hardly be able to speak of a conclusive manuscript tradition in this question. We need only to be reminded of the noteworthy formulation of the title in the group (b) manuscripts in this connection.[173] It indicates sufficiently that also in the Middle Ages this association was felt unsuitable and that therefore attempts were made to justify it by a somewhat artificial title.

---

[170]In the manuscript groups (b), (d), and (c), whose titles begin "de," we might have here an assimilation that is carried over from the Chapter titles of the *Admonitions.*

[171]e.g. *Regula non bullata, Regula bullata,* or the various Letters, respectively.

[172]Cambell, *Les écrits* 34, footnote 124.

[173]Cfr. above p. 155.

But also content-wise this writing does not fit with the *Admonitions,* even if we do not see in this, as Boehmer does, "a very artless indeed, but cohesive exhortation."[174] The tenor of the *Admonitions* is certainly very general, and throughout it strikes at the inner spirit of the Lesser Brothers, while our "Rule for Hermitages" describes in a regulatory fashion the external life of just certain brothers. Not least of all, we can point to the difference of style between the *Admonitions* and the "Rule for Hermitages." These former are in harmony more with the longer writings of the saint, while the small "Rule" appears to be related stylistically to the shorter writings, the *Testament, Letter to a Minister,* and even individual chapters of the *Regula non bullata.* From all of this, we can conclude that this "Rule for Hermitages" probably has been from the beginning an independent work of St. Francis and therefore must be considered in a class by itself.[175]

It is more difficult to solve the question of the relation of this text to the two *Rules* for the whole Order of Lesser Brothers as these are preserved in the present corpus of the Writings. Already Sabatier toyed with the possibility that in this piece of writing "we have a fragment of the *Rule* which was put together about 1217."[176] The opinion of Goetz that we are dealing here with a previous work or a supplement to the *Rule* of the Order has already been mentioned. Both interpretations are conjectures which are not able to be confirmed by the source material with which we are presently acquainted. We might most simply see in this "Rule for Hermitages" a supplement to the *Rule* of the Order. For, as the form of the contemplative, eremitical way of life in the Order more firmly took shape alongside the itinerant preaching, Francis apparently also gave a *forma vivendi* to it, similar to the way he had given such a *forma vivendi* to St. Clare and her sisters.[177] Since this "Rule for Hermitages," however, regulated preferably only the external

---

[174]*Analekten* XXVII and XCI footnote 1.

[175]Cfr. Masseron, *Oeuvres* 109; "une oeuvre distincte"; an assertion which is proved by him very briefly.

[176]*Vie de s. François* 125 footnote 1. This rule of 1217, with which Sabatier works, is, it is true, a great unknown to this day.

[177]*Regula s. Clarae* VI, 3. *Analekten* 35, *Opuscula* 75.

life in the hermitages, it probably should be presumed that for all other matters, the *Rule* of the whole Order which was in force at any given time had to be observed. Our text gave just additional stipulations for those brothers who no longer traveled in the world but stayed in fixed establishments,[178] whose particular form of life had not been taken into consideration in the *Later Rule,* even less than in the *Earlier Rule.*[179]

In this sense, Sabatier might have been right when he saw in our writing one of the perhaps numerous regulations which Francis issued for individual cases and about which much information is retained in later legends.[180]

3. Time of Composition

Neither in the text of this "Rule for Hermitages," nor in the manuscript tradition, do we find any direct statements which make it possible for us to establish with any accuracy its time of composition.[181] The time proposed by Sabataier, "about 1217,"[182] is quite as hypothetical as the cautious proposal of Rederstorff: "This work might have originated about the year 1218; in any case, before the definitive confirmation of the Later Rule in the year 1223."[183] The same indecision is found in the statement of P. Willibrord de Paris: "This juridic text might be possibly later than 1223."[184] Also, none of the authors named here give any sound proof for their conjecture.

Perhaps, from the contents of the text we can present some indirect proofs which will make it possible to pin down somewhat more exactly the question of when this material was written.

---

[178]Cfr. *Regula non bullata* 15; *Analekten* 14, *Opuscula* 43.

[179]Cfr. ibid. 7: "Caveant sibi fratres, ubicumque fuerint, in eremitoriis (eremis) vel in aliis locis, quod nullum locum sibi approprient nec alicui defendant"; *Analekten* 8, *Opuscula* 34. Thus there apparently existed this way of life, which is otherwise not visible in the two existing rules. It is mentioned likewise in the *Letter to a Minister:* "Et istud sit tibi plus quam eremitorium," *Analekten* 28, *Opuscula* 108.

[180]Sabatier and Little II 100ff. Sabatier is accordingly thinking especially of chapter 55 and 82 of his publication of the *Speculum perfectionis.*

[181]Cfr. Boehmer, *Analekten* XLI. Only he has pursued this question minutely for the *Opuscula.*

[182]*Vie de s. François* 125, footnote 1.

[183]*Die Schriften* 94. His statements are almost a literal presentation of the French translation of the writings by Vorreux, *Les opuscules,* 157.

[184]*Les escrits* 179.

First of all, the year 1217 furnishes us with a *terminus post quam*. In this year, the office of minister in the Order was introduced. This is certainly set forth in our text as something known and existing. A certain time period must still be allowed after this terminus until this office arrived at the state of being taken for granted that is evident in this "Rule for Hermitages."

Next, it is striking that this writing does not have any of those strong expressions, which we meet so often in the *Later Rule* and in the *Testament*: *praecipio firmiter, tenantur per obedientiam, per obedientiam iniungo*. In our text, all the precepts are presented in those subjunctive forms which are also used with preference in the *Later Rule* and in the *Letter to a Minister*.[185] We are permitted, therefore, to move time-wise in the vicinity of these writings; at any rate before the final "Rule for Hermitages."

To this terminus also would agree the observation that this writing certainly is to be fixed before the bull *Quia populares tumultus* (December 3, 1224), indeed, before the other bull *Devotionis vestrae* (March 29, 1222), because in our "Rule" there is no indication at all of an oratory, in which the brothers could pray the Divine Office.[186] After the decree of this papal document, such rooms for prayer were introduced. And after that Francis urged "that all the brothers who could, should assemble in the oratory and there sing the psalms with wisdom."[187] However, where had that before been carried out but in the hermitages? That our text might have been composed before the above-named papal documents, can probably also be concluded from the fact that in it there is mention only of the canonical Hours, not however, of the Mass. Perhaps for that reason, the

---

[185]The *Earlier Rule* uses such a formulation only in the final sentence, and, on the other hand, avoids it even in chapter 13 and 19, which are chapters involving penalties. For this latter chapter, a comparison with the tenth chapter of the *Testament* is very revealing in this respect. The plan for a new chapter of the rule found in the *Letter to a Minister* also has a sharp formulation of this kind only in one place.

[186]Cfr. above Part I, pp. 140ff.

[187]2 Celano 197. The pertinent remarks in Esser, *Testament*, 177, should also be considered regarding this question. The opinion expressed there, as if the aforementioned bulls were the foundation for the prescriptions of our rule about the hours of the Office, is not able to be upheld, since we know that Francis and his Brothers also recited the hours of the Office at other times outside of churches and oratories (cfr. 2 Celano 96). In this connection, consider also: Sabatier, *Speculum* 10,18; Lemmens, *Speculum 30*; and Delormé, *Legenda* 16.

expression of the *Rule* of the Order, *divinum officium,* which embraced the prayer of the Hours and the Mass, was avoided. In accord with that, the beginning of 1222, or certainly the end of 1224, would be the *terminus ante quem.* The "Rule for Hermitages" accordingly must have originated in the years 1217 to 1222/24. On stylistic grounds, however, an origin before 1222 is very probable. Along with this still quite wide estimate, the opinion of Ehrle still remains valid: "It is indeed very possible that these regulations touch upon the tradition reaching back to the first years of the foundation of the Order."[188]

4. Interpretation

In the following pages we will attempt to place selected texts from the "Rule for Hermitages" in their historical context in order to draw out their significance for the early history of the Order of Lesser Brothers. In doing that it should become self-evident whether this document is as insignificant for the understanding of St. Francis and his brotherhood as many modern authors have mentioned.[189]

1. *Those who wish to dwell in a religious way in hermitages may be three brothers or, at the most, four; let two of these be the 'mother' and have two 'sons,' or at least one.*

First of all, the expression *religiose stare in eremis* needs to be explained. *Religiose* means neither "blessedly" nor "piously" nor "religiously,"[190] but "in a religious way." For what is described in this "Rule for Hermitages" is the life of members of an Order as it was being attempted at that particular time in many new experiments, often in contrast to the monastic-cloistered life dominant up to that time.[191] The expression *stare* is apparently

---

[188]*ArchLitKirGesch* III, 604.

[189]In the following translation, importance is attached especially to rendering the Latin text as faithfully as possible, in order to avoid from the start all those interpretations which have crept into most of the translations up to this time.

[190]Rederstorff, 94; V.D. Steinen, 82; Bonmann, 54.

[191]A. Mens, OFMCap., *Oorsprong en betekenis van de nederlandse Begijnen en Begardenbeweging* (Antwerp, 1947); he shows, in pages 65 ff., how in this time for many serious-minded Christians, for whom the cloisters of great monastic orders were closed, the eremitical way of life and life as recluses was the only way to a genuine cloistered life; cf. also 323 ff., 226. That in this time "religio" and "ordo" are

used in contrast to the brothers who were still traveling through the world as itinerant preachers, while the brothers in the hermitages have "taken a break."[192] The late Franciscan sources still use the word *stare* in this sense, as when the Delormé's *Legenda* reports of St. Francis: *cum reverteretur ab Urbe, quando scilicet stetit apud dominum Leonem per aliquot dies.*(95) Or the time, according to the *Speculum* of Sabatier (9, 6), when St. Francis remarked to a brother who spoke about his (Francis's) cell: *Ex quo dixisti ipsam esse meam, alius stabit deinceps ibi, et non ego* (13).[193] The term has still been retained also in the title for the 13th Chapter of the so-called *Legenda trium sociorum: de primo loco, quem habuit, et qualiter fratres stabant illic et quomodo inde recesserunt.* This "taking a break" is also already to be observed among the itinerant preachers of the 12th century, who regulary returned to solitude (for them, of course, to their cloister) in order to take a rest, to take a *statio*.[194] For the Lesser Brothers who were traveling around, this could take place chiefly in the hermitages. That there existed such hermitages among them already in 1221 is shown by the *Earlier Rule*,[195] the

---

synonymous concepts, and that the first was even preferably used in the Church for designating an Order, we have demonstrated in another place: Esser, *Ordo fratrum minorum* II, 108 ff.; cfr. also in addition: H. Morton. O.Praem., "De sensu 'Ordinis' saec. duodecimo," *AnalPraem* 37 (1961): 314 -19; and G.G. Meerseman, O.P., *Dossier de l'ordre de la Pénitence au XIIe siècle* (Fribourg, 1961), Register s.v. ordo and religio etc.; especially informative is the research reprinted by him (308f.) of Henricus Ostiensis in his *Summa aurea* (1253) on the extended meaning of the concept "religiosus"; under that term fall all who wear a common dress and follow a definite rule.

[192]Cfr. Esser, *Ordo fratrum minorum* IV, 193. The statement which the *Specula perfectionis* puts in the mouth of Francis fits very well with the evidence cited there: ". . . fratres mei, qui vadant per mundum sustinendo famem et multas tribulationes, et alii fratres, qui morantur in eremitoriis et pauperculis domibus . . ."; Sabatier, *Speculum* 67,17; Lemmens, *Speculum* 20; Delormé, *Legenda* 92. To round out this picture, a very informative parallel is cited from Humbert de Romanis O.P. (1277) who wrote around the middle of the 13th century about the "mulieres religiosae," who had joined the Humiliati: "Hae autem stant inclusae," and that stood in contrast to those who "otiose circumire domos"; see Mens, *Begijnen* 48, footnote 26.

[193]In all these cases genuine tradition has probably been preserved. The last mentioned remark of Francis has been stylistically retouched in 2 Celano 59: "Ex quo Francisci nomen cellae imposuisti, approprians eam mihi, alium sibi quaeras habitatorem; jam ipse ea non morabor de caetere."

[194]Mens, *Begijnen* 23. In this connection the expression "stare ad orationem," which is used over and over in medieval Franciscan writings, likewise gets its full meaning; cfr. p.e. *Earlier Rule* 22; *Analekten* 21, *Opuscula* 55 and below, footnote 45.

[195]Chapter 7; *Analekten* 8; *Opuscula* 34.

Vita Prima of St. Anthony of Padua,[196] and the Life of Blessed Giles of Assisi.[197]

Apparently these hermitages in the Order of Lesser Brothers never were supposed to become large, as eventually among the Carthusians, the Camaldolese, and others. For that reason the number of the brothers dwelling there was restricted by this "Rule for Hermitages." The reasons for that are not presented. But from other sources we know that Francis saw the poverty of his Order better preserved in small fraternities.[198]

The number of the brothers, however, was also not supposed to be too small. There were supposed to be at least three living together. From that we can probably conclude that Francis wanted this small fraternity type of life to prevail over the genuine hermit's life, which he himself and individual brothers led at the beginning of the life of their Order, even if only at intervals. He did not want any hermits living by themselves, but as brothers in a genuine fraternity.[199]

In addition to that, it should be emphasized that this life in the hermitage was designed to be voluntary, thus not an establishment for the whole Order. To be sure, the inclination toward the contemplative life in secluded solitude was peculiar to the Lesser Brothers, as well as to the whole religious movement of their time.[200] But Francis knew that he was obliged just as

---

[196]"eremum Montis Pauli devotus subiit" (7.5); ed. Kerval, *CollEtDoc* V, 36.

[197]"Tunc sexto anno suae conversionis misit (namely, Franciscus) eum ad quoddam eremitorium nomine Fabrione in planitie Perusii (6); ed. Lemmens, *BecAntFranc* I, 43. According to that, such hermitages had already existed in the order around 1215. Likewise, in the case of Giles, the transfer into such a hermitage way of life severed the "vadens per mundum," the life of the itinerant preacher of penance.

[198]Esser, *Ordo fratrum minorum* II, 128; in addition we can also undoubtedly accept the statement of the *Specula perfectionis* that Francis wished "ut fratres non in magna quantitate inlocis coolocarentur, quia sibi difficile videbatur in magna multitudine paupertate observare": Sabatier, *Speculum* 10,6; Lemmens, *Speculum* 30; Delormé, *Legenda* 12; cfr. also Eccleston, *De adventu Minorum in Angliam*, coll. VII, ed. Little 36.

[199]2 Celano 169; LM XII, 2 with *Actus beati Francisci* 16; this kind of hermitage-style living seems above all to have been fostered by the first Brothers of St. Francis: see *AnalFran* III, 40, 43, 46, and others. For the question of the hermitage style of life among the first Lesser Brothers, see also Mens, *Begijnen* page 93, footnote 79, and page 256, footnotes 9 and 12.

[200]Esser, *Ordo fratrum minorum* V, 331 ff. Mens, above all, has justly stressed this strong progressive movement to the eremitical life all over: *Begijnen* 65 ff., 70f., 323 ff.; cfr. also G. Schreiber, *Gemeinschaften des Mittelalters* (Münster i. W., 1948), 420 ff., and other places.

strongly to the service of people, so that he permitted this solitary life for himself only occasionally and for a time, so to speak, as an interruption of his preaching activity.[201] Now, whether or not the brother who chose this life remained always in the hermitage, is not evident from the text of our "Rule." Neither Anthony nor Giles, as their biographies attest, remained continuously in one and the same hermitage. They also interrupted the active or contemplative life from time to time.

Of interest also are the twin concepts *"matres-filii."* Apparently two brothers in the group of hermits held the task of minister, whose authority they represented in the small fraternity. They were similar to the ministers, on whose office in general Francis liked to confer a motherly character,[202] as indeed the love of the brothers for one another is preferably described by him as that of a mother.[203] Consequently, the concretization of this thought in our "Rule for Hermitages" coincides perfectly with Francis's way of thinking.[204]

It is precisely the number that is stated here that distinguishes the Franciscan hermitage from the numerous contemporary forms of this sort. The "Rule for Hermitages" deals with them not in the manner of the *inclusi* or *reclusi*,[205] as Mens makes them appear in numerous examples,[206] but also not as true

---

[201]In the hermitage at *Sarteano* a cell had been erected for him (2 Celano 59), "in quo posset stare ad orationem . . . quando iret illuc": Sabatier *Speculum* 9,1; Lemmens, *Speculum* 29; Delormé, *Legenda* 13.

[202]Esser; *Ordo fratrum minorum* III, 311; cfr. also 2 Celano 137: Brother Pacificus called Francis "mater carissima." Here reference should once more be made to the fact that the copyist of Bs substituted *patres* for *matres* in the whole text of the rule. That apparently seemed to be more appropriate to the German copyist.

[203]*Earlier Rule* 9; *Later Rule* 6; *Analekten* 10 and 32; *Opuscula* 38 and 69; cfr. in addition: *Werkbuch zur Regel des hl. Franziskus* (Werl i.W., 1955) 195f.

[204]J.M. Benoit, OFM, *Le chevalier courtois de Notre-Dame-des-Anges* (Montréal, 1952) 19f., relates the twin-concepts "matres-filii" used by Francis to the twin cloisters of Robert of Arbrissel, in which the abbesses had the governing role; an arrangement by which Robert wished to respect the mysterious union between Mary and John in accord with the words of Jesus on the cross (19f.). However, the comparison "Maria-Martha" in the next sentence of our rule opposes this interpretation.

[205]The strange thing is that there is no mention of such *reclusi* or *inclusi* in the Franciscan literature, insofar as it comes into question here. As far as we know, only in 2 Celano 49 and in the parallel report of that by Bonaventure (LM XI, 9) do we find the remark that Francis stayed in a "cella reclusus" on Mount Alverna. Concerning later instances of the recluse style of living in the Order, cfr. under footnote 86.

[206]Mens, *Begijnen* 23, 48, footnote 26, 67 and other places, but especially 326f.

Anchorites.[207] On the contrary, it treats them as a group of brothers who belong at the same time to a large fraternity, whose ideals of life they share, and to whose minister they are subject in a firm relationship of obedience. This minister primarily has to watch over their life according to the regulations of the whole Order. The brothers in the hermitages are not segregated from the whole brotherhood of the Order.

2. Let the two who are 'mothers' keep the life of Martha and the two 'sons' keep the life of Mary (cf. Lk 10:38-42), and have one enclosure in which each one may have his cell in which he may pray and sleep.

The text of this sentence of the "Rule" was determined by the pericope of Luke 10:38-42 about the visit of Jesus to the house of Mary and Martha, which text has been used in the tradition of the Church even to our day for the justification of the contemplative life as the better part.[208] Also in this, it is again evident how very much Francis wishes to be formed by the gospel. Yet he does not stand entirely alone in this. For instance, the established Orders of the contemporary poverty movements rejected the title "Abbot," and in connection with the Gospel, called their superiors *magister* or *minister*, they also selected for the women the title "Martha" to designate their office.[209] In the same way, the *Regula Anchoritarum* (12th-13th century) among the recluses distinguished between women who fulfilled the serving role of Martha and those that devoted themselves to contemplation like Mary. Yet the latter were *magistrae*,"thus the superiors of the former.[210] Francis therefore stands also here

---

[207]Also this form existed originally among the Lesser Brothers (cfr. above II, footnote 43); still, as the "Vita fratris Rufini" (*AnalFranc* III, 48f.) and other examples show, Francis did not seem to have any particular liking for this.

[208]D.A. Csanyi, S.O. Cist., "Optima pars. Die Auslegungsgeschichte von Lk 10: 38-42 bei den Kirchenvätern der ersten vier Jahrhunderte," *Studia Monastica* 2 (1960): 5-78; E. Laland, "Die Maria-Martha-Perikope Lukas 10: 38-42. Ihre kerygmatiche Aktualität für das Leben der Urkirche," *Studia theol.* 13 (1959): 70-85.

[209]Mens, *Begijnen* 75, footnote 26; 353. The housekeeper of the priest was also called Martha at that time: ibid. 315, footnote 106.

[210]Ibid. 350. Mens also assembles in that place in footnote 50 still more material from the contemporary literature, which clearly shows how very influential this pericope was just at that time. Nevertheless, there was not lacking attempts to unite Martha's readiness to serve with Mary's contemplative prayer: see pages 386 and 403; or "to exchange the role of the Martha with that of the Mary" (page 387).

immersed in the conditions of his time, which he adapted, to be sure, to the life of his brothers.

When it says in the following text: "and have one enclosure," we should not think of an enclosure in our present-day sense, nor even in the sense of that day, but in the literal sense of the *locus conclusus*,[211] the enclosed ground on which the individual cells of the hermits were situated.[212] While the cells of the recluses at that time were closely connected to a church, and thus formed a "complex of hermitages,"[213] the hermitages of the Lesser Brothers we know were chiefly located *in eremo* in solitary places. They were not surrounded by a wall, but by a hedge, "as a sign of holy poverty and humility." The cells were very simple, "made out of clay and wood," frequently built only of twigs,[214] or they were hollows in the hillside.[215]

Our "Rule for Hermitages" does not say clearly whether only the sons lived in this *claustrum* or also the mothers, an ambiguity which, as we have already shown, the later manuscripts wanted to settle. According to the testimony of the first life of St. Anthony, the "cells" were located farther away from the lodgings of the other brothers (7, 8-10). Many other statements of Franciscan sources likewise seem to presume this. The expression "return to the brothers" appears to be typical for these circumstances. As the original text indicates, the cells were

---

[211]Forcellinni, *Totius latinitatis Lexicon II*, 229b. According to the work, the cloisters at that time had the name *monasterium*. From the beginning on, the cloisters of the Poor Ladies of the Second Franciscan Order were called by this expression in the Franciscan sources (see Esser, *Ordo fratrum minorum IV*, 189).

[212]This fact appears to be made clear by the wording: "in claustro, ubi morantur." The copyist of MS$_2$ was thinking on the contrary of a cloister in the usual sense and therefore put this wording: "in quo morantur." A good illustration of the original layout of the hermitages is preserved for us in the "Vita fratris Rufini," *Anal Franc. III*, 48f.): ". . . cum beatus Franciscus cum aliquibus sociis in Monte Subasio in quadragesima majori solitarium moraretur et omnes divisim per montem in cellusis de ramis arborum poenitentiae et orationi vacarent. . . ." Since we are dealing here with an unpremeditated incidental observation, the text deserves our confidence.

[213]Cfr. *Regula anachoretarum*, in: Mens, *Begijnen* 349; in other places he produces plenty of examples concerning this.

[214]Sabatier, *Speculum* 10,16; Lemmens, *Speculum* 30; Delormé, *Legenda* 16.

[215]2 Celano 35 reads: "In remotiore cellula, saxo prominente constructa, vacabat, liberius caelestibus disciplinis"; cfr. also 2 Celano 59 and 169; further *Vita prima s. Antonii* 1,6: "in dicto eremi loco, frater quidam cellam sibi orationibus aptam in crypta quadam construxerat." The Franciscan places still offer today examples of that. We need to think only of the *Carceri* near Assisi and others, even though the small friaries connected with them today are of later origin.

only places of prayer by day and night, and at the same time resting places for sleep.[216]

3. *And let them always recite Compline of the day immediately after sundown; and strive to maintain silence, recite their Hours, rise for Matins; and seek first the Kingdom of God and His justice (Mt.6:33).*

The participation in the choral prayer in the church near which their cells were built, or the discharging of the prayer of the Hours alone, belonged to the life of all recluses.[217] The same held true also for the Lesser Brothers in the hermitages. The course of their day is decided directly by the Hours of the Office. What the *Rule* of the whole order describes in a very general way for all the brothers, is here specified, at least whatever is related to the time of performing this duty. What Office the brothers should pray is not made explicit in this hermitage text. The prescription of the *Rule* of the Order is simply understood in this matter: "The clerics should recite the Office and pray for the living and the dead, as is the custom among the clerics of the Church of Rome."[218] It is important that in the adaptation of this prescription to life in the hermitages, a rather established schedule becomes evident for the first time in the Order. This schedule brings some structure into the life that had been from the beginning rather open, and in its turn must have been very conducive to an accommodation of this life to actual cloister conditions. That this arrangement goes back to St. Francis himself deserves to be firmly maintained. Thus, the development that was set in motion here could not lie completely outside of his own intention!

Whether the brothers in the hermitage performed the Hours in common or alone is not expressly stated. Judging from the practice of St. Francis with which we are already familiar, the first proposal (in common) would probably be our best bet.[219]

---

[216]1 Celano 50; Julian of Speyer, *Vita* 31; 2 Celano 37, 45, 49, 170, and 178; LM IX, 10; XI, 11 and XI, 12.

[217]Cfr. the *Regula anachoretarum* in Mens, *Begijnen* 351 and passim.

[218]*Regula non bullata 3; Regula bullata 3;* cfr. also *Testamentum 4; Analekten* 3f, 31 and 37, *Opuscula* 28, 66, and 79.

[219]*Testamentum* 9; op. cit. 38, or 80f.

Even so, it cannot be established immediately whether the mothers prayed the Office in common with the sons. If the wording is considered closely, the statement that the sons can go to their mothers after Terce seems to dictate against the participation of the mothers. Nevertheless, if we consider that in the hermitages there were supposed to be four or at least three brothers, then we are inclined to assume that this number was chosen in order to guarantee a common prayer according to the ecclesiastical regulation. Thinking along these lines, it also remains possible that the sons went to their mothers after the choral prayer in order to request their nourishment.

Likewise it is not clear whether these friars are considered to be clerics or lay-brothers. Should there also have been lay-brothers there, they could pray the Office of the *Pater-noster* according to the *Rule* of the Order, as the *Regula anachoretarum* also provided for their recluses.[220] The *Specula Perfectionis*, which apply our "Rule for Hermitages" literally in part to the last statements of Francis for the Portiuncula, assign the role of Martha in that passage to the lay-brothers, who are supposed to serve the clerics. Yet, in this application, we are probably dealing with a transferal of later conditions to the early years of the Order.[221]

The silence that is mentioned here from Compline until Terce of the following day goes back to an ancient monastic tradition. This regulation was also known to the authors of the several *Specula Perfectionis*. They speak namely of the *terminus silentii* or *post terminum et constitutionem silentii*[222]; these expressions clearly show that these times of silence had been imposed by law. This silence was likewise practiced in the Order of Lesser Brothers outside the hermitages.[223] Indeed, as the same *Specula* propose, Francis demanded of his brothers that on their

---

[220]Mens, *Begijnen* 351.

[221]Sabatier, *Speculum* 55, 37; Lemmens, *Speculum* 27; Delormé, *Legenda* 10.

[222]Sabatier, *Speculum* 55,25; Lemmens, *Speculum* 27; Delormé, *Legenda* 9. They report also the penal stipulations which St. Francis issued against those who devoted themselves to idle conversation: Sabatier, *Speculum* 82, 6ff.; Lemmens, *Speculum* 35; Delormé, *Legenda* 78. The copyist of MS$_2$ joined just this report and that in the *Legenda* directly to our rule for the hermitages (fol 43a); a combination which certainly deserves special consideration.

[223]Esser, *Ordo fratrum minorum IV*, 206f.; there is also a more detailed account of sources and proofs for this question; see for this matter 2 Celano 19.

preaching journeys they should also observe the strict silence until after Terce.[224]

Apparently, as the testimony from the words of Jesus in Luke 12:31 shows, the Hours of the Divine Office, especially that of the nightly Hour, are for Francis a worship for the coming of the kingdom of God. The quotations which he had prefixed to the corresponding chapter of the *Earlier Rule* also speak of this conviction of his.[225] Perhaps the quotation in our text also attests to the belief of Francis, which he then shared with the whole ecclesiastical tradition, that Jesus is going to come at the hour of midnight to bring to perfection the kingdom in glory.

4. And let them recite Prime at the proper hour and, after Terce, they may end their silence, speak with and go to their mothers. 5. And, when it pleases them, they can beg alms from them as poor little ones out of love of the Lord God. 6. And afterwards let them recite Sext, None and, at the proper hour, Vespers.

Noteworthy here is that Francis wants the individual Hours of the Divine Office to be prayed at the time that corresponds to their name and character. The fact that there is no mention of Holy Mass is probably able to be explained only by the fact that this instruction was given before the adequate papal privileges. Later on in the hermitages, as likewise in the other establishments of the brothers, it will have been permitted "that one Mass be celebrated in the day according to the form of the Holy Church."[226] But whether the brothers before this time left their hermitages in order to attend Mass in some other place is not mentioned.

After Terce the sons can go to their mothers in order to request from them in the spirit of Franciscan poverty what was necessary for their livelihood. What other brothers of the Order were doing, in so far as they solicited alms from door to door, should not be spared to them in a certain sense. By doing that, they would remain aware that they also should live completely

---

[224] Sabatier, *Speculum* 65,14; Lemmens *Speculum* 37; Delormé, *Legenda* 80.
[225] *Regula non bullata* 3; *Analekten* 3; *Opuscula* 27f.
[226] *Epistola ad capitulum* 3; op. cit. 60 or 104, respectively.

poor, dependent entirely on the goodness of God "for the sake of the love of the Lord God."

Here naturally arises the question of how the mothers obtain the sustenance for themselves and their sons—a question which becomes even more difficult because it later says that also the mothers should keep themselves remote from every other person. Perhaps this prescription is not to be pressed too far; then there would always remain the possibility that one of them would provide for the necessities of life by their work or begging.[227]Thus it would have been possible to observe even in the hermitages what Francis wrote in the *Earlier Rule*: "And one should make known his need with confidence to the other, so that he might procure the necessary things for him and thereby serve him. And each one is to love and nourish his brother like a Mother loves and nourishes her child; thereby, will the Lord bestow grace on each one."[228]

For the understanding of this whole matter, it should also be alluded to here that in the Franciscan sources, in the vicinity of the *cellae* or *cellulae,* a *domus* was also often mentioned.[229] This *domus* probably was near the *ostium eremitorii,* thus at a certain distance from the cells of the contemplatives.[230] From that fact there exists the possibility that the *fratres de domo* or *fratres de loco* of the Legends are to be understood as those who led the life of Martha according to the hermitage text. To them the brothers leading the contemplative life descended from their cells.[231] If that is true, we might also be standing before a new

---

[227]Cfr. *Regula bullata* 5 and 6; op. cit. 32, or 68f., respectively. For the brothers who led a life according to our rule near the Portiuncula, the *Specula perfectionis* attest that they occasionally go and help the people with the work in the fields: "et ipsi postea dabant aliquando eis de pane amore Dei": ed. Sabatier 55, 27; ed. Lemmens 27; ed. Delormé 9. St. Bonaventure writes of the hermitage in Greccio that was so far away from the dwellings of men that one could not very conveniently beg (LM VII, 9). That would suggest that the Brothers in the hermitages lived from begging, supposing that we are allowed to generalize this observation.

[228]*Regula non bullata* 9; op. cit. 10, or 38, respectively. A similar sounding admonition is found in: *Regula bullata* 6; op. cit. 32, or 69, respectively.

[229]2 Celano 61 and 178; LM VII, 9; *Intentio regulae* 12; Sabatier, *Speculum* 4,14; 10, 16; 20, 1-4; 67, 17; 82, 13; 100, 1-2; Lemmens, *Speculum* 20, 30, 35; Delormé, *Legenda* 16, 43, 61, 74, 78, and 92.

[230]2 Celano 44 and 45, 61; LM XI, 12 and VII, 9; Sabatier, *Speculum* 20, 4 and 110, 7; Delormé, *Legenda* 32 and 62.

[231]2 Celano 37, 45, 59, 61, 100, and 178; LM XI, 12 and VIII, 9; Sabatier, *Speculum* 20, 4 and 117, 6; Delormé, *Legenda,* 32 and 50.

understanding of the early Franciscan manner of settling down. From the enclosed place with its cells and tiny house, to which an existing or later to be erected Church belonged, developed the *locus fratrum* (*luogho*), which clearly differed from the old abbeys and cloisters, but yet had within it the seeds that could develop in this direction. And that all the more, because evidently the numerical limitation of our "Rule for Hermitages" for those living in the hermitage was not maintained for long.[232]

7. And they may not permit anyone to enter or eat in the enclosure where they dwell.

Francis wanted the area in which the sons spent their time praying to be kept free from all disturbance "so that they would better preserve purity and holiness. For nothing superfluous should be done or spoken in this place, but it should be sanctified by songs and praises of God." With this as a proof, the *Specula Perfectionis* apply our text to the Portiuncula. They even want to propose that Francis also forbade brothers not belonging to that place to enter.[233] In these remarks we can probably see genuine

---

[232]This development is attested to by a report of the *Specula perfectionis*, which certainly deserves reliance for the part coming into question here. According to this report, Francis, a few months before his death, on being asked, expressed his opinion about how the Brothers in the cities should set up their establishments and how they should build them in conformity to his will: "Accepta benedictione ab episcopo, vadant et faciant mitti magnam carbonariam in circuitu terrae, quam pro loci aedificatione acceperunt et ponant ibi bonam sepem pro muro in signum paupertatis et humilitatis; postea faciant fieri domos pauperculos ex luto et lignis et aliquae cellulas, in quibus fratres aliquando possint orare et laborare pro majori honestate et vitanda otiositate. Ecclesias etiam parvas fieri faciant, non enim debent facere fieri magnas ecclesias causa praedicandi populo. . . ." ed. Sabatier, 10, 16-18; ed. Lemmens 30; ed. Delormé 16. That such establishments were a reality in the Order already since 1224 is shown by the corresponding reports about the first establishments of the Lesser Brothers in England, as Thomas of Eccleston has fixed them in his *Chronicle* about the middle of the 13th century (Coll. IV: *De adeptione locorum;* ed. Little 20-24). However, he also clearly points out how buildings similar to cloisters developed from these simple foundations (coll. X: *De mutatione locorum et ampliatione;* ibid. 44-47). At any rate, all of these reports show that the original establishments of the Lesser Brothers were influenced by the model of the hermitages. This is also testified to by the other writings of St. Francis about the kind and way the brothers should build them; see, for example, 2 Celano 56; LM VII, 2; Sabatier, *Speculum* 5, 3; 7,1; 9, 3 and 11; Lemmens, *Speculum* 29; Delormé, *Legenda* 11, 13 and 14.

[233]"Volo etiam, quod nulla persona et nullus frater intret in illum locum, nisi generalis minister et fratres, qui serviunt illis": Sabatier, *Speculum* 55,35; cf. also Delormé, *Legenda* 10.

tradition which clarifies the text of our "Rule" and shows how strenuously Francis wanted the solitude to be protected.

Probably in this sense also is the prescription that the brothers should not eat in the actual *claustrum* to be interpreted. For that, they are to go to the lodging of their mothers. Francis himself acted in such a way as the sources indicate to us: "He had the custom of spending the whole day in one of the solitary cells and not to return to the brothers, except when the need for nourishment forced him." Two visiting brothers did not get to meet him "because he had already withdrawn from the brothers into the cell." Or, "He descended from the cell and came to dinner." Similar customs are reported from the hermitage in Spain: there one day one of the friars "who belonged to the contemplatives" did not come to dinner, because he was in ecstasy.[234] Apparently, however, this prescription pertained only to the common mealtime. For a little nourishment during the day, the hermit took with him "a portion of bread and a container with water."[235] At a stated time a signal called him back to the fraternity of the brothers, so that he might eat with them.[236]

The prescription of our text is thus not only to be understood in the sense of the ecclesiastical law for cloisters, as the manuscripts of group (d) would like it, but very generally in the sense that the quiet of the brothers spending their time in contemplation should not be disturbed by anything or anyone. That point is corroborated further by the expanded text.

8. Let those brothers who are the 'mothers' strive to stay far from everyone and, because of obedience to their minister, protect their 'sons' from everyone so that no one can speak with them. 9. And those 'sons' may not talk with anyone except with their 'mothers' and with the minister and his custodian when it pleases them to visit with the Lord's blessing.

Again we find in the regulation of St. Francis for the Portiuncula, as they are transmitted in the *Specula Perfectionis,* a direct reference to this prescription: "And they themselves

---

[234]2 Celano 45, 61 and 178.
[235]*Vita prima s. Antonii* 7, 8.
[236]Ibid., 7, 10; likewise 2 Celano 178.

should speak to no one except the brothers who serve them and with their minister when he visits them." And the brothers in the role of Martha should never relate to the others "superfluous words or news of the world, or anything else that would not be profitable for their souls."[237] In the special area of prayer devoted to God, nothing disturbing should intrude.

In this section, it is of importance that the mothers are supposed to discharge their duty by order of the minister; thus they are accountable to him. Likewise, the life in the hermitages belongs, in view of that, to the life of the "province," over which eventually the minister has to watch. Therefore, he is also supposed to fulfill his duty of visitation toward these brothers when he deems it to be in accord with the will of God.[238]

The statements of this sentence are even more meaningful, if one considers the fact that the hermitages were perhaps the first stable establishments of the Lesser Brothers. Thus, these hermitages still had no actual minister, since one group governs the other group "in obedience to the minister," who at that time was the only superior of the Province. When the word *custodiant* is used with regard to this, that only shows clearly that the term *custos*, as the text of the *Later Rule* (chapter 8) still shows, was a collective concept for the various offices in the Order. Also, secondarily, it shows that from this *custodire* in the establishments, there was no further step to the designation of the office of *guardianus* for the superiors of the later cloisters, or that *custos* and *guardianus* are synonymous concepts.[239] The superiors of the house also in the following period remain "in obedience to the minister" as regards the carrying out of their office. Thus they never became as independent as the superiors of the old monasteries. Likewise, as is indicated in sentence 10, for set periods of time, they had to put aside their office. Much of what developed later in the Order is thus contained in this small "Rule for Hermitages" as in a grain of seed. Thus we will

---

[237]Sabatier, *Speculum* 55, 36-37: Delormé, *Legenda* 10.

[238]For the expression "cum benedictione Dei," cf. Esser, "Gehorsam und Freiheit," *WissWeish* 13 (1950): 146, footnote 18.

[239]About the designation of the office of guardian, cf. Esser, *Ordo fratrum minorum IV*, 201-05.

not be able to denounce this development as something not
springing from the original Order.

*10. The 'sons,' however, may periodically assume the role of the
'mothers,' taking turns for a time as they have mutually decided.
Let them strive to observe conscientiously and eagerly everything
mentioned above.*

The *Earlier Rule* attests that even the office of the minister is
not given permanently, but is exchangeable. Thomas of Celano
reports that in the Spanish hermitage the alternation by the
governing and obeying brothers took place in a weekly
rotation.[240] This prescription of our text is, therefore, thoroughly
in the framework of what was customary at that time in the
Order. It is, however, also another proof that Francis does not
"regulate" so much, but gives free elbow-room for the brothers'
own judgment. Thus, likewise here, he wishes only that the
mothers do not have their office permanently. They should not
appropriate some other office.[241] The last sentence of our "Rule"
is, therefore, also completely according to the thinking of St.
Francis, particularly springing from his all-embracing attitude of
poverty. Precisely in that lies the difference between the life in
the hermitages of the Lesser Brothers and that of the other
contemporary forms of this life outside the Order. Francis truly
knew how to integrate into the spirit and life of his Order this
universally popular and cherished desire of his time—a desire
that corresponded also to his own deepest yearnings.[242]

---

[240]2 Celano 178.

[241]Cfr. *Regula non bullata* 17; *Admonitiones* 4; *Analekten* 16 and 43; *Opuscula* 46 and
8.

[242]In connection with this point, one might compare also the following
admonitions of Francis, which, according to the *Specula perfectionis* , he delivered to
the itinerant preachers among the Brothers: "Licet enim ambulatis, tamen
conversatio vestra sit ita humilis et honesta, sicut si in eremitorio aut in cella essetis.
Nam ubicumque sumus et ambulans, habemus semper cellam nobiscum: frater enim
corpus est cella nostra et anima est eremita, quae moratur intus in cella ad orandum
Dominum et meditando de ipso. Unde si anima in quiete non manserit in cella sua,
parum prodest religioso cella namu factu." When he then joined with this reminder
the exhortation to "keep silence until Terce," we can clearly detect what significance
the way of life established in our rule was supposed to have also for the apostolic-
active life of the Lesser Brothers (Sabatier, *Speculum* 65,14-17; Lemmens, *Speculum* 37;
Delormé, *Legenda* 80). In this way Francis also conducted himself when he, while one
time on a journey, in spite of a persistent rain, stopped in order to pray his Office in
complete calm, "ac si fuisset in ecclesia vel cella" (Sabatier, *Speculum* 94, 5). The same

Conclusions

1. The *Rule* for the life of the Brothers in hermitages is without doubt a work of St. Francis and has been preserved for us in a form which still approximates very closely the lost original text. Its manuscript tradition is very uniform as far as contents. The grammatical variations can be explained for the most part from the history of the text.

2. Together with the two *Rules* for the whole Order which have been preserved for us (*Earlier Rule and Later Rule*) together with the *Testament* of St. Francis, the text that we have investigated here offers some valuable information about the original life of the Lesser Brothers. Its loss would be irreparable for many an important insight. Above all, it helps in understanding more precisely the often cryptic statements of the other sources (biographies and chronicles).

3. On the basis of this better understanding of the sources, it can be affirmed that the hermitages, as the first form of Franciscan establishments, received the significance of a model for the "settling-down" of the original itinerant preachers.

4. The life of a hermit, which was such a great ideal of medieval piety and aspired to in many and various forms, and which also constantly stood beaming and enticing before Francis and his brothers, remained something like the one pole which stood as a shaping influence in the apostolic life of the Lesser Brothers. Francis attempted to bind both together. Thus it could be said that the hermitage style of life was even in a certain sense the symbol of his inner life.

---

circumstances are also at the basis of the *Epistola ad ministrum* of St. Francis. Thus we are dealing here not with an isolated statement.

Finally we should refer in this matter to the fact that, according to some reports of Salimbene, the form of the old recluse style of life also still existed in the Order of Lesser Brothers in spite of our rule: "Alique morabuntur in Civitatibus juxta ecclesiam fratrum in heremitorio omnino reclusi et habebant fenestram, per quam loquebantur, et erant inutiles ad confessiones audiendas et ad consilia danda. Hoc vit Pistorii et alibe etiam." This is exactly the form of the recluse way of life, as it is described by Mens for many sections of Europe. It proves that in practice, this way of life was stronger than the wish of St. Francis for integration.

5. For the early history of the Order of Lesser Brothers, therefore, these factors with their significant and powerful influence must not be overlooked. Without them every presentation remains incomplete.

A "Rule for Hermitages"

by

Ignatius Brady, OFM[*]

This "Rule for Hermitages" is an aspect of Franciscan life that goes back very far in our history. A book by Fr. Luciano Canonici, OFM, called *Itinerari Francescani*, published in 1972, is a guidebook of Franciscan places, mostly in Umbria. What comes out of the book is how many of these old friaries or convents began as hermitages. And I don't think we really should be surprised, because almost from the beginning of the Order, the eremitical life drew many of the friars. In fact, First Celano 34-35 tells us that when Francis and the eleven were coming back from their first visit to Rome and Innocent III approved the *Propositim*, they arrived at Orte and found a very nice spot in the woods and spent much time there. At that time they began to debate among themselves whether they should become hermits or follow an apostolic life.

In First Celano 35 it says: "They began to have in that place commerce with holy poverty." Remember the word *commercium* doesn't mean in our sense *commerce* only, but an experience of holy poverty. The account continues: "because once they have put aside solicitude for earthly things only the divine consolation gave them joy." And they began to realize some delights of the interior life. And "they all conferred together . . . whether they should dwell among people or go to solitary places. But Francis, who did not trust in his own skill, but had recourse to holy prayer . . . chose not to live for himself alone but for God who

[*]Lecture delivered at the Franciscan Institute, St. Bonaventure University, summer 1977.

died for all" (1Cel 35). And therefore he chose an apostolic type of life so "he might win for God the souls the devil is trying to snatch away." But even if they decided that they were to live as or be apostles, nevertheless, the tendency to the solitary life constantly manifested itself in the Order. And in the life of Francis we do know that, even though in imitation of Christ, as he reminded the friars, they were to win souls for God, Francis himself constantly felt the need for periods of solitude and inner prayer in out-of-the-way places. And as a result, it was not long before the Order, which was not supposed to own the property, nevertheless acquired the use of many solitary places for the pursuit of deeper prayer and penance.

I don't know that anybody has been able to pinpoint just what was the first hermitage, second, and so forth. Within the first five years or so, the friars must have acquired so many of these places that they asked Francis to give them a practical guide for their life in such a hermitage. And so the result is the document you want to study. It's a quasirule. Francis doesn't say that it's binding under sin or anything like that, but it does set forth partly the fruit of experience and partly the suggestion of Francis himself. For us it is not only a precious testimony to the early life of the Order, but it still has meaning for us and even more so in our own day.

Now let us look directly at the historical data about the text. The title of the work is very uncertain. It's called "Religious Life in Hermitages." In two manuscripts at least it's called in Latin *De Religiosa habitatione in eremo* [On Dwelling in a Religious Way in the Desert]. The word *eremo/eremus* is not in the original title. I don't think they started using the word "desert" that early; "desert place" yes, but near the end it could have been used because that word was very much in the religious vocabulary in the Middle Ages. If you look up history you'll find St. Romuald and the Carthusians used this word "desert"— *eremus*—as a common expression for a place of solitude. So we should just be content with "Religious Life in Hermitages." In fact, Fr. Esser said if there isn't any official title, he's just going to call it the "Rule that was given for Hermitages."

It doesn't have a binding character. It's not a Rule in a strict or legal sense. Therefore, it would not mean that in every place it was followed to the letter. And even if in many of the manuscripts of the writings of Francis it comes after the *Admonitions,* I think that was accidental. I don't think that means it was written at the same time the *Admonitions* were written.

As far as dating is concerned, in the form we have it, it comes after 1217 simply because in the text it talks about the *Custos.* In the Assisi manuscript you have *Minister* instead of *Custos.* There is a certain imprecision in Franciscan language in that early period where the provincial was sometimes called *Custos.* The point is that the office of the provincial minister was established in 1217. Consequently, this has to be written after that date. According to Fr. Esser's research, it has to be written before 1222 at the latest, because in March 1222 the friars obtained permission to have a proper oratory in their hermitages.

Before that date, they had a prayer room, but it didn't give them the right to have an oratory in the sense of having a fixed altar. That came in 1222. And this "Rule" might well have been written before 1221 because the Rule of 1221 takes hermitages for granted. We read in the Rule of 1221, chapter 7: "No matter where they are, in hermitages or elsewhere, the friars must be careful not to claim the ownership of any place." In our Franciscan language, the Latin word *locus* in the Middle Ages became the Franciscan word for wherever they lived—a place. And they used that word because it didn't have the connotation of property, such as words like "house," "castle," *domus* or *domicilium* —"domicile." I think Francis would have kept away from these words that implied property.

What was the significance of having an oratory? There is no distinction made in the hermit's world, but with priests there, they had the obligation of Sunday Mass. And in order to have a chapel or oratory, they would have to get permission from Rome or from the bishop.

In 1224 the friars got the right to reserve the Blessed Sacrament. Certainly the "Rule for the Hermitages" was written before that. And if they had had an official oratory, I think there would have been some mention of it in the text. And the date could be pushed back a litle further. Francis went to the Holy Land 1219-20, and in some sense, resigned his office as General Minister or leader when he came back in 1220. It's probable that this text must date to some period before he left for the Holy Land. In all probability the Friars in the Chapter of 1217, which is one of the last Chapters to which all the friars came, must have asked Francis for some direction in respect to hermitages. There is nothing here for sure, but I think you can push the date of composition back to 1217-19.

Another point that could be raised here—and I don't think I know the answer for it—was this text composed before or after Francis heard about how some of the friars lived in Spain? If you look at Second Celano 178, you have a very interesting description there: "It happened that a certain Spaniard, a cleric, devoted to God" came down to Italy. I suppose he was on his way to Rome and had heard already about Francis and wanted to meet him. He told Francis how the friars lived in Spain:

> "They live in a poor hermitage and they have so established their way of living that half of them take care of domestic needs and the other half spend their time in contemplation. In this way each week those who lead the active life exchange with those who lead the contemplative life. . . ." Thus the Spaniard said, does it happen in our land. St. Francis could not contain himself for joy, sprinkled as he was with such fragrance of his sons (2Cel 178).

This account raises a question that I can't answer. Were they inspired by this "Rule for the Hermitages" of Francis or was Francis inspired by their example to write the "Rule for the Hermitages"? I don't know which to say. Celano almost implies this is the first time Francis heard about this, and he was so delighted with the account. Therefore, he suggested that would be the way it be done elsewhere. I don't know if you could jump to that conclusion or not. But that's about all I could say now.

We should pass over to the importance of this movement in the early life of the Order. And here it comes out of this paragraph of Celano that very early there was a Franciscan tendency to this hidden life through a life in solitude or in the desert. And it was not confined to something around Assisi, but certainly spread up and down Italy and to the other areas also, such as Spain. For example, in the *Earlier Rule*, chapter 7, when Francis says: "No matter where they are, in hermitages or elsewhere . . .," he's just taking it for granted that this was a normal situation. Or if you read the life of St. Anthony, we know that when Anthony came to a Chapter and didn't belong to any particular group, the Provincial Minister of Bologna took him and he was sent to a hermitage near Bologna.

If you read the life of Brother Giles, you will find that he had more than one hermitage. When we look at a map of Franciscan places, so many of them indicate where friars lived, but the distinction between hermitage and a monastery or convent is not clear. Anything that's up in the mountains was certainly a hermitage; for example, Monte LaVerna. And then around Assisi, the Carceri and Monteripido were hermitages. In fact, Giles, at the end of his life, was there for several years. And the whole Rieti valley was filled with hermitages—Greccio, Poggio Bustone, Fonte Colombo. One can say that half the Franciscan dwellings, at least in the first part of the thirteenth century, were hermitages.

When we read this text, we're going to find out that there's a real difference here in the Franciscan hermitage from other types of hermitages, both as far as the place is concerned and the life therein. They are quite different from Camaldoli. Camaldoli is very close to LaVerna, about twenty miles away. But that's an entirely different type of hermitage than anything you have as Franciscan.

At Camaldoli, when you come in the front gate off the highway, there is a big abbey which is a community center. Then to go to the hermitage you have to go way up two or three miles into the woods. There you find a stone wall completely around it, a great enclosure and a large church. When you first go in, a path leads up the center, and then there are a series of stone cottages along this path. When you go into one of them, you find that it's quite convenient and also quite cold in the wintertime. It's got a little bedroom, a living room, a workroom, a little chapel, and a wood room where one can chop wood in order to keep the place warm in the winter. In each one of these cottages there's a monk who is a hermit. Way up the hill is a chapel, and around that there are cells which look into the chapel. They are used by solitaries who are practically walled in. They said there was a monsignor who worked for years in the Vatican and got tired of the work. He came to Camaldoli and became a solitary and was in the same cell for some twenty years before he died. But the other hermits in these different cottages come down, for example at midnight, for their office. They come down occasionally for meals together.

The hermitage as Francis envisages it is quite different from other traditions because it's not solitary only, not a recluse in the strict sense, although there were apparently developments even among friars on that point. The Franciscan chronicler, Salimbene, says that at Pistoia he found friars who were walled up to a church. What would these people do in these places? Regarding life in the thirteenth-century hermitages, no one has given us a great deal of history about them. But we do have enough to be able to put a picture together in some way.

For example, it's helpful to read the *Legend of Perugia 14-16*. This doesn't necessarily concern itself with a hermitage, but it does give an idea how or what Francis had in mind for friars in general. It's pretty close to what he wants in a hermit.

The story is that Francis was at Siena for treatment for his eyes very close to the end of his life, in spring of 1226:

> He lived in a cell where an oratory was built after his death. Lord Bonaventure (a lay person) who had given the brothers the land on which their friary was erected, said to Blessed Francis one day: "What do you think of this friary?" The Blessed Francis answered: "Do you want me to tell you how the friaries of the brothers should be built?" (LP 14)

Then he goes on to give a description which really is based on experience, based on the type of hermitages the friars already had:

> When the brothers arrive in a city where they do not have a residence, and they find someone who wants to give them a piece of land to build a friary with a

garden and the necessary space, they must first of all decide that the area is adequate, and not to exceed it; they must never lose sight of holy poverty. . . . (LP 14)

Then they are to go to the bishop and get permission from him (LP 15); and the reason is because the bishop rules the diocese and he has concern for people. Then in LP 16, after they had the blessing of the bishop let them start working on the friary. They don't get a contractor to do it. They do it themselves. "Let them go and dig a large ditch around the property" (LP 16), like a dike. It might not be so much a ditch as piling the earth up to make sort of a barrier. And "let them plant a good hedge in place of a wall"(LP 16). The stone wall would be against poverty and humility. "Let them have poor and small houses built of earth and wood and a few cells where the brothers may sometimes pray and work more at ease and be especially safe from useless chatter. Let them also have churches built"(LP 16).

So you get a piece of land, you dig your ditch around the place, you plant your trees and bushes, and you put a few huts out in the garden. And then you build a kind of central house, an oratory if you obtain permission. And at least as this "Rule for Hermitages" has it here, there are two brothers who are "Marys" and two brothers who are "Marthas." After a week, they exchange roles.

The hermitage place was pretty high up from civilization. This is what Francis calls the *claustrum*; that is not a cloister in our sense, but rather an enclosure in the woods and, perhaps more often than not, up in the mountains. Somehow it would be surrounded by a ditch and a hedge. And then each one would be in the hermitage proper, will have his own hut. And he will live there in silence, in solitude.

Then in regard to the house, there is nothing in this text or even in the document, as far as I can see, about how the house was made, how many people were there. I believe that the passage we have from Second Celano 178 about the friars in Spain, seems to have been more than two living there, kind of a small active community which would take care of the material needs, go begging if necessary, raise vegetables or something like that, provide contact with the outside world, and then take care of whatever else friar-hermits would need. We have stories about that. There is one about a friar who goes into ecstasy and the others have to go and find him.

These people in the house would have the contact with the outside world and gradually this house may have become much larger. It's like the Carceri today. At the Carceri every generation of friars kept adding buildings on to the house.

Was every friary like this? No, I don't think so. As far as the houses in the towns, they took what they could get, at least from the beginning. In fact, in the *Anonymous of Perugia*, John of Perugia was a disciple of Blessed Giles. He gives an account of the early days when one of the friars first went out and tried to stay with secular priests. Sometimes the priests wouldn't even look at them. So then they tried to stay with good lay people. Then eventually they tried to get some kind of a cubicle of their own. Certainly they were able, within the lifetime of St. Francis, to establish some simple place in practically every main town in Italy.

It was always the aim of the friars of the Middle Ages to have houses at least in such relation to each other that you would get from one to the next in a day's walk. In fact, all through Germany in the Middle Ages, the friars all went out in groups or pairs and were able to get from one house to the next in the space of a day.

Francis then suggests in this "Rule" that the number of people would be two "Marys" and two "Marthas." But the account from Second Celano 178 regarding the friars in Spain shows that there would be more than two and two. I believe you find in Second Celano 61 an account about Greccio, the famous story about Francis being at the hermitage there and finding the friars were going all out at Easter for a little celebration. And Francis pulls out the rug from under them. It would imply that there were quite a number of people in the community, so that already in Francis's time we can see the number exceeded two and two. Then in Second Celano 59, regarding the hermitage of Sarteano, the passage implies there are more than two and two in the house. What was Francis's idea in limiting it to smaller houses? I suppose, more or less, to foster detachment or the idea of solitude. But I don't know that he saw a small number as something to be insisted upon.

One other thing before we consider the order of the day, and that is about the spiritual set-up in the house, how they lived. Francis says they lived with the rhythm of the Office. But this rhythm comes from the Rule. I don't know if it comes out of the natural practice. And there is no mention of a guardian or any other kind of local minister. Rather, he sees it as a simple way of living which is a real exercise in brotherhood.

And it is very interesting that he would use "Martha" and "Mary" as the examples to be followed. The psychologist would say that it was his mother's influence on him. His father put him in a prison at home and his mother let him out. In both Rules one of the most beautiful passages is where Francis describes the love of friars one for another: "If a mother has such care and love for her son born according to the flesh, should not someone love and care for his brother according to the Spirit even more diligently?"(RegNB 9:11; RegB 6:8)

Lastly, regarding the order of the day in these hermitages, certainly this "Rule for Hermitages" doesn't give us everything, but it does imply that there was some kind of regulation of the day in a friary. So don't think that everything was free and easy and open in Francis's time. There was some kind of order, at least in the rhythm of the liturgy.

[Here a student asked: Are you talking about the hermitages or about the friary?] I am talking here about the hermitage. I am trying to stick to this "Rule for Hermitages." What is in this to some extent, I think, would be implied in regular friaries. The point here that Esser brings out if you read his book *Origins of the Franciscan Order* (page 175 and following), you have people who sometimes say that Francis couldn't be bothered about order. This shows that he is not against it. Maybe it's something new in the growing Order. But there is an order today that is pretty much established by the rhythm of the liturgy. So they come from their cells to the oratory for the Office. And it doesn't say what Office they were to say because that was only determined later when they took one psalter that was common in Europe and took the rest of the Office from the Roman Curia.

And then the important point here in regard to the order of the day—there is nothing in this writing that says two must be clerics and two must be lay. This is important because it shows that to Francis it didn't matter much.

There is a very interesting development in Second Celano 19 and following. It is an account of Francis's love for the Portiuncula. And it's pretty much in words that would imply that the Portiuncula was considered a hermitage. In fact, I saw in some place, and I can't remember where, a very old print which was very unhistorical in the way it was done, but there's some basis for it even in Celano when he talks about where the cell of Francis was located at the Portiuncula. This old print had the whole thing walled off, and within was the little chapel of the Portiuncula. And then all along the wall, there were little huts. The whole idea was that the Portiuncula was a model hermitage. In fact, if you read Second Celano 19, there's strict discipline and each one had his cell. Francis apparently had a cell way up back in the woods. He tried to get as far away as possible from anything interfering with his interior life.

The point here is that the account in Second Celano 19 makes no reference to clerics or laics, but if we go to the *Mirror of Perfection* 55, about the life of the friars at the Portiuncula, we read:

> I wish this place always to be under the direct control of the General Minister. . . . The clergy are to be chosen from among the better, more holy, and more suitable of the friars, who best know how to recite the Office and who are fully professed in the Order. . . . The lay brothers chosen to serve them are to be holy men, discreet, humble and honest.

See what has happened here? This two and two business, the two that were in the enclosure were now considered only clerics while the two who were out or who were "Martha" become the lay brothers only.

Then finally, in this order of the day, there is an emphasis in this "Rule for the Hermitages" on silence. That's an old monastic tradition, but there was silence because it was demanded by the very nature of the place. Another factor is that the two changed off every two weeks or every week or something like that.

The conclusion is that this writing of Francis says a whole lot to us today because it reemphasizes for us one basic aspect of our Franciscan vocation, namely, that ours is a mixed life, a life of prayer and contemplation, as well as action. And that brought with it from the very beginning the problem of achieving not just a balance, but rather an integration or synthesis of these two elements. And that's why in the Rule, Francis insists on the primacy of the Spirit of prayer and devotion.

Today in our quest for houses of prayer, people are going back to this "Rule for Hermitages." They also are going back to other developments down the centuries of the Order's history, because there's all the difference in the world between the thirteenth-century hermitage as Francis pictures it and the friars lived it, and what was developed later for the house of recollection or a *ritiro*. So, I believe we have a lot to learn by going back to St. Francis!

Vestiges of Eremitism in Francis of Assisi:

A Summary

by

Benedikt Mertens, OFM[1]

Translated from the German
by
Josef Raischl and André Cirino, OFM

[The following points may be useful in drawing some conclusions about the material of this chapter. Eds. note]

1. The biographies of Francis of Assisi and his writings point to an eremitism that was contemporary with his times. However, scholars say whatever influence there is, whether geographic, biographic, or literal, that might appear in the written sources, has not been historically proven.

2. Knowledge of this contemporary eremitical movement is very important for the broader interpretation of the earlier Franciscan movement and for its biographical influences on Franciscan life.

3. It can be said that Franciscan eremitism created an impact upon the eremitical tradition just as the Franciscan model of life was a force upon the poverty movement and the religious orders of the time.

4. Common ideals of the eremitical tradition taken up by Francis include solitude and separation from the world, an intense and inner life of prayer, evangelical poverty, strict asceticism and silence. These elements were also well-known in the eremitical Orders and among the recluses of his time. His gospel reasoning for periodic eremitism as well as his willingness

to preach, show similarities with some French hermits and preachers of the 11th and 12th centuries. His tendency toward a radical poverty and penance can only be understood against the background of the poverty movement and the lay penitents who often looked for an eremitical way of life.

Within the various biographies of Francis, traditional eremitical language appears: *vacare Deo* = to be empty for God, *eremi vastitas* = desert emptiness, *loca solitaria* = solitary places. The motive of the demon's gift and the close relationship with animals is eremitical language as well. This language of eremitical circles is often appropriated by the biographers themselves.

There is also congruence between the organization of life in Francis's "Rule for Hermitages" and eremitical traditions. The enclosure as fence and border of the solitary territory, for example, is common in eremitical as well as cenobitical settings. For the same reason, the cells that are spread out in this place are without order as at Camaldoli, Fonte Avellana or Mount Carmel. Liturgical prayer times provide a daily schedule according to the monastic and eremitical customs, and the strict silence of night is also part of that tradition. Finally, the biblical images of Martha and Mary (Lk 10:38-42) used to illustrate roles of service/prayer fall squarely upon contemporary eremitism of the early 13th century.

5. Francis's creative contributions to the eremitical movement of the High Middle Ages can be shown in various elements. For instance, during the Founder's lifetime, the Friars Minor were the first to combine the eremitical element—as an occasional experience—with itinerant preaching and working in a kind of mixed life. Eremitism became an inner attitude within the itinerant life.

The "Rule for Hermitages" limited to three or four the number of friars who could stay in a hermitage, thus separating it in a unique way from any classical *Reklusen und Anachoretentum*, as well as from the large number of eremitical communities and their Rules.

Francis's eremitism is born from an intuitive desire and becomes a necessary element of his contemplative relationship to God. His ideal and point of comparison are not the great hermits but a radical realization of Gospel life, an imitation of Christ, a looking at Jesus' stay in the desert. Contrary to many medieval eremitical expressions, Francis's eremitism does not evolve out of struggle with contemporary monks or canons. Further, Francis's eremitism makes no reference to Eastern desert writers or to monastic or premonastic eremitical ideals. Thus monastic or eremitical terms such as *lectio divina*, unordered and radical asceticism or the recitation of the psalter cannot be found in Franciscan eremitical writings.

Poverty always exists in the very concept of eremitism. However, Francis radicalized poverty by the provisional character of the hermitage as he conceived it: there is only a symbolic enclosure made of hedges, as well as the cells (sheltered spaces or caves) that hint at eremitical stability. According to the *Earlier Rule*, the Friars Minor refused any property, even hermitages, as a form of settlement, and lived a marginalized existence, even under threat of bandits. Finally, the begging for alms, proper to the mendicants' poverty and lack of security, becomes integrated into the hermitage.

Francis's "Rule for Hermitages" expresses the value of fraternity in unique ways. For instance, the friars are invited to share daily (their experiences of God in prayer) and they exchange roles (Martha/Mary) to preserve fraternal life from a hierarchical order. This last element of the Franciscan "Rule for Hermitages" breaks with the strict order and contraposition of the active life and the contemplative life, as well as with the separation of clerics from lay people. Thus lay people for the friars had access to religious eremitical life at a time when other congregations limited them to serving the clerics.

Endnote

[1] B. Mertens, "In eremi vastitate resedit," 285-374, 365-67.

Chapter Four

Further Historical Development

of the Eremitical Experience

in the Order after Francis

Introduction

We view chapter four as a bridge between the eremitical experience of the first Franciscans as presented in the preceding three chapters and the experience of this eremitical document in our own day as presented in chapter five.

Aware of the complex historical developments in the eremitical experiences of the Franciscan Order down through the centuries, Costanzo Cargnoni enlightens us about *The Houses of Prayer in the History of the Franciscan Order.* Having given a definition of the overall meaning of the "Franciscan Houses of Prayer" and their relation to the reform movements, Cargnoni (relying above all on the studies of Dacian Bluma, OFM and Melchior de Pobladura, OFM Cap. as a pattern) expounds his interpretation in four parts to show the historical evolution of the Houses of Prayer in the Franciscan Order.

The first part treats Franciscan Hermitages (13th-16th centuries) and their relation to the movement of the Spirituals, to those geographic areas of development, and to their spiritual content. Much is said about the rich experience of the Spanish eremitism of Peter of Villacreces.

The second part examines Houses of Gatherings (16th-18th centuries), the reasons for their rise, their general Statutes, their historical evolution, their structure and spiritual content and the method of teaching in character formation.

The third part examines Monasteries for Retreat (17th -19th centuries), which began with the "Riformella" of Blessed Bonaventure of Barcelona. Cargnoni insists again upon the "Spiritual Content," with the intent of signifying by means of adequate, selected legislative texts, the active force of apostleship and prayer. He rewrites the nineteen suggestions of St. Theophilus of Corte for the superiors of retreats and touches upon the initiatives attempted by the Capuchins in the 18th century.

The fourth and last part relates the drastic experience of those living in deserts or in solitude (16th-18th centuries). These begin with St. Peter of Alcantara, Blessed Bonaventure of Barcelona, St. John Joseph of the Cross, and St. Leonard of Port Maurice. Many original texts are quoted which give us a better understanding of the spirit which inspired these strong contemplative experiences. It all serves to demonstrate historically that the Franciscan Rule, on which every experience of the Houses of Prayer pertaining to the Order is based, cannot be observed "spiritually" without the earnest desire to live a life of prayer and of contemplation.

Grado G. Merlo treats *Eremitism in Medieval Franciscanism* up to the 15th century, and Mertens arches over the remaining centuries to give us only a glimpse of this complex historical material.

For the reader who desires to know more of this history of these intervening centuries we would suggest the following:

Dacian Bluma, OFM, offers a study on the eremitical elements of the history of the *Vita Recessualis*;

Melchior De Pobladura, OFM Cap., has written about the desert experience.

Houses of Prayer

in the

History of the Franciscan Order

by

Costanzo Cargnoni, OFM Cap.[1]

Translated from the Italian by

Nancy Celaschi, OSF

The Difficulty of Synthesizing the Material

It is not easy to explain such an intricate and complex history in a few pages. We are dealing with 700 years of the development of concrete experiences and achievements which show many nuances in what motivated the establishment of Houses of Prayer within the Franciscan community. They are based on a knowledge and a choice found deep within various historical factors and which bounce from highs to lows and vice versa with many legislative interventions. They are shaded by the lights of various geographical and cultural environments and are finally also enriched by similar experiences in non-Franciscan monasticism, although they are then filtered by an attentive Franciscan sensitivity.

The difficulty does not come only from a lack of documentation about the variety of geographical regions or the establishment of houses of prayer for which, alongside an abundant documentation (especially concerning recent centuries and some geographical areas), there is a desert, a truly eremitical and inaccessible solitude of documentation which prevents a complete analysis of the contemplative experience. The difficulty is compounded especially by a confusion of terms.

The Meaning of "Houses of Prayer"

What is the real meaning of the term "Houses of Prayer"? What sense is there in saying "Houses of Prayer"? The very fact that the plural is used shows the multiplicity and variety of its historical forms, such as the architectural structure of church buildings changes with the progression of time and according to various geographical areas, although always expressing the same reality.

Drawing near to the term, however, and meditating on it, I have discovered facets of meaning and expressions that are diverse and at the same time consistent and complementary.

The idea of the "house of prayer" did not originate with the friars, but with Jesus Christ: "My house shall be called a house of prayer. . . " (Mt. 21:13). "The hour is coming when you will worship the Father neither on this mountain nor in Jerusalem. . . . But the hour is coming, and is now here, when true worshipers will worship the Father in Spirit and truth" (Jn. 4:21, 23). "Destroy this temple and in three days I will raise it up" (Jn. 2:19). "When you pray, go to your inner room, close the door, and pray to your Father in secret. And your Father who sees in secret will repay you" (Mt. 6:6).

A house of prayer demands secrecy, its desert, its hermitage, its solitude, because the Father "sees in secret"; it demands a certain amount of cloister, retreat and recollection ("Close the door and pray"); it requires a precise choice of time and place ("When you pray, go to your inner room"); it demands a passage and a passion-death-resurrection experience ("Destroy this temple . . ."); and finally it requires a renewal in the Spirit ("True worshipers will worship the Father in Spirit and truth").

St. Francis grasps the idea immediately and puts it into practice, in the process offering the essential core of what will become diverse experiences and forms of houses of prayer in the history of the Order. The variety of expressions and the spiritual wealth of the contemplative program of St. Francis and the first

Franciscans have already been studied by Fr. Octavian Schmucki.[2] Here I would like to give an overview of a simple, intuitive subdivision. The term "houses of prayer" can be interpreted in many ways, which I should like to reduce to three: 1) a generic, universal meaning; 2) a specific, particular, historical meaning; 3) a current meaning.

1. A Generic, Universal Meaning

Each friar is a "house of prayer." Therefore, wherever the friars are must be a house of prayer. Thus every friary is a house of prayer. The Friar Minor is a contemplative prayer journeying through the world. Without prayer, a house of prayer would be useless. This is Francis's final insight: "Although you are travelling, your conduct must be as upright as if you were in a hermitage or in your cell. Wherever we are, wherever we go, we bring our cell with us. Our brother body is our cell and our soul is the hermit living in that cell in order to pray to God and meditate."[3] Prayer is the "architect" of the "house of prayer."

Thus the merely material and exterior concept is surpassed, but not ruled out: "Whether they are in hermitages or in other places" the brothers "must always give themselves totally to prayer or to some good work."[4] Since the power of a living spiritual ideal is so great, St. Francis and the Order after him sense a need to "shape" it, to express it in visible, external dimensions. At the beginning it is but a rough draft, and then symbolic touches are added. Then, with the development of time, strong, unbreachable walls are added, separating them from the world and, at the same time, defending and nourishing the spirit with which the brothers are to travel through the world.

2. The Specific or Particular Historical Meaning

This refers to the concrete expression of an idea, the incarnation of the word, if I may dare to say so; it is the historical appearance of a grace, of a charism. Here the term "houses of prayer" synthesizes its various historical forms throughout 750 years of Franciscan living. In this regard, as we shall see later, there are four "moments" of development, four phases which follow a certain chronological evolution without continuity, and which represent a historical translation of the idea of a house of prayer. These can be divided as follows: the hermitages from the 13th to the 15th and 16th centuries; the houses of gathering, found in the 16th and 17th centuries; the *ritiros* of the 17th to 19th centuries; the deserts or solitary places in the 16th to 18th centuries.

No one can fail to imagine the possibility of interference or influences of other contemporary prayer experiences found in other religious Orders and various regions. Consider, for example, the "desert saints" of the Discalced Carmelites, the eremitical experience of the Benedictines, Carthusians, Camaldolese. Then, too, there is the influence of the mysterious, profound eremitical strain that has filtered into all the religious Orders, the modern ones included. However, it would be necessary to make some precise comparisons of the content of the various experiences in order to see their differences. A Franciscan "desert" is both like and unlike a Carmelite "desert" or a Camaldolese hermitage.[5]

3. Current Meaning

In the flourishing of so many experiences or attempts at renewal, it would seem that the establishment of "houses of prayer" are seen as a better guarantee for a concrete, valid renewal. It would seem that the Franciscan Order as a whole is speaking the same language today, with no division or distinction.

In fact, and here I am referring particularly to current Capuchin legislation, we find people speaking of *"ritiros"* for a temporary experience of prayer and penance; of "contemplative fraternities," which foresee a longer period of prayer experience; and last of all, almost summarizing the whole, there are plans for "fraternities of *ritiro* and contemplation" as a leaven of prayer life capable of stimulating the other communities as well. Then, too, there is even a desire for inter-obediential and international houses of prayer.[6]

Houses of Prayer and Franciscan Reforms

At this point there is a further elaboration to be made, one which I shall express by way of a question: Is it possible to distinguish between houses of prayer and Franciscan reform movements? It seems we should reply that it is possible to make such a distinction, although very difficult. This is because all the Franciscan reforms, those absorbed by the Order and those that became autonomous, always begin from a radical experience of prayer which finds its natural setting in insecure, solitary, abandoned, and poor places.

This would necessitate an analytical study of the individual cases, looking at the different experiences of reform in the Franciscan Order, and studying the initial expressions of the contemplative eremitical life. This task is too complex, especially because the number of individual and collective reforms, often independent of one another although contemporary and spread in various regions, have still not been given their proper understanding, interpretation, and synthesis in studies of Franciscan history.[7]

It can be said that a "house of prayer" is always the soul of a reform, a renewal. At the same time the idea of reform connected to the houses of prayer has often created difficulties for the house of prayer. There is a continual pendulum swinging between particular renewal and general redimensioning of the community of the Order. It seems that the various initiatives are authentic only if they are "sponsored from above," or at least "controlled from above." Ultimately it is a reflection of a Church which consistently rejects doctrinal and structural pluralism. Let us consider an example: around 1525, when a desire for reform throughout the Church had created some tension within the Franciscan Order (which also had to go through the difficulties created by the Capuchin reform), a Spanish Recollect friar, P. Francisco Ortiz, proclaimed during a chapter that the reform had to come from on high; otherwise it would be like a hole in water. He said:

> You yourselves know that we need reform. Indeed, to speak truthfully, this reform must begin, as does ointment, with the head, that is, the Pope. Then let it descend to the beard, that is, the general minister; and to the arms, that is, other prelates; and to the attendants, that is, the last novices. . . . Otherwise, as a matter of fact, our Order cannot be reformed. And as

long as such a great Order remains disordered, the
whole world will be unreformed. Read the author of
the *Conformities* that you may know how the world
should be reformed: the Order must first be reformed;
then our society, in which no one dare wear our habit in
public. But holy brothers are sustained by God in the
forests as once were the children of Israel in the
desert.[8]

This tells us about an idea that was widespread at that
time. Reforms, however, were usually begun by simple, zealous
friars, and then had their effect in every project and human logic
of a juridical or disciplinary nature.

Essential Retrospective Bibliography

However, in the end it is the idea which supports the
synthesis of Fr. Dacian Bluma in *De vita recessuali in historia et
legislatione OFM.*[9] Having traced out the historical development
of houses of prayer in the Order and the persistent Franciscan
vocation to a life of recollection, he shows the relationship
between various houses of prayer and the ministers general of the
Order who promoted them or supported them as the only means
for preserving the unity of the Order. The merit of this synthesis,
which also emphasizes the fundamental importance of the
contemplative life in the Franciscan vocation, is in the
comparison of the various official documents and the statutes
concerning the houses of prayer, although some particular
statutes are omitted because they apply to only a limited
geographical area. This is the reason why many interesting
things with suggestions for the reform in progress are omitted,
such as the statutes of Blessed Bonaventure of Barcelona for the
convents of the *ritiro*, those of St. John Joseph of the Cross and of
St. Leonard of Port Maurice for deserts or solitudes and those, for
example, of Ven. Gesualdo of Reggio for the Capuchin friaries of
the *ritiro*.

Another clear and suggestive synthesis can be found under the
heading of *"Déserts"* (*Les déserts dans l'Ordre de saint François*),
edited by Fr. Melchior de Pobladura for the *Dictionnaire de
spiritualité,* and printed in 1957.[10] It is remarkable how many

Franciscan books and studies have not taken up such a vital topic, such a necessary one, in order to offer a complete and definitive synthesis of the phenomenon.

Various articles, particular or geographically limited studies, have appeared in some reviews, especially with direct reference to eremitism in Europe, which is eliciting the interest of many medievalists, even among anticlericals.[11] Perhaps the time has come to take up the vast range of this topic and study it thoroughly, in such a way that there can be a good historical awareness to accompany and balance the charismatic dynamism of the various experiences now underway or "in hope of good will."

It is truly a "charismatic" element of the Franciscan life, which directly touches the founding charism and Franciscan spirituality. This is the reason it continually arises in the history of the Order and can encounter tension and resistance which can be explained by the authorities' and ministers' fear of seeing friars escape from the control of their obedience.[12]

Perspectives for Research into and a Definition of Franciscan Houses of Prayer

In this regard, before looking at the various elements and geographical areas where it developed, I felt it opportune not to give an outline of the external development of the houses of prayer —which I will, however, do very briefly—but rather to insist on the spiritual content of the various experiences, their apostolic strategy, their motivation and original historical purpose, making use of precise spiritual literature and followed with attention and hope by official and particular legislation. It is obvious that the topic would lend itself to many other historical, sociological, and spiritual considerations which I am not capable of making.[13]

Synthesizing the many historical experiences, I would make this essential definition: by a "Franciscan house of prayer" I mean a group of friars (no fewer than three or four) who come together and want to live together in a certain place, usually somewhere isolated and remote from other dwellings, in order to observe the *Rule* of St. Francis spiritually. Therefore, I would emphasize:

1) the element of community or fraternity;
2) the spiritual observance of the *Rule*;
3) the eremitical or contemplative element.

In the spiritual observance of the *Rule* I include ecclesial apostolicity, that is, the communion with the superiors (Apostolic See, bishops, ministers general, provincials, and all the friars) and the flourishing of various ministries, services, and charisms in the Church, especially the *ministerium verbi*, the proclamation of the Word.

For the sake of clarity I will use four terms which by now have become consecrated by use, and which express the historical evolution of houses of prayer in the Franciscan order: hermitage or *romitorio*, house of gathering, *ritiro*, desert or solitude.

1. The Franciscan *Romitorio* (13th to 16th Centuries)

St. Francis and the Spirituals

The constitution of the hermitage or *romitorio* is first of all tied up with the power and example of St. Francis and then of the Spirituals. These are two powerful forces: St. Francis and the interpretation of the Spirituals. The latter are concerned with the "spiritual" interpretation of the *Rule*. For them the *romitorio* is the place par excellence where this spiritual observance is possible, the true place of the Franciscan spirit.

St. Francis does not speak of friaries, but rather only about the *eremus* or the *locus*, and almost never of a *domus*.[14] The Spirituals treasure these words of Francis in their hearts and put them into practice: they want nothing other than the *romitorio*. This is a demand and a choice for radical contemplation and poverty, but concentrated to a great degree, so much so that it never stopped suggesting and fomenting renewal and Franciscan reforms.[15]

The Spirituals interpreted the Franciscan freedom to have recourse to one's ministers when a friar knows that he cannot observe the *Rule* spiritually in the following manner, as was explained many centuries later, for example, by a Capuchin from

Brescia, Fr. Gaudenzio Lollio (†1769), in his commentary on the *Rule*, entitled *Lo spirito della serafica regola*: when our *Rule* is no longer observed "those who truly love the purity of the *Rule*" ask their ministers and even, if necessary, the Apostolic See, for the "freedom to withdraw to some poor, solitary friary where, in simplicity and quiet spirit they can see to its pure observance."[16]

The urban evolution of Franciscanism quickly establishes a polarity between the hermitages and the friaries in the city. As a result of the heated spiritualistic debates, a certain type of history dominated by these controversies contributed in some way to fostering a suspicion of the Franciscan *romitorio* and those who lived there.

Also of historical significance is the fact that in the oldest lists of statistics, for example, in the *Provinciale vetustissimum* or in the statistics given for 1282—no distinction is made between friaries and hermitages. In fact, some places that are clearly hermitages are called friaries, and some hermitages are not counted.[17] Certainly the division and distinction would not have pleased Francis. However, the Spirituals' flight to the hermitages emphasized the distinction between "house" and "dwelling/ hermitage," for which reason the Constitutions of Narbonne state: "Each house within province boundaries will have hermitage dwellings relatively close to it," although not everybody accepts this interpretation.[18] The hermitage becomes a trampoline where the Franciscan and Spiritual reforms are launched; but despite all their extremism, the hermitage helped to safeguard an essential aspect of Franciscan life, which perhaps was too neglected in the competition against the Dominicans in scientific study and organized apostolate and the consequent urban settlements.

The Franciscan hermitage phase, in the sense that at that time within the Order there was no other alternative for the zealous friars, begins with St. Francis, and is heightened with the Spirituals in the 13th-15th century. It is given a balanced renewal in the early observance of the 14th-15th centuries and blossoms in the houses of gathering in the 16th century and those following.

Areas of Geographical Development

The areas of geographical development are first of all in south-central Italy, particularly the classical hermitages of Umbria, the Marches, Tuscany, and the provinces of Naples and Genoa; then in Provence and often Tours and Spain. However, a list of Franciscan hermitages from the 13th-15th centuries has never been compiled, also because what often began as a hermitage developed into a friary. It began with a first stage which might have had a small church or an abandoned country chapel, some kilometers away from any town, and ended up becoming a small city. Then the first settlement of an eremitical type would have disappeared or been absorbed by other places of solitude or hermitages or remained as a reminder of the heroic beginnings for the zealous friars.[19]

In 1294, with the support of Pope Celestine V, Fr. Liberatus of Macerata and Angelo Clareno and their followers formed the Poor Hermits, or the Celestini. They did not last long, but the name that they adopted is of significance. From the Speco of Subiaco their hermitages spread out to Tivoli and included the hermitages of St. Lucia, St. Blaise, St. Maria of Gallicano, Selva Matutina, St. Mary of Monte Santo, among others. They took the name of Clareni in 1302, in a series of ups and downs, and lasted until the 16th century.[20]

In 1334 John della Valle received permission to live in the hermitage of St. Bartolomeo di Brugliano near Foligno. In 1350 Gentile of Spoleto, a layman, has four hermitages: the Carceri, Giano, Eremita, and Monteluco, with the possibility of accepting novices and therefore with a certain degree of autonomy from the Province. The infiltration of the spirit of the *fraticelli* brings about a crisis in the reform five years later.[21]

In 1368 we see the beginning of the balancing work of Paoluccio Vagnozzi Trinci from Foligno, who gets back the hermitage of Brugliano. In 1390 there are 22 hermitages of Paoluccio Trinci. Faloci Pulignani offers a list of these hermitages: Brogliano a Pischia, Monteluco near Spoleto, the Carceri, Greccio near Rieti, Fonte Colombo near Rieti, Poggio Bustone, Stroncono near Narni, the Eremita, Monte Giove (La Spineta), La Scarzola, Giano of Spoleto, Perugia, La

Rocchiocciola in Assisi, San Damiano, Farneto near Perugia, Montegiove near Perugia, Forano in the Marches, Massa, Montefalcone, Camerino, Cessa Palombo, and Morro.[22]

Structure and Spiritual Contents of the Italian Hermitages

As for the structure of these hermitages, that is, the daily life of the ardent, solitary friars, little or nothing is known. No particular rules are extant. The *Rule* of St. Francis, his Testament, the "Rule for Hermitages" and the example of the Portiuncula are more than enough. Therefore silence, solitude, continuous prayer, penance, poverty, manual labor, and a strict separation from the world constitute the eremitical life meant to foster contemplation, which everything else must serve. The external apostolate is extremely limited, but not absolutely ruled out. However, it is always directed towards a life of prayer.[23]

It is difficult to "take the pulse" of this prayer, reconstruct the daily rhythm of the contemplative life in Franciscan hermitages. A few cells—five or six, perhaps—of wood or branches or masonry, separated or joined to one another by a wall of bushes or wood or stone, dancing mystically around a focal point represented by an abandoned church ("we were glad to stay in poor or abandoned churches")[24] or a chapel or oratory. In this walled off space the separate cells were the place for the intimate prayer of the hermits who used the garden for a bit of manual labor. The hermitage of La Verna, for example, is a radical isolation in a wilderness setting, mysterious solitude, everything built around the chapel of the Stigmata, placed as it were like a watchtower, totally isolated from the rest of the solitude. The caves or rocky caverns express a sense of inner penetration and the rocky outcroppings suggest a motivation of spiritual "ascension."[25] It is an environment transfigured by penitential contemplation, as if the contemplative spirit of St. Francis had left its image in the rocks and the structures of the cells, the caves and the woods, which otherwise would have been left without a spiritual echo. It is precisely solitude in the solitude. For this reason the houses of prayer in the Order should be like a cell within a cell, a separation in an area for fleeing the world, in an evangelical-Franciscan sense.

Another circumstance can be noted. It is not a question of a total eremitism. In the Franciscan Order there are only hermits who live with other hermits, although a purely contemplative vocation is not totally extraneous to it.[26] It is always a minority, like a voice crying in the wilderness. Blessed Bernardino Aquilano of Fossa writes in his *Chronica Fratrum Minorum Observantiae*: "A few good brothers attempted at once to gather together, and to be separate from the common life of the brothers, and, in accord with their fragile human condition, to observe the *Rule* simply."[27]

Furthermore we can note a certain influence of Camaldolese eremitism, but represented with a new spirit. This influence is repeated in some way for the Capuchins and the solitudes of St. John Joseph of the Cross. The Camaldolese hermitage is something like the ancient *laura*, a village of isolated cells built around a church. Different from the Carthusian type with its adjacent cells opening up onto a common cloister, the Camaldolese hermitage has no cloister and the cells are to be a certain distance (six to ten meters) apart from one another. One of the characteristics of the Camaldolese is that the hermit is also allowed to be a recluse, thus having radical isolation in a place that is already isolated.[28]

Another point that seems to be important and noteworthy is also the influence of the spirituality of the desert fathers, and in particular of Cassian and St. John Climacus, obviously setting aside the writings of the early Franciscan tradition which are more decisive. For example, John Climacus' *Scala Paradisi* was translated into Latin by Angelus of Clareno himself and for the first time was rendered in Italian by Clareno's disciple, Gentile of Foligno.[29] It is a whole prayer journey, what the Fathers call "mental and cordial," and its fruits are detachment from sensible beauty in order to be able to see God in them, humility, compunction, tears, a clear vision of self (as in a mirror), perfect purity and ineffable joy. It is a search for a place of the heart in order to see the light of Tabor.[30] Bernardino of Fossa tells us that Climacus' *Scala Paradisi* "in our community is held in high regard. For it teaches spiritual living; it teaches the temptations of demons and the vices, that these may be avoided.

And how we may follow the paths of virtue, it explains in a marvelous manner."[31]

Prayer and Formation in the Hermitages

The content of this contemplative prayer can be understood by reading some passages of the *Fioretti* of St. Francis which describe the contemplative experience of some of the holy friars from the Marches, such as Conrad of Offida, Peter of Monticello, and especially John of La Verna, who lived for the most part in hermitages. Reflection on the passion of Christ is almost the total catalyst for their mental prayer, as a way to approach the Father and lose themselves in the mystery of the Trinity.[32] The spiritual freedom they enjoyed in the quiet of the eremitical life allowed them greater spontaneity in prayer, including in their bodily acts and expressions. They made frequent use of gestures such as praying with outstretched arms, standing, kneeling, prostrate on the ground, or doubled over. It was an imitation of the Seraphic Father and a reminder of the stigmatization; the figure of the seraph of La Verna had fixed such postures in the memory of the friars and later in the writings and in iconography.[33]

Bernardino of Fossa also mentions this aspect in his Chronicle:

> As the brothers persevered in holiness of life, in regular observance, in intense devotion and especially in applying themselves to prayer, esteem for them among the people increased significantly. When they went to beg alms, they were not embarrassed to pray the Our Father with arms extended in the form of a cross. Further, while they awaited the alms, they kept making genuflections. In their places of solitude, they were thought to pass day and night in many tears and in calling to mind the sufferings of Jesus our Savior. Many young people began to change their ways because of the influence of their holy life.[34]

So we see that the solitude of the hermitage was not isolation, disdain, noninvolvement or misanthropism, but a catalytic experience for people and a leaven for new vocations. We should make this observation right away: How is it possible to accept young people in the hermitage? The tradition of the desert fathers said that the desert was not for beginners. St. Benedict, foreseeing the possibility of the anchoritic life for his monks, had written in chapter one of his *Rule* that "these hermits are not novices filled with fervor. They have had a long trial period in the monastery. They have learned to fight against the demons. They have drawn profit from the experience of many others. They have trained in the singular combat of the desert with other brothers."[35] Therefore they must have had a long period of trial in the *cenobium* before being able to live in solitude. Yet the Franciscans living in the hermitages manage to find young novices, even children. This helps highlight the direct relationship between eremitism and the reform of the Order.[36] Let us, however, leave this question aside because it takes us too far off the topic. It does, however, reappear in the Spanish eremitical experience.

Spanish Hermitages

If it is difficult to analyze the spiritual content of the Italian hermitages; we are in a better position in what concerns the Spanish hermitages of the 14th and 15th centuries. For this we have the thorough study of the origins of the Observant Movement in Spain, which appeared in 1957 in *Archivio Ibero-Americano*; it was also clearly synthesized by Fr. Isidoro of Villapadierna of the Capuchin Historical Institute. There are also the articles by Fr. Luis Carrión.[37]

Towards the end of the 16th century and the beginning of the 17th there was a simultaneous explosion of three reforms: the eremitical reform which consisted of a constellation of hermitages not federated with one another; the Villacrecian reform which was composed of groups of friaries of "conventual hermitages" following precise regulations; and the "Regular Observance," which can be found in Italy and the rest of Europe. The centers of the reform are the three provinces of Castille, Aragon, and Santiago. In the latter province the eremitical movement began in 1392 with the friar Gonzalo Mariño and two other friars who obtained from Boniface IX permission to found some hermitages "for the welfare of their souls and peace of heart" but "subject to the customary obedience." The first hermitage is that of St. Lawrence of Trasouto near Santiago. In 1407 there are already seven hermitages, and in 1432 their number has risen to 12 or 13. In 1448 they were definitively absorbed by the Observant reform.[38]

In the province of Castille the foundation of hermitages was promoted by friar Peter of Villacreces who obtained permission from Benedict XIII in 1395 to withdraw *én vida hermetica conventual*. The first hermitage is Our Lady of Salceda. In the first years of the 15th century there are Our Lady of Aguilera or Domus Dei and S. Mary of El Abrojo or Scala Coeli. Fra. Peter of Santoyo, a disciple of St. Anthony of la Cabrera, founded other hermitages: St. Mary of Grace in Villasilos in the diocese of Palencia; St. Mary of Consolation, known as Calahorra; St. Mary of Hope in Valdescopeso near Medina; and St. Mary of Mercy near Paredes de la Navas. In 1454 these eight hermitages form the custody of St. Mary of the Minors under obedience to the Conventuals.[39]

In the interim other independent hermitages spring up in Castille alongside the reform friaries of the Observants. The first is that of Holy Spirit of the Mount, in the Kingdom of Valenza in 1403; with it, three others form the first Observant custody in Spain in 1424.[40]

In this plurality of eremitical reforms we can see some coincidence with the ideals of the Spirituals in what concerns the literal observance of the *Rule* and the use of the early Franciscan literary sources. However, this eremitical movement is independent of similar Italian or French experiences. How can this be explained? As the historians tell us, it can be explained from "their direct contact with the written sources of the first generations of Franciscans," which was facilitated by the compilations which were being spread throughout Spain in the early decades of the 16th century "through the work of the *scriptoria* [writing rooms] of the friaries of the community. The only historical similarity between the Spanish hermits and the Spirituals can be seen in the fact that both of them drew on the same sources to encourage a return to the primitive ideal."[41] Their reference to St. Francis is very strong.

The Experience of Peter of Villacreces

At the Council of Constance, Peter of Villacreces received from Martin VI and Nicholas V some briefs of approbation in order to observe "all the constitutions which our father St. Francis, as his death drew near, made for St. Mary of the Angels and other hermitages."[42]

Villacreces's hermitages should not be understood in the strict sense of the word, as places for the eremitical life, but as small, poor, and humble residences as distinct from the imposing ones of the large friaries. However, there was the possibility of living there the ancient eremitical experience. St. Peter Regalado had a "hermit's cell" in the garden of the friary, where he would withdraw to pray. A text from the process of the canonization states that: "Many times rapt in ecstasy, he ordinarily entered to pray in a hermitage which was within the garden of the friary of Aguilera and every time he was in prayer, he would leave the hermitage aflame. . . ."[43]

These hermitages were governed by detailed regulations which structured every minute of the day and night: the *Memoriale religionis* [schedule of religious services] or *Memoriale religionis de oficios activos y contemplativos*, which were Villacreces's norms for the friaries of La Aguilera and El Abrojo; the *Memoriale de la vita y ritos de la Custodia de S. María de los Menores* and the *Constituciones de la Custodia de S. María de los Menores*.[44] With this legislative corpus it is possible to reconstruct the rhythm of prayer in these hermitages, which at the beginning could house no more than 12 friars.

There were five hours of sleep before Matins and one hour after. The Divine Office, which was normally recited in plainsong, took seven hours on ferial days or work days, eight hours on Sundays and feasts, nine hours on Easter and other solemnities. A small organ was allowed. Before each canonical hour there was fifteen minutes of meditation besides the two hours established; a half hour every Prime and None; an hour after Compline, with a quarter hour of modulation on the steps of the *Passio* of pseudo-Anselm in order to inflame the hearts which were still arid. There were other devotions, such as a nocturnal procession "for benefactors and malfactors, prelates of the Order and absent friars." Altogether, Villacreces' hermits spent 12 to 13 hours a day in the Liturgy of the Hours and meditation.[45]

Spiritual reading was made in common: on Friday the reading was from the Gospel, the *Earlier Rule* and the *Later Rule*, the Testament, their own regulations and other primitive Franciscan texts such as the *Flores* and the chronicles. On the other days Scripture was read on a three-year cycle, and St. Bonaventure's *Regula novitiorum* in a one, or two–year cycle. The readings also indicate some of the sources of spirituality: much space is given to readings from monastic literature, such as the works of Cassian, John Climacus, St. Bernard, St. Jerome, and others.[46]

There was absolute silence throughout the day. From mid-September to Easter, vigils were held in the vigil room by the light of a few small candles, always in silence. Each friar devoted himself to the study of the Divine Office or some other study, in writing and correcting devotional books, doing some other work, such as drawing, mending, sewing, and the like.[47] It was a difficult commitment.

The community was governed by a "president," and after him there was a "formator," or master of postulants, novices, young professed and serving boys. Therefore we see that in these hermitages even very young boys were accepted, and submitted to a rigid discipline. Villacreces's favorite disciples were St. Peter Regalado and Lope de Salazar y Salinas, who were still very young when they were received in the hermitage of La Aguilera.[48]

Their prayer life is described briefly in chapter 12 of *Memoriale religionis*: "The contemplative offices, which all the active offices of Religion must serve, are as follows: 'pray devoutly, meditate in holiness, contemplate loftily.' The Abbot Isaac speaks very much about this. These offices, founded in evangelical poverty and perfect humility, are the principal purpose of all Religion." Note the classic triplet: *oratio —meditatio—contemplatio*. It is a whole commitment to meditation and contemplation, a "continuous work of holy prayer, devotion and pious meditation," with great emphasis on liturgical celebration.[49]

Certainly there was a lack of that happy freshness and simple spontaneity which marked the life of St. Francis and the early hermitages, but the intensity of the mental and vocal prayer which inspired the Villacrecian hermitages is almost proverbial.

2. Houses of Gathering (16th to 18th Centuries)

Observants and Houses of Gathering: Various Motives

The Observants, who obtained permission from the Council of Constance to have their own Vicars General, were against the Villacrecian hermits because they were under the Minister General and did not want any division; their only desire was to be a special witness within the Order, a sign that there was still "a little remnant which observed that special type of eremitical and contemplative life which St. Francis and his closest companions embraced in the *ritiros* of the hermitages."[50] However, in 1471 they were definitively suppressed and absorbed by the Observant wave.

In 1487 the search for the eremitical life sprang up anew when Juan de la Puebla and his beloved disciple Juan de Guadalupe, under the immediate jurisdiction of the Minister General, began within the Observant reform a discalced reform, which was sometimes called the reform "of the holy Gospel" or "of the Capuche." The model they chose was the form of life in the hermitage of the Carceri.[51] It would be perfected by St. Peter of Alcantara in the hermitage of Pedroso, which is more properly a desert or solitude experience, as we shall see later. It was then that the Vicar General Martial Boulier, in the 1502 chapter in Castille, decreed that every province should have some friaries in solitary places for the more zealous friars. This was the birth of the "houses of gathering," which would be organized twenty years later.[52]

In this case, too, the basic motive is the purer observance of the *Rule* in order to maintain the unity of the Order. The number of reform movements was increasing, and it was necessary as well to find some way of creating an outlet for the more zealous friars. For this reason the Minister General Francesco Lichetto allows some friars to live an eremitical life at Fonte Palombo and in

1519 creates the houses of gathering. Stefano of Molino, a Spaniard belonging to the Roman Province, is the leader of these friars, and finds support in the new Minister General Francisco Quiñones of los Angeles. Thus in the provincial chapter of Palencia held in 1523 clear statutes were given to some houses of gathering, which were reconfirmed as an alternative for the friars who were encouraged by their conscience.[53]

We should not overlook the fact that in a single decade many reforms would begin: the Recollects in France in 1523; the Capuchins in Italy in 1525/28; the Reformed in Italy in 1532; the Alcantarines, and others. As usual, Quiñones wanted to preserve the unity of the Order. We should take note of the purpose expressed in the regulations for these houses of gathering:

> Knowing from first-hand experience, from my visit to the Spanish provinces, the great inconveniences caused from not granting the good desires of the religious, and the restlessness to be found in the friars who are led by their conscience, and ask to go to other provinces in order to observe the *Rule* with greater purity, quiet and severity . . . I order by power of obedience that five houses of gathering (*"casas de recogimiento"*) be established in the Province: the friaries of l'Aguilera, Abrojo, Vadescopeço, Villasilos, and Calahorra.[54]

In a manuscript of a chronicle of the Province of the Immaculate Conception, we find that Quiñones, and the Province were appealing more to the mitigated system of Pedro Santoyo than the rigorous one of Villacreces.[55] Quiñones' initiative for Spain was also repeated in Italy, as if to offer an alternative to the Capuchin reform. Thus in 1525/26 there were five places, including Fonte Palombo and Greccio, for these *reformati* who, with the approval of Clement VII, received their own constitutions in 1532.[56]

In his historical survey Fr. Bluma says that at this point it is difficult to describe the evolution of the houses of gathering from their relationship to a given reform because it is not always easy to distinguish to which reform movement they belonged.[57] This shows that we are dealing with an official institution which was looked upon favorably by the ministers, generally accepted by the whole Order in its reforms, but not by the

Capuchins, who suddenly separated and became autonomous, returning to the most stringent forms of the solitary life with many Spiritualist traces and similarities to Villacreces' reform and the primitive observance.

General Statutes and Historical Evolution

Several sets of general statutes exist for houses of gathering: in 1582 Francisco Gonzaga prescribes Quiñones' norms for the reformed and recollect houses; in 1595 Bonaventure of Caltagirone reissues these adapted norms for the Belgian and French Recollects and, in 1621, for those of Spain. In 1676 relations between the houses of gathering and provinces are underlined for the cismontane Observant provinces; in 1684 the shorter form of the statutes is republished in Italian by the Minister General Sormano and is to be found repeated up until the end of the 19th century.[58]

Bluma summarizes the purposes to be found in the evolution of the houses of gathering:

1) a place of prayer and solitude;
2) a "seminary" for the education of the youth of the province;
3) a means of reform.

It should also be noted that the houses of gathering are influenced by the *ritiros,* and the juridical legislative terminology speaks of a *recessus* when referring to houses of gathering and *ritiros* alike.[59]

Structure and Spiritual Content

What was the daily prayer routine in these houses of gathering? Basically, it was not very different from what was specified in Villacreces' norms, although it was of a more mitigated tone, since the Recollect friars who worked with Quiñones in formulating the 1523 statutes had lived in the hermitage friaries of Peter of Villacreces and had known St. Peter Regalado.[60]

At 4:45 each morning the sacristan knocked on the doors of the cells and the religious headed to the choir. At five they prayed Prime, which was always sung in a plainsong. Then the community had a half hour of mental prayer, until 6:00 or 6:15; then came meditation, which was omitted when a Mass was sung after Prime, e.g., on Saturdays in honor of the Blessed Virgin and on Mondays for deceased benefactors and the souls in purgatory. In addition to the Liturgy of the Hours and continuous obedience, mental prayer was the friars' main task: "The entire exercise of the religious has to be reading, prayer, meditation, and contemplation," that is, *lectio, oratio, meditatio, ontemplatio*. This is the great lesson of the monastic tradition as described, for example, by Guigo the Carthusian in his treatise *Scala claustralium*: "Seek it in reading, and you will find it with meditation; keep on pounding away at prayer, and you will enter into it with contemplation. Reading brings nourishment to the mouth, meditation chews it and cuts it up, prayer draws flavor from it and contemplation is the flavor which brings joy and refreshment."[61]

The *recollect* was always to have particular times of mental prayer, day and night, divided as follows: an hour of prayer after Compline and a half hour after Terce all through the year; from mid-September to Easter, another whole hour after Matins; from Easter to September, 45 minutes after None and on fast days before dinner, after the main Mass, when the bell was rung. The meditation after Matins was always based on the life and passion of Christ.[62]

During the time for meditation, all the friars—with the exception of the novices and postulants who were subject to their masters—could freely choose the most apt place for their need, such as the church, choir, cloister, oratory, chapter hall, or the chapels in the friary. Anyone who took care of other things during prayer time was reprimanded and had to go with the novices for prayer for a week. The guardians had to be very diligent to know how the friars were spending their prayer time. They were all to prepare for meditation by reading spiritual books.

At nine in the morning the large bell rang and everyone came to choir to chant Terce and celebrate the community Mass which was obligatory for everyone except for preachers and confessors on

Sundays and feasts. After Mass they recited Sext and None and made another half hour of meditation, which lasted until 10:45. At 11 they ate dinner in complete silence, with chapter of faults on Monday, Wednesday, and Friday. During Advent and Lent they performed penitential practises on Tuesday, Thursday, and Saturday: they ate while sitting on the bare earth, they kept the *restraint* in their mouth, kissed the feet of their brethren and lay prostrate at the refectory door so that all the other friars had to step over them; these practices were often performed by the novices. After their frugal meal, everyone, without exception, went to wash the dishes while chanting the gradual psalms. At 12:30 the bell rang again for silence and siesta. At 2 p.m. a light knock at the door called the friars to prepare to celebrate the liturgy for the following day. At 2:30 the bell tower called them together for Vespers. After Vespers there was manual labor until Compline, which was celebrated with full solemnity, at 5:15. At 7:00 p.m. they went to the refectory for supper. Eight o'clock was bedtime, preceded by the use of the discipline on specified days and during Lent. Fifteen minutes before midnight the sacristan knocked on the doors of the cells to call them to Matins. At midnight precisely the bell rang, and Matins, which lasted about two hours, was followed by mental prayer.

To summarize, every day the friars in the houses of gathering spent three hours and 45 minutes in mental prayer, with the novices spending much more time; they also spent approximately seven hours reciting the Liturgy of the Hours "in a most devout tone."

Thus we see that their life was shrouded in silence, prayer, penance, and poverty.[63]

Formative and Pedagogical Element

It is interesting to note the formative and pedagogical element in relationship to the novitiate and young professed: "It is decreed that in each Province of this family of the Observance three or four Convents of Recollection should be established. They are to be a first and second novitiate. They are also to serve the entire Province as houses of spiritual retreat and seminaries of perfection."[64]

The second novitiate meant that before being admitted to studies, the professed had to spend at least a year in the houses of gathering, and this was written into law.

The way of life drafted by the General Chapter in 1676 and published, with the approbation of Innocent XI three years later, prescribed in eleven articles two-and-a-half hours of mental prayer each day.[65] In Spain and Latin America there was a proliferation of these houses, but not so in other places: the ministers often had to intervene to enforce the regulations.[66] The decadence was especially strong in the 18th century. The renewal movement was expressed in a new type of house of prayer, the *ritiro*.

3. The *Ritiro* (17th to 19th Centuries)

The "Riformella" of Blessed Bonaventure of Barcelona

The "Riformella" or *ritiro* movement can be considered a real gem among the houses of prayer and had a wonderful development, which was confined almost entirely to Italy. The founder was Blessed Bonaventure of Riodoco, commonly called Bonaventure of Barcelona.[67] The movement had a charismatic origin. This lay brother withdrew to a life of prayer in a Spanish hermitage, and felt an irresistible inspiration of the Spirit calling him to Rome for this purpose. In obedience he came and expressed his plan to a few friars. The Minister General, Michelangelo of Sambuca, heard about the matter and reacted in opposition to everything new, "which often arises from human malice" as it says in the *Chronologia historico-legalis*.[68] He forbade the Spanish lay brother to speak about it, and reprimanded him severely. The year was 1659. There was violent opposition against the *ritiro* movement. There were at least 80 written complaints about it sent to the Minister General, and the quarrel reached the courts of Vienna and Madrid.

The opposition came from both friars and ministers who, with all good intention, wanted to preserve the unity of the Order, which they believed was threatened by this institution. Bonaventure of Barcelona, however, was supported by "protectors" with great influence with the Holy See, and in 1662 he presented a strong appeal to the Sacred Congregation, in which he listed the purpose of the *ritiro* movement:

1) in order that we may better observe the *Rule* of our Holy Father St. Francis;
2) that we may be one with the sentiments of the seraphic constitutions;
3) for an increase of solitude and most humble and naked poverty of spirit;
4) to rediscover in total self-denial and the most determined separation from people, the sense of withdrawal and poverty which St. Francis practiced so much.

These four motives were summarized at the end of the appeal in this phrase: "our only intention is to serve God in the pure and literal observance of the *Rule*."[69]

On November 25, 1662, Bonaventure of Barcelona and 11 other friars received the friary of Our Lady of Grace near Ponticelli (Rieti); in 1666 he obtained the friary of St. Angelo di Montorio in Rome; one year later he received the friary of Saints Cosmas and Damian in Vicovaro; 10 years later, in 1677, they were given St. Bonaventure on Rome's Palatine hill. These friaries of the *ritiro* movement would form their own custody in the 19th century, independent from the provincial and directly obedient to the General, but at the beginning they were under obedience to the Minister Provincial of the Roman Reformed Province.

After the death of the founder in 1684, *ritiros* also developed in Tuscany, at Monte alle Croci in Florence, and at Palco di Prato. This growth was the work of the Venerable Pius of S. Colomba.[70]

Reasons for the Development of the *Ritiros*

The idea of Blessed Bonaventure always inspired the development of *ritiros* hand in hand with the spread of the houses of gathering made obligatory for the Order of Friars Minor of the Observance with the decree of 1676. Among the great driving forces behind the spread of the *ritiro* at the end of the 17th and throughout the 18th century were Blessed Thomas of Cori, who founded Civitella (Bellegra) in 1684 and Palombara in 1703; St. Theophilus of Corte, who founded the *ritiro* of Fucecchio in 1736; Blessed Leopold of Gaiche who founded the *ritiro* at Monteluco (Spoleto) in 1788. Another great name was St. Leonard of Port Maurice, who was responsible for the spread of *ritiros* in Tuscany.[71]

The *ritiros* enjoyed greater success than the houses of recollection because, as Fr. Anastasi writes, they enjoyed no privileges or special exemption, but the friars who lived there determined to observe the *Rule* in union with the Province. Besides, they all had an apostolic outreach, which found its dynamism in the life of contemplative solitude and most perfect observance of the *Rule*.[72]

Different *ritiros* had different origins. Let us look at a few examples.

Some Examples

In 1761 six religious signed an appeal to the Definitors gathered together at Lastra di Signa. In the appeal we read: "They ask for a friary so that . . . they might have the ability to continue the exercise of the missions, without the service of the choir being impeded, night or day, by the absence of the preachers; this friary could be Montepulciano where, since it is the formation house the young friars could be well trained, the city edified and the Lord glorified." The Definitory granted the request, "provided that, for the common good of the Province, the Definitory always retains the authority to remove from said convent one or the other of those who dwell there."[73]

In 1707 Fr. Antonio of Montebufo, Vice Commissary General, had ordered the Riformati Province to begin a *ritiro*. The Sacred Congregation for the Regular Discipline did the same for all Friars Minor a year later. In Antonio of Montebufo's circular letter we read:

> Since a number of religious have zealously asked to withdraw to friaries where they can live a more exact observance of the *Rule* and Statutes in order to tend entirely to perfection there, far from corruption, and often adding that such friaries are not to be found in their province, they ask to be sent to the sacred mountain of La Verna, the sanctuaries of Umbria and

the Rieti Valley, or also to transfer to the *ritiros* in Rome, I for my part did not want to impede them in fulfilling these seraphic sentiments which I am glad to see enkindled in the hearts of my religious, and, on the other hand, not being certain that these desires and impulses are of a true spirit, in order not to err, and to satisfy them as much as I can, I hereby order that in the very next congress that they shall have, the ministers provincial and definitors should designate one of their friaries more adaptable to this purpose, where the *Rule*, Apostolic Constitutions and those of the Order can be observed with total rigor and in all things within and without the brightness of the Riformato *Rule* and Regular Discipline may be maintained; they should send here only those religious anxious to profit from it and to remain fervent and serve the Lord in prayer, solitude, humility and poverty. Once the friary has been designated, the designation will be communicated to the province through a circular, inviting those whom the Lord inspires. . . . They should be careful not to allow anything in those friaries which not only could lead to, but not even reflect the slightest shadow of separation from the province and the absolute government of the provincial. . . . In these friaries, which are to be dedicated entirely to the spirit, devotion and prayer, there can be no study, nor lectors, nor any other religious, except for what is done in friary. These friaries do not need to accept financial offerings for Masses.[74]

In the General Chapter of 1762 the problem of the *ritiros* was also discussed. Benedict XIV also attended and, advised by his great friend, St. Leonard of Port Maurice, he recommended that all the capitulars establish at least one *ritiro* in their province.[75]

The *ritiros* were often supported and aided by lay nobility and ecclesiastics. This is true, for example, of Monteluco, begun in 1788 by Bl. Leopold of Gaiche, a Reformed friar, with the help of Fr. Felice of Poggio Catino of the Roman Province, who was also the founder of the *ritiros* of Greccio and Sezze. An eyewitness tells us that these friars lived exclusively from begging almost every day, but accepting no money; their poverty was very strict, and they shared everything in common: bare and simple cells, rough food, frequent periods of abstinence and fasting (almost eight months a year), manual labor with the recitation of prayer, continuous strict silence, strict cloister; they went out only to beg or to minister to the spiritual needs of others; "one can say that their prayer was in some way uninterrupted: usually they spent eight or nine hours a day in common prayer, and much more time in extraordinary prayers; morning and night, without exception, long nightly disciplines"; in short, "uniformity of practice, readiness for all the Hours of Office, austerity of life, punctual and voluntary obedience, mutual respect, religious simplicity, and most of all a sense of withdrawal and complete detachment from every little thing."

After his tiring missions among the people, Bl. Leopold would withdraw to what he called his "rest quarters" at Monteluco, and meticulously lead the hermit's life, so that a great number of religious, ecclesiastics and seculars would come from all over to visit that holy place and to make a retreat there from time to time.[76]

Legislation and Spiritual Content

The *ritiros* were looked upon kindly by the ministers, but not all of them; originally they were only for the professed, but they later became novitiates, and this brought about an explosion of beauty. The whole evolution of the *ritiros* was accompanied by thorough, lengthy, minute but changing legislation. The Statutes of Bl. Bonaventure of Barcelona were like the *seminarium aliorum statutorum* and inspired the 12 *Rules* of Bl. Tommaso of Cori; the *Avvisi* of St. Theophilus of Corte; the *Rules* of St. Leonard of Port Maurice; the regulations of the Ministers General Clement of Palermo (1759) and Paschal of Varese (1774); and the particular Statutes of Venantius of Celano in the mid–19th century, which were reworked by Dionysius Schuler in 1905. Just before the last war, in 1937, Fr. Leonardo Bello recommended the *ritiros*.[77] Then there was a general decline, and today they are once again being introduced.

By reading these various legislative documents we can attempt to reconstruct the spiritual atmosphere of the *ritiros* in which, as Clement of Palermo explains in his constitutions, "the most fervent zealots of the regular observance and greater perfection of spirit should attend not only to observe meticulously all the precepts of the *Rule*, but even all the counsels contained in it."[78]

Great emphasis was placed on the liturgy. Only Gregorian chant was used. Two-and-a-half hours a day were dedicated to mental prayer; night Matins lasted approximately two hours, while the celebration of Prime and Terce took forty-five minutes, Vespers a half hour, and the same for Compline. After Compline the friars went in procession to the altar of St. Francis, while singing the *Salve, sancte Parens*, and the *Si quaeris miracula* of St. Anthony. On Saturday the litany of the Blessed Virgin was sung at her altar. After dinner they would go to choir reciting the *Miserere*; once there they chanted the *Tota pulchra* and, having recited the *De profundis*, they would head in procession to the kitchen to wash the dishes. During the evening in church they would recite the litanies in two parts, earn the "pardon" with six *Paters*, *Aves* and *Glorias* with outstretched arms, and added other prayers for a half hour.[79]

It is interesting to note what was written about spiritual lectures in common. In chapter 11 of Clement of Palermo's constitutions we read:

> Each week four lessons are to be given without possibility of dispensation: on Monday the explanation of the Holy *Rule*; on Wednesday from mystical theology or the spiritual life; on Saturday a conference on moral cases; on Sundays after Vespers the catechism for both clerics and lay brothers. . . . The lecturers are warned not to explain the *Rule* according to their whim . . . . Then, too, in the lesson on mystical theology, the lecturer should take care in treating of vocal prayer, meditation and contemplation, not to fall into the errors of the Quietists; in such a delicate subject, in order to avoid any fall, they should avail themselves of the teaching of our Seraphic Doctor St. Bonaventure, of St. Peter of Alcantara, of St. Teresa, and of Cardinal Lauria in his treatise *De Oratione*.[80]

The *ritiros* were also a great incentive for days of recollection and retreats. A study of this topic would be very interesting. In the particular *Statutes pro Sacri Recessus directione* by Fr. Bernardino of Bisignano (1684) we read:

> Every year each one will try to make two retreats, by which they renew their fervor and refresh their spirit, and the ministers should show their readiness for this, so that these retreats can be made with exactness and be fruitful, with the acquisition of firm virtues, especially in the self-denial which is the principal foundation of the edifice of the spiritual life.[81]

Like clinics of the spirit, specializing in prayer and penance, people frequently brought to the churches of the *ritiros* people possessed by demons. Called together by the guardian, all the friars would pray together for the spiritual liberation of those persons, but they did not perform exorcisms.[82]

Anyone coming to the *ritiro* had to appear before the whole community and renounce "every form of pre-eminence and every title of 'paternity' or any other form of honor, being content with only that of 'friar minor'" because, as the legislative text tells us, "anyone who knows the greatness of God is not concerned with this vanity, nor is he displeased to be considered less than others, because whoever enters the *ritiro* should die totally to himself."[83] The minister then would assign him a spiritual director

> so that he might be instructed in this our way of life, and especially about mental prayer and the ceremonies of the mass; and periodically they should have read at table chapter five of the second part of the *Mirror of Discipline* by the Seraphic Doctor St. Bonaventure. . . . This is to be done continuously in the novitiate house, so that each one can better understand what novices chosen by God should be like, that they are to be interior men, truly devout, and gifted with a seraphic spirit.[84]

A large amount of time was devoted to the apostolate, especially preaching, hearing confessions, celebrating Mass, helping the dying, going to the hospitals "once every week or two weeks in order to serve, confess, and teach Christian doctrine to the poor sick people."[85]

The *ritiro* was to be a true fraternity, a home filled with peace and charity:

> The ministers will show mercy and love to the brothers, being more rigid in judging than in correcting, so that if any friar, having committed some defect, should confess it publicly in the refectory and give signs of true repentance, nothing should be said to him except the words of Jesus Christ: that is, "vade in pace et noli amplius peccare," because the main purpose of these Constitutions is Charity.[86]

However, the legislation was relentless and lacking in mercy against those who disturbed the unity, peace, and charity:

> Whenever a friar is restless and wandering aimlessly, that is, going from friary to friary, and goes to the workshops when it is not truly necessary, thus showing that he is no friend of withdrawal and silence, and all the more so when such behavior and grumbling should disturb the peace or, if for other reasons, he should not prove to be adaptable for the *ritiro*, he will be sent away in the prescribed manner; if the guardians or discretes do not follow this order, they are to be suspended from office.[87]

> They should be warned to be on their guard against another very pernicious diabolical trick which is enough to send that spiritual edifice up in smoke in a short time: namely, that no schisms or divisions or factions or parties should enter under the guise of zeal. And they should make sure to keep this door closed and guarded with special diligence, so that this scourge cannot enter; once it has come in, it leads to irreparable evil, as unfortunately can be seen from the experience of those religious communities which it did enter, and there is no way of getting rid of it or repairing the damage that it produces each day. Everyone therefore should be warned not to be fooled by the false appearances that he might serve the Lord better together with his followers, or those from the same nation, or of the same party, because all this is a suggestion of the Angel of Light, and woe to those who will not be on their guard, because they will realize it too late, after they have drawn upon themselves the irreparable stroke of divine wrath.[88]

The Role of Ministers according to St. Theophilus of Corte

The ministers are to be the true spiritual leaders of the *ritiros*. This was the firm conviction of St. Theophilus of Corte, who chose to leave the guardians of the *ritiros* some "most prudent reminders,"[89] gleaned from his spiritual experience. These are 19 wonderful reminders that are helpful also for those who must exercise authority today. It is a precise and complete answer to the questions that each minister asks about how to fulfil his office: What should I do? In what way must I "manage" authority, as they say today, in order to be a true spiritual leader? To these anguished questions St. Theophilus replies:

1. Each day offer yourself and all your brothers to the Blessed Virgin Mary, praying to her that you might govern and protect them as if they were hers, knowing that you cannot do anything good without her assistance.

2. Often ask the Blessed Virgin's pardon for not having responded to the help you have received.

3. Be careful to be withdrawn, and to make sure not to give others special privileges without cause; see to the common observance in all things.

4. Do not fail to appreciate any brother, even if he may be defective, but be compassionate and help him to mend his ways; do not complain about him with others, nor allow others to grumble about him, nor ever correct anyone, without first admitting to yourself that you are more guilty than he is.

5. Whenever because of the disobedience of the brothers he is moved by an overwhelming sense of disdain, he should seek to be humble, confounding himself, considering how promptly he would like to be served by others, while he himself serves God so poorly.

6. He should frequently practice the more humble ministries, which are the proper means for acquiring the humility that is so necessary to a minister; and, as far as

he can, he should strive to be the first in performing such acts, in order to lead others to imitate him.

7. He should not be angered when he is admonished about something; he should rather be grateful, and even frequently say that he is very grateful for their admonitions.

8. Since the minister cannot show any preference for his brothers externally, he should always prefer them internally, considering himself unworthy of their company, and seek to be humble, realizing that many of his brothers are making better progress on the way of perfection.

9. In cases of grumbling or disrespectful words against his person, especially when this is not done in public, the minister should act gently; however, in anything pertaining to the honor of God, he must display zeal and emotion, but always with moderation.

10. The minister should be convinced that he has no worse counsellor than himself; he should always be prepared to follow the opinion of others rather than his own, and seek advice not only from the discretes and the elders, but sometimes even from the brothers themselves.

11. Whenever it is possible, he should avail himself of secret correction; when, however, it is necessary to do so in public, he should strive to do so in a spirit of calm, refraining from speaking harshly.

12. Whenever house conferences are held, he should seek to avoid contention, but after each one has given his reasons, in all modesty he should give in.

13. When the minister discovers that the brothers are complaining without cause, especially during visitation, he should not show anger; rather, after a modest excuse (defense), if he should judge it proper, he will forget about the whole thing, reminding himself that if he does not have the faults he was blamed for, he probably has many other worse ones of which he is not even aware. He

should accept that difficulty as coming from the hand of God who is taking the opportunity to free him from vainglory, or as penance for his past sins.

14. He should not expect gratitude for governing well, or having done good to others; he should realize he has done his duty, as the servant of all, and remember that if the brothers show their gratitude for his good treatment, that itself would be a large part of the reward for his efforts. If, however, they are ungrateful, his whole reward will be given him in the next life: and so be it.

15. Be vigilant in the important things, such as the Divine Office, which is to be recited with due pause and seriously; in the celebration of the Mass he should see to the observance of the rubrics; in poverty he should see to it that there should not be a surplus of things, and that there should be moderation in the food; in regard to silence, it should be practiced exactly.

16. Once the minister has experienced the fidelity of the officials, he should not always be hanging around to check on them; however, he must not forget to go to the gate every once in a while to see how they are acting.

17. When the minister realizes that he has notably upset his brother, he will try to pacify him.

18. In all things he will seek external and internal peace, never getting upset over anything in this life; and if by chance he should be upset, he should hurry and seek peace of heart, forgetting for a while the one who has fallen into defect, and considering rather the ineffable goodness of God who is willing to pardon his every defect; he in turn will acknowledge his lowliness before God and perform some penance, but with gentleness.

19. Last of all, he will try to look upon his brothers as creatures of God, or even as sons of the blessed Virgin, entrusted to his care; and he will seek to satisfy them in everything he can, and never leaving them mortified or in need; he should be mindful of the reward prepared for

him if he takes good care of them and of the harsh judgment waiting for him if he is neglectful.

What wisdom and light can still be found in these by those today who want the ministers to be the spiritual leaders of the community! Joy should be the condiment for all, as we read in the Constitutions of 1759: "a joyful soul is a very effective means for achieving that state of perfection that is the goal chosen by those who come to the friaries of the strict observance."[90]

The Capuchins and the *Ritiros*

The *ritiros* also have an interesting history among the Capuchins. However, two hundred years would go by before this idea would wind its way into creating problems for the Capuchin Order. As the "Friars Minor of the eremitical life,"[91] the Capuchins began with a tenacious, almost Spiritualist recreation of the strongest aspects of the early Franciscan hermitages, isolated and remote from all inhabitants, almost veritable deserts, with an intense life of mental prayer, four hours a day for the lukewarm, as we read in the Constitutions of Albacina; but the devout and fervent friars will not be satisfied with one, or two, or three hours, but they will spend all their time in prayer, meditation and contemplation; and, with the institution of the reclusion or hermit's cell for the more contemplative friars, as we find in no. 79 of the Constitutions of 1536 which is a reiteration of no. 42 of the Constitutions of Albacina:

> It is also hereby ordered that in every place where it is possible to do so, in the woods or any place granted to the friars, [there should be] one or two small cells, remote from the common habitation of the friars, so that if any friar wants to live the anchoritic life (if his minister feels he is suited for it) he may quietly in solitude, with the *vita angelica*, give himself entirely to God, according to the guidance of the Holy Spirit. And at the same time, so that they may in quiet enjoy God, it is hereby ordered that there they should not speak, except to their spiritual director, who will be like a mother in providing for him, according to the pious desires of our seraphic Father, as we find in the *Conformities*.[92]

Other characteristics emerging from the primitive Capuchin life was a bare, unadorned liturgy, total silence, a "desperate" but joyful poverty, an untamed austerity, and a zeal for charity that made them preach with the power of the Holy Spirit.[93]

After the Council of Trent and the dark night of the soul caused by the news-making apostasy of Bernardino Ochino, the Capuchins had spread beyond Italy. In the interim, as Mattia Bellintani of Salò writes, "when young men came from the world, it was necessary to introduce studies, accommodate friaries that were already far away, near the country and cities, at least for the care of the infirm, and thus there was some loss of that spirit of ferment experienced by the first founders."[94]

The friaries of the Capuchins who came to the cities became centers of apostolate that were organized and institutionalized. The Constitutions and various interventions of the Ministers General had succeeded in maintaining for more than two centuries a commitment to the regular observance which Pope Benedict XIV considered the only surviving example of evangelical poverty.[95] However, in the second half of the 18th century, the more sensitive friars began to notice that there was a split between legislation and living. They understood that they could no longer keep pace. On the one hand were the constitutions, a masterpiece of spirituality, which always ran ahead, while on the other hand the friars felt constrained, while the novelties of the enlightenment had taken hold of many of them.

It was in this period that they began to think of renewal. The strongest incentive came from the splendid flourishing of the *ritiros* which spread the odor of virtue and recharged the Franciscan Order with apostolic zeal. This example inspired some Capuchins for more than 30 years, from 1755 to 1789; and two Ministers General, Paolo of Colindres and Erard of Radkersburg, encouraged the initiative.[96] It was a grass roots activity of a few religious which they developed in the various Capuchin provinces.

Fr. Cherubino of Nice wrote Constitutions for the *ritiro* established in Cittaducale in 1763. However, it did not last very long. The mentality of the Order was against the idea of a *ritiro* as Fr. Cherubino understood it:

> As a hermitage or *ritiro* I want a convent in which the
> Holy *Rule* and the Constitutions of the Order are
> observed to the letter—according to the mind of Jesus
> Christ and our seraphic founder—as far as human
> frailty allows; a convent in which abuses and
> relaxations of discipline having been banished, the
> ancient observance flourishes anew: a convent, that is,
> in which people believe in mortification, prayer,
> silence, and every other virtue, and in which
> everything is done to enable people to follow freely the
> movements of the Holy Spirit without any disturbance
> or human respect; in which, last of all, there is a
> special profession of religious perfection.[97]

That was unheard of! Imagine speaking of a reform of the
"last and most perfect reform" of the Franciscan Order! These
perpetrators were silenced as fanatical, idealistic, individualistic, or too independent. Many ministers provincial responded
that *ritiros* were not needed where observance and regular
discipline flourished as a *Rule*; everyone could live austerely in
the normal convents: the situation would create a scandal for the
seculars and disunity for the provinces.[98]

In the Province of Parma, Miguel de Pamplona and others
tried this out. In Genoa another small group of friars made the
move; in the province of Reggio Calabria Ven. Gesualdo of Reggio
succeeded in establishing the *ritiro* of Terranova which attracted
many zealous friars, and it seems that the institution was
somewhat successful. In Spain the idea of the *ritiro* was spread by
Juan de Zamora who, with typical Iberian subtlety, avoided
speaking of a *ritiro*, but called his new institution a "College of
Missionaries." Other unsuccessful attempts were made in Poland
and Austria.[99]

Reading the regulations drawn up by these Capuchins who
had the original ideas and by those responsible for their
organization, one can find the same concepts already included in
the statutes for the *ritiros* created by the Friars Minor of the
Observance and of the Reform: at the center is charity; the means
to it are interior prayer, spiritual reading, solitude, austerity,
poverty, and so forth. Many concepts can be inferred from the
Constitutions. Twice a year they had to make a 10-day retreat.

They were accused of seeking a life of idleness for contemplative souls and giving thought to exercising the works of mercy and the various types of apostolic and pastoral ministry. It was not hard for Gesualdo of Reggio to give the lie to these preconceived notions, proving rather how the religious of the *ritiro* were continually intent on preaching during Advent and Lent, of giving 8-day and 10-day retreats to the seculars who came to the *ritiros* for that purpose and to monks in their monasteries; they visited prisoners, the sick and the dying, taught catechism not only to the faithful, but also to the priests scattered about the mountainous regions. And he added peaceful thoughts worthy of a saint:

> Stay humble and charitable. . . . Those who oppose you have their own good reasons. They will think that *ritiros* are something new and scandalous. They must be excused, sympathized with, and loved, (because) their opposition stimulates the love of those who seek them, and tries those who seek them. Even if they were to win, we would not lose anything. If through *ritiro* we want to find God and please God, whether or not we gain our goal, we have done our part; and God has been served by us, and our holy Father has been satisfied and . . . if we persevere, we will receive a reward. I shall close by saying that in prayer we must implore the grace that, if it is a good thing, it has to come from God, and can be obtained by prayer. If, however, our desires are fooling us, prayer will also free us from them.[100]

These plans and projects were upset by the French revolution and snuffed out by the crises within the provinces following the suppression effected by the antireligious governments.

The idea of the *ritiro* came up again among the Capuchins at Capodimonte (Naples) through the initiative of Ferdinand I in 1817 through a ruling which was not, however, taken up within the Order.[101] Toward the middle of the 19th century, once the provinces were painstakingly reorganized, the same idea was brought up again in 1851 for novitiates and houses of study or student houses which the Superiors wanted to transform into *ritiros*.[102]

However, let us go on to the last and most radical example of houses of prayer in Franciscan history, perhaps the one that is most disconcerting to us today, who are overwhelmed by activity and who talk and write too much.

4. Deserts or Houses of Solitude (16th to 18th century)

Relationship between *Ritiro* and Desert

"The purpose of the *ritiro* is the perfection of Franciscan life," Father Gori writes; "the purpose of solitude is the perfection of the contemplative life. In the *ritiro* the friars lived a mixed life—contemplative and active; in the desert they lived only the contemplative life. The dwelling of the religious in the *ritiro* was ordinarily stable; in the solitude, however, by virtue of the constitutions, it was of a temporary nature."[103]

The desert exercises a continual allure in Franciscan life. We might say that the primitive hermitages of St. Francis and of the Franciscan reform movements were veritable deserts. However, as to organized and regulated houses of prayer, in the entire history of the Order there are only four clear examples, all of them having a spiritual connection with one another, and ranging from the 16th to 18th centuries. It is no accident that the founders are four saints: St. Peter of Alcantara, Bl. Bonaventure of Barcelona, St. John Joseph of the Cross, and St. Leonard of Port Maurice.

Four Saints and Four Accomplishments

a. St. Peter of Alcantara

St. Peter of Alcantara immediately takes us back to his "ideal" little convent of Pedrosa in Estremadura, with a little church and larger chapel divided from the rest with a wooden gate, a little cloistered area, just a few meters, and cells as small as tombs. The saint wrote special statutes for those who lived there in 1560 and, one year later, promulgated other regulations. The statutes are no longer extant, but their substance is probably contained in the *Ordinazioni della Provincia di S. Giuseppe.* They could expect three hours of daily prayer, one hour of manual labor, various vocal prayers, confession twice a week: divine office "in a low, even, clear tone, with time for pauses; nothing is to be changed; prayer is to be slow, well enunciated and with sufficient pauses." Theirs was an extreme poverty; no more than eight cells, and all the parts of the convent had a precise size, based on spiritual, not architectural, criteria. Further on we read: "It is so ordered that in all the houses one or two hermitages should be built in the garden, or even outside of it, wherever it can best be accommodated; there should always be a friar or two there, busy in prayer and sometimes in reading or some manual labor; and these should go off for weeks or months at a time, as shall be determined by the guardian, or the custos, or the provincial or the commissary general."[104]

It would be interesting to compare the little convents of St. Peter of Alcantara with those of the first Capuchins. There is the same concern, and one does see some striking similarities, but there is no mutual interference.[105] St. Peter of Alcantara's experience seems to be typical. The others experience pretty much the same thing, but with some original touch.

b.   Blessed Bonaventure of Barcelona

Blessed Bonaventure of Barcelona, founder of the *ritiros*, created the hermitage of Sant'Angelo for the religious of Santa Maria della Grazie in Sabina: this was a nucleus of solitary cells for four, and then for seven, religious. In a spiritual treatise[106] Bonaventure explains the deep contemplative meaning of this solitude:

> In what school, and from what teacher, can one learn in many years such solid and real knowledge as one can learn in a few months or days from Holy Solitude? O blessed solitude, O blessed withdrawal!. . . Because of holy solitude and this blessed *ritiro* much more will be asked of us solitary friars minor, imperfect as we are. . . . If, my brothers in the Lord, we want to taste divine and heavenly things, we must *purify ourselves* and *exercise* and *go higher*. In the first stage one smells the perfume of this heavenly sweetness; in the second stage one tastes it, and in the third stage one imbibes it.
>
> *In the first*, then, we must purify ourselves of all sin, of all inordinate affection, of all temporal consolations, and of all imperfect love for creatures; because, as St.

Bernard says, that person is totally mistaken who thinks he can mix the heavenly sweetness with our ashes, and the divine balsam with our poisoned tastes, and the gifts of the Holy Spirit with the delights and pleasures of this world; however, later, when these things shall be purged from our soul by tears and trembling and purified by sighs of sorrow, it can enjoy the divine things because it is right, St. Augustine tells us, that the soul should always feel sadness if it leaves the Creator and goes in search of pleasure and delights in itself and in creatures; as the glorious St. Gregory says it so wonderfully in his morals on the words of Job: before eating, I sigh. The food of our souls is to pasture in the contemplation of the sovereign light; therefore we sigh before eating because whoever in this exile will not humble himself with tears will not taste the celestial desires, nor enjoy the eternal homeland. Those who fast from the food of truth are those who find joy in the miseries of our pilgrimage.

In the second stage the soul must exercise in doing good works and suffering evil, because blessed are those who mourn, for they shall be consoled; because those whom the love of truth afflicts are pleased by the reflection of consolation. O good Jesus, how many times after countless tears and trembling, you anointed my wounded soul with the ointment of your mercy and sometimes you received it, in a state nigh on desperation, and consoled it with the hope of forgiveness; note that the price of honest things is included; although at the beginning there was some fear, the road to life becomes easier in the course of time with the sweetness of inestimable love. O how much more blessed is the consolation which is divinely given to those who work for Christ.

In the third stage, in which the soul drinks of this sweetness, is the refreshment of the heart, when earthly things are left behind and it is wondrously raised up, not only above itself and the world, but above all creatures, so that it can say, "The Lord has led me into his wine cellar"; that soul enters the divine wine cellar in order to drink the wine mixture of the inestimable Deity and the spotless white milk of the humanity of Christ our Redeemer. O my soul, this is what the true servants of Jesus Christ drink and what God's friends imbibe; O blessed drunkenness, from which comes chaste and holy temperance of body and soul. From it the soul, as if drunken, rejoices in adversity, is strong and secure amid dangers, is prudent and circumspect in prosperity, liberal and merciful in forgiving injuries, and finally restful and quiet and as if asleep while resting in the divine embrace. . . .

Here our souls are cut off from all the things of earth, here they receive those lights which help them to recognize as folly and vain whatever does not serve to unite us more closely to God; here they learn to disdain all created things; here they learn to master themselves and all their passions; here they learn to desire not to take into consideration their bodies and all its needs; here they are united with their beloved spouse, Jesus Christ; here are the amorous talks, here the gentle conversations with the heavenly Father, here, with the Mother of Graces, it obtains everything. . . .[107]

It is the whole experience of the journey of the contemplative life.

c.   St. John Joseph of the Cross

With direct reference to the convent of Pedroso founded by St. Peter of Alcantara, at a very young age St. John Joseph of the Cross founded the solitude at Piedimonte d'Alife in the region of Benevento. It was the first convent erected by the Alcantarines in the kingdom of Naples. An hour's walk away, in a nearby wooded area, he helped create the solitude of St. Mary of the Angels, which he named St. Mary Occorrevole (of the Needy). It was a charismatic foundation. The saint prayed to the Holy Spirit and then was inspired in his choice of a place for the foundation because, humanly speaking, it was the least appropriate. Thus a miniature convent sprang up: a chapel, four cells, the refectory, the hearth, the sacristy, the choir, a small lodge, reception area, cistern, laundry, and the like, altogether approximately 30 meters long and eight meters wide. In order to enter the mud and wattle cells, one had to stoop down and enter sideways. The desert of St. Mary was encircled by two kilometers of walls. Within the enclosure there were five small cells placed at random. The saint also helped in the drafting of a special set of rules, which were then approved by Innocent XI in 1679.[108] At the beginning of 1676, while the construction work was still in progress, he wrote in a letter to his brother Don Tommaso Antonio:

> Besides the little convent which is almost finished in this Madonna, a smaller one is being built, about a quarter mile away from it, as a place for those who are called by the solitude of divine love, where they . . . I will stop, because no one can express what God has prepared for that place. I shall only tell you that there are many little cells, besides the little convent, each of them separated from one another, where the religious can stay in silence; the place was called "il muto," and the religious there must be mute.[109]

The Constitutions of the hermitage of St. Mary frequently remind us of expressions, concepts and spiritual "unction" found in the Constitutions of the first Capuchins. What did St. John Joseph of the Cross want for his "solitude"? He tells us in chapter 1 of these Constitutions:

> The idea of this holy solitude is this: a taciturn and contemplative withdrawal for a few solitary religious who are penitent, detached, and totally dedicated to loving, pure, tranquil, and sweet conversation with God alone. They must therefore live removed from almost all interaction, correspondence, and conversation with the world; removed from every care and solicitude for the temporal; with filial fidelity dependent on divine Providence and, finally, as much as possible, removed and forgetful of all creation, so that without any exterior or interior impediment they can, with freedom of spirit and peace of heart, be attentive to the truer and purged reform of what is within them; and, in that way, unfettered, light and free, they may soar to the heights of the divine and beatifying contemplation; this should be their main study and work.
>
> And so that through the faithful practice of these and other things which can be hoped for from those who follow these constitutions, the adventurous inhabitants of this holy place may lead a life that is more "angelic" than human (at least this is what they are obliged to do) and furthermore, so that they may be and live so, under the motherly and most benign

protection and care of the most glorious Queen of the Angels and of their blessed spirits; seeking yet to follow those holy orders which our Seraphic Father St. Francis wanted to be observed in his beloved convent of St. Mary of the Angels at Assisi, it is hereby ordained that this holy house and blessed place shall be given that same name and title, the Solitude of St. Mary of the Angels.[110]

The example of St. Francis was alive again in its most pure form. The young Alcantarine saint was convinced that he had discovered the hidden treasure, the secret of the spirituality of the Seraphic Father:

It was the will of our Seraphic Father St. Francis (his own will and that of his holy sons who most faithfully served his evangelical spirit and put it into practice) that in his religion there should be some oratories in solitary places, set apart from inhabited areas, to which his sons could retire periodically. And there, through a continuous silence, an eremitical withdrawal, and a quiet and abstract distance from the world, without earthly impediments they may return to and refresh the spirit of holy prayer, which is so necessary for preserving the life of grace and for acquiring the truth of perfection; just as this spirit is enriched by diligence and recollection in tranquil and silent solitude, so too are ruin and dissipation wrought by the always distracting, troubled and dangerous conversation with the world.

Our Blessed Father wanted his beloved and blessed sons to withdraw often to similar hermitages and oratories so that, by living alone with God and by themselves for a time, they could then leave them prepared to bring good to others without harming their own souls. And in this way the wholly apostolic man of God wanted to teach them the true way of practicing the best of the mixed life, that is, not just to live for themselves, but to be useful for others to which that heavenly light told him that his evangelical religion was called; following in this also the example of our divine Redeemer, who for our education fled the crowds to go alone to the mountain, and from the mountain, returned to the crowds. . . . [111]

Father Anselmo of San Gaetano, who lived in a solitude, writes an eyewitness account:

> Continuous silence is rigorously observed; one does not even speak with his Superior in order to ask for necessary items, or for permission to withdraw and pray in some of the separate chapels built for that purpose in the enclosed area within the woods, behind a wall and restricted in order to make it impenetrable by any person; this is done by pulling a lace on a piece of heavy paper which each hermit keeps for this purpose, on which are written all the permissions he could possibly ask and all the things he might possibly need. And there are two other laces for the superior, one for yes and one for no, so that the hermit asks by pulling one, and the superior grants permission or refuses it by pulling the other.
>
> They are not involved in any other work than the continuous exercise of prayer and choir, and in both of these for periods longer than is usually prayed in other convents of the province, and in other pious exercises, which is truly a rather perfect life. Any additional time can be used in private prayer or in choir or in the above-mentioned chapels, or in hoeing the garden for the flowers which are placed before the Blessed Sacrament above the altar; they are to perform such activity contemplating in silence or reciting psalms, hymns and other praises of God in common. Each day there is a spiritual conference to increase their ardor in the service and love of our Lord; nor do they have to worry about eating because at the time of common meals this is brought from the nearby convent of Our Lady of the Needy.[112]

d. St. Leonard of Port Maurice

The great apostle of popular missions, St. Leonard of Port Maurice, visited the *ritiros* during his pilgrimages, and was all too happy to spend some time in them. However he, the great force behind the spread of the *ritiros*, sought to create a solitude like those of the discalced friars in Naples. In 1716 he wrote to the Congregation for Regular Discipline, explaining his intention to imitate the Franciscan origins because "from the beginning of the Order our Seraphic Father St. Francis and his devout companions were wont to build in solitary places, sometimes miles away from any convent, some small oratories where from time to time the fervent religious could withdraw in order to give themselves over to a life that was more penitent, contemplative and segregated from the world." He asked for permission to

> build a solitude, a true hermitage on the top of a mountain, to be called 'Incontro,' five or six miles away from their convent (San Francesco al Monte alle Croci in Florence) where there was already a small church given over to the care of a hermit by the ancestors of the Archbishop of Florence . . . in order to observe in that solitude some more austere constitutions, similar to those confirmed by Innocent XI for the solitude of the Discalced fathers of the Province of Naples.[113]

The statutes which the saint wrote were approved by the Minister General and Pope Clement XI and contain a rather lofty spirituality. Radical courage was needed to embrace them. St. Leonard personally exemplified his life's commitment in his well-known and beautiful *Proponimenti*, his spiritual master-piece.[114]

The "desert" should be totally in effect in the *ritiros*. The religious of these convents, seven or eight at a time, should withdraw to the solitude of the Incontro to make their retreat. The solitude was the soul of the *ritiro*, the *ritiro* of the *ritiros*, like a cell within a cell, so that "by totally withdrawing from the world, one may be able to attend to pure contemplation and, after having acquired greater fervor, return to the convents in order to apply oneself more diligently for the good of one's neighbors." [115]

To be apostles and hermits at the same time: it is the active and contemplative life together. "My vocation, as far as I can tell," St. Leonard said, "is the mission and the solitude. In the mission, always busy for the love of God and in the solitude always busy in God."[116]

These hermits withdrew into the garden, into the little cells, and there gave free rein to their hearts with frequent, devout prayer to God, who sweetened the rigors of their most severe penance. They had nine hours of common prayer daily and used the discipline for a half hour each day; they fasted almost all year long, they kept perfect silence in every place and slept for brief periods on wood, with a wooden block for their headrest. They were not allowed to leave the enclosure or write letters, and they walked barefoot, without even sandals. A contemplative prayer in reparation for the sins of the world and to implore grace for everyone made the whole area fragrant. The saint wanted each province to create a "desert" in order to make the apostolate more effective and dynamic.[117]

"Knowing their imperfection, they lived continuously in the solitude of the desert, with a continuous interchange. In the interest of souls and their own interests too, they would go down from the hermitage and spread out generously in preaching that which they had harvested in solitude with the sickle of contemplation."[118] Theirs was an ascent of the mountain of holy prayer and contemplation, in order to descend like a flaming arrow and inflame the world with the love of God.

Conclusion

Thus with these various historical phases we have come full circle: in the beginning the hermitages, at the end the deserts. More than 700 years of the history of houses of contemplative prayer in the Franciscan Order have taught us that the hermitages of the Seraphic Father and the solitude of St. Leonard are, we might say, like the summit of a pyramid that includes all the friars. How could these contemplative eremitical experiences be held to be unilateral spiritualistic deviations, as some modern historians would have us think?[119] Jean Sainsaulieu goes so far as to accuse Franciscan spirituality (which had a more marked influence on European eremitism) of having "preserved a great morass of asocial institutions and immoral justification in the Mediterranean countries. Franciscan pauperism, as it was lived by the disciples of St. Francis, monks or hermits," according to the French historian, supposedly "led Catholic religious and moral life astray for many centuries."[120]

By their fruit you shall know them. This is the minimum for discernment. It has been said that the yearning for solitude, the allure of the desert, the attraction of the eremitical life are the ceaseless temptation of Franciscanism.[121] It is truly a magnificent temptation if it has produced such wonderful fruits of holiness! Heaven permit that all Franciscans may yield to such a temptation, lay down the arms of resistance, and be overcome by this tempestuous and most gentle experience of God in the desert, which is so necessary for the renewal of Franciscan life!

If every experience of houses of prayer was intended as a return to the example of St. Francis in order to live a more pure, simple, and spiritual observance of the *Rule*, that means that the *Rule* cannot be observed without a serious commitment to the contemplative life, which must have pride of place, and "to which all other things of our earthly existence must contribute" (RegB 5). This is why novitiates and student houses should be true houses of prayer, a prayer lived and nourished by a living experience of the observance of the *Rule*.

It is the "Spirit of the Lord and his holy manner of working" (RegB 10); it is an experience of God in the sense that God tries us, making us journey in the desert for whatever amount of time God chooses, in order to see if we truly love and are faithful to God (cf. Deut. 8:2, ff), and then frees us and accompanies us to the promised land, leads us to the land of the living and makes us heirs and kings of the kingdom of heaven (cf. RegB 6). This is the meaning of the experience of Exodus, of the temptations and death of Christ. It is God's trial. It is God who uses us and wants to work through us. At this point it is better to keep silence and not glory in the experiences of others, but rather listen attentively, adore and taste the word of comfort which he endlessly repeats: "My house shall be a house of prayer" (Mt 21: 13).

Endnotes

[1]C. Cargnoni, "Le Case di Preghiera nella Storia dell'Ordine Francescano," *Le 'Case Di Preghiera' Nella Storia E Spiritualità Francescana,* ed. Fiorenzo F. Mastroianni (Naples: Edizioni Dehoniane, 1978) 55-112.

[2]Cf. O. Schmucki, "Secretum solitudinis; Mentis silentium Il programma contemplativo nell'Ordine francescano primitivo," *Laurentianum* 14 (1973): 177-222; "Die Stellung Christi im Beten des hl. Franziskus von Assisi," *Wissenschaft und Weisheit* 25 (1962): 128-45, 188-212; "Franciscus 'Dei laudator et cultur' De orationis vi ac frequentia in eius cum scriptis tum rebus gestis," *Laurentianum* 10 (1969): 3-36, 173-215, 245-282; "La meditazione francescana," *IF* 48 (1973): 75-89; "La preghiera francescana," *La nostra vita di preghiera,* Supplement to the *Atti dei Frati Minori Cappuccini della Provincia di S. Carlo in Lombardia,* vol. XIV (1974): 107-21.

[3]*Legend of Perugia* 80. Unless indicated otherwise, translations of passages from the early *vitae* are taken from M. Habig, ed., *St. Francis of Assisi: Omnibus of Sources* (Chicago:Franciscan Herald Press, 1973). Hereafter, *Omnibus.*

[4]*RegNB 7.* Unless indicated otherwise, translations from the writings of St. Francis are taken from Armstrong and Brady.

[5]Cf. T. Merton, *Vita nel silenzio* (Brescia: Morcelliana, 1963); Anastasio Del S. Rosario, "L'eremitismo della Regola carmelitana," in *Ephem. Carmeliticae* 2 (1948): 245-62; Francisco del Niño Jesús, "El Deserto en el Carmen Descalzo," *Rev. de Espirit.* 13 (1954): 347-68, 431459; Felipe de la Virgen, "La vida interior en los desiertos de la reforma teresiana en su primer siglo," *ibid.* 21 (1962): 584-600; Paul-Marie de la Croix [Zimmermann], "Les déserts chez les Carmes Déchaussés," *Dictionnaire de Spiritualité* III, 534-39.

[6]Cf. Clemente da S. Maria, "Case di Ritiro nell'Ordine Cappuccino," IF 51 (1976): 26-34; *"Habere Spiritum Domini" Litterae encyclicae quattuor Ministrorum Generalium ad totam familiam sancti Francisci post exercitia spiritualia in monte Alverniae celebrata"* (Rome: Ed. Porziuncola, 1977), 16. "With the wisdom that flows from prayer, the prayer in which our Family engages, let the following be perceived as marks of renewal: the establishment of houses or fraternities of prayer, or of hermitages; participation in the daily rhythms of prayer; diverse gatherings for purpose of praying together, and similar initiatives which are springing up in many places. It seems fitting for those who hold leadership roles in these houses, to convene first regional then international meetings. Moreover, we hope that a special international commission of experts will devote themselves to shedding light on the contemplative and eremitical dimensions of our life, and will present concrete proposals for renewal."

[7]See note 6 above. I must immediately note, to avoid any misunderstandings, that for reasons of space and time, this synthesis is not intended to touch every aspect of ermitism and contemplative life present in the history of the Franciscan Order. I am not able to analyze all the movements regarding the Franciscan Reform. I cover most of all the Spirituals, the Observants, the Villacresans, the Reformati, the Scalzi or Alcantarines, and the Capuchins, while I pass over the Amadeiti, the Colettines or Recollects of France, and lesser-known reforms such as the Saccati, the Capriolani, the Barbanti, the "College of the Missions" and the flowering of houses of recollection and *ritiros* in Latin America in the 17th and 18th centuries. Furthermore, I do not speak of the Second or Third Orders. The Third Order Regular, for example, has had a beautiful flowering of eremitical and contemplative life, as has the Third Order Secular. For the various reforms, I turn to Gratien of Paris, *Histoire de la fondation et de l'évolution de l'Ordre des Frères Mineurs au XI -XIIIe siècle* (Paris, 1928); L. DeFonzo, "I Francescani," in *Ordine e congregazioni religiose*, ed. M. Escobar, I (Turin, 1951) 159-344; H. Holzapfel, *Handbuch der Geschichte des Franziskanerordens* (Fribourg, 1909); other works (L. Brengio, P. Sevesi, J. Moorman) have already been cited.

[8]Cf F.J Meseguer, "Fr. Francisco Ortiz en Torrelaguna. Notas para su biografía," *AIA* 8 (1948): 500f.

[9]This work is the result of a doctoral dissertation, and was published as the 14th work in the series "Studi e Testi Francescani."

[10]It is the first true synthesis printed: cf. Melchior de Pobladura.

[11]Cf. *L'eremitismo in Occidente nei secoli XI e XII. Atti della II Settimana Internazionale di Studi*, 4 (Milan, 1965): there is Meersseman's communication about Franciscan eremitism; *España eremítica. Actas de la VI Semana de Estudios Monásticos. Abadía de S. Salvador de Leyre* (Pamplona, 1970); cf. *Studia monast.* 6 (1964): 210-18; see "Eremitismo," *DIP* III, 1224-44, especially the bibliography on pages 1242-44; J. Sansaulieu, "Ermites en Occident," *DHGE* XV, 771-87; P. Doyere, "Érémitisme en Occident," *DS* IV, 953-82; for further bibliography in English on Franciscan eremitism, see *Omnibus,* 1703f.

[12]Cf. *DIP* III, 1227.

[13]The limitations are understandable. It would be an impossible undertaking to follow the geographic spread of Franciscan eremitism or describe the social and cultural aspects of it. The modern historian's interest is more on the elements of the external relations, such as the relationship between the hermit and his lay or ecclesiastical protector, or between the hermits and the populace, between hermits and the geographic setting and their relationship with the neighboring inhabitants, or the way the hermits managed to live, what social classes they came from, etc.

[14]Cf. Schmucki, "Secretum solitudinis," 7 f, 20 f, 544 ff.

[15]People have often tried to portray the Spiritual influences in a negative light, but perhaps we should really try not to just repeat these criticisms, but to study them better. Is the power of dissent within the Order hidden by healthy spiritual motives or is it these spiritual values which create the tension? Certainly in this case a detailed analysis of the individual historic events is needed, e.g., what is the meaning of the "spiritualism" of the first Capuchins and in what ways did the Spirituals influence Franciscan reform movements?

[16]Gaudenzio of Brescia, *Lo spirito della serafica Regola* (Brescia: G. Rizzardi, 1761) 261.

[17]Cf. *Provinciale Ordinis Fratrum Minorum vetustissimum*, ed. C. Eubel (Quaracchi, 1892) (ed. ca. 1340); *Bullarium Franciscanum* V, (Rome, 1898) 579-605; D. Cresi, "Statistica dell'Ordine Minoritico all'anno 1282," *AFH* 56 (1963): 157-62; for more bibliographical references on the growth of the Order up to 1300 cf. P. Peano and C. Schmidt, "Die Ausbreitung der Franziskaner bis 1300," *Atlas der Kirchen-Geschichte*, ed. H. Jedin, Kenneth Scott Latourette, Jochen Martin, Herder, Freiburg, etc. 1970, 42*-43*.

[18]St. Bonaventure, "Constitutions of Narbonne," *Opere Omnia* VIII (Ad Claras Aquas, 1898) 465; cf. M. Bihl, "Statuta Generalia Ordinis edita in Capitulis Generalibus celebratis Narbonae an. 1260, Assisii an. 1279 atque Parisiis an. 1292 editio critica et synoptica," *AFH* 34 (1941): 67, 11b.

[19]Cf. Sisinio da Romallo, *Il ministero della confessione nei primordi dell'Ordine francescano in relazione ai diritti parrocchiali*, Annali Francescani (Milan, 1949) 71-711 (describes this evolution with rare clarity and objectivity).

[20]F. Tocco, *Studi francescani* (Naples, 1909) 260, 264; P. Sevesi, "S. Carlo Borromeo e le Congregazioni degli Amadeiti e dei Clareni (1567-1570) Con documenti inediti," *AFH* 37 (1944): 104-64; A. Frugoni, "Dai 'Pauperes Eremitae Domini Celestini' ai 'Fratelli de paupere vita,'" *Celestiniana* (Rome, 1954) 125-67. A list of the Clareni's 43 hermitages can be found in P. Sevesi, *L'Ordine dei Frati Minori* I, 297. Angelo Clareno died in 1337.

[21]D. Bluma, 32f; Brengiol, 37-61; J. Moorman, 370 f.

[22]M. Faloci-Pulignani, *Il B. Paoluccio Trinci e i Minori Osservanti* (Assisi, 1920) 39; M. Sensi, "Brogliano e l'opera di fra Paoluccio Trinci," *Picenum Seraphicum* 12 (1975): 7-62; Sevesi, I, 40-42; Moorman, 371ff.; Brengio, 62-132; R. Manselli, "Dagli Spirituali all'Osservanza Momenti di storia francescana," *Humanitas* 6 (1951): 1217-28.

[23]Cf. "Considerations sur la vie érémitique," *Informationes* 2 (1976); 190-99; Melchor, 541f; Bluma, 36. Salimbene of Parma speaks of a hermitage in Campania where "the brothers at that place, in order to be useful and because it was necessary, used to go out, some to beg alms, some to hear confessions, some to preach." (This was in the years from 1240-1245.) Cf. *Cronica*, M.G.H., *Scriptores* t. XXXII (Antwerp-Leipzig, 1905-1913), 569. Of importance also is what Bernardino Aquilano writes in his Chronicle: "In the proliferation of houses, they received the special light of divine grace, namely: they acquired places for building anew apart from cities and inhabited areas. For in acquiring new places they caused harm to no one. Thus they pursued their goals in peace. For had they been willing to accept convents, they'd have incurred the wrath of the conventual fathers, and would have been living in continual enmity. For people cannot be expelled from their own home without

upheaval. A further special grace was this: they constructed houses apart from inhabited areas, remote from people's dwellings. Indeed, it is a most praiseworthy thing to avoid ongoing association with people. These latter, as a result, are themselves highly edified, and the brothers more securely, more admirably shielded. Once an honorable citizen of Aquila remarked to me: 'The remoteness of your houses is truly your salvation'" (cf. Bernardini Aquilani, *Chronica* 15).

[24]St. Francis, *Testament*, 18.

[25]Cf. S. Mencherini, *Guida illustrata della Verna* (Quaracchi, 1907).

[26]*Considerations sur la vie érémitique*, 190 ff.

[27]B. Aquilani, *Chronica*, 3. This chronicle was written in 1480.

[28]Merton, 161, 165. For information on the *laura*, see P. Compagnoni, *Il deserto di Giuda* (Franciscan Printing Press: Jerusalem, 1975) 21-109; E. Morini, "Eremo e Cenobio nel monachesimo greco dell'Italia meridionale nei secoli IX e X," *Riv. di Storia della Chiesa in Italia* 31 (1977): 1-39.

[29]Cf. St. John Climachus, *Scala Paradisi*. Text with introduction, version and notes by Trevisan P. Corona Patrum Salesiana, S.G., VIII I (Turin: 1941) 28-29; J. Gribmont, "La Scala Paradisi, Jean de Raïthou et Ange Clareno," *Chi erano gli Spirituali Atti del III Convegno Internazionale 1975* (Assisi, 1976) 216-20; see also the reflections of Rosalind B. Brooke during the Round Table at the end of the congress (ibid., 269-71).

[30]Cf. I. Hausherr, "La méthode d'oraison hésichaste," *Orientalia Christiana*, IX/2, n. 36 (1927): 110f.

[31]B. Aquilani, *Chronica*, 4.

[32]Especially chapters 41-53.

[33]Cf. V. Faccinetti, *Iconografia francescana* (Saggio), (Milan: ed. S. Lega Eucaristica, 1924); S. Gieben, "Philip Galle's Original Engravings of the Life of St. Francis and the Corrected Edition of 1587," *CF* 46 (1976): 291ff. and n. 136.

[34]B. Aquilani, *Chronica*, 9.

[35]See C. Butler, *Benedicti Regula monasteriorum* (Freiburg: Herder, 1935[3]).

[36]This problem was immediately noticed by witnesses outside the Order in the very first years of the Franciscan experience.

[37]The study appeared in *AIA*, ed. Fidel de Lejarza and A. Uribe (S. II, 17 [1957]), and was published separately with the title of *Introducción a los origines de la Observancia en España. Las reformas en los siglos XIV y XV* (Madrid, 1958). The most important contents of this work were explained in an article by Isidore of Villapadierna, mentioned at the beginning of this work; the article includes an updated bibliography. Of the many works by L. Carrion, I would recommend "Origines de la Custodia," etc. and "Historia documentada," etc., which have already been cited.

[38]Isidore, 247ff.

[39]Ibid., 275 f.

[40]Ibid., 276 f.

[41]Ibid., 277-79.

[42]Cf. "Introducción," 656 and 329-331; Carrion, "Origines," in *AIA* 3 (1915): 175.

[43]Ibid., "El convento de 'Donus Dei' de la Aguilera y algunos bienhechores," *AIA* 10 (1918): 448f., n. 7.

[44]For the text of the "Memoriale Religionis" see ibid., "Memoriale religionis de oficios activos y contemplativos por San Pedro Regalado?" *AIA* 12 (1919): 54-86 and "Introducción," 687-713; for the *Memoriale de la vita y ritos de la Custodia de Santa María de los Menores* and for the *Constituciones de la Custodia de Santa María de los Menores*, see ibid., 714-46, 747-74.

[45]Isidore, 285; Carrión, "Historia," 129-33.

[46]"Introducción," 710 f., 744-46, 858, 863; Carrion, "Memoriale Religionis," *AIA* 12 (1919): 83-84 and 59.

[47]Ibid., "Historia," 132.

[48]Ibid., "Origines," *AIA* 3 (1915): 161-66; "Historia documentada," 460-65.

[49]Ibid., *Memoriale Religionis*, ch. XII, in *AIA* 12 (1919) 82.

[50]Ibid., *Historia*, 468; Isidore, 287.

[51]Ibid., 289; Bluma, 38 F.

[52]Carrión, L., *Historia*, 115ff; see also V. Anjbarro, "El P. Ximenez Samaniego y los origines de la Oservance en España," *AIA* 8 (1948): 450 ff; Melchior, 542.

[53]Bluma, 40 f.

[54]L. Carrión, "Casas de Recollección de la Provincia de la Inmaculada Concepción y Estatutos por que se regían," in *AIA* 9 (1918): 264 f.

[55]Ibid., *Historia* 174.

[56]These constitutions, in Latin, are similar to the Spanish ones (see note 54 above) and can be found in Wadding's *Annales Minorum* XVI, 193-97. The same constitutions were published again in 1526 for the whole Cismontaine family; cf. D. DeGubernatis, *Orbis Seraphicus III* (Rome-Lugduni, 1684), 262-65.

[57]Bluma, 43.

[58]For the 1582 statutes see *CHL* I, 257 and DeGubernatis, *Orbis Seraphicus* III, 365; for the norms of 1595 f: ibid. III, 659-574 and Goyens, 59-76; for the 1621 statutes see *CHL* I, 660-64; for 1676 statutes see ibid., III/2, 171-176; for the 1684 statutes: ibid., III/1, 243-45.

[59]Bluma, 47, 58, 84ff.

[60]Ibid., 39; Carrión, *Historia*, 174.

[61]Guigo II, *Scala claustralium*, ch. 1-2; *PL* 184, 475-76.

[62]"Then let them immediately return to the church. Once the reading is finished (after Matins, it should always be from the life or the passion of Christ), let them give themselves to recollection and prayer." See Goyens, 68.

[63]Carrion, *Historia*, 176-81.

[64]*CHL* II, 143 b.

[65]"In all, let two-and-a-half hours be devoted to mental prayer." Ibid., 144a; III/1, 173 ff.

[66]Bluma, 45; Melchior, 543; *CHL* II, 143; III/2, 179, 250.

[67]Wallenstein, 238-41.

[68]See *CHL* III,1, 291 a; Gori, 161 f.

[69]*CHL* III/1 291 1-b.

[70]Gori, 166 f; *CHL* III/1, 293 a; Bluma, 48 ff.

[71]Ibid, 48-51 with the bibliography cited in the notes. In particular see B. Innocenti, "Le relazioni tra S. Leonardo da P. M. e S. Teofilo da Corte," *SF* 28 (1931): 144-80.

[72]L. Anastasi, "I sacri ritiri nella lettera collettiva dei M. RR. PP. Provinciali," *Vita Minorum* 35/3 (1964): 24 f.

[73]B. Innocenti, "P. Giuliano da Pistoia e i suoi scritti," *SF* 14 (1928): 138-39.

[74]Ibid, 141 f.

[75]Ibid., 144.

[76]See Pacifico da Rimini, min. rif., *Della vita e dell'eroiche virtù del ven. P. Leopoldo da Gaiche min. rif. di S. Francesco nella Provincia Serafica, istitutore del ritiro di Monteluco e missionario apostolico*. 2 vols. (Foligno, 1835) 149-66.

[77] For the Statutes of Bl. Bonaventure see *CHL* III/1, 290-304 and P. Mencinetti, *De SS. Recessuum B. Bonaventurae a Barcinone Statutis* (Studium historico-iuridicum), Romae 1946 (unpublished); for the 12 rules of Bl. Thomas of Core see *CHL* III/1, 498-508; for the 19 *Avvisi* or *Memos* of St. Theophilus of Corte see ibid., IV, 323 1-b; for St. Leonard of Port Maurice, see *Breve Scrittura (sulla natura del Ritiro di S. Bonaventura)*, *S. Bonaventura al Palatino, 1751*, in B. Innocenti, Operette, 277-287; S. Leonardo da Porto M., *Massime necessarie e regolamento per chi s'impiega a fare le sante missioni* . . . in which is found a "breve regguaglio del ritiro di Toscana e modo di vivere nella Solitudine del medmo," in *Collez complete delle opere del B. Leonardo da Porto M.* (Rome, 1853), 2 vols;

for the later regulations see *CHL IV*, 308-328 (Clement of Palermo); *Regole e Costituzioni da osservare in tutti i conventi di ritiro dell'Ordine de'Minori*, decreed and established by the Most Rev. Fr. Paschal of Varese, Min. Gen. (Rome: Salomoni Typography, 1744); *Statuti e Regolamento che il Min. Gen. dell'Ordine* (Venantius of Celano) *propone ad osservarsi nei ritiri dei Padri Missionari dell'Ordine dei Minori* (Rome, 1855); *Statuta pro sacris recessibus* (1905), in *Enchiridion vitae franciscanae*, A. Ghinato, ed. (Quaracchi, 1957) 48-52, published previously in *Acta O.F.M.* 24 (1905) 156-158; *De sacris recessibus* (July 27, 1937), in *Acta OFM* 56 (1937) 263-266 and in *Enchiridion*, op. cit., I, 324-333.

[78]*CHL IV*, 308a.

[79]Ibid., 309 ff., 312 ff., 320 ff; cf. Innocenti, *Le relazioni*, 153 f.

[80]*CHL IV*, 318.

[81]Ibid., III/1, 303 b, n. 25.

[82]"In order to see to the quiet and recollection of the religious, when people possessed by demons are brought to the churches of their convents, the local superiors are not to allow exorcisms to be performed; with all good manners they should say that they are forbidden to do so and, before sending such persons away, they can call all the religious to the choir, ordering them to say some particular prayer for the liberation of the person" (Ibid., IV, 322 a, n. X).

[83] Ibid. III/1, 293.

[84]Ibid.

[85]Ibid., 299a.

[86]Ibid., 298 f.

[87]Ibid., 302 a, n. 6.

[88]Ibid. 304 a, n. 26.

[89]These 19 "reminders" correspond to ch. 17 ("Del modo e pratica di regolarsi i Superiori de' Conventi di Ritiro per ben esercitare il loro Uffizio") of the Constitutions of Clement of Palermo (1759), cited in note 76 above.

[90]Ibid. IV, 328 b.

[91]So they are called in the first Constitutions of Albacina, in the earliest documents of the Holy See, and the first ascetic works of John of Fano.

[92]See Eduardus Alenconiensis, *Primigeniae Legislationis Ordinis Fr. Min. Cap. textus originales*, Rome 1928, 57a, 58 a; see also O. Schmucki, *Das meditativ-kontemplativ Element im Kapuzinerleben nach Ausweis der Frühgeschichte*, in 43. *Provinzkapitel der Bayerische Kapuziner* 6-10. Aug 1973, 168-186; Ibid., "L'indirizzo contemplativo dell'Ordine cappuccino primitivo, in Picenum Seraphicum," 12 (1975) 296-303.

[93]Cf. Methodius of Nembro, *La spiritualità cappuccina*, in *Quattrocento scrittori spirituali*, Rome 1972, 1-27; Optat de Veghel, *La réforme des Frères Mineurs Capucins dans l'Ordre franciscain et dans l'Eglise*, in CF 35 (1965) 5-108.

[94]Cf. Mattia of Salò, *Historia Capuccina*, II, 280 f. in *Mon. Hist. Ord. Min. Cap.*, VI, Roma 1950; for some observations on Capuchin spirituality see also my study: "*Vita della B. Angela da Desenzano*" in "*Historia Capuccina*" *di Mattia da Salò, Agiografia e letteratura spirituale della riforma tridentia* in IF 52 (1977) 187-218.

[95]Cf. *Litterae circulares Superiorum Generalium Ordinis Fr. Min. Cap.* (1548-1803), ed. P. Melchior a Pobladura, Mon. Hist. Ord. Min. Cap., VIII. (Rome, 1960); as for the judgement of Benedict XIV, see the Brief "Inclytum Fratrum Min. S. Francisci Capuccinorum" (March 2, 1743) in *Bull. Cap.*, VIII, 354-55; Melchior A. Pobladura, *Historia Generalis OFM Cap.*, II/2 (Rome, 1948) 99f.

[96]Melchior de Pobladura, "El establecimiento de los conventos de retiro en la Orden Capuchina" (1760-1790), in CF 22 (1952) 53-73, 150-79.

[97]Cf. *Costituzioni originali fatte dal P. Cherubino da Nizza per il ritiro stabilito in Cittaducale. 1763* (Ms. in the Provincial Archives of the Capuchins in Rome, sign. *Cittaducale*); cf. Melchior of Pobladura, "El Establecimiento" 61, n. 12.

[98]Ibid., 62 ff.

[99]Ibid., 150-73: also, Pobladura, "Seminarios de misioneros y conventos de perfecta vida comun. Un episodio del regalismo español (1763-1785)," *CF* 32 (1962): 271-309, 397-433; 33 (1963): 28-81.

[100]Melchior de Pobladura, *Saggio della corrispondenza spirituale del venerabile Gesualdo da Reggio* (Catanzaro, 1969) 101 f. (Terranova: Jan. 3 1779); see also his work, "De scientia et scriptis ven. servi Dei Jesualdi a Rhegio (1725-1803)" *CF* 24 (1954): 110-35, 329-382, especially 337, f; 347, f; 355 f.

[101]See *Direttorio della famiglia del Real Eremo, o sia ritiro de' Cappuccini in Capodimonte* (Naples, 1819); G. Rubinacci, "Il Real Eremo di Capodimonte in Napoli (1819-1865),"*IF* 46 (1971): 3-133.

[102]Cf. "Epistola Venantii a Taurino" (Sept. 30, 1851) in *Bull Cap*. X, 253 b-254 b; he prescribes some rules for novitiates, homes for those in simple vows, and student houses.

[103]102 Gori, 168 f., note 9.

[104]Cf. *Ordinazioni particolari e lettere di San Pietro d'Alcantara*, in S.J. Piat, *Il maestro della mistica S. Pietro d'Alcantara* (translated from the French) (Bari: Ed. Paoline, 1963) 180f.

[105]Ibid., 179-80. In order to understand the spiritual, ascetical, and mystical dynamism of the Alcantarine hermitages, read the work by the Observant minor, Antonio Daza, *Essercitii spirituali delli Romitori instituiti dal Nostro Serafico P. S. Francesco per utilità de i suoi frati*, . . translated from Spanish into Italian by Fr. Luigi of Rome in 1626. It is an interesting and rare commentary on the "Rule for Hermitages," seen from the Alcantarine perspective. Pointing to the example of St. Francis, the author transcribes the text in Latin with the more traditional title of *De religiosa habitatione in heremitoriis*, and then offers a commentary with 20 points or conclusions. Then he treats specifically *Dell'offitio delle Madri* (ch. 3) and *Dell'offitio de figliuoli* (ch. 4). The other ten chapters deal with mental prayer, the "art of all arts," with all the spiritual exercises required by it. It shows the influence of Alcantara's Treatise on prayer and meditation. The Way of the Cross is given great importance. The last chapter (ch. 11) has the precise description of the hermitage and its measurements, as if to offer a standard. There is a "portico to enter the hermitage: it is 22 spans wide and 27 high." Then one comes to the "place of the turn and the adjacent areas: it is 22 spans wide and 10 long; the turn, which is still used in many cloistered monasteries, was the means of communicating with the outside world without breaking solitude and voluntary reclusion. A "well is in the center of the cloister: it is 14 spans in diameter." In the "garden within the convent's cloistered area" there are four cells for those making retreats, as narrow and poor as those founded by St. Francis, each one of them 10 spans square. So that those who are making retreat do not hear one another, each cell should be separated from the others. The central reference point is the "chapel of the cloister, which is 10 spans wide and 27 spans in length. The ceiling should be made of the skulls or bones of the dead." This last detail might strike us as slightly macabre, but it is part of the history of the Capuchin experience. Then we come to the "main dormitory, which in every place must be dedicated to the Immaculate Conception of Our Lady: it is to be 12 spans wide and 33 spans long." The "sacristy is 12 spans wide and 16 long." Another area is the "*via sacra*, and a corridor which faces south, where they can pray stations when making the exercises of the cross: it is 20 spans wide and 85 spans long. And the four pillars in this corridor should be made from old tombstones, out of love of holy poverty." Then, for a slight touch of humor, there is the "water reservoir, 30 spans wide and 16 spans long," and next to it the "room for cooking: 16 spans wide and 15 spans long." There are also "common places" and "two chapels in the garden, each of them 10 spans square" (cf. Daza, *Essercitij*, 101-03).

[106]Wallenstein, 236-56.

[107]Ibid., 250 f., 252.

[108]Cf. Salvatore, 91 ff. The original title of these still unpublished statutes was: *Costituzioni particolari che devono osservarsi nell'eremitico ritiro, detto La Solitudine di Santa Maria degli Angioli in Piedimonte Diocese d'Alife nel Regno di Napoli habitato da Religiosi Minori Scalzi della Provincia di San Pietro d'Alcantara fatte d'ordine dell'Em.mo e Rev.mo Signore, il Signore Cardinale Francesco Barberino Protettore della N.ra Serafica Religione per vigore di facoltà comunicatagli dalla S.M. di Clemen. X. Accettate dal Capitolo Provinciale del 1678 per voti: secreti nemine discrepante e da osservarsi perpetuamente nella medesima Solitudine per commandam. del Nostro Beatissimo Padre Innocentio XI per il suo Apostolico Breve, spedito alli 15 di giugno del 1679.*

[109]Salvatore 23.

[110]Ibid., 96.

[111]bid., 95.

[112]Ibid., 97 f.

[113]Cf. Innocenti, *Opperette* 77f.

[114]A. Cresi, "S. Leonardo da P.M. e l'Incontro," *SF* 24 (1952): 176-197; Ibid., "Il Collegio—ritiro dei missionari dell'Incontro nel primo centenario della fondazione (1853-1953)," *SF* 26 (1954): 44-89; *Costitutzioni da osservarsi nella Solitudine del ritiro della Provincia riformata Toscana* (Florence, 1776); *Proponimenti di S. Leonardo da P.M. tratti dall'autografo,* with introduction and notes by P. Benedetto Innocenti (Florence, 1937).

[115]Gori, 168.

[116]Cresi., *S. Leonardo,* 196.

[117]Ibid., see also Wallenstein, "La Spiritualità di S. Leonardo da Porto M.," *SF* 24 (1952): 24-26.

[118]These are the words of the *Ignea sagitta* of Nicolas Le Gaulois, 7th prior general of the Discalced Carmelites (13th century): cf. *DS* III, 534 f; *DIP* II, 461.

[119]These tendencies clearly appeared in the most recent Franciscan Study Congress at Assisi. See *Francesco d'Assisi e francescanesimo dal 1216 al 1226. Atti del IV convegno internazionale* (Assisi, 1977).

[120]See Sainsaulieu, *Les ermites français* ("Sciences humaines et religions") (Paris: Ed. du Cerf), 167.

[121]See, for example, S. Gieben, "Il richiamo della foresta: la funzione del bosco presso i primi cappuccini," *Picenum Seraphicum* 12 (1975): 290-95.

Eremitism in Medieval Franciscanism

by

Grado G. Merlo[1]

Translated from the Italian by

Nancy Celaschi, OSF

Following their happy father, they went at that time to the
Spoleto valley. They all conferred together, as true followers of
justice, whether they should dwell among people or go to
solitary places (*conferebant . . . utrum inter homines conversari
deberent, an ad loca solitaria se conferre*).[2] Thus in his *First Life*
Thomas of Celano recalls the joys and doubts which Francis and
his first companions faced as they returned from Rome, where
they had met Innocent III.[3] Their joy revolved around the fact
that the Pope had allowed them to continue their religious
experiment. Their doubts concerned the way that experiment
should proceed: Should they witness to Christ among people or
withdraw in solitude? These questions can be rather surprising if
we take into consideration that just a few lines before this
Thomas of Celano referred to Francis's refusal when Cardinal
John of St. Paul tried to persuade him to follow the more
traditional ways, such as the "life of a monk or a hermit"; this
refusal was based on his desire to be conformed to "a higher
desire."[4] If Francis had rejected the life of a hermit suggested to
him by a prelate of the Roman Curia, how is it possible that
when they returned to the valley, he began discussing with the
other friars whether or not they should withdraw to solitary

places? The apparent contradiction can be resolved if we consider that the phrase *ad loca solitaria se conferre* does not convey the idea of formalized models of the eremitical life and that the choice of the life of a hermit would be only externally similar to the type of eremitical life known until that time.

At that time (around 1210) Francis's gospel inspiration must have been quite clear already if he had decided to go to the pope to obtain recognition.[5] What direction he should give to the life of the friars, however, was not quite so clear, given that Francis did not want to waste time with the proven methods which the Church hierarchy suggested, and given that his meeting with the highest Church authorities had not really settled anything.[6]

Inter homines conversari? Ad loca solitaria se conferre? Such a dilemma can be considered the leitmotif for the analysis and interpretation of a large part of the Franciscan event since the end of the Middle Ages (and perhaps for an even longer period).[7] The alternative, either "the desert" or apostolic activity among the people is, in my opinion, connected with a certain difference between Francis's religious plan and its historical expression: a plan that was very fascinating in its basic inspiration, but equally difficult to live in the changing make-up and conditions of the fraternity.[8] In the early stages of the Franciscan adventure the alternative was resolved by alternating, or rather, to borrow an expression from Santé Bortolami,[9] in a "particular type of proclivity for commuting between the hermitage and city": an alternation, or rather a successful synthesis of the two tendencies. In the course of the middle decades of the 13th century, however, the Franciscan "commuter lifestyle" would swing more in the direction of the cities; the balance was destroyed. By 1270 the Order of Friars Minor was fully integrated into urban society.[10] Pastoral ambition, material necessity, and the need for security were wedded to the objective of the "spiritual" conquest of upper-class citizens and participation in the highest cultural institutions. These reasons are also known to us through the theoretical explanations of the Bonaventurian era.[11] Beginning in the middle of the 13th century, these changes involve the development of Italian eremitism in general, urged and sometimes even forced by ecclesiastical authorities to take on the structure of the "mendicant model" and become involved in the urban apostolate,[12] in order to help bring the city dwellers back to the ethical and religious horizon of Roman Catholicism.[13]

The city became the privileged locale for the presence of the mendicants in general and that of the minors in particular. The majority of the Franciscan Order accepted and fostered this urban-centered orientation. Those who did not accept this evolution had no other option than the *loca solitaria*. However, mind you, for them—the zealots of the Rule—it was not merely a discussion about the type of housing, but rather the connection between the mode of bearing witness as Franciscans and the manner of interpreting the heritage of St. Francis. As is general knowledge, it was around the so-called hermitage tradition[14] that a large part of that heritage revolved, or rather, that the beneficiaries disputed the inheritance of a saint whom many considered unique in his way of giving Christian witness. Franciscan eremitism stands at the crossroads of the conflict about the ways and forms of perpetuating the teaching of Francis as an exceptional witness of Christ. The Franciscan hermitages, therefore, took on many practical and symbolic functions. First and foremost, they are places destined to receive the friars who considered it their duty to safeguard the heart of an extraordinary Christian intuition from the deviation and degradation suffered at the hand of the large majority of the Order (until, with the imposition of the Observant Movement, it would become part of a rather singular metamorphosis).

There are places for recollection for small groups, like those who gathered around Caesar of Speyer and Simon of Collazzone in the Spoleto Valley, separating themselves from the "community."[15] There are places of individual "flight." Shortly after the death of Francis, Brother Giles[16] "withdrew not only from familiarity with worldly people, but also from his brothers and other religious," going from hermitage to hermitage and ending his days at Monteripido in 1262. It is to Brother Giles that people attribute the saying: "If we did not have the example of the Fathers who have gone before us, perhaps we would not be in the state of penance in which we are." This saying shows a clear

awareness of the Franciscan connection with the first models of
the anchorite life of the ancient hermits in the Egyptian desert,
passed on to tradition by the Lives of the Fathers, a reference to
the strength of a myth which was among the strongest and most
continuous inspirations of the eremitical life.[17] The reclusive life
of Giles, Caesar, and Simon are an example, although rather
precocious from the chronological point of view, of a phenomenon
destined to intensify during the lengthy dispute between the
zealots of the Rule and the friars of the community. This
phenomenon is sufficiently well-known and we do not need to
develop it more here.

However, it is not entirely superfluous to mention here that
the late Raoul Manselli, commenting on a report by Stanislao da
Campagnola on "the Umbrian spirituals" during the third
congress of the International Society of Franciscan Studies (1975),
suggested the need for caution "in making too close a connection
between the hermitage and dissent" because, in the opinion of
the illustrious Franciscanist, there were eremitical "moments"
brought about solely by the desire to "realize a more perfect
Christian life" in regard to the guidelines contained in the "Rule
for Hermitages."[18] His correct emphasis was a suggestion for
further research, because the aspect mentioned is little known in
the period after 1230. For all we know, institutionalized
Franciscan eremitism seems to have suffered a phase of decline in
the context of the spread of urban Franciscanism, as seems to be
suggested by reports of the abandonment of some hermitages
connected with the figure of St. Francis himself (Greccio, La
Verna, Montecasale).[19] Still hoping for broader studies which
will provide more information on the topic, up to now we can
claim that soon after the death of Francis the hermitages drew
mainly those who did not take to the changes taking place in
the Order of Minors.

Rather, separation from the community when it did not
conform to the Rule and Testament of St. Francis, was seen as an
act of great gospel awareness. Let us consider the words which
Angelus of Clareno places in the mouth of the "great teacher of
holy theology" (Caesar of Speyer) at the time of his conversion

to Franciscan life, and the response attributed to St. Francis himself:

> 'I ask you for one favor: if during my days it should so happen that the friars draw distant from the pure observance of the Rule . . . and because of their opposition I cannot freely observe it in conformity to that holy and perfect intention revealed by God to you, I ask you, with your obedience and license, to be able to withdraw alone or with a few friars and observe it perfectly.' Upon hearing these words, blessed Francis was filled with immense joy and, blessing him, he said: 'What you have asked for has been granted by Christ and me.'[20]

When the evangelical path which God had revealed to Francis was not being followed, or it was no longer possible to follow it within an Order which had abandoned the "perfect observance" of the Rule, solitude was no longer a tragic necessity or an elitist temptation. It was rather a legitimate obligation approved by Christ himself through the holy founder. Clareno's passage, edited almost a century after the first friars took refuge in the hermitages, interprets the past in the light of the problems of the present with the explicit goal of supporting the reasons for the troubled journey of the "authentic" followers of St. Francis. "I ask you . . . to be able to withdraw alone or with a few friars": the legitimate choice of, one could say, a forced eremitical life. For his part, Angelus of Clareno, above and beyond a certain personal inclination for the "desert," was forced into the eremitical life in order to remain faithful to what he, along with others, considered to be genuine Franciscanism.[21]

This constriction seems to have been turned into a liberation of sorts after the meeting with Celestine V in L'Aquila in 1294. The Pope wanted Angelus of Clareno and his "brothers" to observe "the way of life" they had promised and "poverty in deserted places, serving God with simple faith."[22] Institutionalized eremitism seemed to be the best solution for those who wanted to observe strict adherence to the original Franciscanism. The juridical and organizational distinction of the Order of Minors sanctioned these different interpretations. Things were developing differently from what the pope had intended. In alternating periods of severe repression and relative calm for many years the hermitages would be a necessary refuge for Angelus and his companions. It was only 150 years later, and unthinkably so, that the experience of Clareno would finally be restored with full right to the Order of Friars Minor, as part of a complex task of absorbing the various "spiritual" tendencies in the Observant movement. However, we shall discuss this later.

Once the attempt failed to gather the various components of the Franciscan dissent into an autonomous order of an eremitical nature, the "desert" continued to be the place of marginalization, or rather self-marginalization, as well as forced silence. The latter is the case of Ubertino da Casale, isolated in 1305 at La Verna where, among other things, he composed one of two probable versions of his important work, the *Arbor Vitae Crucifix Iesu* [*Tree of Life of the Crucified Jesus*].[23] Ubertino, sent to live with eremitical limitations, was not the type for the hermitage. His strong campaign against the urban tendencies of the Friars Minor, the sign of the friars' adaptation to the world and their distance from St. Francis's original plan, was not caused by nor even accompanied by a propensity for the hermitage. On the contrary, once again a spy with a rather nonsedentary nature helps us see the broader horizons of the religious conflict. With regard to the minors who, wherever possible, had made their dwellings "in the centre of the town squares," thus becoming city-dwellers motivated by "human cupidity" and the search for "fame" and "glory," Ubertino called people back to the pilgrim values of the original witness of Francis of Assisi. He alternated times of contemplation and solitude with presence among people. He wanted the friars' places to be "near the people but placed away from their habitations in places appropriate for solitude."[24]

There is a notable convergence between Ubertino's expressions and what Jacques de Vitry had written a century earlier about the lesser brothers whom he met and admired in Umbria: "During the day they go into the cities and villages, giving themselves over to the active life of the apostolate; at night they return to their hermitage or withdraw into solitude to live the contemplative life."[25] At the beginning of the 14th century the hermitage-city commute was seen as the mobile lifestyle most consistent with the evangelical life, the paradigm for measuring transgressions and infidelity to the Rule and Testament of St. Francis. "To their hermitage or withdraw into solitude" was the way the French prelate's letter described it at that time, 1216, when there was not yet a precise type of Franciscan dwelling. The isolation of their residences was the primary dimension.[26]

In effect, Francis of Assisi's religious inspiration took place along eremitical lines. His very choice of gospel poverty had close connections with the "desert" tradition.[27] Other scholars have already emphasized these connections. However, there is something more precise that should be pointed out. Let us take into consideration a single example. When in his Testament St. Francis takes pains to tell his fratres not to occupy places (churches or poor dwellings or anything which is built for them) which are not in conformity with the "holy poverty" promised in the Rule, and advises them to have an attitude "as pilgrims and strangers" in their regard,[28] it was certainly for reasons of "marginalism." No attachment to things, nor privileges granted by anyone, can be placed above and beyond the desire to witness to Christ precisely in this marginal living which is both socio-topographical and ecclesiastical-cultural at the same time. However, this marginal lifestyle brought diverse results. Exemplary witness and living in places more adept to contemplation which produced holiness, or which were seen as manifestations of holiness by outsiders, attracted a world that needed holiness for individual and collective reasons. People went to the holy places and wanted to bring the holy brothers from the holy places to the city. There is a synergism between the friars' need for holiness and the friars who, in imitation of Christ, could not fail to preach the "good news" for the conversion and support of humanity.

As the hermits of previous centuries had already learned, it was difficult to make space for solitude. However, the Friars Minor experienced an additional complication because, in the meantime, urban society had grown immensely and required new forms of religious presence. If in the past the monks had to resolve the problem of the relationship between hermitage and monastery,[29] in drawing closer to the urban milieu, the Franciscans were forced to deal with the question of maintaining a balance between hermitage and city, or between the desert and the crowd. All this was aggravated by the obvious difficulty in maintaining that balance in the difficult dialogue with the "novelty" expressed by St. Francis and within the process of the Order's tremendous growth, which demanded their assuming various responsibilities and their intimate insertion into the life of the Church and the ecclesiastical hierarchy.[30] In addition to this, there was the encounter and competition with other mendicant groups and with the many more or less spontaneous religious experiences which were also inspired by gospel poverty. However, that is not all.

The evolution of the Order brought with itself a rich, committed theological and cultural debate. From it came a vast amount of ecclesiological, ethical, economic, and political discussion from which has come the "social hypotheses of medieval Franciscanism" about which Ovidio Capitani has written many important pages.[31] The intellectuals among the community and the spirituals alike could not be satisfied with a Christianity *sine glossa*, without gloss. Moving away from the central theme of the poverty/ownership polarity and its anthropological connections, they set about creating a theoretical combination of the apocalyptic, eschatological dimension with the horizontal, or with questions posed by the economic, social, and cultural development of the cities.[32] The results caused the center of Franciscan interest to shift decisively to Christian society as a whole and therefore, to the Church—the Christian society and Church in a crisis about their ideology and foundation. Rightly did Claudio Leonardi, in opening the Fourteenth International Congress on 13th-century Franciscans and Franciscanism in Assisi in this same place, recall that the first half of that century marked the end "without return of the parable of Franciscanism as the principal dynamic force in the history of Christian tradition."[33] Francis's heritage was not passed on to institutions, but was rather perpetuated at the level of mysticism "in a few women"—Angela of Foligno, Clare of Montefalco—"a mysticism" lived at the "personal, private level."[34]

It is the Observant movement which will try to create a synthesis of the patrimony received from a past which was far from linear, one filled with contradictions and contrast. It is the Observants who will attempt to recompose the unity of the interior life and the "social hypothesis" in an innovative plan for restructuring Franciscanism and the Order of Minors and society too.[35] The renewal began in the hermitage: in the solitude of Brogliano Paoluccio of Foligno, according to the 14th-century chronicler Bernardino Aquilano, "rekindled observance in the order."[36] From the experience of Friar Paoluccio and his companions flows the movement destined to restore the original alternating balance between the desert and the crowds. The *Chronica Fratrum Minorum Observantiae* of Aquilano is a text which documents an awareness: an awareness celebrating the observant novelty when it was largely imposed.[37] In the last decades of the 15th century they could clearly explain the affirmation's lines. In the distance the line passed through those who, because of their desire to "observe their Rule of Life without gloss or without reservation" were the object of persecution. Among these was Angelus of Clareno who, independently of the habit he assumed, had never ceased to follow the Rule of St. Francis. It then passed through Brogliano and moved on to Perugia in connection with the city, its authorities and the university world. From here it spread everywhere.[38]

By the end of the 14th century the fruitful bond between hermitage and city had been restored. This bond was then proposed anew as the special way of living for the new Observant settlements "on the outskirts of towns and apart from people's homes." This was noted by an attentive outside observer to whom the following expression is attributed: "Truth to tell, secluding the hermitages means your preservation."[39] To be sure, the hermitage tradition was strengthened by the Observant movement as regards the city as well as the Franciscan hermitages. Hermitages which the collective memory connected with St. Francis, St. Anthony, or Brother Giles (e.g., Monteripido, Santa Maria della Valle del Sasso, San Paolo in Monte and San Giovanni di Camposampiero) were given new life.[40]These and other hermitages became the cornerstones of the Observant movement. No one should believe, however, that the *sequestratio* [seclusion] which the astute person quoted by Aquilano saw as the element of strength and continuity (*conservatio*), meant isolation. Rather, Ugolino Nicolini appropriately pointed out that, from the first years of the 15th century the Observants gathered in the hermitages had guardians coming from the various parts of Italy and Europe. This is evidence of their cosmopolitan nature and their broad relations.[41]

During the turbulent decades of the Great Western Schism and the age of the councils, the Observants were strong on the settlement debate in order to support their claims of being in line with the original Franciscan lifestyle. In doing so, they used the argumentation once advanced by Ubertino da Casale and the Spirituals.[42] A short time later these themes and topics were turned upside down and used against the Observants, who were accused of duplicity and falseness. Their apparently rigorous choices and their preference for seclusion were judged to be mere pretense because their dwellings on the outskirts of the cities were really large, rich, and comfortable houses, and even those who were supposed to live in the woods, attracted by the cities, stayed there "eating and drinking."[43] Not even the Observants, therefore, were able to maintain the balance between the desert and the crowd, and very soon they opted for the latter.

A quick parenthetical observation is required at this point. Following the logic of the Order's internal conflict, we are not able to rid ourselves of the impression that this logic is fruitless from the historian's viewpoint. As an agent of history, the myth of the origins is rather dangerous and ambiguous to evaluate because, with a certain amount of distance from human affairs in their development and particulars, we are always led to judge the past as better than the present.[44]

As for the Observant movement, the concrete human factors meant a complex of the restoration of traditions and offering religious themes to a European society which had a tendency to build things that were institutionally and culturally stronger, more stable and lasting. This is what was done by the "four columns of the Observant reform" and the intellectuals who formed the strong core of the movement first and later of the whole Order. Someone could object that the Franciscan reform movement had an "anti-intellectual attitude" and a "type of auto-didacticism."[45] Is it valid to speak of "Observant" intellectuals? It is a question of words and content. If by the word "intellectuals" we mean professional thinkers who address and respond to the public, wanting to have a direct influence on the historical situation through the use of a professional intellect,[46] there can be no doubt that this definition is truly applicable to a Bernardine of Siena and his followers.

The hermitage is also a place for learning and for training intellectuals. We immediately recall that in the hermitages the manuscript tradition of the Spirituals' texts was preserved because of their "observant" use. Roberto Rusconi has shown this quite clearly.[47] In the hermitage of Colombaio, Friar Bernardino could build his own learning outside the normal scholastic context and, in all probability, began to study the works of Peter John Olivi and Ubertino da Casale. These writings and this culture allowed him to draw up his own religious program to be spread through his preaching activity.[48] Thus it was from the hermitage that a "renewed" Christian, Franciscan proposal went out, one based on the desire to impose a strict compulsory moral law on a society which they wanted to see solidly established and disciplined.

The convents away from the cities and the hermitages could thus become places for the celebration of power in that they were able to guarantee stability and discipline. This topic leads us away from our main consideration, and we cannot treat it here. Let us recall only the case of Our Lady of Graces near Mantua, in which the hermitage/city was complicated by a third element, namely, the power of the "prince."[49] It is common knowledge that in a large part of Europe the Observants enjoyed the favor of those in public authority, thanks mainly to the convergence of the necessities of the 15th-century power structure and the "socio-religious hypothesis" of the Observant branch of Franciscanism expressed in a preaching style that did not seem to make hopeful promises, but rather spread constricting, rigid, ethical, and religious models.[50]

If this seems to be one of the predominant and, in some way, eventually dominant tendencies, the reader can understand how room for an immediate relationship with the divine was to be sought in a mystical, ascetic, contemplative spirituality drawing greatly on the monastic and eremitical traditions, which concerned small groups and isolated individuals. Rather, it was a question of a "countercurrent" which "points at relationships and encounters as an exception, taking place between chosen souls who, in the affective and mystical search for Christ, find their point of contact and their sense of the Church." These are some of the manifestations of that "parabola of withdrawal for long periods" in the religious history of the Late Middle Ages in Italy, as they were so keenly analyzed and explained by Giovanni Miccoli.[51] We seem to have a re–creation of a climate which was proper to the hermits at the end of the 10th century and the following century who lived within the circles of the spirituality of St. Romuald: grand souls, united by a common yearning for a personal perfection nourished by a special love by God and for God.[52] However, in them there was also a "need for order and rationality which met the broadest needs of the society in which they lived and which deserved to translate their spiritual ardor into an important historical factor."[53]

In the 14th and 15th centuries was the eremitical movement still, or once again, capable of being expressed in "an important historical factor"? We have seen that in Franciscanism, and not only in it, there is a heightened split between the religious forms which had derived from the hermitage a capacity for energetic intervention in social situations and religious forms which were either internalized or effectively closed themselves off in elitist, isolated experiences. We also know that the eremitical ideals were common in humanist circles and that a scholar like Paolo Giustiniani, at the beginning of the 15th century, "turned from the rich humanist experience to the extreme simplicity of Romuald, seeking to give new life to the eremitical forms of asceticism and contemplation for the whole gamut of the order to which Romuald called it back."[54] From these unfortunately too rapid references we can see that in the last centuries of the Middle Ages and the first part of the modern era eremitism acts as a force of religious attraction and action, even though articulated in a multiplicity of expressions and levels of realization, and is interwoven at every level. A quick check on the level of iconography has been brilliantly conducted by Daniel Russo, following the evolution of depictions of St. Jerome in Italy from the 13th to 16th centuries. The saint had earlier been depicted majestically as a cardinal in a pose reminiscent of university professors. Beginning about 1370-80 and beyond, however, he is shown as a humble penitent in the desert. In the late 15th century the patron of the humanists is depicted in an elegant study.[55]

Saint Jerome: what a great model of eremitism, not only in art; from the mid 14th century onwards there were many anchoritic initiatives undertaken in the Italian and Iberian peninsulas.[56] There are many similarities with the development and outcome of the earlier mendicant orders (Carmelites, Augustinians, Franciscans, Servites, Saccati). They arise spontaneously in "the desert." After several decades they move towards the city, and frequently end up in the heart of urban areas. Is it a question of an inevitable mechanism or imitations of the "mendicant" organization? As far as I know, we do not have enough data to draw any conclusions. However, we cannot exclude the possibility that Franciscanism had some ties with it and exercised some influence on it. We have more certain evidence of Franciscan ties and influence with reference to the hermitage experience of a Francis de Paola and the prophetic–penitential itinerant preachers. First of all there is the desire to imitate Francis of Assisi, which will be formalized in the very name of the first group gathered around him, "the Society of poor hermits of St. Francis of Assisi in Paola."[57] Secondly, their "golden age" takes place several decades later, in the last 20 or 30 years of the 15th century and the first years of the 16th. The need to return to their Franciscan origins mixes with the themes of the Minorite-Joachimite tradition, sometimes with temporarily explosive results.[58]

The continuity and strength of the Franciscan "myth of origins" are extraordinary. For the most part it is interpreted in an eremitic perspective, and is not limited to the Middle Ages. The "Capuchin reform" will have the same roots.[59] On the other hand, in the Late Middle Ages there was a flourishing of eremitic experiences which historians have often all too easily related to the Franciscan area and underrated as "a singular, significant, but secondary manifestation of the vast, varied lay movement aroused by the mendicants or in some way related to it."[60] Recently Luigi Pellegrini made his point in this regard, highlighting the importance and complexity of the phenomenon of "lay hermits" as well as the difficulty of finding a single way to interpret them.[61] In effect, rural and mountain eremitism stand side by side with an eremitism lived near urban areas, or even in the city itself, although this latter form seems to have progressively decreased from its greatest numbers in the second half of the 13th century until its lowest level in the first decades of the 15th century. This parabola can be deduced by analyzing the individual situations in central Italy and should be studied further in less limited dimensions, using a broader sampling.

In the world of semiurban or urban eremitism we particularly find the presence of women expressed in various ways and forms which were not always respected and preserved in the bishops' attempts to direct them into the modules of recognized religions. "Cellanes," "incarcerate," domestic penitents, hermits, recluses, repentants, and incluses are the characters we find peopling a religious universe which research began to discover but a few years ago. I am thinking especially of the work of Anna Benvenuti Papi,[62] Mario Sensi,[63] Giovanna Casagrande,[64] and Edith Pásztor.[65] Casagrande and Pásztor have shown the dimensions eremitism had reached among women in Europe in the Late Middle Ages, what influence and relationship they had with Franciscanism,[66] and how true is Benvenuti Papi's hypothesis that "the women's religious 'revolution' of the 13th century, which was dying out in the 14th and was relatively revitalized through the Observant regularization of the 15th century, was extinguished in the post-Tridentine tidying up of institutions."[67] However, rather than closing the topic, this opens up for us a whole world of study, as fascinating as it is unexplored.

Endnotes

[1]G.G. Merlo, "Eremitismo nel francescanesimo medievale," *Eremitismo Francescano,* 27-50.

[2]1 Celano 35. See *Omnibus of Sources* 258.

[3]Cf. G.G. Merlo, *Tensioni religiose agli inizi del Duecento* (Torre Pellice, 1983), with material from A. Marini, "La 'novita' francescana tra i movimenti dell'inizio del secolo XIII," *Studi e materiali di storia delle religioni,* 53 (1987): 103 ff.

[4]1 Celano 33. "Indeed, because he was a prudent and discreet man, he began to ask Francis about many things and urged him to turn to the life of a monk or hermit. But St. Francis refused his counsel, as humbly as he could, not despising what was counselled, but in his pious leaning toward another life, he was inspired by a higher desire." See *Omnibus of Sources* 255.

[5]See T. Desbonnets, *From Intuition to Institution: the Franciscans* (Chicago: Franciscan Herald, 1988).

[6]Cf. Merlo, *Tensioni religiose,* 44-47.

[7]Cf. G.G. Merlo, *Dal deserto alla folla: persistenti tensioni del francescanismo in Predicazione francescana e società veneta nel Quattrocento: committenza, ascolto, ricezione,* Acts of the Second International Congress of Franciscan Studies (Padua, 1987), Padua-Vicenza 1989, Le Venezie francescane, n.s., VI/1, 61-77.

[8]A good, precise reconstruction can be found in R. Lambertini and A. Tabarroni, *Dopo Francesco: l'eredità difficile* (Turin, 1989).

[9]S. Bortolami, *Minoritismo e sviluppo urbano fra Due e Trecento: il caso di Padova in Esperienze minoritiche nel Veneto del Due-Trecento,* Acts of the National Congress of Franciscan Studies (Padua, September 1984 and Padua-Vicenza, 1985).

[10]The subject of the connection between the mendicant orders and urban life has been developed extensively following the work of Jacques Le Goff, "Apostolat mendiant et fait urbain dans la France médiéval: L'implantation géografique des Ordres Mendiants Programme-questionnaire pour une enquête," *Annales ESC* 23 (1968): 335-52; Jacques Le Goff, "Ordres mendiants et urbanisation dans la France médiéval. Etat de l'enquête," *Annales ESC* 25 (1970): 924-46.

[11]Cf. L. Pellegrini, *Insediamenti francescani nell'Italia del Duecento* (Rome, 1984) 123-53. Chapter 4 takes up the argument of his previous study "L'ordine francescano e la società cittadina in epoca bonaventuriana. Un'analisi del 'Determinationes quaestionum super Regulam fratrum Minorum" in *Laurentianum* XV, 1974; A.I. Galletti, "Insediamento e primo sviluppo dei frati Minori a Perugia," *Francescanesimo e società cittadina,* 1-32, especially pages 1-8.

[12]Cf. K. Elm, "Italienische" 491-559; B. Van Luijk, *Gli eremiti neri nel Duecento;* F. Dal Pino et al., "Mendicanti, ordini," DIP V (Rome, 1978) 1163-89.

[13]Cf. G. Miccoli, *La storia religiosa in Storia d'Italia II: Dalla caduta dell'Impero romano al secolo XVIII* (Turin, 1974) 707 ff.; 793, ff.; 825, ff.

[14]Cf. Pellegrini, *Insediamenti francescani,* 76. Chapter II takes up from a previous study: "L'esperienza eremitica di Francesco d'Assisi e dei primi francescani," in *Francesco d'Assisi e francescanesimo dal 1216 al 1226,* International Society of Franciscan Studies, Fourth Congress (Assisi, 1977) 281-313.

[15]See Stanislao da Campagnola, "Gli spirituali umbri," *Chi erano gli spirituali* (Assisi, 1976) 79, f., 85, f., 88, f.

[16]Cf. Stanislao da Campagnola, "La 'leggende' di Frate Egidio d'Assisi nei secoli XIII-XV," *Francescanesimo e società cittadina,* 113-143.

[17]Cf. G. Tabacco, *Romualdo di Ravenna*. This valuable work contains two previously published articles. The first was published in *Il Saggiatore Rivista di cultura filosofica e padagogica* IV (1954) and the other in *L'eremitismo in Occidente*; Merlo, *Tensioni religiose*, 50-51.

[18]R. Manselli, Minutes of the sessions in *Chi erano gli spirituali?* 24-26.

[19]Cf. Stanislao da Campagnola, "Gli spirituali umbri," p. 88, n. 50.

[20]Angelus of Clareno, *Chronicon seu Historia septem tribulationum ordinis Minorum*, ed. A. Ghinato (Rome ,1959) 50.

[21]For more information about the writings of Angelus of Clareno, see the thorough study by G. L. Potestà, "Gli studi su Angelo Clareno. Dal ritrovamento della raccolta epistolare alla recenti edizioni," *Rivista di storia e letteratura religiosa*, 25 (1989): 111-43. See also his work "Sull'edizione delle 'lettere' di Angelo Clareno," *Cristianesimo nella storia* VII (1986): 341-52.

[22]F. Accrocca, "I 'pauperes eremite domini Celestini,'" *Celestino V papa angelico*, Acts of the Second International Historical Congress (L'Aquila, 1988) 95 ff. Concerning the connections between Celestine V's eremitical choice and models of holiness, see P. Golinelli, "Monachesimo e santità: i modelli di vita di Celestino V," *S. Pietro del Morrone—Celestino V nel medioevo monastico*, Acts of the Third Historical Congress (L'Aquila, 1989) 45-66.

[23]See G. L. Potestà, *Storia ed escatologia in Ubertino da Casale* (Milan, 1980) 22 f.

[24]See Le Goff, "Ordres mendiants," 942; Potestà, *Storia ed escatologia*, 102 ff., 206-11.

[25] R.B.C. Huygens, *Lettres de Jacques de Vitry (1160-1170-1240)*, éveque de Saint-Jean-d'Acre. Edition critque (Leiden 1960) 75 ff. Jacques de Vitry's Letter of 1216, trans. by Paul Oligny, O.F.M. in the *Omnibus of Sources*, page 1608. According to Pellegrini, "Espressioni di minoritismo nella realtà urbana del secolo XIII," *Esperienze minoritiche*, 73, this part of de Vitry's testimony would be "absolutely generic and telling us very little." For an opposite interpretation, we have a precise analysis by Bortolami, *Minoritismo e sviluppo urbano*, 82-84, showing that the first friars' choices of settlements were inspired by "a particular type of propensity for commuting between the hermitage and city." In other studies we find agreement in the rest by L. Pellegrini "Gli insediamenti degli ordini mendicanti e la loro tipologia. Considerazioni metodologiche e piste di ricerca," "Ordres mendiants" (see note 9) 566-68 and *Insediamenti francescani* (see note 13), 61 ff.

[26]See Pellegrini, *Insediamenti francescani*, 17 ff.

[27]See Merlo, *Tensioni religiose*, 41 ff.

[28]*Opuscula sancti patris Francisci Assisiensis*, K. Esser, ed. (Grottaferrata, 1978) XII, 312 (Test., 24): "Let the brothers beware that they by no means receive churches or poor dwellings or anything which is built for them, unless it is in harmony with (that) holy poverty which we have promised in the Rule, (and) let them always be guests there as pilgrims and strangers." Brady-Armstrong, 155.

[29]See G. Tabacco, "Eremo e cenobio," 326-35.

[30]Cf. Gratien of Paris, *Histoire de la fondation et de l'évolution de l'ordre des frères Mineurs au XIIIème siècle* (Rome, 1982); Bibliotheca Seraphico-Capuccina, 20, first edition, 1928, 63 ff; *Espansione del francescanesimo tra Occidente e Oriente nel secolo XIII* (Assisi , 1979).

[31]O. Capitani, "Ipotesi sociali del francescanesimo medioevale: orientamenti e considerazioni," *San Francesco* (Rome, 1985) 39-57.

[32]An overview of these developments and problems is given in Lambertini and Tabarroni, *Dopo Francesco* (see note 8).

[33]C. Leonardi, "Il francescanesimo tra mistica, escatologia e potere," *I francescani nel Trecento* (Assisi, 1988) 35.

[34]Ibid., 36

[35]I introduced the concept of "Observance" as "innovational restoration" in "Dal deserto alla folla" (see note 5), 65, and was accepted by A. Vauchez in "Conclusions," *Predicazione francescana*, 267, although a typographical error caused the expression to be printed to refer to "restorative installation."

[36]See Merlo, "Dal deserto alla folla," 64.

[37]Cf. Bernardini Aquilani, *Chronica fratrum Minorum Observantiae*, ed. L. Lemmens (Rome, 1902).

[38]See Merlo, "Dal deserto," 64-67. For more on the Franciscan Observance see: *Il rinnovamento del francescanesimo L'osservanza*, International Society for Franciscan Studies, Ninth congress (Assisi, 1985); M. Sensi, *Le osservanze francescane nell'Italia centrale* (Rome, 1985); D. Nimmo, *Reform and Division in the Medieval Franciscan Order from Saint Francis to the Foundation of the Capuchins* (Rome, 1987) 353 ff.

[39]Merlo, "Dal deserto," 66.

[40]Ibid., 63, 72.

[41]U. Nicoloini, "Perugia e l'origine dell'osservanza francescana," in *Il rinnovamento del francescanesimo*, 298.

[42]Cf. Merlo, 70.

[43]Ibid., 71.

[44]See Lambertini and Tabarroni, 5-17 for more concrete considerations.

[45]Cf. Merlo, 75.

[46]Cf. G. Tabacco, "Gli intellettuali del medioevo nel giuoco delle istituzioni e delle preponderanze sociali," *Storia d'Italia Annali 4: Intellettuali e potere* (Turin, 1981) 9 f.

[47]R. Rusconi, "La tradizione manoscritta delle opere degli spirituali nelle biblioteche dei predicatori e nei conventi dell'Osservanza," *Picenum Seraphicum* 12 (1975): 63-137.

[48]Ibid., 83.

[49]See G. G. Merlo, "Francescanesimo e signorie nell'Italia centro-settentrionale del Trecento," *I francescani nel Trecento*, 125 f.

[50]There is an extensive bibliography on this topic. Here I will mention only H. Martin, "La predicazione e le masse nel XV secolo. Fattori e limiti di un successo," *Storia vissuta del popolo cristiano*, ed. J. Delumeau, Italian translation by F. Bolgiani (Turin, 1985) 455-89; R. Rusconi, "La predicazione minoritica in Europa nei secoli XIII-XV," *Francesco, il francescanesimo e la cultura della nuova Europa*, ed. I. Baldelli and A. M. Ramanini (Rome, 1986) 141-65.

[51]Miccoli, 875-975, with the citation on page 915.

[52]Cf. Tabacco, *Romualdo di Ravenna*, (cf. note 17).

[53]Ibid., 20.

[54]Ibid., 119.

[55]D. Russo, *Saint Jérome en Italie Etude d'iconographie et de spiritualité* (XIIIème - XVème siècle), (Paris-Rome, 1987).

[56]See F. Gambacorta, *Luci e ombre nella cristianità del secolo XIV: il beato Pietro Gambacorta da Pisa e la sua congregazione (1380-1933)* (Vatican City, 1964); see also the following entries DIP III: 1191, 1202-1207; "Eremiti di fra Pietro da Pisa," "Eremiti di san Gerolamo di Beltramo da Ferrara," "Eremiti di san Gerolamo di Nicola da Farca Palena," "Eremiti di san Gerolamo di Pietro Malerba," "Eremiti di San Gerolamo dell'Osservanza." See also the entry "Gerolamine e Gerolamini," DIP IV 1098-1105.

[57]See A. M. Galluzzi, *Origini dell'ordine dei Minimi* (Rome, 1967).

[58]See Miccoli, "La storia religiosa," 968 ff.

[59]See Melchior A. Pobladura, *Historia generalis Ordinis fratrum Minorum Capuccinorum* I (Rome, 1947) 21 ff.; G. Abate, "Fra Matteo da Bascio e gli inizi dell'Ordine cappuccino," *Collectanea Franciscana* 30 (1960): 31-77.

[60]L. Pellegrini, "A proposito di eremiti laici," 123.

[61]Ibid., 117-42.

[62]See A. Benvenuti Papi, "Santità femminile nel territorio fiorentino e lucchese," *Religiosità e società in Valdelsa nel busco medioevo* (Florence, 1980), 113-144. "Penitenza e santità femminile in ambiente cateriniano e bernardiniano," *Atti del Simposio internazionale cateriniano-bernardiniano*, eds. D. Maffei, P. Nardi (Siena, 1982) 865-75; "Frati mendicanti e pinzochere in Toscana," 107-35; "Margherita filia Jerusalem. Santa Margherita da Cortona e il superamento mistico della crociata", in *Toscana e Terrasanta nel medioevo*, ed. F. Cardini (Florence, 1982) 117-57; "Le forme comunitarie," 389-449; "Una terra di sante e di città Suggestione agiografiche in Italia," *Il movimento religioso femminile in Umbria nei secoli XIII-XIV*, ed. R. Rusconi (Scandicci-Perugia, 1984) 183-202.

[63]See M. Sensi "Incarcerate e recluse in Umbria," 87-121 (includes important bibliographical references); "La monacazione delle recluse nella valle Spoletina," *S. Chiara da Montefalco e il suo tempo*, ed. C. Leonardi and E. Menestò (Scandicci-Perugia, 1985) 71-121.

[64]See G. Casagrande, "Note su manifestazioni," 459-79; "Forme di vita religiosa femminile nell'area di Città di Castello nel secolo XIII" in *Il movimento religioso femminile*, 123-157; "Movimenti religiosi umbri e Chiara di Montefalco," *S. Chiara da Montefalco*, 53-70.

[65]E. Pásztor, "I papi del Duecento e Trecento," 29-65; "Chiara da Montefalco nella religiosità femminile del suo tempo," *S. Chiara da Montefalco*, 183-267.

[66]However, we cannot omit Rusconi's basic study "L'espansione del francescanesimo femminile nel secolo XIII," *Movimento religioso femminile e francescanesimo nel secolo XIII* (Assisi, 1980) 263-313.

[67]Benvenuti Papi, "Le forme comunitarie," 446.

Historical Development of Eremitical Vestiges

in the Franciscan Order:

A Summary

by

Benedikt Mertens, OFM[1]

Translated from the German by

Josef Raischl and André Cirino, OFM

The knowledge we have gained in this study refers exclusively to the era of the first generation of Friars Minor in Italy. Yet we must not close our eyes to the historical realities of further developments in the Order because of limitations of time and theme.[2]

Although eremitism was anchored harmoniously in the "mixed life" by the intention and practice of Francis, the hermitage became a marginal and problematical phenomenon. After only a few decades with the Order settling in the cities, the fast-growing Order and generous response to the pastoral needs of the communes led to clericalization and conventualism.

Thus the *Constitutions of Narbonne* of 1260, the first constitutions issued in the Order as an interpretation of the *Earlier Rule,* does not mention hermitages. There is only a slight echo heard in the passage talking about "the nearby dwellings" as dependent cells of large convents. These could be places for periodical eremitical withdrawal.

As general minister of this widespread order from 1257 to 1274, Bonaventure knew very well how to defend this development. He thought it was Francis' intention to combine for the first time in his Order the enclosed sanctification of the cenobites, the pastoral ministry of the clerics and the uninterrupted contemplation of the hermits. And he wanted to prioritize this in the city. Consequently, Bonaventure defends the Order's custom of living among the people rather than in lonely places. In his work *Resolutions for the Questions concerning the Rule of the Friars Minor* he uses three basic reasons: first, pastoral work demands one to be close to the people in the city for edification and access to spiritual direction; second, it would be a problem for houses far removed from the city to get enough food; and third, outside the city there is concern for security of the friars and sacred objects.

As a result of such reasoning, the Franciscan hermitage was marginalized, but did not disappear completely. In Second Celano 179, Thomas notes that the hermits had become an irritation and scandal within the order. Thus the harmony of hermitage and apostolate was broken. Eventually, the hermitage became a place of shelter and refuge for the Spirituals.

The Community [all other friars except the Spirituals—eds.] favored urbanization of the Order. They banned the Spirituals[3] who were accused of Joachimism to various hermitages, among whom were John of Parma (1257-87), Thomas of Tolentino, Peter of Macerata (1274) and Ubertino of Casale (1304).

In 1294 some brothers with Peter of Fossombrone (Angelus Clarenus) separated from the Community and joined the foundation of the *Poor Hermits of Pope Celestine*. Even Peter John Olivi, the leader of the southern French Spiritual party, polemicized against this separation.

The Franciscan hermitages of Umbria were resettled only in the 14th century with the beginning of the Observant movement. Their leaders, John of Valle, Gentile of Spoleto, and Paoluccio Trinci, came from the Community, yet were eremitically inspired. Their center was Brogliano [northeast of Foligno—eds.].[4]

By 1400 the introduction of the Observant movement in Spain had strong eremitical beginnings. Simultaneously the reform of Peter of Villacreces included vestiges of the "Rule for the Hermitages."

Later on, the Capuchin Reform (1525-28), which was originally known as the "Brothers Minor of the Eremitical Life,"[5] developed, followed by the houses of recollection from the 16th to the 18th centuries, and *ritiro-friaries* from the 17th to the 19th centuries.

In conclusion, the documentation shows that the eremitical thrust of the first generation of Friars Minor, influenced by the eremitical movement of the High Middle Ages, has resiliently survived through the centuries.

Endnotes

[1]B. Mertens, "In eremi vastitate resedit," 285-374, 367-69.

[2] Cfr. Cargnoni.

"Those who kept yearning for the pure observance of the Rule."

[4]Cfr. U. Nicolini, "L'eremitismo francescano umbro nei secoli XIII-XIV," *Analecta TOR* 131 (1979): 425-42.

[5]"Fratres minores de vita eremitca."

Chapter Five

The Rule for Hermitages

Lived and Experienced Today

Introduction

In this fifth and final section we present to the reader some practical applications of Francis's "Rule for Hermitages" as it is lived and experienced today.

Our first example shows that the "Rule for Hermitages" can be lived and experienced almost anywhere, as it is in the heart of the inner city of the South Bronx, New York. The first article by André Cirino, OFM, outlines the entire "Rule" and how it was lived and experienced at the Little Portion Retreat House. Then in the next article, Sheila Patenaude, FMM, presently residing and working in Harlem, New York City, gives a reflection on the "Rule for Hermitages" as she first experienced it at the Little Portion, using the image of a pink magnolia tree.

Following our premise that this text can be lived and experienced almost anywhere, Helen Budzik, OSF, a pastoral assistant in a parish in York, Pennsylvania, demonstrates how this eremitical experience can be shared with people of a parish community—a unique application. The Raischls open further creative applications of the hermitage "Rule" as they share their insights as a married couple who take up Francis's invitation to solitude.

Two Third Order Regular Friars, John Kerr and David Liedl, share with us their construction of a simple hermitage structure (also in the shadow of a magnolia tree) in the South Bronx. Their local fraternity creatively integrated Francis's brief document into their daily life.

In a most idyllic setting, two Syracuse Franciscan Sisters, Raphael Fulwider and Baptiste Westbrook, live as "resident" hermits with the "Rule for Hermitages" of Francis as their daily guide. In their article they give us a glimpse of their life, as well as a reflection of one of their "guest" hermits, Sister Leonilda Avery.

Next, Franciscan Sister Mary Catherine Gurley, a professor at Assumption College, Worcester, Massachusetts, has gleaned a wide range of solitude experiences and shares them as personal reflections of her spiritual journey.

And last, our anthology concludes with the Lady Clare "speaking" through an article. André Cirino, OFM, writes about an experience at the Monastery of the Poor Clares in Stamford, Connecticut, showing from Clare's writings and the Sisters' way of life how they may have been guided by Francis's text for hermitage living.

Hermitage in the City

by

André Cirino, OFM[1]

Before the summer of 1980, I knew little about Francis's "Rule for Hemitages." During the Franciscan Study Pilgrimage at Assisi I was first introduced to the text and given a chance to live it for a few days in a hermitage at Colfano in the Province of the Marches. During the lectures and explanations of this "Rule,"[2] I began to see potential for living it upon my return to the United States. After returning to the States, I heard Dacian Bluma, OFM, give several talks on the "Rule for Hemitages." At that point, I was convinced that it was possible to experience this "Rule" right where I was in the South Bronx.

During the 800th centenary celebration of St. Francis's birth in 1982, the Friars Minor Province of the Immaculate Conception sponsored a project for the poor in the South Bronx, where the friars had labored for more than eighty years among Italian immigrants. The pastoral team of Our Lady of Pity parish offered the vacant convent as a retreat center for the poor and those whose ministry is with the poor. Retreats were to be offered free of charge. Soon after the dedication of this new ministry at the Little Portion, an opportunity was available to try living the hermitage "Rule." Our first experience was set for spring 1983. Four of us came together, two men and two women, and the Hermitage Experience of the Little Portion was born. (See Patenaude, *Pink Magnolias or Assisi Revisited in the Bronx*.)

The Hermitage Experience was rather simple. It unfolded as follows. The hermits usually gathered on a Friday evening. After an instruction on the content of the "Rule," a schedule was proposed for living according to it, and the hermits began to do this for the next three days. Civic holiday weekends were chosen since, with the addition of the Monday holiday, it was easy for people to be free to extend the Hermitage one more day.

Since the summer of 1980 I have had the opportunity to experience this "Rule for Hermitages" many times, both at the Little Portion and other places. I would like to share some of the insights I have gained.

1. Those who wish . . .[3]

I find that this aspect of voluntarily entering the hermitage sets the tone for the entire experience. I have gathered with many people to live this way, and the experiences have been blessed because the participants truly desired to be there. There is a sense of expectation flavored by enthusiasm and excitement.

. . . to dwell in a religious way in hermitages . . .

During the Franciscan Study Pilgrimage in Assisi, all the participants were assigned to hermitages which were on mountain-tops or in rural areas. So I was truly amazed to learn during our first Hermitage Experience at the Little Portion that our inner-city retreat house was very suitable for living this "Rule." I was further impressed by the comment of a Franciscan sister who works in a hospital in New York City: "We can do this at home!" Monthly days of recollection have been the routine for many religious communities. This sister saw the possibility of living according to the model found in the text during this monthly period of prayer.

. . . may be three brothers or, at the most, four; let two of these be the 'mother' and have two 'sons,' or at least one.

With regard to numbers, the Little Portion had thirteen bedrooms or cells. We have had as few as four and as many as seventeen gather for a Hermitage Experience. With the four it was clear—two were "mothers" and two were "sons."[4] For the seventeen, I made adjustments. Since our hermitage stay at the Little Portion was so brief, each person who signed up was automatically a son/Mary. Of the seventeen, three were mothers/Marthas, and each mother assumed this role for four or five participants. This worked very well. It was not only

Franciscans who were hungry to learn about and experience this. Others who do not belong to the Order and knew little of Francis and less of Clare came to the Franciscan Hermitage Experience and picked up the flavor and rhythm of it all in a short time.

Someone goes into a hermitage for solitude. And we have Francis talking here about three or four brothers. This is because Francis wanted people to be together in solitude—to be in fraternity like the rest of the Order. It is this notion of *fraternity* that distinguishes the Franciscan "Rule for Hermitages" from any other experience of solitude, such as quiet days, *poustinia*, desert days, and the like. Although there is silence during the days of hermitage, participants remark that they are aware that brothers and sisters are "walking this hermitage road" with them. In moments of difficulty, fraternity brings a security in prayer; in moments of joy, it reaffirms their commitment to be part of a Franciscan fraternity. In such a small house (the building was a four–story tenement), people seemed to find space for solitude, which—to judge from their comments—they were happy to share.

2. Let the two who are 'mothers' keep the life of Martha . . .

I assumed the role of Martha with one or more persons, depending on the size of the group. The ratio was usually one Martha to three or four Marys. I have discovered the role of Martha to be an exhausting one, not only from the viewpoint of preparation for prayer and Eucharist, but also because of the work in the kitchen, dining room, chapel and other areas. So usually we were two, sometimes three Marthas. I would invite someone to be a Martha only after he/she had experienced the role of Mary. Because the Martha role is so demanding, I think it is important for the Martha to understand the needs of the Mary by being a Mary first. Comments from various Marthas who have served at the Little Portion verified this for me.

. . . and the two 'sons' keep the life of Mary (cf. Lk 10:38-42) . . .

The first, early friars were itinerants. Although we may not be literally on the road, the intensity of our activity usually keeps us "on the go." We need time just to be (*stare*), like Mary to sit at the feet of the Lord to do the "'one thing required'" (Lk 10:42). I encouraged the hermits to assume the role of Mary even to the point of asking them simply to move from the table after eating and to leave all utensils there. Some people who came for this experience found this deactivation very difficult—they were so used to "doing." So we exaggerated a bit to encourage them to take the time for just "being."

. . . and have one enclosure in which each one may have his cell in which he may pray and sleep.

The early friars had stone caves or cells/huts made of twigs and mud. Our cells at the Little Portion were very simple — a bed, a chair, a lamp, a table with a Bible on it. Many hermits who came to the Little Portion were exhausted people; so they did take significant rest in their cells. One hermit, a wife and mother, recorded in her journal as she awoke the first day: "8:20 A.M. —strange, no reason to rush. To be on God's time—to wake when God wakes me."

During another hermitage experience, a sister shared with us that it was a new experience for her to observe this part of the hermitage text—to pray in her cell. She was more accustomed to community prayer, praying in chapel or a church. After hearing this, a friar decided to try the same thing. He spent the next day entirely in his cell in prayer. With no phone, no work, no personal items, he witnessed to us that he was able to let himself "get cornered by God." He was pleasantly surprised with this experience.

3 . . . and strive to maintain silence . . .

I had discovered this to be a crucial part of our experience at the Little Portion. Silence was observed all day. At lunch and supper, music was played. The silence seemed to become a pregnant experience for the hermits, stemming in part from the atmosphere of fraternity. During the day God moved the hermits. They might have wanted to share their experience with someone, but they held it in silence. So I included a sharing time for the hermits at the end of each day. They could bring all of the experience of silence to birth during the period of sharing.

The amazing result was to witness how deeply the details of this simple text became incarnated in each of them.

. . . and seek first the Kingdom of God and His justice (Mt.6:33).

John Gallen, S.J., once reminded me that the Kingdom of God was not necessarily a place, but an experience of the God who dwells in unapproachable light, who unfolds before us and is revealed to us. And I think that this was experienced by the hermits as they assumed the stance of Mary before God. They search for God. God unfolds before them, and they experience the kingdom that is within.

Moreover, the South Bronx is a place where justice needs to be upheld. St. Bonaventure says justice "makes beautiful what had been deformed."[5] I think that a region like the South Bronx, so pervaded by violence, poverty, and suffering, was in some way made beautiful by the presence of the hermits who gathered at the Little Portion to live this "Rule."

4. And let them recite Prime at the proper hour . . .

It is in this "Rule for Hermitages" that an early example of a schedule of the daily life of the friars is found. At the Little Portion the "Rule" was lived as written, with the sole exception that all the liturgical hours were not recited. In the short time span of three days, praying all the liturgical hours together would leave little time for personal prayer. In his Letter to Leo—at times called the "Gospel of Franciscan Freedom"—Francis told Leo: "In whatever way it seems best to you to please the Lord God and to follow in (God's) footprints and . . . poverty, do this with the blessing of God and my obedience."[6] Taking my cue from this thrust of freedom, I would suggest, in my explanation on the first evening, the following schedule to the hermits, which every group accepted and lived:

9:00 A.M.	• Morning Prayer
12:00 P.M.	• Lunch
4:00 P.M.	• Eucharist
6:00 P.M.	• Supper
7:30 P.M.	• Evening Prayer
8:00 P.M.	• Sharing

Attendance at any scheduled function was completely voluntary. This is supported by Dacian Bluma's comments on the liturgical hours:

> From the simplicity of the "Rule for Hermitages" some things are not clear. For example, were the hours prayed together? Did everyone have to come? If you were having an ecstasy, did you have to leave that and come? Did they have a bell rung so as to come out of their caves, cells, huts? Did the mothers say the hours with the sons? And the brothers who prayed the Office of the Our Fathers, where did they fit in? Very likely, they arranged things for themselves by mutual agreement.[7]

Although this little writing of Francis makes no mention of the Eucharist, we celebrated Eucharist each day during the Hermitage Experience. It was around 1222 that papal approval was given for Mass to be celebrated in private oratories. The friars probably celebrated Mass in the hermitage, because Thomas of Celano says: "One day therefore he went before the holy altar which was erected in the hermitage where he was staying. . . ."[8]

A final note on scheduling: I would mention to the hermits that God might call them in the middle of the night to prayer. I would encourage them to respond, and many have done so.

. . . and, after Terce, they may end their silence, speak with and go to their 'mothers.'

I would tell the hermits at the beginning that this was not a directed retreat, that I would not be meeting with them during the day. I did not encourage sessions for spiritual direction, counseling, or the celebration of the sacrament of reconciliation. If someone asked for a session for whatever reason, however, I did accommodate. This stance preserves the time for them to live the solitude they seek in silence.

As mentioned already, we gathered for sharing for about an hour at the end of each day. Besides building up the hermits' faith, it was a chance for the fraternal aspect of the text to be experienced by all.

5. *And, when it pleases them, they can beg alms from them as poor little ones out of love of the Lord God.*

The seeking of alms was a practice of the entire fraternity. When food did not come from their work, they went out to beg from the table of the Lord. Francis included this begging idea in the hermitage text, possibly to keep the friars in touch with the rest of the fraternity. At the Little Portion, there was no begging of alms for food, but our meals were simple. If hermits desired to fast, I asked that they inform their mother/Martha so as to assist us in planning for meals. One friar who came from a community of more than fifty men remarked that most meals he ate at the friary were on the fast-food style. Slowing down his pace as a hermit and eating in silence introduced him to the food he was eating, leading him to praise God for these simple sustaining gifts of creation that he had previously ignored.

6. *And afterwards let them recite Sext, None and, at the proper hour, Vespers.*

As already noted above (number 4), we did not pray all the liturgical hours. On a longer Hermitage Experience, e.g., eight to ten days, additional liturgical hours other than those scheduled could be added. In our practice at the Little Portion, we left as many hours as possible for personal prayer.

7. *And they may not permit anyone to enter or eat in the enclosure where they dwell.*

Francis usually advised the friars to plant a hedge around their huts when they erected a hermitage. During the entire time of hermitage, the Little Portion was closed to all other activities. This formed a "hedge" around the entire building. The slamming of a door or laughing aloud in an ordinary greeting could disturb this silence and distract the hermits. Thus silence pervaded the entire hermitage area.

8. Let those brothers who are the 'mothers' strive to stay far from everyone and, because of obedience to their minister, protect their 'sons' from everyone so that no one can speak with them.

As one of the mothers/Marthas, I spent my time in the front office by the door and the phone. I had to protect some of the sons/ Marys from business calls as well as from people trying to drop in for a visit with a hermit.

9. And those 'sons' may not talk with anyone except with their 'mothers' . . .

I assigned a mother/Martha to each hermit on the first night so he or she knew with whom they could talk. This was a happy arrangement because the listening and chores were shared by all the mothers/Marthas.

10. The 'sons,' however, may periodically assume the role of the 'mothers,' taking turns for a time as they have mutually decided.

In the short time we had for a Hermitage Experience at the Little Portion, this switch was not made. An exchange should take place during a longer period of time, or in response to the needs of the hermits themselves.

Conclusion

Francis established a rhythm for his life: he was on the road for a period of time; then he would spend a period of time in hermitage. Although we seem largely to have lost this sense of rhythm in the Order today, I think it is very possible for us to re-establish it on the local fraternity level.

For example, I think that members of friaries/convents with an extra room could actually create a hermitage room and give the members of the fraternity the possibility of living the "Rule for Hermitages" on a regular basis. Each member of the house could be given the opportunity of taking a hermitage day (overnight) on a regular (weekly/monthly) basis. The hermit could enter this cell early in the day, join the fraternity for prayers, Eucharist, and perhaps the evening meal. Although one could fast or take meals in silence, the one meal taken with the fraternity could be the one time they could go and speak with their mother (the fraternity). For any specific needs that may arise, members of a fraternity could alternate the Martha role.

Once a fraternity has received some instruction on the "Rule for Hermitages" and lived it for several days, I think the rhythm Francis knew as an itinerant preacher could again become our experience today. I believe it is worth a try.

Endnotes

[1]This article was originally published in the March, 1986, edition of *The Cord* (St. Bonaventure, NY: The Franciscan Institute), pages 89-96.

[2]Lectures and explanations of the "Rule for Hermitages" were given during the "Assisi Experience" by Damien Isabell, OFM; Aaron Pembleton, OFM; Roch Niemier, OFM; and Murray Bodo, OFM.

[3]"Rule for Hermitages" *Gospel Life* 62–63.

[4]Throughout this article I use the expression *sons* as it occurs in Francis's text. I mean sons/daughters, for such was our experience.

[5]St. Bonaventure, *Collations on the Six Days*, First Collation, 34.

[6]Armstrong and Brady, "A Letter to Brother Leo," 48.

[7]Dacian Bluma, OFM, "The Rule for Hermitages," a talk given at the Franciscan Gathering at Tampa, February 7, 1983. (Cassette Enterprises, 1112 Park St., Seffner, FL 33584).

[8]I Cel 92; *Omnibus of Sources*, 307.

Pink Magnolias

or

Assisi Revisited in the Bronx

by

Sheila Patenaude, FMM[1]

Long ago as a teenager, I saw the movie "A Tree Grows in Brooklyn." It had a valid message to convey, but I later discovered that many trees grow in Brooklyn and that the film title gave rise to an incomplete stereotype. But recently, during Easter week, I saw a pink magnolia bloom in the South Bronx, and I realized why one of my students, fiercely proud of living there, reacted so strongly to one-sided "Fort Apache" images of the area.

Sometimes contemplation of a flower spurs "satori" or enlightenment in a Zen Buddhist, but I discovered that a pink magnolia awakened me to my Franciscan heritage. During Easter Week I made a Franciscan Hermitage Experience in the South Bronx at the Little Portion, a retreat house serving the poor in the area and those who work with the poor. Since I teach daily at a high school only three blocks away, I had not planned to go there for a retreat. But I did want once to make a retreat that would span both Holy Week and Easter week, so as to relive prayerfully the death/ resurrection mysteries of Christ. Four places where I had applied were closed during Easter week, but then I learned that André Cirino, OFM, was directing a Franciscan Hermitage Experience at that time. I consoled myself that during my Holy Week Triduum elsewhere, I would gaze at beautiful trees and a lake so the inner city atmosphere of my daily work grind would not be too bad for a few days!

Little did I realize what I was getting into. The first morning I looked out my street window—gazed at the desolate, garbage-ridden vacant lot across the street, where once had stood a gutted building—and muttered "Oh Lord!" But that afternoon I went out on the roof, and two doors away in the back yard of a neatly renovated apartment building, were a children's swimming pool and a fully blooming pink magnolia tree! I could hardly believe my eyes, and I felt like crying when I realized not only the pride and sense of beauty of the residents, but how much they cared to stay and stubbornly rebuild in beauty where others had moved out.

When we were asked to reflect on what the Hermitage Experience meant for us, by an association of ideas, that pink magnolia tree reminded me of the pink Easter tulips in the Little Portion's chapel, a sign of love and resurrection. It reminded me, too, of the pink rosebushes I saw in our convent garden in Assisi years ago, blood-stained "descendants" of the rosebushes in which Francis himself rolled during temptation. And the curly redwood St. Francis shrine in an upstairs sitting room, where I often prayed during the Hermitage Experience, brought me back to my first Franciscan roots in California, a Palm Sunday procession at Santa Barbara's Old Mission when I was 15, and where the first desire to become a Franciscan was born within me. Yes, truly these hermitage days were a rediscovery of my Franciscan roots and of an indigenous Franciscan experience now starting to be revived in practice. It is one thing to read or pray about Franciscan spirituality, but quite another thing to live out this aspect of it in the actual simplicity of radiant Franciscan joy and transparency.

Francis himself spent about half his converted life in hermitages, but his "Rule for Hermitages" is not too well-known, because it was voluntary and thus not incorporated into the official 1223 Rule approved by Pope Honorius. St. Bonaventure and St. Bernardine of Siena, in their zeal for many friars to pray in the hermitage style, built larger enclosures than the ones Francis intended for four at the most, his idea being to maintain poverty and simplicity. I was also unaware of the fraternity atmosphere of his Hermitage "Rule" and expected merely a few days of private, silent reflection. The first evening, however, André went over the "Rule for Hermitages" with us, sharing spiritual insights. Not only was it to be an in-depth time of silence, prayer, and deepening of one's own spiritual life, which it certainly was, but it also had a period of sharing built right into the experience. We did this each evening, and although I was the oldest participant, it was a real learning experience to listen to the prayerful, simple, and deeply Franciscan insights of the other three: André, a young woman preparing to enter the Franciscan Sisters of the Poor, and a young man preparing to enter a group of Secular Franciscans. We also shared after the psalms of Office and the Gospel homily at Mass, by song or by the equally strong bond of silent pauses, by words, liturgical gesture, and guitar. This fraternal experience, as well as the interdependence of Martha/Mary and mother/son roles, brought us all closer to the Risen Lord, to St. Francis, and to one another. (Ironically, the two men were the mothers and the two women the sons.)

Another little-known aspect of Franciscan hermitage is that although the Carceri was on the slope of Mount Subasio, some hermitages such as the Portiuncula were near outcasts, lepers, or the poor districts of towns—not necessarily out in the wilderness. Our experience in the heart of the South Bronx, therefore, was not out of keeping with the original intention of Francis. Indeed, despite his encouragement to silence, the hedge enclosure, and the mothers' protection of their sons from outside distractions, Francis encouraged solitude for all. For him, solitude was never an ivory-tower escape from the world, but was a temporary withdrawal in order to return to activity balanced with the spirit of the Risen Christ, bringing the cell and enclosure of the heart along, encountering reality with his sacramental view of the universe.

One day I especially realized this when I went out for a short walk in the neighborhood to get some exercise. My first thought was that if I happened to meet two of my students who lived around the corner it might break my hermitage recollection. One had moved to the South Bronx and a Catholic school only recently, and still attended a Pentecostal Church even though she was a Catholic. The other, a woman ex-offender whom I had taught the previous year in Harlem, had spent time in prison for embezzlement, was a recovered alcoholic, but was still struggling to overcome habits of cheating and dishonesty that were survival tactics from childhood. As I walked past these two students' apartments, I suddenly realized that the Jesus Prayer I was saying in rhythm to breathing exercises was not merely a means to maintain recollection outdoors, but also a powerful way to reach out and touch someone with the power of the Risen Jesus, using His Name as tangibly and forcefully as St. Peter did in his post-Easter sermons and healing.

Yes, as André mentioned once during those days of silence, the South Bronx is similar in some respects to the desolate ruins of Jerusalem to which the Israelites returned after the Babylonian Captivity. Yet the Jews did not give up on the ruins, but set to work to rebuild, just as many Bronxites are doing today. The South Bronx is being rebuilt spiritually as well as physically, as witnessed by houses of prayer proliferating there—not only Little Portion, but Christ House a few blocks away, a combination house of prayer for the neighborhood and hostel for young men from the streets. The South Bronx is being reborn in the magnificent and moving liturgies of St. Augustine's Gospel Choir and in Hispanic parishes, in the loving warmth and determination of families who refuse to move from the area because they nourish the seeds of hope, and intuitively sense the death/resurrection mystery being re-enacted there. It is being reborn in pink magnolia blossoms in back yards, and in the pink, blue, and yellow renovated apartment buildings on 142nd Street, springing up amid the gutted and burnt ruins around them.

Christ is dying still in the South Bronx, in families that disintegrate when encountering hardships after emigrating from Latin America or the Caribbean, in families frustrated by unemployment, in youth sucked into drugs or crime, in the general death throes characteristic of urban decay everywhere. But Christ is also rising in the myriad signs of determination to emerge and rebuild, in the spiritual rebirth of hearts and souls, in the empowerment and healing provided by teachers, counselors, and pastors. And where the Crucified and Risen Christ is, there also is Francis, his follower, and the followers of Francis. That is why, for me, those days were really an experience of "Assisi revisited." That is why, amid the experience of being evangelized and gifted by the poor in the South Bronx, I shall never forget the pink magnolia blossoms in a backyard.

Endnote

[1] This article was originally published in the June 1984, issue of *The Cord* (St. Bonaventure, NY: The Franciscan Institute) 162-66.

The Rule for Hermitages

for a Parish

by

Helen Budzik, OSF

I realized that I was truly a Franciscan in heart as well as name during a Franciscan pilgrimage to Assisi, Italy, in the summer of 1985. This discovery began during our journey from Rome to Assisi, when we visited various Francicscan hermitages of the Rieti Valley and I was introduced to the contemplative dimension of the life of St. Francis. It became even more clear when I discovered the "Rule for Hermitages" during our preparations for a visit to the Carceri.

Those who wish . . .[1]

Even after the pilgrimage ended I knew that I was one of the "those who wish . . ." for whom Francis had written his simple instruction. My own desires for a greater balance between the active and contemplative dimensions of my life over the next four years, however, led me along circuitous paths until my spiritual director suggested the possibility of creatively adapting the "Rule for Hermitages" for use within my own ministerial setting—St. Joseph Parish, York, Pennsylvania.

The next morning, after (coincidentally?) the Gospel of Martha and Mary was proclaimed at the parish morning Mass, one of the parishioners asked if I would consider beginning a contemplative prayer group in the parish. Our subsequent conversation revealed her long-felt desire for support in time given to contemplative prayer. This led us to invite parishioners interested in contemplative prayer to participate in a small-group, one day experience.

. . . may be three brothers or, at the most, four . . .

Initially, four women responded. Why did they come?

> ". . . to fill a need to put aside all of my duties and distractions and give my thought and myself to God for a time."

> ". . . to spend time in quiet with God—a time especially set aside to be open to listening, just being—alone yet communally as in 'where two or more are gathered in my name. . . .'"

> ". . . for some time I had felt the need to find spiritual companions to pray with, who would be at ease discussing the Bible and sharing spiritual insights. . . . When I was growing up, I had wanted to become a contemplative nun."

As the project unfolded, it became a once-a-month gathering over several years.

. . . and strive to maintain silence . . . and seek first the Kingdom of God and His justice (Mt.6:33).

The format planned for the day was simple:

9:30 A.M.	• Arrival and Coffee
10:00 A.M.	• Morning Prayer
10:20 A.M.	• Contemplative Prayer
12:30 P.M.	• Simple Lunch and Sharing
1:30 P.M.	• Departure

For the initial day's experience, the above format was adjusted to begin half an hour earlier to accommodate additional time at the end of the day to explore future possibilities. The coffee time at the beginning, designed initially as a getting-to-know-you occasion, was continued each month to allow those gathering to enter the day with an awareness and support of each other. Not long into the experience, however, we saw the need to keep this time to a minimum to avoid becoming a "koffee klatch." Contemplative prayer was the primary focus.

. . . let two of these be the 'mother' and have two 'sons,' or at least one. Let the two who are 'mothers' keep the life of Martha and the two 'sons' keep the life of Mary (Cf. Lk 10:38-42) . . .

In our adaptation of the "Rule for Hermitages," the role of the mother, or Martha, usually included providing the hermitage space, the coffee and simple lunch, and morning prayer. Martha prevented any intrusions on the solitude and saw to whatever else supported the role of Mary. In general, once a Mary entered Martha's home, her stance was one of being. Martha took care of the doing. As the experience continued through its first year, other members of the women's families became extended Marthas. In some instances husbands and children provided quotes and artwork for morning prayer services or helped clean and add special touches to rooms around the home to facilitate the contemplative experience.

As Mary, each person spent the time in contemplation in whatever way suited her. When, over the course of the three years of monthly experiences, these women spoke about their contemplative experiences with each other, the diversity and flexible use of methods was evident. Contemplation sprang from spiritual reading, praying the rosary, taking a walk, sitting before the Blessed Sacrament, gazing out a window or engaging in the techniques of centering prayer. In a relatively short period of time, those participating found this monthly opportunity for contemplation meeting their need for balance in their active lives. To this end, they periodically evaluated their experiences, fine-tuning the format and its elements accordingly.

When recently asked to reflect back over their three years together, the women described experiences common to each:

"Above all, I remember the peace of mind and heart, how restful it was 'spending time with God.' Words cannot describe the warm loving embrace felt during contemplative prayer."

"Peaceful . . . joyful . . . longing to return . . . closeness to all who participated . . . the desire to be with others in the solitude of contemplative prayer. 'O God, it is good for us to be here.'"

"Warm, caring relationships. . . . In a small group it's easier to be open and experience the joy."

The 'sons,' however, may periodically assume the role of the 'mothers,' taking turns for a time as they have mutually decided.

For the first day's experience, I assumed the role of "Martha," working from the premise of my previous hermitage experiences—that one should be a Mary first. When this initial experience brought a "day-a-month" commitment from the group, a previous Mary joined me as Martha for the second experience. With each successive experience that first year, another Mary joined the previously new Martha so that for each monthly experience there were two Marthas and three Marys—four, when another woman joined the group. By the end of the first year, all those participating agreed that, given the nature of the one-day experience, only one experienced Martha was needed.

Changing from Mary to Martha brought surprises to several of the women. One woman spoke of initially not wanting to exchange roles. "In becoming 'Martha,' however, I realized how good I felt allowing others to be Mary. I also learned that when there really wasn't that much to do, I could sit and be quiet in between preparations."

Several discovered that the contemplative stance wasn't incompatible to being Martha in this setting. They also spoke of how the experience brought a contemplative dimension to their activities outside of their time together. One woman was surprised by the joy she felt after preparing morning prayer for the first time. Another found that preparing morning prayer facilitated a contemplative stance for her, even as a Martha.

. . . and have one enclosure in which each one may have his cell in which he may pray. . . . And they may not permit anyone to enter . . . in the enclosure where they dwell.

The initial gathering location was my convent, which provided sufficient interior as well as outdoor space—weather permitting—for solitude. The sisters with whom I lived readily supported our efforts, planning their day to prevent intrusions. Subsequent gatherings took place at the home of a Martha. Our daytime schedule facilitated ample space in each home as other family members were usually at school or work. Retired spouses graciously supported our attempts at an enclosed environment by planning activities away from home for the day.

. . . And let them always . . . recite their Hours . . .

Morning Prayer at the beginning of our day allowed us to quickly enter into a contemplative atmosphere. Most found that the music of these prayer experiences "especially set the mood for the day." Another aid was the concluding prayer, which recalled biblical experiences of solitude and centered on asking God's blessing of this space and those gathered within it. Because of its particular value as "a way of moving into our quiet," this prayer became a standard element of Morning Prayer.

Morning prayer also put us in touch with the prayer of the larger Church. Intercessions, both prepared and spontaneous, allowed us to carry each other's concerns as well as those of our parish and our world into our contemplation in an attitude of trust in and dependence upon God and with the confidence that comes "when two or three are gathered in my name. . . ."

. . . and, after Terce, they may end their silence, speak with and go to their 'mothers."

After the several hours of time dedicated to contemplation, we gathered for a simple lunch. Given the time limits of the day, this was a time to "speak with . . . their mothers" and each other. This sharing was, most often, a time to speak about our prayer and faith experiences during the time of solitude. Initially, there were many questions about prayer and spirituality. Gradually, this time became not only a sharing of their experiences of God in solitude, but also an experience of God in itself. One woman observed: "Especially nice is the sharing of thoughts and feelings which occur during our solitary prayer time. At times, God hovers in our midst."

Let them strive to observe conscientiously and eagerly everything mentioned above.

Both the rhythm of moving in and out of our monthly hermitage experience as well as the rhythm within our hermitage days brought a sense of rightness to our lives. For one woman it imaged the evangelical life of the early Christians. For another it was her connection between Francis and Clare and her own evangelical vocation as a Secular Franciscan.

Our monthly hermitage experience continued for three years before changing life circumstances for some of the women led to a decision to temporarily suspend the experience. Looking back a couple of years later, those who had participated acknowledged its long-term fruits as well:

> "I still do much spiritual reading and believe I have a greater understanding of what I read. And, laying this reading aside, I ponder over what God is trying to say to me."

> "It has helped me to cope with life. . . . I have more confidence in prayer . . . and in acceptance instead of repeatedly begging God for something. . . . I listen more to God, trust God."

> "What was true in the experience still holds true: time set aside to be with God is important to my life. Without it, there is a void."

We do not know what the future holds. But as we continue on our life's journey, we do so with a greater appreciation of the contemplative desire God has nurtured in us through our hermitage experience. As for my own desires to live out of the contemplative dimension of my Franciscan vocation, they were again confirmed during a return visit to Assisi in the summer of 1993. Perhaps I will find yet another way to creatively adapt the "Rule for Hermitages." As I explore further possibilities, this parish experience continues to be a sign of promise for the future.

Endnote

[1]"Rule for Hermitages," *Gospel Life* 62-63.

The Rule for Hermitages
for Married Couples

by

Bernadette and Josef Raischl

Translated from the German by
Bernadette and Josef Raischl and André Cirino, OFM

Francis's way of living the Gospel attracted people from all
levels of society to his new movement, so that in the early years
lay women and lay men, both single and married, sought to join
him. The Secular Franciscan Order was born among lay people who
through the centuries have walked in the footsteps of Francis and
Clare. So it would not be extraordinary to speak of married couples
adapting the "Rule for Hermitages" to their lives in the world.

Francis was born into the family of Pica and Pietro Bernardone,
where he lived with one sibling, Angelo. The sources paint Pica as
a loving, caring mother and Pietro as patriarch of his clan. One can
imagine Pica protecting her two sons as they grew up in Assisi at
the close of the 12th and beginning of the 13th centuries. From this
very family structure we already have overtones of the first verse
of the "Rule for Hermitages" in which Francis employs the images
of mothers/sons. It is significant to note that as Francis looks to the
family model when he writes his words about solitude, he does not
choose "patriarch" or even "father." He chooses the maternal
image to convey more of the fraternal closeness he desires for his
family.

Our family at the present time is the same as the Bernardones:
we, Bernadette and I, have two sons, Jona and Elia. I, Josef, am a
social worker with Hospice in the city of Munich and Bernadette is

a nurse on leave from her job while nursing Elia and caring for the boys. Bernadette has been in training for dance therapy for almost four years. Our family life keeps us constantly on the move to the point that at times we find ourselves meeting in the city of Munich to transfer our children to the other as one finishes work and the other moves on to a course or work.

Right after Elia's birth in 1993, we found ourselves exhausted and in desperate need of space and quiet, "desiring . . . peace of spirit."[1] We could say with Bonaventure, we were "seeking this peace with panting spirit."[2] So like Francis, who sought solitude on mountain tops (LaVerna) or near lakes (Lake Trasimeno), we withdrew for four days to a beautiful house run by the Sacre Coeur Sisters near the Bavarian Sea bordering the Bavarian Alps. We left Jona with his cousins and took Elia with us since Bernadette was still nursing him at that time. With the hermitage text as a guide, we share our experience.

1. Those who wish to dwell in a religious way in hermitages may be three brothers or, at the most, four; let two of these be the 'mother' and have two 'sons,' or at least one.[3]

The most important reason for us to seek solitude these days was to have time just *to be*, allowing each other some time alone while alternating the care for our son Elia. In the Latin version of the "Rule" Francis uses the verb *stare*, conveying the meaning of being or simply taking a break from one's daily way of life, and in that sense to live and spend time in solitude. During our first day in the quiet we simply wanted "to land." Since a great amount of our energy goes out to our children, we decided we would spend some time praying and thinking about our direction with them.

We began our reflections by looking back upon our history. Before the conception of our son Elia, we had suffered a miscarriage. Taking some clay, Bernadette shaped it into a coffin, and this coffin became our cradle for Christmas. Through the use of clay and paint we began to see God's creative energy at work within us, especially in our giving birth to new life—our second son Elia.

The first part of the text speaks about 'three brothers or four." This worked well for us as a couple, with the Sisters caring for other needs. We plan in the future to invite at least one other married couple so as to allow us even more time in the role of Mary.

2. Let the two who are 'mothers' keep the life of Martha and the two 'sons' keep the life of Mary (Cf. Lk. 10:38-42) and have one enclosure in which each one may have his cell in which he may pray and sleep.

Since we were in the role of Mary, our stance emanated from our experience. Bernadette is a professional dance therapist. She decided to use dance as a means to demonstrate our development as a couple with special emphasis on our relationship. The movement of the dance, supervised by God's loving care and goodness, was insightful, thrilling, and exciting for us.

Our children became part of our contemplative gaze. We took turns caring for our younger son Elia. Rather than keeping us away from God, our boys, Jona and Elia, share their contemplation in the way they play and simply stay with toys or things. They teach us every day how to contemplate; they seduce us, too, just *to be* with them. So we brought paint and clay with us for our contemplative time.

As mentioned already, the Sisters served as Marthas in all that was necessary for our stay in their beautiful house, taking special care of the meals, the house, and the lovely garden. The old, bent tree of their garden, with its deep roots and branches stretching wide towards the sky, spoke to us of "being" and simply "letting go."

While the Sisters were the primary Marthas, admittedly the alternation of our son Elia was another aspect of this active role. The alternation gave the other contemplative time and space. With older children, we would opt for a longer time of solitude.

3. And let them always recite Compline of the day immediately after sundown; and strive to maintain silence, recite their Hours, rise for Matins; and seek first the Kingdom of God and His justice (Mt.6:33).

6. And afterwards let them recite Sext, None and, at the proper hour, Vespers.

In the morning and evening, we would share some prepared prayer times together, by reading and singing. (Francis mentions the *Liturgy of Hours* in this verse as well as in verses 4 and 6.)

Verse 3 mentions the word "silence." Being married and having a young family, this aspect of our life is precious and taken whenever circumstances allow. We experienced a most profound silence in the solitude of the nearby forests and lakes. We walked this area about two hours each day. We drank in the silent beauty of the trees, birds, paths, the fresh mountain air, and the crystal-clear lake waters. All of this brought us in touch with the God who saves, the God of life, the very life which is given to each one of us on our journeys and in our relationships.

Francis uses only one verse of Scripture in this writing, Matthew 6:33: "Seek first the Kingdom of God." As a married couple with children, we see this verse preserving this document from becoming too rigid, since the demands of life for married couples are different than those placed on celibates. We see a baby's needs as synonomous with the kingdom's presence. We have Jesus' statements in mind: "Let the children come to me, and do not hinder them. The kingdom of heaven belongs to such as these"(Mt. 19:14). And in response to the question: "'Who is the greatest in the kingdom of heaven?' Jesus called for a little child to come and stand among them. Then Jesus said, 'I assure you, unless you change and become like little children, you will not enter the kingdom of Heaven. Those who make themselves as humble as this child are the greatest in the kingdom of Heaven.'"(Mt. 18:1-4)

4. And let them recite Prime at the proper hour and, after Terce, they may end their silence, speak with and go to their 'mothers.'

While we came apart primarily for the silence and solitude, we took Francis's option to speak not only with our mothers who served us, but also to share together during the day so as to discern God's movement both in our personal, individual lives and in our marriage. We learned once again that communication is vital to all human relationships, especially that of marriage. In our daily struggle to coordinate our needs with the needs of our children, we are constantly threatened with foregoing personal communication by yielding to the demands of hyperactivity. The hermitage experience helped us deepen the nature of our marital communication.

5. And, when it pleases them, they can beg alms from them as poor little ones out of love of the Lord God.

In coming to the Sacre Coeur Sisters' house, we came as poor little ones in need of the silence and solitude which they provided. With a family it takes much planning to withdraw this way. Needless to say, the results enhanced and strengthened us as a couple.

7. And they may not permit anyone to enter or eat in the enclosure where they dwell.

Living in a hermitage experience for these four days took us away from the daily activity of our work and from distractions such as the telephone. We were enclosed in the silence/solitude of the lakes and mountains, reading what St. Bonaventure calls the "Book of Creation."

8. Let those brothers who are the 'mothers' strive to stay far from everyone and, because of obedience to their minister, protect their 'sons' from everyone so that no one can speak with them.

One of the fruits of our experience of solitude has been brought back home with us. We invited people from the parish to join one of us for a morning of contemplation before going to work. The arrangement is very simple: one of us enters into silence for thirty minutes with our guests in our basement, waiting for God to touch our hearts. The other's task is to prepare breakfast for the children while "protecting their sons" (the people at prayer) in the basement from any disturbance.

9. And those 'sons' may not talk with anyone except with their 'mothers' and with the minister and his custodian when it pleases them to visit with the Lord's blessing.

In the future, if we should be able to repeat this experience with other married couples, we could alternate the Mother/

Martha role for preparation of meals, prayers, and care of children or infants.

10. The 'sons,' however, may periodically assume the role of the 'mothers,' taking turns for a time as they have mutually decided. Let them strive to observe conscientiously and eagerly everything mentioned above.

The silence/solitude, even though it had to be interrupted by taking turns with our son Elia, drew us closer to the Center. Since the exchange of roles is part of our daily experience, caring for Elia did not interrupt our quiet stance. The difference during these days was the silence we could anticipate once we exchanged roles with each other.

As a conclusion to our reflections on this experience, we realize how much we value time and space for silence, solitude, and simply being before God. We are searching for like-minded people to accompany us on our journey. Our contemplation time at home with other parishoners is one way we are exploring the possibilities. The memories of all God did and showed us during our four days encourage us to continue seeking God's face in solitude.

Endnotes

[1]St. Bonaventure, *The Soul's Journey into God*, ed. Ewert Cousins (New York: Paulist Press, 1978) Prologue 2 (p. 60).
[2]Ibid.
[3]"Rule for Hermitages," *Gospel Life* 62–63.

Our Lady of the Angels

A Hermitage Attached to a Friary

by

John Kerr, TOR, and David Liedl, TOR

It is Sunday night and darkness shrouds the city. In a little chapel, vigil candles burn softly as five friars finish night prayer. A brother rises with taper in hand to light an oil lamp from the sanctuary candle. Holding the lamp, he bows in unison with another brother and leads him in silent procession out to a small shelter. They embrace, and the brother who carried the lamp leaves it with the blessing, "May God give you peace!" The ritual is over; hermitage has now begun.

When one of our fraternity steps into a Bronx, New York, night and Our Lady of the Angels hermitage,[1] we re-create an experience St. Francis began 800 years ago. The South Bronx may seem an unlikely place, and the way we live out Francis's vision a unique style, but our form of hermitage has served us since 1984. Guided by the Holy Spirit, the simple directives of Francis's "Rule for Hermitages," and our own experience, we have sought to face the shadows and hope of our lives and enter into a life-giving encounter with Jesus Christ.

We intentionally begin hermitage with the night prayer of the Church. Night prayer's images of shadows, darkness, and death, the cry for protection, and the hope of meeting again the Risen Christ parallels our experience of hermitage. Through it, we have felt the depth of our powerlessness—when the "demons" attack us, as Francis knew so well—and the glory of illumination, and quite often the poverty of boredom and restlessness.

For our protection, we call upon Our Lady of the Angels as night prayer draws to a close. We have dedicated our hermitage to her, for whom Francis held a loving devotion. The reader prays using words of the Marian Antiphon of St. Francis in his *Office of the Passion*: "Holy Virgin Mary, among all the women of the world there is none like you; you are the daughter and handmaid of the most high King and Father of heaven; you are the mother of the most holy Lord Jesus Christ; you are the spouse of the Holy Spirit."[2]

The reader continues in words that summarize so well both our hope and our experience: "We entrust to your care our brother, N.N., that he may experience in his solitude the abiding presence of the Father; in his silence the powerful Word of Jesus; and in his prayer the intimacy of union with the Holy Spirit."

When the brother accompanying the hermit leaves him, he returns to the others praying silently in the chapel. With the invocation, "May the all-powerful Lord grant us a restful night and a peaceful death," night prayer ends. We sense this night not an end, but a beginning. Although we have released once again one of our brothers to the darkness, we also know the hope of new light to be enkindled within him and, subsequently, within all of us.

Solitude: The Abiding Presence of the Father

The space that enfolds our brother in hermitage is far from the rocky crags of Poggio Bustone, the lush wooded hills of Fonte Colombo, or the panoramic vistas of La Verna. Francis himself might be surprised to find a hermitage set in a ghetto of one of the largest cities in the world. Surrounded by abandoned buildings and rubble-filled lots, and down the street from a shelter for 800 homeless men, Our Lady of the Angels illuminates an area plagued by harshness and suffering.

Despite the fact that the enclosure borders the street and the hermitage is only ten feet from the house, it is like another world. It bears color and life. Between the street and the yard grows a thick green hedge planted years ago by the Christian Brothers who previously occupied our house, forming an enclosure, a natural divider to the street. A brown, six-foot stockade fence bordering the hedge adds intimacy and protection. Plantings of yew and Rose of Sharon soften and color the fence line.

Within the enclosure, fern, pachysandra, hosta, and flowering clematis create a colorful carpet around the base of a magnificent magnolia tree. (See article by Patenaude. Hermits seem to love this tree. Eds.) In mid-April the tree bursts with exotic pink blossoms—an event our neighbors appreciate as much as we do. It contrasts sharply with its only competition on the block—an eight-foot stick, the sole survivor of an urban planting project three years ago. The magnolia shades the hermitage in the sweltering hot days of the city's summer and offers a pleasant perch for the occasional birds that stray into the ghetto.

Through nature and the work of various gardeners, our enclosure yard creates a visual delight that is so characteristic of the places to which Francis fled to pray. However, any attempt to fashion an environment respectful of solitude is compromised by the reality of the inner city. Hedges, fences, and hermitage walls may discourage intruders. (A memorable exception to that is the night one of the brothers awoke to see a man's arm reaching through the window to unlatch the door, but that's another story!) In the city, though, noise always intrudes: pedestrians, fire engines, ambulances, air traffic, and from September to May the children from our parish grade-school only a few feet away.

To pray in a place that most would never accept as solitude challenges us to a spiritual and emotional discipline. Certainly there are times when noise is an intrusion, but for the most part we have learned either to ignore it or bring it into prayer. Contemplation in the city demands the ability to find an inner chamber where one can retreat to the solitude.

When the first brothers of our fraternity moved to the South Bronx in 1976 to begin an intentional community dedicated to simplicity, prayer, service, and fraternity, there was no talk of such solitude on our premises. The rhythm that evolved with the arrival of new brothers included times of communal and private prayer, occasional full days of prayer, and retreats. In our life, we have always emphasized prayer and fraternity over the apostolate. This was our disposition when the idea of adopting the "Rule for Hermitages" began to come alive in the heart of one of the brothers. The cause was quickly taken up by all, and soon the front yard was being redesigned and the structural parts ordered from a company that specializes in prefabricated pool cabanas!

Over four weeks the hermitage dream began to shape up piece by piece. We assembled the basic structure, installed two windows, added insulation and interior pine wood walls, and stained and varnished the floor. We finished it with simple furnishings—a fold-up desk, bench, oil lamp, mattress for the floor, and a small woodstove—to transform a pool cabana into a homey sanctuary for prayer. After we planted the enclosure garden, we placed a graceful cement-cast statue of Our Lady of Wisdom at the base of the magnolia tree, a visual reminder of the new life that came from the *fiat* of the second Eve. From the beginning, we understood intuitively that the hermitage could become a place of regeneration, incarnation, and birth, a place in which we could remember—as the Prologue to our TOR Rule reminds us—that we are "spouses, brothers and mothers of our Lord Jesus Christ" (1EpFid 7).

Francis addressed the environment in which he desired his brothers to live in two of the ten verses of the "Rule." Consequently, we gave plenty of time and thought to create from what was available a space that was set apart, well-ordered, and serene.

Silence: The Powerful Word of Jesus

Commentaries on this writing point to Francis's unique contribution to the eremitical tradition in his emphasis on the reconciliation of solitude and fraternity. At least six of the ten verses of the text refer to the relationship that exists between those living in hermitage. Assisted by Franciscan researchers and passionate promoters of the "Rule for Hermitages," we began to reflect as a fraternity on the relationship described by Francis as mother and son.

In the regular cycle of our fraternal life, we designate one person to withdraw from his active apostolate and serve the needs of the fraternity. While his principal responsibilities involve the preparation of meals, taking care of food donations, shopping, and answering the door and phone, he also gains some quiet and space in the working day to relax, pray, and read. We realized before the hermitage project began that we already utilized the role, in part, described by Francis as mother. Through further discussion we expanded the responsibility of this friar who takes care of the needs of all the brothers to include special solicitude for the needs of the friar who has entered into hermitage.

If the friar in hermitage has any need, he is free to ask the mother to attend to it. On the other hand, the mother is responsible for protecting the space and silence of the son as much as he requests. This primarily involves taking messages or redirecting people at the door until that time when the brother finishes hermitage. (Admittedly, even after all these years, few outsiders understand the arrangement. A typical response from some of our senior shut-ins is: "Oh, he's in the box, huh? What did he do wrong now?")

This same sense of protection of the hermit's solitude and silence extends beyond just the mother to all members of the fraternity. As in the orignial text, no one but our minister and the mother is allowed to enter the enclosure space to speak to the hermit, and then only for serious reasons. This value presented a practical difficulty some years ago when we realized that the water spigot for the hose was located in the enclosure yard. For a while it meant watering summer gardens during the time the hermit was out of the enclosure.

Any communal concerns or personal issues which might disrupt the hermit's emotional balance or prayerful stance are not spoken about by the fraternity when the hermit is present in the house. Knowing there will be no intrusions helps the hermit to relax, let his defenses down, and be more open to listen and attend to the voice of the Spirit in the silence.

Prayer: The Intimacy of Union with the Holy Spirit

If there is one word that characterizes the tenor of the hermitage "Rule," it is "flexibility." There really can be no other approach if one considers the hermitage as a place of encounter with the Spirit of God. Francis embodies so well the freedom experienced by the children of God, both in his life and in the "Rule for Hermitages."

Enfleshing the hows and whys of being in hermitage has been our greatest struggle. In practical application, we have changed much from how we once observed the instructions of Francis to what has evolved as our current practice. From the beginning, we were aware of the fraternal dimension of this "Rule," the respect paid to enclosure, the stress Francis laid on common and liturgical prayer, and the rather odd stricture against taking meals in the hermitage. What perhaps we paid less attention to in the beginning was the necessary flexibility to allow for the operation of the Holy Spirit in each individual.

All of us were eager to "try it out." Fortified with enthusiasm and devotion, we confidently stepped into hermitage armed with a few simple rules. 1) Once every six weeks each brother was to go into the hermitage from after Sunday night prayer until Wednesday morning prayer. 2) The only reading material allowed was a Franciscan-oriented book and the Scriptures. 3) No work of any sort was allowed. 4) The hermit was to join the fraternity for morning prayer, evening prayer, and Eucharist. 5) The main meal of the day was to be eaten with the fraternity. All other meals were to be eaten privately and only in the house.

The first thing to change when we tempered rules with flexibility was the mandated frequency and length of stay. It is too easy to gloss over the first three words of the text: "Those who wish to dwell in a religious way in hermitages. . . ." As a fraternity we have affirmed the value of being exposed to the experience of hermitage. We no longer expect it, though, of everyone for three days every six weeks. Instead, we have set flexible parameters respectful of individual differences and needs and, at the same time, consistent with the other values we have chosen for our life.

The restriction on reading material was actually based on a misunderstanding of a presentation on the "Rule." The reading of Scripture continues to be an important practice for us, but we no longer confine other reading to just Franciscan works. Whatever can draw an individual into the presence of God determines the choice of supplementary material.

The restriction on work was not practical for five men aged 26-40. Given a small enclosure and the vigor of youth, we soon learned the importance of providing time and space for exercise or physical labor. Now the hermit may engage in any activity which helps him to relax and channel his energy. We still emphasize that the activity *not be work-related.* Here, respect for individual differences is paramount: what may seem like work for one person may not be for another. Activities that we often do are splitting wood, gardening, creative craft work, exercising, and writing.

What led us originally to insist the hermit join the fraternity for morning prayer, evening prayer, and Eucharist was Francis's clear desire in the "Rule for Hermitages" that his brothers ought to pray with the mind of the Church. Here, too, experience has tempered our living of the value. While connection into community prayer is still emphasized, our primary value is the friar's alert attendance to God's presence. We have allowed for different sleep patterns so each friar can establish a rhythm of prayer more attuned to his nature. Francis's joy at hearing of the friar in Spain who faulted himself for being late to dinner because of a rapture (2Cel 178) evidences that all principles bend before the movement of the Spirit.

Lastly, we come to that strange little dictate in the "Rule for Hermitages" that no meals should be eaten in the hermitage. Perhaps because of its novelty, this is the one norm which has remained unchanged from our earlier practice. In our fraternity much stress has been laid upon the sharing of food as a sacred event, a moment associated with the mystery of Eucharist. For this the hermit is still called to join the fraternity for the main meal, to partake of food in an act of fraternal thanksgiving.

All of our guidelines and changes have come through long and sometimes painful deliberations since June 15, 1984, when the building and enclosure were blessed. Those changes came as we listened to the Spirit and each other. What remained constant was our gratitude for the chance to encounter God in solitude, silence and prayer in the heart of the Bronx. It is when God in all mystery and humility comes to dwell among us again that we know the sacredness of our hermitage.

We returned to our hermitage over and over again because it became, without question, a meeting place with the holy. In those wonderful moments when we received in this place what God offered, Our Lady of the Angels, Bronx, New York, took its place with the hermitages of Sant' Urbano, Monte Casale, Greccio, and all the other holy places of sacrament that are so much a part of our Franciscan heritage and tradition.

Endnotes

[1]San Damiano Friary in the Bronx closed in 1994.
[2] See *Omnibus of Sources* 142.

The Rule for Hermitages

A Daily Way of Life

by

Raphael Fulwider, OSF, Baptiste Westbrook, OSF, and Leonilda Avery, OSF

Brief History of Hermitage and Resident Hermit-Sisters

In Sacred Scripture hills are frequently places of encounter with God. And even today a hilltop can offer, along with its panoramic view, the possibility of a new perspective on life to those who ascend it seeking silence and solitude.

The Hermitage of the Sisters of St. Francis of Syracuse is located on just such a hill. Overlooking an area of both residential and commercial centers, Alverna Heights, as it is called, is, nevertheless, sufficiently removed from them to afford the seclusion that St. Francis so often sought for prayer.

Founded in 1973, the Hermitage was a graced outcome of the many initiatives taken after Vatican II that aimed at a return to the spirit of the Founder. But it was the sisters who pursued Franciscan Studies at St. Bonaventure University who were most instrumental in educating the community about Francis's legacy, in presenting to the Chapter of 1971 a proposal for establishing a hermitage.

For some sisters the awareness of the priority given to contemplation by Francis validated the longing they themselves felt for a life in which prayer could be given primacy. Many other sisters, though they felt no personal call to the hermitage life, supported it as an appropriate option within the community.

The Hermitage began with one resident hermit in a very small building on Alverna Heights, but many sisters took advantage of the hermitage facilities for prayer. Small, primitive huts were erected in the woods to allow for periods of greater solitude.

Over the 20 years of its existence, the Hermitage has developed both as a building and a way of life. The addition of simple, mobile units to the original structure has resulted in a four-bedroom complex that accomodates both resident and guest hermits. The adoption of Francis's "Rule for Hermitages" as the guideline for the life of the hermits has brought a much needed clarity to the identity and mission of the Hermitage.

The very existence of a "Rule for Hermitages" reveals a unique feature of Franciscan eremitical life: it is not a solitary endeavor but a truly fraternal life. Francis describes two roles for hermits: mother (or Martha) and son (or Mary). Prayerful solitude for the sons is safeguarded not by some physical barrier but by the careful attention of another hermit, a mother. Likewise, the sons who abandon themselves to prayer rely not on some previous provision but on the loving activity of the mothers to provide for all their needs. These roles were to be exchanged periodically, fostering the mutuality of trust and trustworthiness in both action and contemplation.

Francis further prescribes a sharing of the Liturgy of the Hours, meals, and even conversation to maintain the fraternal bonds. The prescriptions of Francis's text are simple and clear. But equally clear in its wording is its intention to be flexible. The "Rule for Hermitages" is at the service of contemplation and should never create disturbance or tension that would interfere with the Spirit's activity. The hospitable flexibility of this "Rule" is what allows for its use today as a foundation for life.

In keeping with their reality of daily involvement in active ministry, the resident sister-hermits at Alverna Heights have adapted the "Rule for Hermitages" to their own situation. Morning and Evening Prayer are prayed in common Sunday through Friday. Midday Prayer is prayed privately when the sisters are outside the hermitage. Whenever possible, Morning Prayer is preceded by a time of adoration of the Blessed Sacrament, and Evening Prayer is followed by a time devoted to a personal consciousness examen.

The roles of Martha and Mary are alternated day by day. Martha is responsible for preparing meals, washing dishes, answering the phone and doorbell, and attending to everyday household chores, to allow Mary greater leisure for prayer. As limited as it is, this giving and receiving of personal service can heighten awareness of God's provident attention to the smallest details of our lives.

Silence is observed except at the evening meal, which has proven to be the best time for fraternal sharing when there are no guests in the hermitage. The planning of activities, resolving of conflicts, and all other essential communications are carried out in meetings arranged in a context of prayer, so that the Holy Spirit may direct, as fully as possible, every aspect of hermitage life.

In the early days of the hermitage, visits to friends and family, attendance at social gatherings, and even writing letters were strictly limited. At present such activities are not seen as entirely incompatible with the choice to live in the hermitage. The hermits themselves are entrusted with the determination of the elements needed for a balanced life.

During the course of a year, approximately six weekends are reserved for Hermitage Experiences. On such weekends, the resident sister-hermits generally assume the role of Martha, offering interested persons a time of silence and solitude for prayer, lived according to Francis's instructions.

Ordinarily such experiences begin with an orientation on Friday evening and end after the evening sharing on Sunday. Following the schedule of the hermits is offered as an option, not a requirement. The one absolute requirement is that each participant respect the silence and solitude of the others, and allow God to work in each person according to his/her natural rhythms.

Once a person has made a Hermitage Experience, and has demonstrated a grasp of and appreciation for Francis's way of being a hermit-in-fraternity, he/she is welcome to come to the hermitage as Mary or Martha at a time agreed upon with the resident hermits. Sisters will frequently spend an extended period in the hermitage, particularly during the months of clement weather, when the woods can offer their unique contribution to hearing the Word of God.

It goes without saying that hermitage life is not immune to the vagaries of human existence: plans that go awry, hopes that are not quite fulfilled, misunderstandings, mistakes, and human weakness in its various forms. But it is a life lived in faith in Jesus Christ, who calls people to journey along the limitlessly diverse paths that lead to an infinite, loving, Three-Person God.

A Guest Hermit-Sister's Weekend Experience

It was a chilling Friday in February when seven of us met at the Hermitage to participate in the second "Hermitage Experience." It was early evening, the wood fire danced and crackled, lending a cozy atmosphere to our quietly excited conversation. None of us had known who else was coming until we actually arrived. We were seven diverse people from varied apostolates, all looking forward to something that we had come for voluntarily, without quite being able to define it yet.

We listened attentively as the "Rule for Hermitages" was explained. We understood that we were all Marys and three sisters would serve as our Marthas. For the sake of convenience, we were assigned at random to a Martha in case we should need anything. There was a suggested schedule briefly outlined for us. The weekend was designed to give us a taste of Hermitage living, and some ideas of how it could be incorporated into the life of our Community to serve our spiritual growth and development.

We awakened and had breakfast on our own. Some of us were surprised that as Mary, we were not even allowed to stack our dishes or carry them into the kitchen. Martha served us entirely, and we were free to "sit at the feet of Jesus." At this point, some of us discovered one difference between "retreat" and "hermitage." We were encouraged not to catch up on work we might have brought with us, write letters, solve puzzles, or enjoy quiet games for relaxation. We were to "sit at the feet of Jesus." Jesus alone was to be our companion in silence, the object of our thought, the friend accompanying us in our solitude, the teacher leading us to Beauty, to Truth, to God.

We went our separate ways, coming together for Eucharist, prayer, and meals that were taken in silent gratitude. They were delicious and attractively prepared. As the silent hours passed, some walked outside in natural beauty; others remained in chapel; others sought Jesus in spiritual reading or tapes; and still others simply sat, lost in their own contemplation. It is impossible to set down each individual's experience during this sacred time.

There were some things common to us all, however, which I should like to mention in order to give some idea of what was able to be shared or observed. Saturday and Sunday nights, we gathered, again before a roaring fire, to speak of our thoughts or experiences. This was optional and we could speak or remain silent as the Spirit moved. Sometimes moments passed in wordless contemplation of the inner privacy of minds, while the dying embers shed an atmosphere of quietude over all. The remarks that were made, however, conveyed some new discoveries by those who offered them.

One Sister who had begun to notice that nothing was "still" around us, nothing without motion, exclaimed: "I never knew solitude was so exciting." Another Sister had found herself watching the struggles of a solitary, small bird, attempting to cling to the topmost branch of a tree tossing and swaying in the winds of a violent snow squall. One hermit mentioned that some forms of meditation often focus upon little things. With the large events of our busy lives removed for a time, we were all beginning to realign our priorities. Things that were so important last week could now be seen as definite distractions from the dynamism of God's creation surrounding us but unnoticed in the hectic rush to meet scheduled deadlines.

So it was that we came to our departure time on Monday afternoon. We understood now why we were told that we must be Mary before we could be Martha. We had to understand that Martha was not just waiting on Mary. She was assisting Mary in her call to contemplation and joining her in prayer at designated times. Martha is not subordinate to Mary. She is equal to and necessary for her! Mary has "chosen the better part," but Martha is not excluded.

As we left to return to our varied apostolates, several people offered to serve as Martha in further Hermitage Experiences. All of us felt renewed, refreshed. Some people felt changed somehow, and many felt that others should do this, at least once.

Franciscan Hermitage in the 20th Century

A Personal Reflection

by

Mary Catherine Gurley, OSF

A number of years ago—I had been in religious life about a dozen years at the time—I was with a group of sisters from my own community sharing in an afternoon/evening of prayer and reflection. We were asked to go apart for a while, to think back on what attracted each of us to religious life, and to this particular congregation. I surprised myself when I realized that in the quiet and the spaciousness of our retreatlike surroundings I had taken myself to the very edge of the property and had found a place on the grass where I sat looking out over the evening rush hour traffic. I was so close to the road I could hear the hum of the radios! Why, I wondered, had I chosen such a noisy place when there were so many secluded, quiet nooks available? My second surprise came when I realized that my answer to the question we were asked to ponder—what attracted us to this particular branch of religious life—was going to be "the spiritual depth and professional stance" of these women in community whom I had come to know when I was a teenager. Without consciously doing so I had opted for a place of noisy contemplation and in that strange place understood also that my initial call to religious life had a similar paradox to it.

It was not, however, until years later, when I began to participate in Franciscan hermitage weekends, that my experience of the mixed messages of that day started to make some sense. I began to understand that in the lived experience of hermitage, as presented in Francis's "Rule for Hermitages," many disparate elements of the spiritual life come together and that a 13th–century presentation of hermitage has important relevance for me as a 20th–century Franciscan. Indeed, I found in this text and my experience of it an easy rhythm that brings into a balance at least three of the conflicting elements we face as present–day disciples: 1) the active life versus the contemplative life; 2) our dual need for solitude as well as for community; 3) the issue of living either a life of separateness or one of connectedness in relationship. A brief review of each of these modern-day tensions should show the relevance of the hermitage experience for today, at least as I have experienced such. First, the active-contemplative dimension.

The call of the Gospel to be perfect (Mt. 5:48), or as translated by some, "to be perfected," is a clarion call that has for ages sent Christians in two directions: some to the deserts and mountaintops of prayer, some for service to the inner cities, the rural outskirts or the foreign missions. So often we Christians have looked for the imitation and following of Jesus in an either-or way. We are either active or contemplative; we work in the vineyard or pray in the cloister; we are a Martha or a Mary. The dichotomy, of course, doesn't hold up for long; for the committed followers of the gospel will soon find that their desert prayer must necessarily lead them to their neighbors and, conversely, their work among the dispossessed becomes mere "do-gooding" unless sustained by prayer. Inevitably, a serious following of the Gospel must encompass both active and contemplative dimensions.

We need not look far for models of this twofold engagement with God. In Jesus we have the example of one who preached to crowds, healed and counselled the weary, challenged the politicians, taught the apostles, visited with friends, and played with children. This same Jesus prayed in the desert, in the hills, in places alone, or surrounded by disciples. So balanced were the active and contemplative sides of Jesus that he cannot be defined or understood if one were to focus solely on one dimension to the exclusion of the other.

Francis was the same. His prayer at San Damiano and his rebuilding of the tiny church there are but one act. His staying in Bernard's house and his spending the night in prayer were equally significant in Bernard's conversion. His question of the brothers, "What do you think, brothers, what do you judge better? That I should spend my time in prayer or that I should go about preaching?" (LM XII:1) raised the issue in precise terms. His answer to himself was just as precise: "And because we should do everything according to the pattern shown to us in him as on the heights of the mountain, it seems more pleasing to God that I interrupt my quiet and go out to labor" (LM 12:1).

As a final point, however, it must be remembered that Francis's choice was not an either-or decision. In his own life— half of which, scholars tell us, he spent in hermitage—and in his "Rule for Hermitages," Francis outlined a way of life that was active-contemplative. His preaching was the fruit of his contemplative praise of his God; what he witnessed in his preaching he brought back into a contemplative stance before his God. This duality was what was resonating with me that afternoon when I prayed with the traffic and realized I was drawn to Franciscanism by the example of women who were equally prayerful before God and busy professionals in God's vineyard.

This interplay of the active and the contemplative is at the heart of Franciscan hermitage, drawn directly from the Gospel narrative of Martha and Mary (Lk. 10:38-42). As Francis wrote in this "Rule," the brothers were to assume, when in hermitage, the role of either a Martha or a Mary. The Marthas, the "do-ers," were to care for and protect from unnecessary distraction the brothers who were the Marys, those who sit in prayer at the feet of Jesus. To Francis each role was equally important, for his instruction also directs that after a space of time the roles be reversed; the Marthas become Marys, the Marys assume the responsibilities of Martha. I have personally found it very enlightening to experience both roles as renewing and refreshing. While I obviously love the luxury of being a Mary, the Martha role, even at times when I have been most frantically in need of hermitage, has always been spiritually refreshing, so well-integrated are the active and contemplative dimensions of Franciscan hermitage.

Besides the being-doing dichotomy of modern life—and, again, part of my little understood "praying in the traffic" that afternoon—is another phenomenon of Franciscan life and solitude that literally overwhelmed me the first time I committed myself to a hermitage weekend. I realized that for a Franciscan praying in solitude and praying with community are synonymous. Let me put the experience into context.

The ardent disciples of our day have taken seriously the vineyard dimension of the Christian life and live their ministries on the high side of overextended. Worn out, and justly so, by the pace and intensity of ministry and by the burdens of others that they so readily take on as their own, they seek the isolation of the desert or the solitude of the retreat house for the needed peace and space for prayer and spiritual reenergizing. I identify with such people, and as the passing years give me greater wisdom born of grace and experience, I find that the dividing line between time for ministry and space for prayer becomes less well-defined and that the one flows in and out of the other far more gently and frequently. At times, however, I just need to run, to escape it all, to be alone with God. So it was the first time I read an announcement for a FRANCISCAN HERMITAGE EXPERIENCE. I signed up immediately and set off to be alone. Alone!

In Franciscan solitude, I was to learn, we are not alone. Francis, like Jesus, sent the disciples out in pairs, admonishing them to pray together while on the journey. Francis, himself, always took a brother with him, that they might sing God's praises together. Even when each brother went his separate way into the solitary seclusion of the cave to pray, they stayed within hearing distance of one another, to support each other, to care for the other's needs. In the hermitage rule Francis carefully provides for such companionship, for he directs that "three or four" gather together, provides for prayer in common, designates the assignments of Martha and Mary roles to those in the hermitage together, and outlines basic elements of fraternal living for all. In Franciscan solitude one does, indeed, stand alone in contemplative awe before her/his God, but never in an isolated manner. Always there is the echo of Francis, "God gave me brothers" and the repetitive phrase of Clare, "together with my sisters." No one in the Franciscan family prays alone, especially in hermitage.

My first opportunity to live Franciscan hermitage was, therefore, something of a surprise to me. I wanted and expected solitude, and while I had ample time and space for prayer and rest, I was also constantly aware that I was part of a very intense and supportive praying fraternity of Marys and Marthas. The whole was truly greater than the sum of the parts. Carried in Franciscan fraternity, I met God as Mother-Father of all of us there, yet without diminishing my own stance before the Almighty. My sisters and brothers were not people from whom I needed to escape so that I could pray; we were a fraternity of solitary pray-ers in relationship with one another, participants in the relational language and intention of Francis's idea. When I left hermitage that weekend, and whenever I've returned to hermitage periodically since, it is never a separating experience of "now I work—now I pray" or "this I do with others—this I do alone." Hermitage unifies it all for me. Truly, Franciscan solitude celebrates the refrains "God gave me brothers" and "together with my sisters" and gives me another insight into why it now seems so natural for me to be able to pray within sight and sound of traffic!

In addition to the active-contemplative dichotomy and the solitude-fraternity question, the third condition of modern life that the experience of hermitage addresses is the issue of separateness vis-à-vis interconnectedness, a deep concern of many segments of society. Ours is a fractured culture, the end product of which can often be isolation and separateness. Large impersonal cities, sprawling and sterile developments, isolated farms, huge corporations, and factories that separate their workers into a multitude of employee divisions, large regional schools, carbon-copy shopping malls, impersonal services—the list could get quite long—all tend to isolate people. Moreover, living as we do in what some call a global village where we are today more keenly aware of all who share the planet with us, we are also, ironically, less neighborly and more isolated than ever, living in our own carefully designed and structured corners. Fear and violence have also pushed us into isolation, causing us to move farther apart, to separate ourselves behind brick and mortar barriers, or, perhaps, psychological or prejudicial ones. Oftentimes, sad to say, the sheer number of involvements, however good, can result in our drowning in our own whirlpool of activities. We can become so busy in the little worlds of our own making that we shut out all other worlds and become very separated ministers.

Illustrative of this discussion of separateness and interconnectedness is an essay from the field of physics that I read recently. The essay was discussing the division of matter into two phenomena. The one was made up of tiny particles (ions) that are in constant motion and continually bumping into one another. The other was described as waves of energy (a sound wave, for example) emanating from some matter and constantly crisscrossing with other such waves. The essay went so far as to state the belief that all of creation, including people, are made up of these ions and waves. The ions, I suggest, represent the isolation of which I write; the waves represent the interconnectedness that we seek, some way in which to be in touch with one another, to know that our lives have "connected" with something or someone significant.

Here, too, I have found hermitage to be a place of necessity for my own modern-day survival. In hermitage I have always met sisters and brothers not of my own choosing, but always in the end, real gift. Like the waves of interconnectedness described in the essay, the fraternal nature of the hermitage experience is a place where stories and lives, faith and prayer connect, and the walls and barriers of separateness begin to disappear. In the structure of hermitage we can be strangers and aliens no longer. Once the connections are made, and each time new connections are made, we become people who can never quite be comfortable again behind any barriers between brother and sister. In my own life I find myself seeking hermitage as much to connect as to pray. Indeed, the two are of the same source.

So it seems that on that day so many years ago when I sought the edges of the property and prayed within sound and sight of the rush hour traffic, I was merely responding to elements in myself that I had yet to discover, elements that probably drew me to Franciscan life in the first place. I was responding, also, I suspect, to deeper elements of the human person that Francis probably recognized intuitively when he wrote his "Rule for Hermitages." Because we are so very human, all ages will struggle with these active-contemplative, individual-communal, separate-interconnected paradoxes that life presents. We of the twentieth century, however, are particularly susceptible to these contradictions. As praying people we look for healing measures that will slow the pace, close the empty or overcrowded places, ease the aloneness, satisfy the yearning for connection. In a word, we look for God and, in God, we look for the faces of our sisters and brothers. The lived experience of Francis's "Rule for Hermitages" responds to these longings and places us firmly on the ground to which Francis and Clare continually call us: "God gave me brothers," and "together with my sisters." The "Rule for Hermitages" is an over-arching rule for every 20th-century Franciscan whose life is lived close to the rush hour traffic.

Clare and The Rule for Hermitages

An Experience at the Poor Clare Monastery

in Stamford, Connecticut

by

André Cirino, OFM[1]

In the fall of 1990 I conducted a retreat for the Monastery of Poor Clares in Bordentown, New Jersey. The retreat centered on the prayer of Francis and Clare. Toward the end of the retreat, we examined prayer in the solitude of Francis in light of the "Rule for Hermitages." After an explanation of the "Rule," we spent the last three days experiencing its rhythm. At the end of the time one of the Poor Clares handed me a sheet of paper with a list of the many quotes from the writings of Clare which she felt paralleled Francis's text. I took the list home with me, where it sat on my desk for several months until Easter week, when I made my own annual retreat at the Monastery of Poor Clares in Stamford, Connecticut. Alone in the quiet for the week, I was able to pick up the rhythm of their life. And then the list came back to me as well as the parallelism between the "Rule for Hermitages" and Clare's writings. I would like to go through the "Rule for Hermitages," sharing the list as well as some commentary from the rhythm I experienced at the Stamford Monastery.

1. *Those who wish to dwell in a religious way in hermitages may be three brothers or, at the most, four; let two of these be the 'mother' and have two 'sons,' or at least one.*[2]

In the *Mirror of Perfection* we read:

When the friars have received the blessing of the Bishop, let them go and mark out the boundaries of the land which they have accepted for their house, and as a sign of holy poverty and humility, let them plant a hedge instead of building a wall. Afterwards let them erect simple huts of clay and wood, and a number of cells where the friars can pray or work from time to time in order to increase their merit and avoid idleness (*SP* 10).

This gives us an idea of the way the early friars lived. Most of the surviving hermitages we see today—Carceri, LaVerna, Poggio Bustone, Greccio, to name a few—are on secluded mountains, and one can still see remnants of caves friars would have used.

Clare writes, in two different texts:

The Abbesses are bound to observe it [poverty and] . . . are not to receive or hold on to any . . . property . . . except as much land as necessity requires for the integrity and the proper seclusion of the monastery; and this land is not to be cultivated except as a garden for the needs of the sisters (*RegCl* VI.4-6).

Let both the sister who is in office and the other sisters exercise such care and farsightedness that they do not acquire or receive more land around the place than strict necessity requires for a vegetable garden. But if, for the integrity and privacy of the monastery, it becomes necessary to have more land beyond the limits of the garden, no more should be acquired than strict necessity demands. This land should not be cultivated or planted but always remain untouched and undeveloped (*TestCl* 16).

The Stamford monastery (on diocesan property) is an old house on twenty-two acres of land. The sisters make use of the land for prayer in solitude and for a small garden. The monastery presently has four members, so they almost literally align themselves with this part of the "Rule for Hermitages." On this land, the sisters are able to experience solitude—a solitude in fraternity—as Francis indicates in the first verse of the hermitage "Rule."

Francis uses the term *mother*, a term he uses in the *Later Rule* (6:8); the same term was used to refer to him in Second Celano 137. Clare uses the term when she writes: "elect another as abbess and mother . . ." (*TestCl* 24). The term *mother* conveys not only concern and work, but also an attitude that is delicate, sensitive, warm, affectionate, tender. These qualities are evident in abbesses and also in the sisters themselves. There is a general mother-attitude in all to safeguard the solitude of their lives. This will be treated further in the second verse below.

2. Let the two who are 'mothers' keep the life of Martha and the two 'sons' keep the life of Mary (cf. Lk. 10:38-42) and have one enclosure in which each one may have his cell in which he may pray and sleep.

We saw above how Clare in her *Testament* calls herself "mother and servant." One who assumes the role of mother or Martha assumes the role of servant, of work. Clare writes: "The sisters to whom the Lord has given the grace of working are to work faithfully and devotedly [beginning] after the Hour of Terce, at work which pertains to a virtuous life and to the common good" (*RegCl* VII.1).

The Stamford monastery had many works going on each day, including for example, cooking, cleaning, raking leaves, cutting wood, spiritual direction, preparing liturgies, sewing and weaving. All seemed to facilitate the solitude that permeates the monastery. For the most part the work seems to be done in solitude so as to preserve the atmosphere of prayer for each other. And to preserve this solitude Clare calls all the Sisters to "obey their mother . . . so that seeing the charity, humility, and unity they have toward one another their mother might bear all the burdens [work] . . . lightly" (*TestCl* 20).

3. And let them always recite Compline of the day immediately after sundown; and strive to maintain silence, recite their Hours, rise for Matins; and seek first the Kingdom of God and His justice (Mt.6:33).

Here Francis begins to delineate a schedule for the friars in hermitage that includes the Liturgy of the Hours. Clare writes: "The sisters who can read shall celebrate the Divine Office according to the custom of the Friars Minor . . ." (RCl 2:1). The Monastery at Stamford had its Office of Readings (matins) about 11:30 A.M. In the solitude and silence of my week there, I frequently heard the voices of the sisters chanting parts of the Divine Office in much the same way I have experienced the chanting of the office at the Protomonastery in Assisi.

In writing about silence, Clare reproduces almost exactly the words of the third verse of the "Rule for Hermitages" when she writes: "The sisters are to keep silence from the hour of compline. . ." (*RegCl* V.1).The silence Francis desires is a profound experience of the hermitage text, deepening the solitude. Clare says: "They should keep silence continually in the church, in the dormitory, and, only while they are eating in the refectory" (*RegCl* V.2). In my week at the Stamford Monastery—a small building—during the day voices or noise never broke into my silence, or rather I should say, the atmosphere of silence created by the Sisters.

4. And let them recite Prime at the proper hour and, after Terce, they may end their silence, speak with and go to their 'mothers.'

Francis here seems to be laying out a schedule, a time-table for the friars to set the rhythm of the hermitage. Clare approximates this statement of this verse when she writes: "The sisters are to keep silence from the hour of Compline until Terce, except those who are serving outside the monastery" (*RegCl* V.1). Those serving outside the monastery would be the mothers, performing the Martha-tasks for the community. Then a few verses down in chapter V, almost as if Clare is seeing them all as mothers to each other, she says: "However, they may briefly and quietly communicate what is really necessary always and everywhere" (*RegCl* V.4). Clare picks up on the silence and the speaking that we find in the fourth verse of the "Rule for Hermitages."

At the Stamford Monastery the sisters prayed morning prayer at 7:00 and mid-morning prayer at 9:30, being very much in silence all this time. Both in the morning before 10:00 and in the evening after night prayer, the sisters take advantage of silence to be Mary to whatever degree they feel called. Around mid-morning (Terce) the sisters seemed to take up their Martha/mother roles for one another—cooking, cleaning, running errands, and the like.

5. And, when it pleases them, they can beg alms from them as poor little ones out of love of the Lord God.

Francis might have wanted to keep the Marys in touch with the rest of the fraternity who went about seeking alms for needs, for food. For the seeker of alms, Clare writes: "Each should make known her needs to the other with confidence" (*RegCl* VIII.9). And for the one from whom the alms are sought, Clare says:

> I also beg the sister who will have the office [of caring for] the sisters . . . [to] be prudent and attentive to her sisters just as a good mother is to her daughters; and especially, let her take care to provide for them according to the needs of each one from the things [alms] which the Lord shall give (*TestCl* 19).

While alms were not sought for literally at the Stamford Monastery, the people of the area brought alms to the sisters in diverse forms—food and new song books to name two of which I am aware—the people themselves acting almost like mothers to the sisters to preserve their prayer of solitude, which prayer the people value. People also at times drive the sisters to appointments and run errands so they can remain in solitude.

6. And afterwards let them recite Sext, None and, at the proper hour, Vespers.

Francis further delineates a schedule based on the Liturgy of the Hours. And Clare approaches this suggestion of the Hours when she asks "the sisters who can read [to] celebrate the divine office according to the custom of the Friars Minor" (RCl 3:1).

At Stamford the Poor Clares prayed mid-day prayer together after the mid-day meal. Vespers is usually 5:00 P.M.

7. And they may not permit anyone to enter or eat in the enclosure where they dwell.

Since the brothers were on the road preaching the gospel, engaged in the active ministry, when they returned and spent time in hermitages, Francis wanted to preserve their silence. So he "hedged" them in and spoke of enclosure for them. Clare has much to say about enclosure in chapters five and eleven of her *Rule*. Without getting into the details of grilles, locks, doors, and the like, Clare says: "The sisters shall not allow anyone to enter the monastery. . ." (RCl 11: 8). While she is aware of "evident, reasonable, and unavoidable" (RCl 11: 8) necessity, her words here in this chapter on enclosure come very close to those of Francis.

During the week people telephoned or came to the Stamford Monastery. The sisters "hedged" themselves in by the use of a telephone-answering machine during prayer time and times of silence. And one sister would be available to respond to those who came to the door, thus "hedging off" the others in their solitude.

8. Let those brothers who are the 'mothers' strive to stay far from everyone and, because of obedience to their minister, protect their 'sons' from everyone so that no one can speak with them.

Here Francis is urging the mothers to protect themselves as well as the sons who are in the stance of Mary. For protection of the mothers themselves, Clare writes:

> The sisters who serve outside the monastery should not delay long unless some evident necessity demands it. They should conduct themselves virtuously and speak little, so that those who see them may always be edified. And let them zealously avoid all meetings or dealings that could be called into question. . . . They may not dare to repeat rumors of the world inside the monastery. And they are strictly bound not to repeat outside the monastery anything that was said or done within which could cause scandal (RCl 9: 6-11).

Clare insures protection of the solitude of the sisters—as Marys— when she writes: "The sisters are to keep silence. . . . The sisters may not speak at the parlor or at the grille without the permission of the abbess or her vicar" (RCl 5: 1, 5).

As I remember during my stay at Stamford, the abbess had to drive a sister to an appointment. She let me know this, as well as the time of her return, for our planned celebration of Eucharist. There was need to go forth, but the return was precise, for I sensed the sisters' desire to reenter their rhythm of solitude. This or any appointment is insignificant to mention, other than the fact that the appointments took them away from the rhythm of their solitude; on their return I witnessed the desire to resume this rhythm, to return to God, to their Center. A woman also came for spiritual direction from one of the sisters. This was announced to all to make us aware of someone entering, which awareness assured all of the preservation of the rhythm of solitude.

9. And those 'sons' may not talk with anyone except with their 'mothers' and with the minister and his custodian when it pleases them to visit with the Lord's blessing.

Francis provided a way for ministers to be in touch with the friars who were in hermitage for long periods of time. Having no means of communication such as those to which we are accustomed, Francis allowed the ministers to come and speak with the brothers. Other than this exception, the sons did not speak with others.

Clare says: "The sisters may not speak . . . without permission of the abbess or her vicar . . . [and] should speak very rarely at the grille. . ."(RCl 5: 5, 9).

The Stamford Monastery, in comparison to some that I have seen, is small. Some people came to see the sisters or pray in their chapel or on their grounds. People would approach to speak with them. Words were briefly exchanged. I observed one sister on a bright, sunny day clearing leaves from a large flower bed. A man approached to speak. He pulled up a chair, sat and spoke. The sister, listening and making occasional responses, continued her clearing. I smiled to myself as I observed this scene.

However, even with this intrusion, she preserved her Martha rhythm by continuing to work as she listened and responded. When he left, her silence surrounded her once again.

10. The 'sons,' however, may periodically assume the role of the 'mothers,' taking turns for a time as they have mutually decided. Let them strive to observe conscientiously and eagerly everything mentioned above.

From 2Cel 178 we know that the friars in Spain living in hermitage exchanged roles. We read: "In this way each week those who lead the active life exchange with those who live the contemplative life and the quiet of those giving themselves to contemplation is changed for the business of work."

Clare sees the role of abbess as that of "mother" (TestCl 19-20). Today, the role of abbess is very much taken up with the "business of work" for the sisters and the monastery itself. It seems as if the work load of the abbess, akin to that of the brothers and sisters of the First and Third Orders, makes her in her mother-role more a member of those branches while she is in office. And in the fourth chapter of her *Rule* Clare provides for the election of abbess as well as her council, exchanging roles with others in the community (*RegCl* IV.17-18).

In all monasteries today, the exchange of abbesses and their council—the Martha —takes place by election to terms of office, so these sisters are able to exchange this work role for a contemplative role within the rhythm of community solitude once again. As abbess and council, they worked to preserve this solitude. Now others are chosen to do the same, as once again, they enter the embrace of communal solitude.

In the Stamford Monastery, the sisters take every Friday as a quiet day, doing only necessary chores, with one sister completely free from all work. The sisters exchange roles every Friday to partake of "contemplation" while the other attends to the "business of work."

Conclusion

In the early years, the Order was experienced more as a Franciscan movement rather than as the numerical divisions we live with today: First, Second, or Third Order. From the beginning, Francis spent time in caves, in solitude. Dacian Bluma, OFM, claims that Francis spent up to half of his converted life in hermitages. Clare joined the movement in these early years. Both of them valued solitude and contemplation. And while Francis preserved his experience for us in his "Rule for Hermitages," it seems that Clare picked up this same rhythm as she and her sisters lived as contemplatives in the solitude of San Damiano. And, in the list of quotes from Clare's writings handed to me at Bordentown, the Sister who wrote the list picked up the same rhythm in those writings as we shared an experience of the "Rule for Hermitages" together. This was verified for me during my stay at the Stamford Monastery. It seems that in regard to contemplation and solitude in the early Franciscan movement, there is much harmony between Francis and Clare.

Endnotes

[1] This article was originally published in *The Cord* (July-August 1991): 195-202. It has been slightly re-edited for this publication.

[2] "Rule for Hermitages," *Gospel Living* 62–63.

ABBREVIATIONS

Acta SS	*Acta Sanctorum*
AF	*Analecta Franciscana*
AFH	*Archivum Franciscanum Historicum*
AIA	*Archivo-Ibero-Americano*
AnalPraem	*Analecta Praemonstratensia*
Annales ESC	*Annales: Economies, Sociétés, Civilisations*
ArchLitKirchGesch	*Archiv für Literatur- und Kirchengeschichte des Mittelalters*
Bull. Cap.	*Bullarium Cappucinorum*
CChrCM	*Corpus Christianorum*
CF	*Collectanea Franciscana*
DCBNT	*Dizionario de teologia biblica*
DHGE	*Dictionnaire d'histoire et géographie ecclésiastique*
DIP	*Dizionario Istituto Perfectione*
EtFrNS	*Etudes Franciscaines Nouvelle Série*
FranzStud	*Franziskanische Studien*
GLNT	*Grande Lessico del NT*
IF	*L'Italia Francescana*
LA	*Linguistica Antverpiensa*
MF	*Miscellanea Francescana*
MGH	*Monumenta Germaniae Historica*
MGH SS	*Monumenta Germaniae Historica, Scriptores*
MMS	*Munstersche Mittelalter-Schriften*
NF	*Neerlandia Franciscana*
PL	*Patrologia Latina*
RAM	*Revue d'ascétique et de mystique*
RBen.	*Revue Bénédictine*
Rev. de Espirit.	*Revista de Espiritualidad*
SF	*Studi Franciscani*
SP	*Studia Picena*
Studia theol.	*Studia Theologica*
TRE	*Theologische Realenzyklopädie*
WissWeish	*Wissenschaft und Weisheit*

Franciscan Solitude

Bibliographic Compilation of References

Abate, G. "Fra Matteo da Bascio e gli inizi dell'Ordine cappuccino." *CF* 30 (1960): 31-77.

——. "Il primitivo breviario francescano (1224-1227)." *MF* 60 (1960): 98.

Accrocca, F. "I 'pauperes eremite domini Celestini.'" *Celestino V papa angelico*. Acts of the Second International Historical Congress. L'Aquila, 1988.

Aelred de Rievaulx. *La vie de recluse*. . . . Ed. C. Dumont. *Sources Chrétiennes* 76. Paris, 1961.

Alberigo, J., J. A. Dossetti, et al. *Conciliorum oecumenicorum decret*. Bologna, 1973.

Alberzoni, M.P. "Penitenti e terziari a Milano fino agli inizi del XIV secolo." In *Prime manifestazioni di vita comunitaria maschile e femminile nel movimento francescano della Penitenza (1215-1447)*. Eds. R. Pazzelli and L. Temperini. Rome: Commissione Storica Internazionale T.O.R., 1982.

Alszeghy, Z. "Fuite du monde." In *Dictionnaire de Spiritualité* 5 (1964): 1575-1605.

Anastasi, L. "I sacri ritiri nella lettera collettiva dei M. RR. PP. Provinciali." *Vita Minorum* 35/3 (1964): 24-25.

Angelus of Clareno. *Chronicon seu Historia septem tribulationum ordinis Minorum*. Ed. A. Ghinato. Rome, 1959.

Anjbarro, V. "El P. Ximenez Samaniego y los origines de la Oservance en España." *AIA* 8 (1948): 450 ff.

Aquilani, Bernardini. *Chronica fratrum Minorum Observantiae*. Ed. L. Lemmens. Rome, 1902.

Ariès, P., and G. Duby. *Histoire de la vie privée II. De l'Europe féodale à la Renaissance*. Paris, 1985.

Autenrieth, J. "Einige Bemerkungen zu den Gedichten im Hortus deliciarum Herrads von Landsberg." *Festschrift B. Bischoff.* Stuttgart, 1971.

Bachea, M. "La cripta triastila di San Benedetto al Subasio." Atti dell'Accademia Properziana del Subasio, 1956.

Balderich of Dol. *Vita Roberti.* II, 11. *PL* 162, col. 1049 C.

Barsotti, S. *Un nuovo fiore serafico, il beato Giovanni Cimi, confessore pisano, soldato ed eremita, fondatore dei fratelli della penitenza ed uno dei fondatori della Pia Casa della Misericordia.* Quaracchi, 1906.

Bartoli, Marco. "Analisi storica e interpretazione psicanalitica di una visione di S. Chiara d'Assisi." *AFH* 73 (1980): 449-72.

Battistoni, A. "La Compagnia dei Disciplinati di S. Giovanni Evangelista di Porta della Pace in Pisa e la sua devozione verso frate Giovanni soldato." *Bollettino della Deputazione di storia patria per l'Umbria* 65 (1968): 205, 207-209, 220-21.

Baumann, B. "Jutta di Disibodenberg." *Bibliotheca Sanctorum.* Vol. 1. 1032-33.

Benoit, J.M. *Le chevalier courtois de Notre-Dame-des-Anges.* Montréal, 1952.

Benvenuti Papi, A. "'Velut in sepulchro,' Cellane e recluse nella tradizione agiografica italiana." In *Culto dei santi, istituzioni e classi sociali in età preindustriale.* Ed. S. Boesch Gajano and L. Sebastiani. L'Aquila-Rome, 1984.

—. "Donne religiose nella Firenze del Due-Trecento: appunti per una ricerca in corso." In *Le mouvement confraternal au Moyen Age, France, Italie, Suisse.* Rome, 1987.

—. "Le forme communitarie della penitenza femminile francescana." In *Prime Manifestazioni di vita communitaria maschile e femminile nel movemento francescano della penitenza (1215-1447).* Eds. R. Pazzelli and L. Temperini. Rome: Commissione Storica Internazionale T.O.R., 1982.

—. "Margherita filia Jerusalem: Santa Margherita da Cortona e il superamento mistico della crociata." In *Toscana e Terrasanta nel medioevo.* Ed. F. Cardini. Florence, 1982.

—. "Penitenza e santità femminile in ambiente cateriniano e bernardiniano." In *Atti del Simposio internazionale cateriniano-bernardiniano.* Ed. D. Maffei and P. Nardi. Siena, 1982.

—. "Santità femminile nel territorio fiorentino e lucchese." In *Religiosità e società in Valdelsa nel busco medioevo.* Florence, 1980.

—. "Umiliana dei Cerchi Nascita di un culto nella Firenze del Dugento." *SF* 77 (1980): 87-117.

—. *Il movimento religioso femminile in Umbria nei secoli XIII-XIV.* Ed. R. Rusconi. Scandicci-Perugia, 1984.

—. *In castro poenitentiae: Santità e società femminile nell'Italia medievale.* Rome, 1990.

Besse, J. "Anachorets." *Dictionnaire de Théologie Catholique* 1 (1909): 1134-41.

Bevegnati, Giunta. *Leggenda della vita e dei miracoli di Santa Margherita da Cortona.* Trans. E. Mariani. Vicenza, 1978.

Bienvenu, J.-M. "Roberto d'Arbrissel." *DIP* 3.

—. *L'etonnant fondateur de Fontevraud, Robert d'Arbrisse.* Paris, 1981.

Bihl, M. "Statuta Generalia Ordinis edita in Capitulis Generalibus celebratis Narbonae an. 1260, Assisii an. 1279 atque Parisiis an. 1292 editio critica et synoptica." *AFH* 34 (1941): 67, 11b.

Bluma, Dacian, OFM. "The Rule for Hermitages." Presentation given at the Franciscan Gathering, Tampa, February 7, 1983. (Cassette Enterprises, 1112 Park St., Seffner, FL 33584).

—. "De vita recessuali in historia et legislatione O.F.M." *Studi e Testi francescani* 14. Rome, 1959.

Bocher, O. "Deserto,"*DCBNT,* 464-65. Bologna, 1976.

Boehmer, H. *Analekten zur Geschichte des Franciscus von Assisi.* Tübingen, 1904.

Bonaventure. "Constitutions of Narbonne." *Opere Omnia.* Vol. 8. Ad Claras Aquas, 1898.

—. "The Life of St. Francis." *Bonaventure.* Ed. and trans. E. Cousins. The Classics of Western Spirituality. New York, 1978.

Bonmann, O. *Die Schriften des hl. Franziskus von Assisi.* Freiburg im Br., 1940.

Bonnet, S., and B. Gouley. *Gelebte Einsamkeit: Eremiten heute.* Freiburg/Basel/Vienna, 1982.

Book of Margery Kempe, The. Ed. S. Brown Meech and H. E. Allen. London, 1940.

Bortolami, S. *Minoritismo e sviluppo urbano fra Due e Trecento, il caso di Padova in Esperienze minoritiche nel Veneto del Due-Trecento.* Acts of the National Congress of Franciscan Studies. Padua, September 1984, and Padua-Vicenza, 1985.

Brancaloni, L. "Il Monte Subasio e le Carceri di S. Francesco." In *Frate Francesco* 1. 1924.

Brengio, L. "L'osservanza francescana in Italia nel secolo XIV." In *Studi e testi francescani* 24. Rome, 1963.

Brentano, R. "Catherine of Siena, Margery Kempe and a 'caterva virginum.'" In *Atti del Simposio internazionale Cateriniano-Bernardiniano*. Ed. D. Maffei and P. Nardi. Siena, 1982.

—. "Death in Gualdo Tadino and in Rome (1340, 1296)." *Studia Gratiana* 19 (1976): 98.

Busson, G. and A. Ledru. "Actus pontificum Cenomannis in urbe degentium." *Archives Historiques du Maine*. Vol. 2. 1901.

Butler, C. *Benedicti Regula monasteriorum*. Freiburg: Herder, 1935.

Cacciamani, G. "La Réclusion dans l'ordre camaldule." *RAM* 38 (1962): 37-54; 273-87.

—. *Le reclusione presso l'ordine camaldolese*. Camaldoli, 1960.

Cadderi, A. *La beata Margherita Colonna (clarissa)*. Rome, 1984.

Caesari Heisterbacensis monachi Ordinis Cisterciensis Dialogus miraculorum I-II. Cologne, Bonn, and Brussels, 1851.

Cambell, J. *Les écrits de saint François d'Assise devant la critique*. Werl/Westf, 1954. Also in *FranzStud* 36 (1954): 82-109; 205-264.

Canonici. L. *L'Umbria con frate Francesco*. Assisi, 1979.

Capitani, O. "Ipotesi sociali del francescanesimo medioevale, orientamenti e considerazioni." In *San Francesco*. Rome, 1985.

Caponeri, M. Rossi. "Nota su alcuni testamenti della fine del secolo XIV relativi alla zona di Orvieto." In *Nolens intestatus decedere*. Perugia, 1985.

Cargnoni, C. "Le Case di Preghiera nella Storia dell'Ordine Francescano." In *Le 'Case Di Preghiera' Nella Storia E Spiritualità Francescana*. Ed. Fiorenzo F. Mastroianni. Naples: Edizioni Dehoniane, 1978.

Carpentier, E. *Acta SS Oct.* 9. Brussels, 1858.

Carrion, L. "Casas de Recollección de la Provincia de la Inmaculada Concepción y Estatutos por que se regían." *AIA* 9 (1918): 264 -65.

—. "Origines." *AIA* 3 (1915): 175.

Casagrande, G. "Forme di vita religiosa femminile nell'area di Città di Castello nel sec. XIII." In *Il movimento religioso femminile in Umbria nei secoli XIII-XIV.* Ed. R. Rusconi. Perugia-Florence, 1984.

—. "Forme di vita religiosa femminile solitaria in Italia centrale." In *Eremitismo nel francescanesimo medievale.* Assisi: Società Internazionale di studi francescani, 1991.

—. "Presenza di Fraticelli nell'area di Bettona." *AFH* 74 (1981): 323, 325, 327.

Catalogus codicum latinorum bibliothecae regiae Monacensis, 2. Munich, 1876.

Cavanna, N. *L'Umbria francescana illustrata.* Perugia, 1910.

Cenci, C. *Documentazione di vita assisana 1300-1530.* Vol. I. Grottaferrata, 1974.

Cerafogli, E. *La Baronessa santa Filippa Mareri.* Vatican City, 1979.

Chartier, M. C. "Reclus." *Dictionnaire de Spiritualité* 13 (1988): 221-28.

—. "Regula solitariorum" *DIP* 7 (1983): 1598-1600.

Chiappini, A. "S. Filippa Mareri e il suo monastero di Borgo S. Pietro de Molito nel Cicolano." *MF* 22 (1921): 65-119.

Chiaretti, G. "Eremiti del Monteluco." *DIP* 3, 1167-75.

"Chiese e conventi degli ordini mendicanti in Umbria nei secoli XIII-XIV. Gli archivi ecclesiastici di Città di Castello." Ed. G. Casagrande. Perugia, 1990.

Cirino, A."Vita della B. Angela da Desenzano." In *"Historia Cappuccina" di Mattia da Salò, Agiografia e letteratura spirituale della riforma tridentia. IF* 52 (1977): 187-218.

Clay, L. M. *The Hermits and Anchorites of England.* London, 1914.

Clotilde of Sainte Julienne. *Histoire d'un glorieux passé: Sainte Julienne de Cornillon, Sainte Eve de Saint-Martin et la Fête de Dieu.* Brussels-Paris, 1924.

College, E. J. *A Book of Showings to the Anchoress Julian of Norwich.* Toronto, 1978.

Collez complete delle opere del B. Leonardo da Porto M. Rome, 1853.

Constable, G. "Aelredo de Rievaulx e la monaca di Watton Un episodio agli inizi della storia dell'Ordine Gilbertino." *Sante, regine e aventuriere nell'Occidente medievale.* Ed. D. Baker. English translation: "Aelred of Rievaulx and the Nun of Watton: An Episode in the Early History of the Gilbertine Order." In *Medieval Women*, Ed. Derek Baker. Oxford, 1978.

—. "Eremitical forms of monastic life." In *Istituzione monastiche e istituzioni canonicali in Occidente (1123-1215)*. Milan, 1980.

—. "Eremitical Forms of Monastic Life." In *Monks, Hermits and Crusaders in Medieval Europe*. London, 1988.

—. "Contemplazione ed Evangelizzazione nella vita apostolica." In *Lettura spirituale-apostolica delle Fonti Francescani*. Ed. G. Cardopoli and M. Conti. Rome, 1980.

—. "Contemplazione ed Evangelizzazione nella vita di San Francesco." In *Lettura spirituale-apostolica delle Fonti Francescane*. Ed. G. Cardiapoli and M. Conti. Rome, 1980.

—. "La Sacra Scrittura nell'esperienza e negli Scritti di san Francesco (Criteri ermeneutici.)" In *Lettura biblico-teologica delle Fonti Franciscane*. Rome, 1979.

—. *La missione degli Apostoli nella Regola Francescana*. Genoa, 1972.

"Costituzioni of S. Rodolfo." In *Annales Camaldulenses*. Vol. 3. Venice, 1758.

Cresi, A. "Il Collegio-ritiro dei missionari dell'Incontro nel primo centenario della fondazione (1853-1953)." *SF* 26 (1954): 44-89.

—. "S. Leonardo da P.M. e l'Incontro." *SF* 24 (1952): 176-97.

—. *Costitutzioni da osservarsi nella Solitudine del ritiro della Provincia riformata Toscana*. Florence, 1776.

—. *Proponimenti di S. Leonardo da P.M. tratti dall'autografo*. Introduction and notes P. Benedetto Innocenti. Florence, 1937.

Cresi, D. "Statistica dell'Ordine Minoritico all'anno 1282." *AFH* 56 (1963): 157-62.

Crosara, F. *Le Constitutiones e le Regulae de vita eremitica del B. Rodolfo Prima legislazione camaldolese nella riforma gregoriana*. Rome, 1970.

Csanyi, D.A. "Optima pars. Die Auslegungsgeschichte von Lk 10: 38-42 bei den Kirchenvätern der ersten vier Jahrhunderte," *Studia Monastica* 2 (1960): 5-78.

D'Alençon, Edouard. *L'abbaye de Saint-Benoit sur Mont Soubase près d'Assise*. Couvin, 1909.

da Barberino, Francesco. *Regimento ecostumi di donne*. Ed. G. Sansone. Turin, 1957.

da Campagnola, Stanislao. "Gli spirituali umbri." In *Chi erano gli spirituali*. Assisi, 1976.

—. "La 'leggende' di Frate Egidio d'Assisi nei secoli XIII-XV." In *Francescanesimo e società cittadina*. Perugia, 1979.

da Rimini, Pacifico. *Della vita e dell'eroiche virtù del ven. P. Leopoldo da Gaiche min. rif. di S. Francesco nella Provincia Serafica, istitutore del ritiro di Monteluco e missionario apostolico*. 2 vols. Foligno, 1835.

da Romallo, Sisinio. *Il ministero della confessione nei primordi dell'Ordine francescano in relazione ai diritti parrocchiali. Annali Francescani*. Milan, 1949.

da S. Maria, Clemente. "Case di Ritiro nell'Ordine Cappuccino." *IF* 51 (1976): 21–34.

—. "Habere Spiritum Domini." *Litterae encyclicae quattuor Ministrorum Generalium ad totam familiam sancti Francisci post exercitia spiritualia in monte Alverniae celebrata*. Rome: Ed. Porziuncola, 1977.

Dal Pino, F.A. *I frati Servi di S. Maria dalle origini all' approvazione*. Vol. 1. Louvain, 1972.

Dal Pino, F. A. et al. "Mendicanti, ordini." *DIP* 5 (Rome, 1978): 1163-89.

Daza, Antonio. *Essercitii spirituali delli Romitori instituiti dal Nostro Serafico P. S. Francesco per utilità de i suoi frati. . . .* Trans. Fr. Luigi of Rome in 1626.

De Gaiffier, B. "Hagiographie du Picenum Vie de S. Elpidius, Passion de Ste. Franca." *Analecta Bollandiana* 75 (1957): 288-89, 294-98.

De Gubernatis, D. *Orbis Seraphicus* III. Rome-Lugduni, 1684.

de la Croix, P. M. [Zimmermann]. "Les déserts chez les Carmes Déchaussés." *Dictionnaire de Spiritualité* 3: 534-39.

de la Virgen, Felipe. "La vida interior en los desiertos de la reforma teresiana en su primer siglo." *Rev. de Espirit.* 21 (1962).

de Pobladura, Melchior A. *Historia generalis Ordinis fratrum Minorum Capuccinorum*. Vol. 1. Rome, 1947.

—. *Historia Generalis OFM Cap*. Vol. 2. Rome, 1948.

—. "De scientia et scriptis ven. servi Dei Jesualdi a Rhegio (1725-1803)." *CF* 24 (1954): 110-35, 329-382.

—. "El establecimiento de los conventos de retiro en la Orden Capuchina (1760-1790). " *CF* 22 (1952): 53-73, 150-79.

——. *Saggio della corrispondenza spirituale del venerabile Gesualdo da Reggio.* Catanzaro, 1969

——. "Seminarios de misioneros y conventos de perfecta vida comun. Un episodio del regalismo español (1763-1785)." *CF* 32 (1962): 271-309, 397-433; 33 (1963): 28-81.

De sacris recessibus. Acta OFM 56 (1937): 263-66

Dechanet, J. *Guillaume de Saint-Thierry: Lettre aux frères du Mont-Dieu (Lettre d'Or).* Paris, 1975.

Del Corno, C. *Giordano da Pisa e l'antica predicazione volgare.* Florence, 1975.

Del S. Rosario, Anastasio. "L'eremitismo della Regola carmelitana." In *Ephem. Carmeliticae* 2 (1948).

Delaruelle, C. E. "Les érmites et la spiritualité populaire." *L'Eremitismo in Occidente, nei secoli XI e XIII.* Milan, 1965.

Delarun, J. "Jeanne de Signa, érmite toscane du XIVème siècle, où la sainteté ordinaire." *Mélanges de l'Ecole française de Rome* 98 (1986): 161-99.

——. *L'impossible sainteté: La vie retrouvée de Robert d'Arbrissel.* Paris, 1985.

——. *Robert d'Arbrissel fondateur de Fontevraud.* Paris, 1986.

Delormé, F-M. *La "Legenda antiqua S. Francisci":texte du Ms. 1046 (M.69) de Perouse.* Paris, 1926.

DeParis, W. "Rapports de Saint François d'Assise avec le mouvement spirituel du XIIe siècle." *EtFrNS* 12 (1962): 129-42.

de Ricci, S. *Census of Medieval and Renaissance Manuscripts in the United States and Canada,* I. New York, 1935

Desbonnets, T. *From Intuition to Institution: The Franciscans.* Chicago: Franciscan Herald Press, 1988.

de Veghel, Optat. *La réforme des Frères Mineurs Capucins dans l'Ordre franciscain et dans l'Eglise. CF* 35 (1965): 5-108.

Di Costanzo, G. *Disanima degli scrittori e dei monumenti resguardanti S. Rufino, Vescovo e martire di Assisi.* Assisi, 1797.

Direttorio della famiglia del Real Eremo, o sia ritiro de' Cappuccini in Capodimonte. Naples, 1819.

Dominici, G. *Regola del governo di cura familiare.* Ed. D. Salvi. Florence, 1860.

Dörr, O. *Des Institut der Inclusen in Süddeutschland Beiträge zur Geschichte des alten Mönchtums und des Benediktinerordens.* Münster, 1934.

Doyère, P. "Erémitisme en Occident." *Dictionnaire de Spiritualité* 4 (1960): 953-82.

—. "Ermites." *Dictionnaire de droit canonique* 5 (1953): 412-29.

Duby, G. "Les chanoines réguliers et la vie économique des XIème et XIIème siècles." In *La vita comune del clero*. Vol. I.

Duft, J. "Die Ungarn in Sankt Gallen." *Bibliotheca Sangallensis*. Vol. 1. Zürich-Constance, 1957.

Eduardus Alenconiensis. *Primigeniae Legislationis Ordinis Fr. Min. Cap. textus originales*. Rome, 1928.

Ehrle, F. "Die Spiritualen, ihr Verhältnis zum Franciscanerorden und zu den Fraticellen," *ArchLitKirchGesch* III, 604.

Elm, K. "Die Stellung der Frau in Ordenswesen: Semireligiosentum und Häresie zur Zeit des heiligen Elisabeth." In *Sankt Elisabeth, Fürstin, Dienerin, Heilige*. Sigmaringen, 1981.

—. "Italienische Eremitengemeinschaften des 12. und 13. Jahrhunderts: Studien zur Vorgeschichte des Augustiner-Eremitenordens." In *L'Eremitismo in Occidente nei secoli XI e XII*. Milan, 1965.

—. *Beiträge zur Entstehung des Wilhelmitenordens* (Münstersche Forschungen 14). Cologne/Graz, 1962.

"Epistola Venantii a Taurino" (Sept. 30, 1851). *Bull Cap*. X.

"Epistula seu tractatus ad fratres de Monte Dei." In *Etudes de philosophie médiéval*, 19. Ed. M.M. Davy. Paris, 1940.

Esser, K. *Anfänge und ursprüngliche Zielsetzungen des Ordens der Minderbrüder*. Leiden, 1966.

—. *Das Testament des heiligen Franziskus von Assisi Eine Untersuchung über seine Echtheit und seine Bedeutung, Vorreformationsgeschichtliche Forschungen, 15*. Münster, 1949.

—. *Die älteste Handschrift der Opuscula des hl. Franziskus von Assisi (cod. 338 von Assisi)*. *FranzStud* 26 (1939): 129-142.

—. "Die Regula pro eremitoriis data des heiligen Franziskus v. Assisi." *FranzStud* 44 (1962): 383-417. Reprinted in *Studien zu den Opuscula des hl. Franziskus von Assisi* (Rome, 1973): 137-79.

—. "Eine Expositio regulae Ordinis fratrum minorum aus dem 14. Jahrhundert." *FranzStud* 37 (1955): 18-52.

—. "Gehorsam und Freiheit." *WissWeish* 13 (1950): 146.

—. *Il Testamento di S. Francesco d'Assis*. Milan, 1978.

—. *Opuscula Sancti Patris Francisci Assiensi: Bibliotheca Franciscana Ascetica Medii Aevi*, 12. Collegii S. Bonaventurae ad Claras Aquas: Grottoferrata, 1978.

—. *Ordo fratrum minorum. Über seine Anfänge und ursprünglichen Zielsetzungen. FranzStud* 42 (1960): 95-129 and 297-355; 43 (1961) 171-215 and 309-347.

Esser, K. and L. Hardick. *Die Schriften des hl. Franziskus von Assisi, Franziskanische Quellenschriften,* 1. Werl/W, 1956.

Fabiani, G. "Monaci, eremiti, incarcerati e reclusi in Ascoli nei secoli XII e XIV." *SP* 32 (1964): 141-59.

Faccinetti, V. *Iconografia francescana* (Saggio). Ed. S. Lega Eucaristica. Milan, 1924.

Faloci-Pulignani, M. *Il B. Paoluccio Trinci e i Minori Osservanti.* Assisi, 1920.

Fink, K. A. *Chiesa e papato nel Medioevo.* Bologna, 1987.

Fleischacker, J. "Studien zu einer Eremitologie, Idee und verwirklichung des Einsiedlergedankens im Kapuzineorden von den Anfängen bis heute im deutschen Sprachraum." Unpublished dissertation. University of Graz, 1988.

Forcellini, E. *Totius latinitatis lexicon.* London, 1828.

Fortini, A. *I Fioretti delle Carcerelle.* Venice, 1956.

—. *Nova Vita di S. Francesco.* Assisi, 1959.

Francesco d'Assisi e francescanesimo dal 1216 al 1226. Atti del IV convegno internazionale. Assisi, 1977.

Francis and Clare, The Complete Works. Tr. R. Armstrong and I. Brady. New York, 1982.

Francisco del Niño Jesús. "El Deserto en el Carmen Descalzo." *Rev. de Espirit.* 13 (1954): 347–68, 431–59.

Frugoni, A. "Dai 'Pauperes Eremitae Domini Celestini' ai 'Fratelli de paupere vita.'" In *Celestiniana.* Rome, 1954.

Fuhrmann, H. "Zur Benützung des Registers Gregors VII durch Paul von Bernried." In *Studi Gregoriani.* Vol. 5.

Fumi, L. "Eretici e ribelli dell'Umbria." *Bollettino della Deputazione di Storia Patria per l'Umbria* 5 (1899): 218-19.

Gagnan, D. "François au Livre de la Nature 3, Le solitaire." *EtFrNS* 21 (1971): 211.

Galletti, A. I. "Insediamento e primo sviluppo dei frati Minori a Perugia." In *Francescanesimo e società cittadina: il caso di Perugia.* Perugia, 1979.

Galluzzi, A. M. *Origini dell'ordine dei Minimi.* Rome, 1967.

Gambacorta, F. *Luci e ombre nella cristianità del secolo XIV, il beato Pietro Gambacorta da Pisa e la sua congregazione (1380-1933).* Vatican City, 1964.

Garampi, G. *Memorie ecclesiastiche appartenenti all'istoria e al culto della B. Chiara da Rimini.* Rome, 1755.

Gatti, M. *Le Carceri di San Francesco del Subasi.* Assisi, 1969.

Gaudenzio of Brescia. *Lo spirito della serafica Regola.* Brescia: G. Rizzardi, 1761.

Gemeinschaften des Mittelalters Recht und Verfassung, Kult und Frömmigkeit. Münster, 1948.

Gesta abbatum monasterii S. Albani a Thoma Walsingham . . . compilata, Rerum Britannicarum Medii Aevi Scriptores, 28/4. Ed. H. T. Riley. London, 1867.

Ghidelli, C. *Atti degli Apostoli.* Turin, 1978.

Gieben, S. "Il richiamo della foresta, la funzione del bosco presso i primi cappuccini." *Picenum Seraphicum* 12 (1975): 290-95.

—. "Philip Galle's Original Engravings of the Life of St. Francis and the Corrected Edition of 1587." *CF* 46 (1976): 291ff.

Giordani, B. "Acta franciscana e tabulariis bononiensibus deprompta." *AF* 9 (Quaracchi, 1927): 113, 771.

Goetz, W. *Die Quellen zur Geschichte des hl. Franz von Assisi: eine kritische Untersuchung.* Gotha, 1904.

Golinelli, P. "Monachesimo e santità, i modelli di vita di Celestino V." In *S. Pietro del Morrone–Celestino V nel medioevo monastico.* Acts of the Third Historical Congress. L'Aquila, 1989.

Golubovich, H. *Caeremoniale Ord. Minorum vetustissimam. AFH* 3 (1910): 65.

Gougaud, L. "Cellule." *Dictionnaire de Spiritualité* 2 (1953), 396-400.

—. *Ermites et reclus.* Ligugé, 1928.

Gratien of Paris. *Bibliotheca Seraphico-Capuccina.* Vol. 20. First Edition, 1928.

—. *Espansione del francescanesimo tra Occidente e Oriente nel secolo XIII.* Assisi, 1979.

—. *Histoire de la fondation et de l'évolution de l'ordre des frères Mineurs au XIIIeme siècle.* Rome, 1982.

Gregorii Episcopi Turonensis Libri Historiarum. Vol 10. Ed. B. Krusch and W. Levison. *MGH SS* I/I. Hanover, 1951.

Gribmont, J. "La Scala Paradisi, Jean de Raïthou et Ange Clareno." *Chi erano gli Spirituali Atti del III Convegno Internazionale* 1975. Assisi, 1976.

Gribomont, J., P. Rouillard, and I. Omaechevarria. "Eremitismo." *DIP* 3 (1976): 1224-44.

Grundmann, H. "Neue Beiträge zur Geschichte der religiösen Bewegungen in Mittelalter." *Archiv für Kulturgeschicht* 37 (1955): 129-92.

———. *"Religiöse Bewegungen in Mittelalter."* Berlin, 1935.

Guillou, A. "Il monachesimo greco in Italia meridionale e in Sicilia nel medioevo." *L'eremitismo in Occidente nei secoli XI e XII.* Milan, 1965.

Haag, H. *Teufelsglaube.* Tübingen, 1974.

Habig, M. *Omnibus of Sources.* Chicago, 1973.

Hausherr, I. "La méthode d'oraison hésichaste." *Orientalia Christiana* 9/2, n. 36 (1927): 110f.

Herrad of Hohenbourg. *Hortus deliciarum [Garden of Delights]: A Reconstruction.* Ed. R. Green. Vols. 1-2. Studies of the Warbourg Institute. London-Leiden, 1979.

Heuclin, J. *Aux origines monastiques de la Gaule du Nord, Ermites et reclus du V au XI s.* Lille, 1988.

Hinnebusch, J. F. *The Historia Occidentalis of Jacques de Vitry: A Critical Edition.* Fribourg, 1972.

Hogg, J. "Kartäuser." *TRE* 17: 666-73.

Holdsworth, G. "Christina of Markyate." In *Medieval Women.* Ed. D. Baker. Oxford, 1978.

Hollenstein, J. M. *Karthäuserspiritualität.* Ms. Pleterje, 1984.

Holtzgartner, K. *Chronik des Benefiziumbezirks, Zweite Chronik.* Haader, 1978.

Holzapfel, H. *Manuale Historiae Ordinis Fratrum Minorum* 60.

Hoste, A. *Aelrede Rievallensis opera omnia.* CChrCM I. Turrnhout, 1971.

Hubert, J. "L'érémitisme et l'archéologie." In *L'eremitismo in Occidente nei secoli XI e XII.* Milan, 1965.

Huizinga, J. *Herfsttij der Middeleeuwen.* Haarlem, 1928.

Huygens, R. B. C. *Lettres de Jacques de Vitry (1160-1170-1240)*, *évêque de Saint-Jean-d'Acre*. Edition critique. Leiden, 1960.

Il rinnovamento del francescanesimo L'osservanza. International Society for Franciscan Studies, Ninth Congress. Assisi, 1985.

"Inclytum Fratrum Min. S. Francisci Capuccinorum" (March 2, 1743). In *Bull. Cap.*, VIII, 354-55.

Innocenti, B. "Le relazioni tra S. Leonardo da P. M. e S. Teofilo da Corte." *SF* 28 (1931): 144-80.

—. "P. Giuliano da Pistoia e i suoi scritti." *SF* 14 (1928): 138-39.

Introducción a los origines de la Observancia en España. Las reformas en los siglos XIV y XV. Madrid, 1958.

Ioannis de la Haye. *Sancti Francisci Assisiatis Minorum Patriarchae, nec non S. Antonii Paduani eiusdem Ordinis opera omnia*. Paris, 1641.

Irblich, E. *Die "Viborada." Bibliotheca Sanctorum* 12 (Rome, 1961): 1072-73.

—. *"Vitae s. Wiboradae" Ein Heiligen-Leben des 10. Jahrhunderts als Zeitbild*. Constance, 1970.

Jacobilli, L. *Vite dei Santi e beati dell'Umbria*. 3 vols. Foligno, 1647, 1656, 1661.

Jacques de Vitry. *Vita b. Mariae Oigniacensis* [Life of Blessed Marie d'Oignies]. *Acta SS*, Iuni V, 547-72.

Kittel, G. "Eremos." *GLNT*. 3: 893-94.

Kurze, W. "Zur Geschichte Camaldolis im Zeitalter der Reform." In *Il monachesimo e la riforma ecclesiastica (1049-1122)*. Miscellanea del Centro di Studi Medievali. Vol. 6. Milan, 1971.

Kürzinger, J. *Atti degli Apostoli*. Vol. 1. Rome, 1958.

La Vita comune del clero nei secoli XI e XII. Milan, 1962.

Lagrange, M.J. "Evangile selon Saint Marc." In *Etudes Bibliques*. Paris, 1966.

Laland, E. "Die Maria-Martha-Perikope Lukas 10: 38-42. Ihre kerygmatiche Aktualität für das Leben der Urkirche." *Studia theol.* 13 (1959): 70-85.

Lambertini, R., and A. Tabarroni. *Dopo Francesco, l'eredità difficile*. Turin, 1989.

Lampen, W. "De S. P. Francisci cultu angelorum et sanctorum." *AFH* 20 (1927): 3-23

Laqua, H. P. *Traditionen und Leitbilder bei dem Ravennater Reformer Petrus Damiani 1042-52. MMS* 30. Munich, 1976.

Laurent, L. *Yvette, la sainte recluse.* Paris, 1980.

Lazzarini, A. *Il miracolo di Bolsena.* Rome, 1952.

Le Bras, G. *Institutions ecclésiastiques de la étienté médiévale. Préliminaires et Ière partie,* Book 1. *Histoire de l'Eglise.* Vol. 12. Tournai, 1959.

Le Goff, Jacques. "Apostolat mendiant et fait urbain dans la France médiéval: L'implantation géografique des Ordres Mendiants, Programme-questionnaire pour une enquête." *Annales ESC* 23 (1968): 335-52.

—. "Ordres mendiants et urbanisation dans la France médiéval: Etat de l'enquête." *Annales ESC* 25 (1970): 924-46.

Leclercq, J. "L'Erémitisme en Occident jusqu'à l'an mil." *L'Erémitismo in occidente nei secoli XI e XII.* Milan, 1965.

—. "La crise du monachisme aux XI e XII siècles." *Bulletino dell'Istituto storico italiano per il Medio Evo* 70 (1958): 19-45.

—. "Reclus." *Dictionnaire d'archéologie chrétienne et de liturgie* (1948).

—. "Solitude and Solidarity, Medieval Women Recluses." *Medieval Religious Women.* Vol. 2. *Peaceweavers.* Ed. L. Thomas Shank and J. A. Nichols. Kalamazoo, 1987.

—. *La femme et les femmes dans l'oeuvre de Saint Bernard.* Paris, 1983.

—. *La spiritualité du Moyen Age.* Ligugé, 1961.

—. *La spiritualité du Moyen Age.* Paris, 1966.

—. *Saint Pierre Damien ermite et homme d'Eglise.* Rome, 1960.

Leclercq, J., and H. Rochais, eds. *Sancti Bernardi Opera.* Vol. 7. Rome, 1974.

Lehmann, L. *Tiefe und Weite Der universale Grundzug in den Gebeten des Franziskus von Assisi.* Werl, 1984.

Lekai, J. *The Cistercians Ideals and Reality.* Ohio, 1977.

Lemmens, L. *Opuscula sancti patris Francisci Assisiensis.* Quaracchi, 1904.

Leonardi, C. "Il francescanesimo tra mistica, escatologia e potere." In *I francescani nel Trecento.* Assisi, 1988.

—. *Alle origini della cristianità medievale, Giovanni Cassiano e Salviano di Marsiglia.* Spoleto, 1978.

—. *Dall'eremo al cenobio.* Milan, 1987.

Leonardi, D. *La lettera d'oro*. Florence, 1983.

Leyser, H. *Hermits and the New Monasticism. A Study of Religious Communities in Western Europe, 1000-1500*. London, 1984.

"Liber de doctrinis vel liber sententiarum seu rationum Beati viri Stephani primi patris religionis grandmontensis." *CChrCM* 8: 7.

Liber de restauratione sancti Martini Tornacensis. Ed. G. Waitz. *MGH SS* 14: 306.

Litterae circulares Superiorum Generalium Ordinis Fr. Min. Cap. (1548-1803). Ed. P. Melchiore a Pobladura (Mon. Hist. Ord. Min. Cap., 8). Rome, 1960.

Lunardi, G. "Giovanni da Matera." *DIP* 4: 1233.

—. "Pulsano." *DIP* 6: 1113-14.

Male, E. *L'art religieux en France*. Paris, 1898-1908.

Mann, J. B. *L'ordre cistercien et son gouvernment des origines au milieu du XIIIème siècle*. Second edition. Paris, 1951.

Manselli, R. "Dagli Spirituali all'Osservanza Momenti di storia francescana." *Humanitas* 6 (1951): 1217-28.

—. *Il secolo XII, religione popolare ed*. Rome, 1983.

—. *Il soprannaturale e la religione popolare nel Medio Evo*. Rome, 1985.

—. *La religiosità popolare nel Medio Evo*. Bologna, 1983.

Martène, E. *De antiquis ecclesiae ritibus libri*. Vol. 2. Antwerp, 1736.

Martin, H. "La predicazione e le masse nel XV secolo. Fattori e limiti di un successo." In *Storia vissuta del popolo cristiano*. Ed. J. Delumeau. Italian translation F. Bolgiani. Turin, 1985.

Martini, C. M. *Atti degli Apostoli*. Rome, 1970.

Martyrologium Franciscanum. Rome, 1938.

Masseron, A. *Saint François d'Assise: Oeuvres latines et Cantique de frère soleil*. Paris, 1959.

Mattia of Salò. *Historia Capuccina*, Vol. 2. Mon. Hist. Ord. Min. Cap., Vol. 6. Rome, 1950.

Meerseman, G.G. *Dossier de l'ordre de la Pénitence au XIIe siècle*. Fribourg, 1961.

Mencherini, S. *Guida illustrata della Verna*. Quaracchi, 1907.

Mencinetti, P. *De SS. Recessuum B. Bonaventurae a Barcinone Statutis (Studium historico-iuridicum)*. Rome, 1946 (unpublished).

Menestó, E. *Il processo di canonizzazione di Chiara di Montefalco*. Perugia-Florence, 1984.

Mens, A. *Oorsprong en betekenis van de nederlandse Begijnen en Begardenbeweging.* Antwerp, 1947.

Menzel, O. "Die 'heilige' Liutbirg." *Deutsches Archiv.* 2 (1938): 189-93.

Merlo, G.G. "Eremitismo Nel Francescanesimo Medievale." In *Eremitismo Nel Francescanesimo Medievale.* Assisi: Società internazionale di studi Francescani, 1991.

—. *Dal deserto alla folla, persistenti tensioni del francescanismo in Predicazione francescana e società veneta nel Quattrocento, committenza, ascolto, ricezione.* Acts of the Second International Congress of Franciscan Studies. Padua, 1987; Padua-Vicenza 1989.

—. *Tensioni religiose agli inizi del Duecento.* Torre Pellice, 1983.

—. *Tensioni religiose agli inizi del Duecento.* Torre Pellice, 1984.

Mertens, B. "'In eremi vastitate resedit' Der Widerhall der eremitischen Bewegung des Hochmittelalters bei Franziskus von Assisi." *FranzStud* 74 (1992): 285-374, 288-319.

—. "Eremitica Francescana: Ein historischer Streifzug." *Thuringia Franciscana; NF* 47 (1992): 355-85, 355-59.

Merton, T. *Vita nel silenzio.* Brescia: Morcelliana, 1963.

Meseguer, F.J. "Fr. Francisco Ortiz en Torrelaguna: Notas para su biografía." *AIA* 8 (1948): 500ff.

Methodius of Nembro. *La spiritualità cappuccina,* in *Quattrocento scrittori spirituali.* Rome, 1972.

Meuner, G. *La règle des Recluses, dite aussi le livre de la vie solitaire* (Ancren Riwle). Tours, 1928.

Miccoli, G. *La storia religiosa in Storia d'Italia II, Dalla caduta dell'Impero romano al secolo XVIII.* Turin, 1974.

Mitarelli, G. B., and A. Costadoni. *Annales Camaldulenses.* Vol 4. Venice, 1759.

Molinari, P. *Julian of Norwich, the Teaching of a 14th century Mystic.* London, 1958.

Molmenti, P. G. *La storia di Venezia nella vita privata Dalle origini alla caduta della Repubblica.* Vol. 1. La grandezza. Bergamo, 1927. 2nd edition, Trieste, 1973.

Mongelli, G. "Guillaume de Verceil." *DHGE* 22: 1038-42.

Moricca, U., ed. *Dialogi.* Rome, 1924.

Morin, G. "Rainaud l'ermite et Ives de Chartres, un épisode de la crise du cénobitisme aux XI et XII siècles." *RBen* 40 (1928): 99-115.

Morini, E. "Eremo e Cenobio nel monachesimo greco dell'Italia meridionale nei secoli IX e X." *Riv. di Storia della Chiesa in Italia* 31 (1977): 1-39.

Morton. H. "De sensu 'Ordinis' saec. duodecimo." *AnalPraem* 37 (1961): 314 -19. and

Nicolini, U. "L'eremitismo francescano umbro nei secoli XIII-XIV." *Analecta TOR* 131 (1979): 425-42.

—. "Perugia e l'origine dell'osservanza francescana." In *Il rinnovamento del francescanesimo* .

Niederst, R. *Robert d'Arbrissel et les origines de l'Ordre de Fontevrault*. Rodez, 1952.

—. *Robert d'Arbrussel et les origines de l'Ordre de Fontevrault*. Paris: Rodez, 1981.

Nimmo, D. *Reform and Division in the Medieval Franciscan Order from Saint Francis to the Foundation of the Capuchins*. Rome, 1987.

Nolli, G. *Evangelio secondo Marco*. Rome, 1978.

Oliger, L. "Documenta originis Clarissarum." *AFH* 15 (1922): 81.

—. *B. Margherita Colonna*. Rome, 1935.

Oury, G. "Fontevrault." *DIP* 4: 127-29.

Paludet, G. "Vita comunitaria e contemplazione." In *La comunità Esperienze dello Spirito*. Vol. 2. Vicenza, 1978.

Pantoni, A. "San Benedetto al Subasio." *Benedictina* 2 (1948).

Paolucci, T. Locatelli. "Santuario di Santa Maria delle Carceri presso Assisi." *MF* 13.

Papi, M.D. *Il Trattato del Terz'Ordine o vero"Libro come Santo Francesco istituì et ordinò el Tertio Ordine de Frati et Sore di Penitentia et della dignità et perfectione o vero Sanctità Sua" di Mariano da Firenze*. Rome, 1985.

Papini, N. *Storia di s. Francesco d'Assisi, II*. Foligno, 1827.

"Passio sanctorum Benedicti et Iohannes ac sociorum eorundem." *MGH SS* 10. Hanover, 1888.

Pásztor, E. "Chiara da Montefalco nella religiosità femminile del suo tempo." In *S. Chiara da Montefalco e il suo tempo*. Ed. C. Leonardi and E. Menteso. Perugia-Florence, 1985.

—. "Gli angeli nelle visioni medioevali." *Prospettive nel mondo* 14 (1989): 69-70.

—. "Ideali dell' eremitismo femminite in Europa tra i secoli XII-XV." In *Eremitismo Nel Francescanesimo medievale.* Assisi: Società Internazionale de Studi Francescani, 1991.

Peano, P., and C. Schmidt. "Die Ausbreitung der Franziskaner bis 1300." In *Atlas der Kirchen-Geschichte.* Ed. H. Jedin, Kenneth Scott Latourette, and Jochen Martin. Herder, Freiburg, etc., 1970.

Pellegrini, L. "A proposito di eremiti laici d'ispirazione francescana." In *I frati Minori e il Terzo Ordine Problemi e discussioni storiografiche.* Acts of the 23rd Study Congress of Medieval Spirituality. Todi, 1985.

—. "L'esperienza eremitica di Francesco d'Assisi e dei primi francescani." In *Francesco d'Assisi e francescanesimo dal 1216 al 1226.* International Society of Franciscan Studies, Fourth Congress. Assisi, 1977.

—. "L'ordine francescano e la società cittadina in epoca bonaventuriana. Un'analisi del Determinationes quaestionum super Regulam fratrum Minorum." *Laurentianum* 15 (1974).

—. *Insediamenti francescani nell'Italia del Duecento.* Rome, 1984.

—. *Specchio di donna L'immagine femminile nel XIII secolo, gli "exempla" di Stefano Borbone.* Rome, 1989.

Penco, G. "L'eremitismo irregolare in Italia nei secoli XI-XII." *Benedictina* 32 (1985): 204.

—. *Storia del monachesimo in Italia.* Milan, 1983.

Perquin, W. *St. Franciscus' Word.* Antwerp, no date..

Pertusi, A. "Aspetti organizzativi e culturali dell' ambiente monacale greco dell' Italia meridionale." In *L'eremitismo in Occidente nei secoli XI e XII.* Milan, 1965.

Piat, S. J. *Il maestro della mistica S. Pietro d'Alcantara* (translated from the French). Bari: Ed. Paoline, 1963.

Piazzoni, A. M. *Guglilemo di Saint-Thierry, il decline dell'ideale monastico nel secolo XII.* Rome, 1988.

Pierucci, C. "La vita eremitica secondo s. Pier Damiano." *San Pier Damiano nel IX centenario della morte.* Vol. 4. Cesena, 1978.

Plastaras, J. *Il Dio dell'Esodo.* Turin, 1977.

Potesta, G. L. "Gli studi su Angelo Clareno. Dal ritrovamento della raccolta epistolare alla recenti edizioni." *Rivista di storia e letteratura religiosa* 25 (1989): 111-43.

—. *Storia ed escatologia in Ubertino da Casale*. Milan, 1980.

Profili, L. "Carceri, Santuario." *Dizionario Francescano*. Padua, 1983, 157-66.

Rando, D. "Il Convento di S. Maria Mater Domini di Conegliano nel Duecento, condizionamenti politici ed esperienza religiosa." *Le Venezie francescane* 2 (1985): 55.

Regole e Costituzioni da osservare in tutti li conventi di ritiro dell'Ordine de'Minori, decreed and established by the Most Rev. Fr. Paschal of Varese, Min. Gen. Rome: Salomoni Typography, 1744.

Rigaux, B. *Testimonianza di Luca*. Padua, 1973.

Rigon, A. "Dalla regola di S. Agostino alla regola di Niccolò IV." In *La "Supra montem" di Niccolò IV (1289), genesi e diffusione di una regola*. Ed. R. Pazzelli and L. Temperini. Rome, 1988.

Ronzani, M. "Penitenti e ordini Mendicanti a Pisa sina all'inizio del Trecento." *Mélanges de l'Ecole française de Rome* 89 (1977): 741.

Rotzetter, Anton. "Geist und Geistesgaben." *Seminar Spiritualität*. Vol. 2. Zurich, 1980.

Rouillard, C. R. "Regole per reclusi, 5. 'Ancren Riwle' or 'Ancrene Wisse.'" *DIP* 7 (1983): 1535.

Rubinacci, G. "Il Real Eremo di Capodimonte in Napoli (1819-1865)."*IF* 46 (1971): 3-133.

Rusconi, R. "L'espansione del francescanesimo femminile nel secolo XIII." In *Movimento religioso femminile e francescanesimo nel secolo XIII*. Assisi, 1980.

—. "La predicazione minoritica in Europa nei secoli XIII-X." In *Francesco, il francescanesimo e la cultura della nuova Europa*. Ed. I. Baldelli and A. M. Ramanini. Rome, 1986.

—. "La tradizione manoscritta delle opere degli spirituali nelle biblioteche dei predicatori e nei conventi dell'Osservanza." *Picenum Seraphicum* 12 (1975): 63-137.

Russo, D. *Saint Jérome en Italie: Etude d'iconographie et de spiritualité (XIIIème - XVème siècle)*. Paris-Rome, 1987.

Sabatier, P. *Vie de S. François d'Assise*. Paris, 1894.

—, ed. *Speculum perfectionis*. Paris, 1898.

Sabatier, P. and A.G. Little, eds. *Le Speculum perfectionis*. British Society of Franciscan Studies, XIII. Manchester, 1928.

Sabbe, E. "Notes sur la réforme de Richard de Saint-Vannes dans les Pays-Bas." *Revue belge de philologie et d'histoire* 3 (1928): 551-70.

Sainsaulieu, J. "Ermites II. Occident," *DHGE* 15: 771-87.

———. *Les érmites français, "Sciences humaines et religions."* Paris: Ed. du Cerf.

St. John Climacus. *Scala Paradisi.* Text with introduction, version and notes by Trevisan P. Corona. Patrum Salesiana, *Studi Gregoriani,* VIII I. Turin, 1941.

Sakur, E. *Die Kluniacense in ihrer kirchlichen und allgemeingeschichtlichen Wirksamkeit bis zur Mitte des XI. Jahrhunderts.* 2 vols. Halle, 1892-1894.

Samaritani, A. "Conventualizzazione di eremiti e pinzocchere a Ferrara tra Medioevo e Umanesimo (metà sec. XIII-metà sec. XV). Contributo documentari." In *Prime manifestazioni di vita comunitaria maschile e femminile nel movimento francescano della Penitenza (1215-1447),* 301-58. Eds. R. Pazzelli and L. Temperini. Rome: Commissione Storica Internazionale T.O.R., 1982.

"Santità femminile nel territorio fiorentino e lucchese; considerazioni intorno al caso di Verdiana da Castelfiorentino." In *Religiosità e società in Valdelsa nel basso Medioevo.* Società Storica della Valdelsa, 1980.

Sassi, R. "Incarcerati e incarcerate a Fabriano nei secoli XIII e XIV." *SP* 25 (1957): 67-85.

Schmid, J. *L'evangelio secondo Marc.* Brescia, 1961.

Schmitz, P. *Histoire de l'Ordre de Saint-Bénoit.* Vol. 7. Maredsous, 1956.

Schmucki, O. "Die Stellung Christi im Beten des hl. Franziskus von Assisi." *WissWeish* 25 (1962): 128–45, 188–212.

———. "Franciscus 'Dei laudator et cultur' De orationis vi ac frequentia in eius cum scriptis tum rebus gestis." *Laurentianum* 10 (1969).

———. "L'indirizzo contemplativo dell'Ordine cappuccino primitivo." *Picenum Seraphicum* 12 (1975): 296-303.

———. "La meditazione francescana" *IF* 48 (1973): 75–89.

—. "La preghiera francescana." *La nostra vita di preghiera,* Supplement to the *Atti dei Frati Minori Cappuccini della Provincia di S. Carlo in Lombardia* 14 (1974).

—. "Secretum solitudinis: Mentis silentium Il programma contemplativo nell'Ordine francescano primitivo." *Laurentianum* 14 (1973): 177-222.

—. *Das meditativ-kontemplativ Element im Kapuzinerleben nach Ausweis der Frühgeschichte. Provinzkapitel der Bayerische Kapuziner* 6-10 (Aug. 1973): 168-186.

Schnackenburg, R. *Vangelo di Marco.* Vol. 1. Rome, 1969.

Schneider, A. *Die Cistercienser Geschichte, Geist, Kunst.* Cologne, 1986.

Schreiber, G. *Gemeinschaften des Mittelalters.* Münster/W, 1948.

Scriptores ordinis Grandmontensis. CChrCM.

Sensi, M. "Brogliano e l'opera di fra Paoluccio Trinci." *Picenum Seraphicum* 12 (1975): 7-62.

—. "Incarcerate e penitenti a Foligno nella prima metà del Trecento." In *I frati Penitenti di San Francesco nella società del Due e Trecento.* Ed. Mariano d'Alatri. Rome, 1977.

—. "La Beata Angela nel contesto religioso folignate." In *Vita e spiritualità della beata Angela da Foligno.* Perugia, 1987.

—. "La monacazione delle recluse nella valle Spoletina." In *S. Chiara da Montefalco e il suo tempo,* edited by C. Leonardi and E. Menestò. Scandicci-Perugia, 1985.

—. *Le osservanze francescane nell'Italia centrale.* Rome, 1985.

—. *Vita di pietà e vita civile di un altopiano tra Umbria e Marche (secc. XI-XIV).* Rome, 1984.

Sevesi, P. "S. Carlo Borromeo e le Congregazioni degli Amadeiti e dei Clareni (1567-1570). Con documenti inedit." *AFH* 37 (1944): 104-64.

—. *L'Ordine dei Frati Minori.* Vol. 1.

Sisti, A. *Marco.* Rome, 1974.

Spidlik, T., and J. Sainsaulieu. "Ermites." *DHGE* 15 (1963): 766-87.

Spidlik, T., P. Rouillard and M. Sensi. "Reclusione." *DIP* 7: 1229-45.

Stachnik, R., A. Triller, and H. Westpfahl. *Die Akten des Kanonisationsprozess Dorotheas von Montau.* Cologne-Vienna, 1978.

Statuta magnificae civitatis Asisii (Perusiae per Hieronumum Francisci Baldasarris de Carthulariis, 1543, die XI Augusti) fol. 7.

Statuta pro sacris recessibus (1905). In *Enchiridion vitae franciscanae.* Ed. A. Ghinato. Quaracchi, 1957. Published previously in *Acta O.F.M.* 24 (1905): 156-58.

Statuti e Regolamento che il Min. Gen. dell'Ordine (Venantius of Celano) *propone ad osservarsi nei ritiri dei Padri Missionari dell'Ordine dei Minori.* Rome, 1855.

Steinen, W. von den. *Franziskus und Dominikus. Leben und Schriften.* Breslau, 1926.

Sticca, S. "S. Pietro Celestino e la tradizione eremitica." *Bullettino della Deputazione abruzzese di storia patria* 70 (1980): 235-84.

Storia delle donne Il Medioevo. Ed. C. Klapisch-Zuber. Bari, 1990.

Tabacco, G. "Eremo e cenobio." *Spiritualità clumniacense.* Todi, 1960 .

——. "Gli intellettuali del medioevo nel giuoco delle istituizioni e delle preponderanze sociali." In *Storia d'Italia Annali 4, Intellettuali e potere.* Turin, 1981.

——. "Romualdo di Ravenna e gli inizi dell'eremitismo camaldolese." In *L'Eremitismo in Occidente nei secoli Xi e XII.* (Milan, 1965).

——. *Vita Romualdi des Petrus Damiani.* Rome, 1957.

Talbot, C. H. *The Life of Christina of Markyate, a Twelfth Century Recluse.* Oxford, 1959.

——. "The *De Institutis Inclusarum* of Aelred of Rievaulx." *Analecta Sacri Ordinis Cisterciensis* 7 (1951): 167-217.

——. The "*Liber Confortatorius*" *of Goscelin of St. Bertin.* Studia Anselmiana. Rome, 1955.

Taylor, V. *Marco.* Assisi, 1977.

Temperini, L. "Fenomini di vita comunitaria tra i penitenti francescani in Roma e dintorni." *Prime manifestazioni di Vita Comunitaria Maschile e Femminile nel Moviemento Francescano della Penitenza (1215-1447).* Eds. R. Pazzelli and L. Temperini. Rome: Commissione Storica Internazionale T.O.R., 1982.

Testa, E. "Il deserto come ideale." *LA* 7 (1957): 15.

Thomas, C., and X. Léon-Dufour. "Deserto." In *Dizionario di teologia biblica.* Turin, 1968.

Tocco, F. *SF* (1909): 260-64.

Turbessi, G. "La solitudine dell'asceta come espressione ideale della vocazione cristiana." *Benedictina* 8 (1954): 43-55.

Turner, V.W. *The Ritual Process.* London, 1974.

Valensin, A., and G. Huby. *Vangelo secondo san Luca, Verbum Saluti.* Rome, 1953.

Van Luijk, B. *Gli eremiti neri nel Dugento con particolare riguardo al territorio pisano e toscano Origine, sviluppo ed unione.* Pisa, 1968.

Vauchez, A. "L'idéal de sainteté." *Movimento religioso femminile e francescanesimo nel secolo XIII.* Assisi, 1980.

——. *La sainteté en Occident aux derniers siècles du Moyen Age d'après les procès de canonisation et les documents hagiographiques.* Rome, 1981.

——. *La spiritualità dell'Occidente medievale.* Milan, 1978.

——. *Les laics au Moyen Age: Pratiques et expériences religieuses.* Paris, 1987.

Violante, C. "L'eremitismo." *Studi sulla cristianità medievale.* Milan, 1972.

——. "Western Eremitism in the 11th and 12th centuries." *Eremitismo* (1965): 19-23.

"Vita Liutbirgae." *MGH SS* 4: 158-64.

Vita Sanctae Clarae de Cruce. Ed. A. Semenza. Vatican City, 1944.

Vita Stephani c. XXXII. "De Heremitis Calabriae." *CChrCM* 8: 121.

Von Walter, J. *Die ersten Wanderprediger Frankreichs Studien zur Geschichte des Mönchtums.* Vol. 1. Leipzig, 1903.

Vorreux, D. *Les opuscules de saint François d'Assisi.* Paris, 1955.

Vuolo, A. "Monachesimo riformato e predicazione, la 'Vita' di San Giovanni da Matera (sec. XII)." *NSMed.* 27 (1986): 69-121.

Wadding, L. *B.P. Francisci Assisiatis Opuscula,* Antwerp, 1623.

——. *Opuscula b. p. Francisci Assisiatis.* Neapoli, 1635.

Wallenstein, "La Spiritualità di S. Leonardo da Porto M." *SF* 24 (1952): 24-26.

Walz, A. "Die Miracula Beati Dominici der Schwester Cäcilia." *Archivum Fratrum Praedicatorum* 37 (1967): 40-41.

Warren, A. K. *Anchorites and their Patrons in Medieval England.* Berkeley-Los Angeles-London, 1985.

Watterich, J.M. *Pontificum Romanorum . . . Vitae.* Vol. 1. Leipzig, 1962.

Werkbuch zur Regel des hl. Franziskus. Werl/W, 1955.

Westpfahl, H. *Dorothea von Montau.* Meitingen, 1949.

Willibrord de Paris. *Les écrits de saint François d´ Assise.* Paris, 1959.

—. *Franziskus von Assisi Die Werke Die Blümlein.* Hamburg, 1958.

—. *Le message spirituel de s. François d´Assise dans ses écrits.* Blois, 1960.

Wilmart, A. "Eve et Goscelin." *RBen* 46 (1934): 414-38; 50 (1938): 42-83.

Wirkenhauser, A. "Sull'edizione delle 'lettere' di Angelo Clareno." *Cristianesimo nella storia* 7 (1986): 341-52.

—. *Atti degli Apostoli.* Brescia, 1962.